Mastering
Public Administration

Mastering Public Administration

From Max Weber to Dwight Waldo

Second Edition

Brian R. Fry

University of South Carolina

Jos C. N. Raadschelders

University of Oklahoma

CQ PRESS

A Division of SAGE
Washington, D.C.

CQ Press
2300 N Street, NW, Suite 800
Washington, DC 20037

Phone: 202-729-1900; toll-free, 1-866-4CQ-PRESS (1-866-427-7737)

Web: www.cqpress.com

Photos: 19, Getty Images; 55, 85, Corbis/Bettmann; 113, Lyndall Fownes
Urwick Archive, Henley Management College, Henley-on-Thames; 141, 180,
211, AP Images; 258, American Political Science Association; 302, file photo.

Cover design: Paula Goldstein, Blue Bungalow Design
Composition: Judy Myers

∞ The paper used in this publication exceeds the requirements of the
American National Standard for Information Sciences—Permanence of
Paper for Printed Library Materials, ANSI Z39.48-1992.

Printed and bound in the United States of America

13 12 11 10 09   2 3 4 5

Library of Congress Cataloging-in-Publication Data

Fry, Brian R.
  Mastering public administration : from Max Weber to Dwight Waldo /
Brian R. Fry, Jos C. N. Raadschelders. – 2nd ed.
      p. cm.
  Includes bibliographical references and index.
  ISBN 978-1-933116-82-2 (alk. paper)
  1. Public administration–History. I. Raadschelders, J. C. N.
II. Title.
  JF1341.F78 2008
  351.092'2–dc22

                                                2008003221

To my wife, Lois, and my son, Mark,
who give meaning to my life and
inspiration to my work
B. R. F.

To Julie, Kitty, and John
J. R.

About the Authors

Brian R. Fry is a distinguished professor emeritus in the political science department at the University of South Carolina. He previously taught at Stanford University and was a fellow at Stanford's Hoover Institution on War, Revolution, and Peace. He has served on the Executive Council of the National Association of Schools of Public Administration and on the editorial boards of a number of journals in public administration and public policy. In addition to his academic work, Fry has acted as a consultant to government agencies in South Carolina and California.

Jos C. N. Raadschelders is professor and Henry Bellmon Chair of Public Administration in the department of political science at the University of Oklahoma. He is also the managing editor of the *Public Administration Review*. His interests include the nature of the study of public administration, administrative history, public sector ethics, civil service systems, political-administrative relations, church-state relations, and water management.

Contents

Introduction

The intellectual genesis of this book is probably not unusual. The idea arose more than two decades ago from a casual request to Brian Fry by a colleague who was looking for a single reference that would summarize the work and significance of Frederick Taylor and the Scientific Management movement. Fry was hard-pressed to render appropriate advice. General textbooks continue to deal with the subject too briefly. Books on the specific subject are too long. Excerpts in readers are not comprehensive. What Fry's colleague wanted was a single source of manageable length that would summarize, in a fairly comprehensive manner, the works and contributions of a major author in the field of public administration. In this second edition of the book that Fry wrote in response to this need, we intend to provide an updated source covering a collection of leading authors in the field.

A key to the success of this effort is the list of authors chosen for inclusion. It should be noted at the outset that, though we will consider the current status of the field of public administration in the final chapter, this book is not meant to be a treatise on the current status of the field of public administration. It is more concerned with origins—how we got where we are—than with current status. Consequently, we shall focus on authors who have been pioneers in public administration and whose work largely shaped the current contours of the field. These authors are Max Weber, Frederick W. Taylor, Luther H. Gulick, Mary Parker Follett, Elton Mayo, Chester Barnard, Herbert A. Simon, Charles Lindblom, and Dwight Waldo.

The diversity of these authors reflects the diversity of the field of public administration. Several disciplines are represented: Gulick, Simon, and Waldo were trained in political science; Mayo in psychology; Follett in English, political economy, and history; Weber in economics and law; Barnard in economics; Lindblom in economics and political science; and Taylor in mechanical engineering. The level of education also varies,

FIGURE I-1
Timeline: Lives of Major Theorists

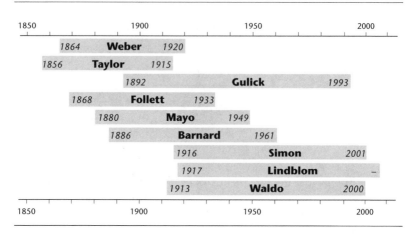

ranging from Barnard, who never received an undergraduate degree, through Weber, Gulick, Simon, Lindblom, and Waldo, who earned PhDs. Follett had an undergraduate degree, and Taylor and Mayo held master's degrees. The list is almost evenly split between academics and practitioners, though there is substantial overlap in those categories. Taylor, Barnard, and Follett were primarily practitioners; Mayo, Weber, Simon, Lindblom, and Waldo are, or were, basically academicians. Gulick has a legitimate claim to membership in both groups.

The significance of these authors is perhaps best revealed by placing them in the context of the history of the study of public administration in the United States. There are at least three broadly identifiable approaches in that study: the Classical approach, the Behavioral approach, and the Administration-as-Politics approach. Representatives of each approach are included among the authors treated in this volume.

The Classical Approach

The beginning of the self-conscious study of public administration in the United States is usually traced to Woodrow Wilson's 1887 essay, "The Study of Administration." Though the direct impact of his ideas was limited, Wilson's thoughts about the study of public administration as expressed in that essay were widely shared during the Classical period. Writing in response to an age of widespread governmental corruption (especially virulent during the 1840s–1870s) and in the spirit of the reform movement that sought to develop administrative answers to the challenges of demographic growth, industrialization, and urbanization,[1] Wilson argued that administration should be separated from political and policy concerns. According to Wilson, public administration should be concerned solely with the "detailed and systematic execution of public law."[2] As for political officials and politics, they should set the tasks for administration but not be "suffered to manipulate its offices."[3] Given this separation of administration from politics, Wilson suggested that the task of the public administrator was not significantly different from that of any administrator: the selection of appropriate means to accomplish given ends.

Based on the preceding postulates, Wilson called for the development of a science of administration, the objective of which should be the discovery of general principles to guide administrators in the efficient performance of their duties. The principles were to be based on systematic and empirical investigations performed on a comparative basis. The call for comparative analysis entailed the examination of administrative techniques successfully employed in other settings—for example, in other political and constitutional systems or in the private sector—and a determination of the applicability of those techniques to the practice of public administration in the United States. Wilson was particularly adamant in asserting that there is no difference between public and private administration. In Wilson's words, "The field of administration is a field of business. It is removed from the hurry and strife of politics.... It is a part of political life only as methods of a countinghouse are a part of the life of society; only as machinery is part of the manufactured product."[4]

Wilson's separation of politics from administration, his proposed search for a science of administration, and his assertion that business techniques are applicable in the public sector all became a part of the dominant image of public administration in the Classical period. Wilson did not make this happen; it was the *Zeitgeist*. Policy and political matters were conceptually divorced from administrative matters, leaving efficiency in execution as the legitimate area of concern for students and practitioners of public administration. Scientific procedures were espoused, if not fully adopted. And many of the techniques suggested to improve the efficiency of public-sector operations were based on private-sector practices.

Two major groups in the Classical period were the Scientific Management movement, on the one hand, and what March and Simon refer to as the *Departmentalists* and Mosher calls "Administrative Management," on the other hand.[5] Together they formed what was considered the "administrative theory" of the day. Scientific Management, usually identified with Frederick Taylor since he coined the term, focused on the performance of routine and repetitive physical tasks. The objective of Scientific

Management was to discover the basic principles of motion involved in the performance of physical tasks and then to determine the "one best way" of performing any task. The primary tool of analysis in this endeavor was the time-and-motion study. Though its analyses were conducted largely in the private sector, Scientific Management attracted a large number of enthusiasts in the public sector.

The Departmentalist approach formed a logical complement to the Scientific Management movement and is represented in this volume by the works of Luther Gulick. Whereas the primary focus of Scientific Management was the performance of physical tasks, that of the Departmentalists was the formal organizational structure. Accordingly, while the basic tool of analysis of Scientific Management was the time-and-motion study, that of the Departmentalists was the formal organization chart. The general problem addressed by the Departmentalists was the identification of the tasks necessary to accomplish an organizational objective and the grouping and coordination of those tasks in a way that would maximize organizational efficiency. The lexicon of the Departmentalists is familiar: terms such as *chain of command, span of control,* and *line and staff* are common fare even for those acquainted only peripherally with the literature on organizations. The principles deduced by the Departmentalists are equally familiar. Though, among scientists, they may have been in a state of some disrepute since the late 1940s (see the Simon and Waldo chapters), these principles appear to enjoy renewed appreciation since the late 1990s.[6] Obviously, among applied social scientists and practitioners, the Departmentalists' principles were never totally abandoned. Some of their basic principles—that authority should be commensurate with responsibility, that there should be unity of command in the organization, and that the chain of command should not be circumvented—have become deeply ingrained in our administrative culture.

The Departmentalists, as had the advocates of Scientific Management, sought to establish a science of administration that would be equally applicable in the public and private sectors, though their analyses were not as systematic as those of Scientific Management. Moreover, the Departmentalists attempted to derive specific applications from preordained general principles rather than relying on generalizations built inductively from an accumulation of specific observations, as had Scientific Management.

The combination of Wilson's definition of the field and the Scientific Management and Departmentalist prescriptions for organizational management and structure (relying heavily on hierarchy as a primary mechanism for control and coordination) constituted the core of the Classical approach to public administration. Max Weber's work, too, should at least be mentioned in regard to the Classical approach. Though his work defies either precise classification or delimitation, Weber is related to the

Classical approach in two basic ways. First, Weber takes the same position as the Classical authors on the appropriate relationship between the politician and the administrator. For Weber, the bureaucrat should be the neutral servant of his political masters, which is precisely the position embodied in the Classical politics-administration dichotomy. Second, Weber's formulation of the ideal-type bureaucracy, perhaps the most famous summary statement of the attributes of that ideal-type, bears a close resemblance to the kind of organization widely prescribed in the Classical approach. Despite those similarities, it would be a mistake to suggest that Weber's influence was limited to the Classical approach. His influence has, in fact, been pervasive. Weber's support for a value-free social science and his sociological interests are related to similar concerns in the Behavioral approach. His concern with power relationships in society is similar to the basic focus of the Administration-as-Politics approach.

A caveat is probably in order here. Though we have referred to a logical progression and a correlation of ideas, it is often difficult to draw causal linkages among those ideas. Wilson expressed concerns and proposed formulations that were widely accepted in the Classical approach. But there is little evidence that Wilson's essay was widely known among the authors of the Classical period.[7] There is a direct relationship between the Scientific Management and Departmentalist approaches, for Taylor's ideas were widespread and frequently cited in the Departmentalist literature. But it is likely that few, if any, of the authors of the Classical approach had read Weber, whose writings did not become well-known in the United States until after the Second World War. Weber probably knew of the Scientific Management movement, for he had visited the United States in 1904. Whether his subsequent work was influenced by his contact with American ideas we'll never know, but it is doubtful.

The Behavioral Approach

Though the Classical approach was dominant in the United States before 1940, it did not go unchallenged. In this period, the seeds were sown for the subsequent flowering of the Behavioral approach. This approach defies brief definition. James W. Fesler ascribes the following characteristics to the Behavioral approach: it entails the study of actual behavior, usually taking the individual as the preferred unit of analysis; it is multidisciplinary in focus; it calls for "rigor" in the use of scientific procedures; and it proscribes prescription (that is, it is primarily descriptive in intent). As the word is employed here, *Behavioralism* incorporates a diversity of perspectives, including the Human Relations movement, Simon's model of decision making, organizational humanism, and contingency theory.[8] The Behavioral approach was not much concerned with the Classical definition of the field of public administration. As had the Classical authors, the Behavioralists sought an organization theory that, it was assumed, would be applicable in both public and private settings, but the political environment was more ignored than conceptually separated as it had been in the Classical approach. Simon, one of the few students of public administration who identified himself with the Behavioral approach, did suggest that a fact-value dichotomy be substituted for the politics-administration dichotomy, but this formulation was generally viewed at the time as simply another twofold division of the administrative world closely akin to that of the politics-administration dichotomy in intent, if not entirely in substance.[9] The major thrust of the Behavioral approach was organization structure and management, not definition of the field, and here the differences from the Classical approach are substantial.

The Behavioral approach sought to modify, though seldom to eliminate, the hierarchical organizational structures so ardently espoused by Classical authors. This modification was thought to be necessary in order to appeal to a wider range of human needs and thus effectively motivate man in the organization. Accordingly, the Behavioral approach supported a number of changes in organizational structure and process. Whereas the Classical approach emphasized executive decision-making responsibilities, the Behavioral approach argued for more participatory decision-making procedures. Supervision under the Classical approach was to be basically "production-oriented," while the Behavioral approach supported a more "employee-oriented" style of supervision. The Classical approach (particularly Scientific Management) preached the benefits of specialization, but the Behavioral approach counseled job enlargement (that is, expanding the range of work functions performed) to give employees a greater sense of satisfaction from the performance of their tasks. The Classical approach urged a restricted span of control to ensure close supervision, while the Behavioral approach suggested a wider span of control to prevent close supervision and allow sufficient latitude for the expression of self-initiative and self-control on the part of the worker. The Classical authors demanded centralization in the name of control and coordination; the Behavioral authors insisted on decentralization to give more members of the organization a greater sense of control over their own destinies.

These contrasts in managerial style were derived, in large part, from more fundamental conceptual differences between the two approaches—most basically, in their notions about the relationship between man and the organization. In the Classical approach, there was what might be called a "mechanical view" of man in the organization.[10] It was assumed that man was involved only segmentally in the organization (that is, work was only one of many interests and not necessarily the primary interest), and that the member of the organization sought instrumental rewards that could be used to obtain basic satisfactions elsewhere. Given this conceptualization of the relationship between man and the organization, and assuming that money is the primary instrumental reward, it was felt that man's behavior in the organization could be controlled by the judicious manipulation of monetary incentives.

The Behavioralists constructed a substantially different scenario, viewing man's behavior as more variable (less manipulable) than had been presumed by Classical authors. In part, this difference reflected the perception that man is, or should be, more totally involved in the organization and should expect intrinsic, rather than merely instrumental, rewards from the organizational experience. These social and psychological rewards extend beyond money and are less easily manipulated than are monetary incentives. Moreover, there are forces affecting man's behavior in the organization that are either beyond the control of the organization or at least more difficult for the organization to control. Internal to the organization are informal groups, a major focus of analysis for the Behavioral approach, which often elude organizational control but act as major determinants of individual behavior. Beyond the organization lie a variety of social forces that influence behavior in the organization but are likely to escape organizational control.

All of this meant, according to the Behavioralists, that the organization must learn to respond to a wider range of human needs if it is to effectively motivate man in the organization, let alone control his behavior. Organization man may be malleable, but he is not necessarily compliant. The organization cannot simply assume obedience to its directives; it must actively seek the consent and compliance of its participants. Indeed, the question of how best to secure compliance is a major theme—perhaps the central theme—of the Behavioral literature.

There were also some major differences between the Classical and Behavioral approaches in the methods employed to realize the common ambition of constructing a science of administration. The Classical approach, as has been mentioned, was largely deductive and normative in its emphasis. The Behavioral approach, in contrast, was more inductive and descriptive in emphasis, pursuing much of its research in the logical-positivist tradition stressing the operationalization of concepts, the use of systematic techniques of analysis in the testing of hypotheses, and generalization based on an accumulation of empirical findings. Normative attributions about organizations were not so much abandoned as deferred, pending the acquisition of more descriptive information.[11] It was maintained that we should not try to prescribe how organizations should operate (normative analysis) until we know more about how they actually operate (descriptive analysis).

The works of Mary Parker Follett, Elton Mayo, and Chester Barnard are all integral to this developing challenge to the Classical organizational paradigm and precursors to the development of the Behavioral approach. Follett's work, the earliest of these precursors, anticipated by more than two decades some of the central themes of the Behavioral period. Most prominent among Follett's ideas were her insights about the nature of authority in the organization. In contrast to the Classical literature, which maintained that coordination flows from the exercise of authority and that authority resides in the apex of the organizational pyramid, Follett argues that authority flows from coordination and that it is neither supreme nor delegated. Instead, authority is pluralistic—existing at many points in the organization—and "cumulative"—arising from below instead of descending from above. Moreover, Follett argues that authority is exercised increasingly on the basis of the objective demands of the situation rather than according to personal and arbitrary mandates. Finally, Follett contends that authority is not a final moment of decision embodied in a command, but a reciprocally conditioned relationship among hierarchical superiors and subordinates in a series of interactions that precede, and determine, final choice.

Mayo's famous research at the Hawthorne Plant of the Western Electric Company in the late 1920s and early 1930s laid much of the conceptual and empirical foundation for the Behavioral approach. Indeed, this research led directly to the Human Relations movement, a major component of the Behavioral approach. Mayo's research focused on social and psychological factors in human behavior in the organization, with particular emphasis on informal group activity. Mayo asserts that informal groups develop within the organization in response to needs and expectations not effectively served by the formal organization, and that they adopt norms of behavior that are not necessarily the same as those of the organization. Moreover, these informal groups, which are nowhere described in the organization chart, exert significant influence on individual behavior in the organization. Mayo contends that management must learn to deal with these groups, and to respond to the needs and expectations expressed therein, in order to achieve the objectives of the organization. By directing attention to the social and psychological aspects of organizational behavior, the Western Electric researches set the stage for a continuing empirical investigation of the relationship between changes in the organization (with particular emphasis on style of supervision), worker satisfaction, and productivity as emphasis shifted to precisely those elements of human feelings, passions, and sentiments that were largely either avoided or ignored in the Classical literature on organizations.

Barnard provides a conceptualization of the organization that is supportive of both Follett's ideas on authority and Mayo's assertion that subordinate needs must be satisfied to achieve organizational effectiveness. Barnard asserts that the organization is a system of exchange in which each participant makes contributions in return for inducements offered by the organization. Both organizational inducements and individual contributions are subjectively evaluated by each participant, and an individual's participation will continue only as long as the participant perceives that the value of the inducements received from the organization exceeds the value of the contributions required by the organization. Why, then, should the organization pay attention to subordinates? Because each subordinate subjectively evaluates the balance of contributions required and inducements received, and will terminate his association with the organization if these expectations and needs are not being met. This view of the organization prompts Barnard to formulate a concept of authority in a manner generally consistent with that of Follett. Barnard defines authority as "the character of a communication (order) in a formal organization by virtue of which it is accepted by a contributor to or 'member' of the organization as governing the action he contributes." [12] In short, authority lies in the consent of the governed. As such, it resides in a relationship between a superior and a subordinate, not in a position, and it is exercised only on acceptance of a directive, not on its issuance. By so defining authority, Barnard emphasizes the role of subordination and the importance of compliance.

If Follett, Mayo, and Barnard were precursors of the Behavioral movement, Simon was an important part of the movement itself. His distinctive contribution was to shift the focus of analysis to decision making in the organization. More specifically, Simon argued that the science of administration should be founded on the factual premises of administrative decision making. In examining decision making, Simon sought to reconcile the rational-choice model of economic theory (which was at least implicit in Classical administrative theory) with the emergent findings on human behavior in the organization. In Simon's hands, the image of man is transformed from the "lightning quick" and omniscient calculator of the economics literature into an empirically more realistic decision maker limited in cognitive and analytical abilities, who chooses alternatives that are likely to be merely satisfactory rather than optimal.

This revised view of the decision maker is relevant to the organization in that it enjoins the organization to devise ways to cope with the probable limits on rationality in human decision making. The primary organizational strategy for dealing with human decision-making frailties is to devise appropriate decision premises so that organizationally rational decisions can be made despite the likelihood of individually nonrational processes. This likelihood means that the organization should alert the individual to decision situations (by structuring stimuli in the organizational environment) and provide decision rules that can be mechanically applied to render an organizationally correct outcome.

This strategic insight returns Simon to the central theme of the Behavioral approach—the problem of compliance. The problem is simply translated from a question of authority in general to a question of getting the subordinate to recognize and apply the appropriate decision rule. This process he sees as largely a problem of providing appropriate inducements so that individuals will respond in the desired manner.

As was the case with the Classical authors, there are both interesting relationships, and a lack thereof, among these authors and between these authors and those of the Classical approach. Follett was known, but not extensively cited, by the authors considered here. One of her pieces did appear in the famous *Papers on the Science of Administration*. Mayo was similarly included in the *Papers*. Interestingly enough, Mayo considered his work to be more a complement to, than a substitute for, the Classical formulation. As he put it, there are three dimensions to management: the application of science and technical skill (the primary emphasis of Scientific Management), the systematic ordering of operations (the primary emphasis of the Departmentalists), and the organization of teamwork and cooperation. Mayo sought to redress what he perceived to be an imbalance in previous works by stressing the problem of securing teamwork and cooperation. Though the relationship between Mayo's work and that of Barnard seems obvious, Barnard denies that Mayo had any influence on his ideas about the organization. In contrast, the relationship between Barnard and Simon is both evident and acknowledged; Simon relies heavily on Barnard's conceptualization of the organization as a system of exchange. There are also some intriguing relationships between Simon and the Classical authors, especially those in the Scientific Management movement. In particular, Simon's continuing stress on hierarchical control and coordination—here exercised through the formulation and induced application of decision rules—would appear to be more closely akin to the Classical stance than to that of his Behavioral brethren.

The ideas of this set of authors have also had substantial impact on their successors, or contemporaries, in the Behavioral approach. The Human Relations movement, a direct outgrowth of research at the Western Electric Company, sought ways of restructuring the organization and revamping managerial styles to become more responsive to a wider range of social and psychological needs in the organization. A related, but more negative approach, focused on bureaucratic organizations and their dysfunctional consequences, is exemplified by the writings of authors such as Robert Merton, Philip Selznick, and Peter Blau. Combined, these approaches pronounced a need for change and stimulated a search for alternatives to the hierarchical structures so warmly embraced in the Classical literature.

As we move into the more contemporary literature, we find that the Human Relations approach, in turn, prompted its own reaction. One response addressed the empirical difficulties encountered by that approach in the attempt to sort out the relationships among organizational characteristics, worker satisfaction, and productivity. To state the matter briefly, it was found that the suggested changes in the organization did not, as had been expected, always lead to higher levels of satisfaction, nor were higher levels of satisfaction always associated with increased productivity. The response to these empirical difficulties came in the form of the Contingency approach. Contingency theory suggests that the Human Relations approach made the same mistake as had the Classical authors in assuming that there is one best way of managing all organizations. The Contingency approach suggests that management is a relative and adaptive process in response to environmental stimuli and that the appropriate style is contingent on a number of organizational considerations. The task assumed by the Contingency approach is to stipulate the conditions under which a particular approach is likely to be successful.

A second response to the Human Relations approach was what has been called *organizational humanism*. Based originally on the conceptual apparatus of humanist psychologist Abraham Maslow, organizational humanism is more concerned with the morality of the Human Relations movement than with its empirical difficulties. Here it is argued that the Human Relations approach, like the Classical approach, is simply concerned with raising productivity. The only difference, it is argued, is that whereas the Classical approach relied primarily on command, the Human Relations approach employs more sophisticated forms of psychological manipulation. Organizational humanism, in contrast, attempts to establish the intrinsic value of the satisfaction of human needs in the organization, rather than viewing it simply as a means for increasing productivity.

The Administration-as-Politics Approach

The second major challenge to the Classical paradigm came in the form of the Administration-as-Politics approach, which, in combination with the Behavioral approach, questioned every fundamental premise of the Classical perspective. Whereas the basic difference between the Classical and Behavioral approaches concerns the way organizations should be structured and managed, the basic difference between the Classical approach and the Administration-as-Politics approach lies in their differing definitions of the field of public administration. In direct contrast to the Classical approach, the Administration-as-Politics approach maintains that it is impossible, and undesirable, to separate politics from administration. Consequently, public administration is inherently different from private administration, and the distinguishing characteristic of public administration is the political milieu in which the public administrator is required to operate. Moreover, this approach questions the possibility of separating facts and values. The combination of its rejection of the politics-administration dichotomy and its reservations about the fact-value dichotomy means that the Administration-as-Politics approach considers public administration to be art, craft, and science—and perhaps more art than craft or science.

The politics-administration dichotomy is rejected on both empirical and normative grounds. Empirically, it is argued that even casual observation reveals that administrators are involved in political and policy concerns. The size and complexity of modern government warrant the exercise of administrative initiative in the formulation of policy and the exercise of administrative discretion in its implementation, and both activities centrally involve the administrator in policy and political processes. Normatively, it is maintained that separating the administrator from policy and political matters deprives society of the creative input of those likely to be best informed about the programs they administer and tends to insulate the administrator from the legitimate demands of the public he is charged with serving.

Given the rejection of the politics-administration dichotomy, the central challenge for the Administration-as-Politics approach is to seek a satisfactory reconciliation of the necessity of administration and the requirements of democracy. This concern manifests itself in two forms: a focus on the concept of administrative responsibility and an emphasis on the public policy process itself. The focus on administrative responsibility has concentrated on defining an appropriate role for the administrator in a pluralistic political environment. Whereas the Classical approach stressed a position of neutrality regarding policy matters, the Administration-as-Politics approach counsels a role of policy advocacy, but with some variance in defining the standards on which that advocacy should be based. At first, the emphasis was placed on professional standards as the appropriate base, but it was later switched to representing clientele interests. This shifting emphasis culminated in what has been called the *new public administration*, which stresses participation both within the organization, in a spiritual alliance with organizational humanism, and in the practice of clientele representation, whereby the administrator is charged with a special responsibility for representing those interests not adequately reflected through the formal electoral process or by elected representatives. This latter charge meant, for the most part, an obligation to represent the interests of minorities and the poor.

The second development in the Administration-as-Politics approach has been an analytical interest in the processes by which policy is formulated, adopted, implemented, and evaluated. In part, this interest has led to increasing concern with the techniques of policy analysis, such as planning and evaluation. More generally, there has been a focus on the policy process with particular emphasis on the role of the administrator at various stages of the process.

We have included the works of Charles Lindblom and Dwight Waldo in this volume. Lindblom is introduced (for the first time in this new edition) because of his ideas about the interaction between markets and politics and how this interaction influences policymaking, as well as for his specific ideas about what social science ought to be. Waldo is included, in part, because his work is illustrative of the concerns of the Administration-as-Politics approach, those concerns being stated most forcefully in his book *The Administrative State*. Also, he is widely recognized as perhaps the chief chronicler of the early development of the field of public administration and as one of its most astute critics.

The diversity of the field of public administration is reflected both in the selection of authors included in this volume and in the history just recounted. There are two basic reasons for this diversity. First, public administration is notoriously a borrowing discipline—if, indeed, *discipline* is the right word. It has borrowed heavily from economics, business administration, sociology, psychology, and political science, drawing what cohesiveness it possesses more from its object of analysis than from its intellectual parentage. The second factor promoting diversity in public administration is its sometimes unnerving tendency to be cumulative rather than substitutive in its development—in other words, the field tends simply to add new ideas to old rather than to substitute the new for the old. Take the ideas of the Classical period, for example. The staying power of those ideas is attributable both to the prescriptive nature of that literature (that is, it tells you what to do if something is wrong and focuses on factors largely under the control of the organization) and to the basic truth that formal organizational structure has an important influence on behavior in organizations. As a result, many of those ideas still live, sometimes in different manifestations, such as what is now called *management science* and the new emphasis on organizational design, and sometimes in much the same incarnation, as is the case with industrial engineering. The result of this cumulative development is a field whose ideas and perspectives, though often complementary, sometimes exist in a state of uneasy internal tension. We will address both these issues in more depth in the final chapter.

The Method of This Book

In 1989 this was the first book of its kind in the United States.[13] It was/is focused on American authors, but it is useful to a wider readership, because of the influence of American scholarship in public administration and organization theory across the globe, especially since the Second World War (we will revisit this issue in the last chapter). More importantly, our method—that of providing an intellectual biography situated in the author's environmental context—emphasizes each author's substantive contributions and avoids an American bias in the reconstruction of the development of a field of study.[14] We merely reconstruct and summarize the thought of nine authors. A European-based study of intellectual biographies is available and accessible in English.[15]

Meanwhile, research employing a biographical approach has been slowly increasing in volume since the first edition of this book.[16] Why? When Frank Marini reviewed a study on Waldo, he wrote, "I came away from this book realizing that the field could profit from additional works of oral history cum intellectual biography."[17] In his review of a study on Barnard, Gideon Kunda observed that it was a "welcome addition to the all-too-short list of attempts to take seriously the oft-noted but rarely actualized need for a contextualized historical perspective on management and organization theory."[18] Indeed, it would not hurt the study of public administration one bit to follow the example of the study of business administration, where the intellectual biography has become quite popular. Indeed, the number of titles in that field is so large that there is little point in even beginning to list them, but the Tonn study on Mary Parker Follett (cited in chapter 4) serves as a good example.

Our book aims to travel the happy middle road between a full-blown biography of one individual and the cursory, often stereotypical treatment characteristic of handbooks and specialized overviews. What H.L. Schachter wrote about the literature on Frederick W. Taylor is applicable to any author who has made a mark in the literature:

Time limits force textbook, compendium, and article writers to summarize the works of major theorists. Some simplification is necessary to make sense out of mounds of possibly relevant data and to give the history of management theory a sense of drama, coherence, and temporal gain. But simplification should not imply partiality. Simplicity eliminates trivia and noise. Partiality yields a lopsided view of an experiment or of a theorist's work. Oversimplification or partialization of Taylor's work has led a dysfunctional human relations/engineering dichotomy. A review of Taylor's writings shows that he urged managers to realize that technical success requires enhanced human relations.[19]

All the authors in our volume have met with such partiality, and we hope that our presentation of their ideas and theories in the context of their lives and times will help to establish a more nuanced view of these authors.

Let us conclude this introduction with some comments on the possible uses of the book and its construction. *Mastering Public Administration* can serve in a number of roles. The introductory course at the graduate levels is, we think, the most obvious setting for the adoption of this book. Before publication of the first edition, Fry had incorporated readings from the manuscript in an introductory course at the graduate level and had met with a positive response, though from an admittedly biased sample. That setting should not be the limit of its utility, however. The book, now revised and expanded, should also be useful in courses on administrative/organization theory, decision-making theory, personnel administration, and PhD field seminars. Selected chapters may be useful in fields such as public policy (the Simon and Lindblom chapters) or collective bargaining and labor relations (Follett, Mayo, Barnard). Given the diversity of the authors covered, some chapters (or the entire book) may be of value in fields such as business administration and social work.

The book is not meant to be a substitute for a general textbook, which places the authors in a broader context; nor is it a replacement for selected excerpts from the authors themselves, which expose the student directly to the words and ideas of the authors and allow the instructor to emphasize particular points. We think this book is best regarded as a supplemental text and best used in conjunction with other resources in a manner that allows the instructor to capitalize on the comparative advantages of each of the media of presentation.

In regard to construction, a number of comments are in order. One important issue is the body of authors omitted from consideration. We believe that few would quarrel with the selection of subjects included in the book, but the exclusions are likely to be more controversial. One does not have to contemplate the matter at any great length to assemble a much longer list of worthy contributors to public administration, particularly within the generous confines of the field as defined here. We can only plead limitations of time and space and signal our intent to expand the coverage if this second edition is well-received—indeed, we would welcome suggestions in this regard. Another consideration is the writing style. We have tried to be faithful to each author's style and tone, attempting to write these summaries as the authors themselves might have done. In so doing, we have attempted to segregate personal evaluations and confine them to a section of "summary and conclusions."

Finally, a word about the sequencing of the chapters. Authors are grouped according to the relationships among their ideas. Weber and Waldo serve as bookends for the others. Weber provides a useful beginning by placing the study and practice of public administration in the broader historical context of the processes of rationalization in society. His contribution is also logically related, as noted earlier, to the works of the Classical period. The Weber chapter is followed by chapters on Frederick Taylor and Luther Gulick, representatives of the Scientific Management and Departmentalist perspectives. This opening section is followed by chapters on Mary Parker Follett, Elton Mayo, and Chester Barnard, whose works signal the nascent stages of the Behavioral approach. Next comes Herbert Simon, who borrows heavily from the previous authors (particularly Barnard), represents some major elements of the Behavioral approach, and introduces a focus on decision making. The chapters on Charles Lindblom and Dwight Waldo exemplify the Administration-as-Politics approach. Waldo provides a natural endpoint to the main body of the book and a fitting bridge to the concluding chapter by virtue of his review and assessment of the development of the enterprise of public administration in the United States.

NOTES

1. On the reform period, see, especially, Richard Hofstadter, *The Age of Reform: From Bryan to F. D. R.* (New York: Vintage Books, 1955); and Richard J. Stillman II, *Creating the American State: The Moral Reformers and the Modern Administrative World They Made* (Tuscaloosa: University of Alabama Press, 1998).
2. See Woodrow Wilson, "The Study of Administration," *Political Science Quarterly* 2 (June 1887): 212. There is some controversy about whether Wilson really meant to separate politics/policy and administration. His statements in the article are confusing, if not contradictory, and admit of differing interpretations. Our conclusion is that Wilson did intend to suggest such a separation, though with reservations.
3. Ibid., 10.
4. Ibid.
5. James C. March and Herbert A. Simon, *Organizations* (New York: Wiley, 1958), 22; Frederick C. Mosher, *Democracy and the Public Service* (New York: Oxford University Press, 1968), 55. Mosher does not use the phrase "administrative management," but characterizes the fifth period (1937–1955) in the evolution of civil service concepts as a "government by administrators: the management period."
6. For instance, Gulick's intuitive theories about span of control have now acquired empirical backing. See references to Meier and Bohte in chapter 3.
7. See Paul P. Van Riper, "The American Administrative State: Wilson and the Founders—An Unorthodox View," *Public Administration Review* 43, no. 6 (November–December 1983): 478–479. See also Paul P. Van Riper, *The Wilson Influence on Public Administration: From Theory to Practice* (Washington, D.C.: American Society for Public Administration, 1990); and idem, "Some Anomalies in the Deep History of U.S. Public Administration," *Public Administration Review* 57, no. 3 (1997): 219. Wilson, though, is not always consistent in the expression of his ideas; see Jos C. N. Raadschelders, "Woodrow Wilson on the History of Government: Passing Fad or Consti-

tutive Framework for His Philosophy of Governance?" *Administration & Society* 34, no. 5 (2002): 589–591.

8. James W. Fesler, "Public Administration and the Social Sciences: 1946 to 1960," in *American Public Administration: Past, Present, Future,* ed. Frederick C. Mosher (University: University of Alabama Press, 1975), 114–115.

9. There is some question about whether or not Simon should be classified as a Behavioralist. We do so for two primary reasons. First, he fits the general criteria proposed by Fesler as cited above. Second, he attempts to incorporate many of the findings of the Behavioral approach in his own work. Third, he identifies himself as a Behavioralist, clearly distinguishing himself from behaviorism in psychology. See Herbert A. Simon, "Human Nature in Politics: The Dialogue of Psychology with Political Science," *American Political Science Review* 79, no. 2 (1985): 295.

   There are some difficulties with such a classification. Most significantly, Simon has little in common with the analysis of the Human Relations movement or with the organizational humanists—also classified as part of the Behavioral approach—in regard to the affective elements of organizational behavior, the importance of the satisfaction of human needs in the organization, or the appropriate organizational responses to such considerations.

10. While the use of the machine metaphor originates with Descartes' animal-machine, it was not until the publication of *Man-Machine* in 1747 by Julien Offray de La Méttrie that human behavior was assumed to be completely determined by external stimuli. It shocked people to realize that this theory basically eliminated free will and altruism. See Lynn McDonald, *The Early Origins of the Social Sciences* (Montreal/Kingston: McGill-Queen's University Press, 1993), 102, 163.

11. Some have argued that normative attributions were not so much deferred as they were hidden. As we see in later chapters, a substantial portion of the Behavioral approach, particularly in the form of the Human Relations movement, has been challenged as ideologically based and involving unstated or unwarranted assumptions about the nature of man and/or his relationship with the organization. See, especially, the following chapters on Elton Mayo and Dwight Waldo.

12. Chester I. Barnard, *The Functions of the Executive,* 30th Anniversary ed. (Cambridge: Harvard University Press, 1968), 163.

13. A comparable publication one year earlier in the Netherlands contains intellectual biographies of American, German, and French authors, one Norwegian, one Canadian, and one Dutchman: Michel Crozier, Robert Dahl, Anthony Downs, Murray Edelman, Christopher Hodgkinson, Harold Lasswell, Charles Lindblom, Michael Lipsky, Niklas Luhmann, Renate Mayntz, Henry Mintzberg, Johan Olsen, Vincent Ostrom, Edward Quade, Fritz Scharpf, Herbert Simon, Alain Touraine, Gerrit Van Poelje, Dwight Waldo, and Aaron Wildavsky. See A.F.A. Korsten, Th.A.J. Toonen, *Bestuurskunde. Hoofdfiguren en kernthema's* (Leiden/Antwerpen: H.E. Stenfert Kroese bv, 1988).

14. In her review of O.E. Williamson's edited volume on Barnard (see chapter 6), Michael Rowlinson observes that there is a clear American bias, given that organization theory "... is presented as if derived from a few classic texts ..." (e.g., Barnard, Simon, Selznick) and completely ignoring European roots. See Michael Rowlinson, review of O.E. Williamson, in *Journal of Management Studies* 34, no. 1 (1995): 154.

15. Nico Nelissen, Marie-Louise Bemelmans-Videc, Arnold Godfroij, Peter de Goede, eds., *Renewing Government: Innovative and Inspiring Visions* (Utrecht: International Books, 1999). This volume provides discussion of the works of Michel Aglietta, Michel Crozier, Robert Dahl, Robert Denhardt, Norbert Elias, Robert Golembiewski, John Kingdon, Henry Mintzberg, Mancur Olson, David Osborne and Ted Gaebler, Pierre Rosanvallon, and Cees Schuyt—predominantly American and French authors, plus one Canadian, one Dutchman, one German.

16. See, e.g., Norma M. Riccucci, *Unsung Heroes: Federal Execucrats Making a Difference* (Washington, D.C.: Georgetown University Press, 1995); Stillman, *Creating the American State.*

17. Frank Marini, review of Brack Brown and Richard J. Stillman, *A Search for Public Administration: The Ideas and Career of Dwight Waldo* (College Station: Texas A&M University Press, 1986). In *Public Administration Review* 50, no. 6 (1990): 683.

18. Gideon Kunda, review of William G. Scott, *Chester I. Barnard and the Guardians of the Managerial State* (Lawrence: University Press of Kansas, 1992). In *Administrative Science Quarterly* 39, no. 3 (1994): 529.

19. Hindy Lauer Schachter, "Frederick Winslow Taylor and the Idea of Worker Participation: A Brief against Easy Administrative Dichotomies," in *F. W. Taylor: Critical Evaluations in Business and Management,* ed. John C. Wood and Michael C. Wood (London: Routledge, 2002 [1989]), vol. III, 338.

Chapter 1

Max Weber:
The Process of Rationalization

To include the works of Max Weber in a volume on the study and practice of public administration in the United States may have seemed somewhat unusual at the time the first edition of this book was published, but, in view of the vast literature that has appeared on his work since then, Weber is clearly back in fashion. Indeed, according to Thomas Kemple, "metaphors of awe and veneration abound" next to acknowledgments of "the fragmentary, unfinished, and ambiguous quality of his work."[1] Weber, a German scholar of catholic interests and extensive knowledge of economics, law, history, and sociology (of administration, religion, music, and so on), was neither much read nor often noted in this country until half a century after the beginnings of the field of public administration as an object of self-conscious study. The reason for considering Weber here is that he places public administration, including public administration in the United States (of which he was quite conscious), in a broad historical context and describes its development as part of the more general process of rationalization in Western societies. The purpose of this chapter is not to attempt to summarize Weber's works—that would be an impossible task in the space available. The scope of Weber's interests and the reach of his intellect are truly awesome. Instead, our more modest ambition is to place Weber's ideas about administration in the broader setting of his more general concern with processes of rationalization and patterns of domination. His analysis of the social and historical context of administration and, more particularly, of bureaucracy may well be Weber's distinctive contribution to the literature on public administration and probably accounts for his lasting impact on the field.

Weber clearly saw administration in general, and bureaucracy in particular, as vital to these historical processes. Indeed, Weber asserts that domination is exerted through administration and that legal domination requires bureaucracy for its exercise. Moreover, Weber considered bureaucracy to be the most rational and efficient form of organization yet devised by man. In this stance, Weber, who may have penned the most famous statement on bureaucracy, uses the term in a manner opposite to its common meaning, both before and after he wrote. Moreover, Weber contends that bureaucracy embodies a concept of justice familiar to Western systems of jurisprudence. In the case of bureaucracy, the "equal application of the law" is simply translated into the equal (and impersonal) application of the rule.

Despite his general admiration for bureaucracy, Weber was also aware of its flaws. As an organizational form, bureaucracy subjects the individual to an oppressive routine, limits individual freedom, and favors the "crippled personality" of the specialist. As a potential political force, bureaucracy becomes a danger when it oversteps its proper function and attempts to control the rule of law rather than being subject to it. Weber argues that the bureaucrat should stay out of politics and limit himself to the "impartial administration of his office," and that he should subordinate his personal opinion on matters of policy to his sense of duty.

There are obvious relationships between Weber and the authors of the Classical period. His call for bureaucrats to be the neutral servants of their political masters echoes Wilson's admonition that administrators should be responsible only for the efficient execution of the law. His description of the "ideal-type bureaucracy" is similar in form and process to organizations widely prescribed by the Classical authors. But to limit Weber's influence to the Classical approach alone would be misguided. His call for the construction of a value-free social science corresponds to the ambition and stated intent, if not the accomplishment, of the Behavioral approach. His overall concern with power relationships in society is similar to the concerns of the Administration-as-Politics approach. In short, Weber's influence, although often indirect, has been pervasive in the field of public administration.

Life

Max Weber was born in Erfurt, Thuringia, Germany, on April 21, 1864. His family numbered among its members a long line of persons distinguished in the professions, especially the Lutheran clergy. Weber's father, Max Weber Sr., was a prosperous right-wing politician whose governmental posts included a seat in the Reichstag, while his mother, Helene Fallenstein Weber, was a cultured liberal woman of the Protestant faith and the daughter of a well-to-do official.

Weber was a sickly child, suffering from meningitis at an early age, and the object of his mother's brooding concern. As a student in his pre-university years, Weber had a recognized talent but was perceived as lacking ambition by his teachers, who were not much impressed by this stringy young man with sloping shoulders.[2]

In 1882 Weber commenced the study of economics, philosophy, and law at the University of Heidelberg. He also began to change from a slender, withdrawn adolescent into a large, pompously virile young man. Joining heartily in the social life of a dueling fraternity, he engaged in drinking bouts and fell into debt. After three semesters at Heidelberg, Weber moved to Strassburg to serve a year in the military. Here, the man who would later become a recognized authority on bureaucracy suffered under what he considered to be the stupidity of barracks drill and the chicanery of junior officers. He rebelled against attempts to, in his words, "domesticate thinking beings into machines responding to commands with automatic precision."[3] On receiving his officer's commission, however, Weber learned to see the brighter side of army life.

The next year Weber resumed his studies, this time at Göttingen University in Berlin. In 1886 he took his first examination in law, and he subsequently took up the practice of law in Berlin. Three years later, Weber completed a PhD and subsequently qualified as a university teacher by writing a thesis on Roman and agrarian legal history. In 1892 he obtained a position teaching law in Berlin.

The following year Weber married Marianne Schnitzer, who was a second cousin on his father's side and, reputedly, something of a beauty. She was to become one of the leading exponents of women's rights in Germany. After his marriage, Weber embarked on the life of a successful young scholar in Berlin, and his early academic years were filled with both practical studies directed at public policy issues and more scholarly works. He soon accepted a chair in economics at the University of Freiburg, having found economics to be more challenging than legal history, and in 1896 he became a professor of economics at Heidelberg.

Complications in Weber's life began shortly after his appointment at Heidelberg. Weber's father unexpectedly collapsed and died, leaving the son suffering from exhaustion and anxiety and forcing him to suspend his regular work. In fact, Weber would not resume that work full-time for a period of three-and-a-half years. Although he suffered repeated set-backs, Weber published a book review in 1903, and he also became the associate editor for the *Archiv für Sozialwissenschaft und Sozialpolitik*. By the following year, his writing productivity was returning to its previous level, and Weber visited the United States, where he delivered a paper and toured the country. An inheritance received in 1907 enabled him thereafter to focus entirely on his writing.

Weber spent the war years as a hospital administrator; after the war, he served as a consultant to the German Armistice Commission in Versailles and to a commission that drafted the Weimar constitution.[4] In 1918 Weber spent the summer in Vienna, where he gave his first university lectures in nineteen years. He still experienced compulsive anxieties, however, and had to use opiates in order to sleep. Weber accepted an academic position in Munich in 1919, but held it only for a short time before his death from influenza at the age of fifty-six on June 14, 1920.[5]

Weber has been graphically described by a personal associate, who noted that he spoke in an exquisite German that was entirely different from his labored writing style and that he had a volcanic temperament coupled with occasional coarseness.[6] Weber was capable of both great impetuosity and righteous indignation. He had an ascetic drive for work and was considered by his colleagues at Heidelberg to be a difficult person with a demanding conscience and a rigid sense of honor.[7]

Weber did not consider himself to be a scholar, and although he chose an academic career, he held a regular academic position (that is, teaching and research) for only five years. Reportedly more at home on a political platform than in an academic setting, Weber was, in the context of his times, a "liberal" and a "nationalist." As a liberal, he fought against both conservatives, who sought protection for agriculture and bureaucratic control of industry, and the Marxists.[8] As a nationalist, Weber believed in force as the last argument of any policy, and he developed a German tendency to "brutalize romance and to romanticize cynicism."[9] In Weber's words, "Policymaking is not a moral trade, nor can it ever be."[10] As both a nationalist and a German patriot, Weber perceived the German culture to be worth preserving against the Russian menace and the rising Slavic tide. He even had fleeting political ambitions of his own. Presented with an opportunity to be nominated for election to the National Assembly in 1918, however, he refused to make any effort on his own behalf and lost the nomination.

Religion, as we see later in this chapter, played an important role in Weber's sociology, but he described himself as "religiously unmusical."[11] Although Protestantism was integral to his family, Weber rejected conventional "church" Christianity and was indifferent toward religion in general. He was apparently equally repulsed by his father's philistinism and his mother's piety. Nonetheless, Weber's writings on religion start from a Protestant viewpoint and offer the ideas generated by Protestantism as the wave of the future.[12]

Weber's Sociology

Widely acknowledged as one of the founders of modern social science, Weber conceived of sociology as a science with the objective of interpreting and understanding social conduct. Weber's own ambition was to examine the relationships among economic institutions and actions and all other social institutions and actions constituting a given social structure.[13]

Though Weber acknowledged that sociology is not confined to the study of social action, it was the main focus of his analysis. He viewed the world of man in society as "a world of unit social acts, ordered by the need to make choices for an always uncertain future in terms of some principle of choice which we call a value."[14] In analyzing social action, Weber hoped to go beyond statements of "lawful regularities" (the limited preoccupation of the natural sciences) to the definition of the causal and motivational forces that produce systems of action in social situations. More precisely, Weber's work is concerned with examining and explaining individual, purposive, rational social actions.

Weber's focus on motivated behavior means that he is interested in what he calls "meaningful" action, not merely reactive behavior. Processes that are not the results of motivations are to be considered only conditions, stimuli, or circumstances that further or hinder motivated individual action. Moreover, the affective and irrational components of human behavior are relegated to the status of "deviations" from rational behavior as Weber concentrates on ideal-type rational behavior, such as that exhibited in the formal elements of law and pure economic theory.[15] Weber's sociology thus focuses on the single deliberate action of the individual that is directed toward affecting the behavior of others. The intention of the act is primary, and the success, failure, or unanticipated consequences are of only secondary importance.

Weber asserts that individual actions fall into categories and that they can be combined into social structures. His intent is to understand the categories and structures of social actions as they have appeared in history. In classifying social actions, Weber's distinctions are based on degrees of rationality, ranging from rational expediencies such as economic actions, which are the most understandable of motivated actions, through the pursuit of absolute ends and affectual actions flowing from sentiments, to instinctual behavior and traditional conduct. Weber groups social actions by their determinants and orientations. Purposive, rational conduct is determined rationally and is oriented toward discrete individual ends. Affectual conduct is both determined by, and oriented toward, feelings and emotions. Traditional conduct is determined by, and oriented toward, historical precedent. These categories of social action yield three kinds of social structure: *society*, which is based on rationally expedient social action; *association*, which is based on affective social action; and *community*, which is based on traditional social action.[16]

Weber's approach to sociology is one of the primary alternatives to a Marxist perspective, and it was clearly intended as such by the author. Weber felt that Marx had only a partial perspective on history and had unduly emphasized material interests in his analysis. In contrast, Weber argues for causal pluralism, in which factors such as nationalism and ethnicity join material interests as determinants of social actions. Although Weber agrees with Marx's belief that ideas are powerless unless joined with economic interests, he denies that ideas are simply reflections of those economic interests. Weber emphasizes the autonomous role of ideas and is concerned with the relative balance between "ideal" and "material" factors in history.[17] This viewpoint is most dramatically stated, of course, in Weber's famous analysis of the relationship between Protestantism and capitalism, in which he argues that the particular form of capitalism that arose in the West was, in large part, a product of the ideas and ethics of Protestantism. (We will have more to say on this subject later.)

This emphasis on the importance of ideas leads Weber to distinguish between class and status and to identify the latter as the primary basis of social dynamics. According to Weber, while class is based solely on economic power, status is determined by social estimates of honor and a style of life.[18] Weber maintains that society is a composite of positively and negatively privileged status groups, within which the positively privileged status groups attempt to preserve their style of life through the monopolization of economic opportunities. Consequently, for every idea or value, one should seek out the status group whose ideal and material interests are served. Conflicts among the divergent interests of status groups are resolved in social patterns of compliance and domination.[19]

A final distinction between Marx and Weber arises on the role of class struggle in their formulations. Weber does not deny the importance of class struggle, but he rejects the idea that class struggle is the central dynamic of society. Instead, he emphasizes the forces of rationalization and their organizational counterpart, bureaucracy. Human behavior is thus guided not only by economic interests but also by social affinity (status) and by a legitimate order of authority that depends on a bureaucratic structure for its exercise.

Weber's Methodology

Weber's methodological objective is to make possible the treatment of social phenomena in a systematic and scientific manner, and, to this end,
he emphasizes the importance of both quantitative and qualitative methods and research. Though it is little known, he "pioneered the large-scale
empirical programs that really did not take off until the 1920s."[20] We,
however, will focus on Weber's comparative, historical approach to the
causal analyses of social action since it is more germane to the matter of
assessing his impact on the field of public administration.

The first crucial element of Weber's methodology is his use of the
ideal-type construct. Weber believes the construction of ideal-types to be
essential to causal analysis, and it is part of his broader effort to codify the
concepts of the social sciences. He asserts that two kinds of meaning can
be ascribed to social behavior: a concrete meaning and a theoretical or
"pure" type of subjective meaning. The problem with concrete meaning
is that there is a bewildering variety of actual social phenomena, each of
which is complex in its own right. Consequently, most concepts in the social sciences are necessarily abstractions from reality, not "presupposi-
tionless" descriptions, and they are not likely actually to appear in their
full conceptual integrity.[21]

The ideal-type is intended as a mental construct that categorizes
thought and helps to capture the "infinite manifoldness of reality."[22]
More precisely, the ideal-type is the conceptual construction of elements
of reality into a logically precise combination that represents historical
phenomena but that may never be found in its ideally pure form in concrete reality.

It is important to understand what Weber's ideal-type is *not*. The ideal
type is not a description of reality, which is too complex to be seized and
held. It is not a hypothesis, though it can be used to generate hypotheses.
Most emphatically, it is not a normative model. As Weber puts it, the
ideal-type "has no connection at all with value judgments and it has nothing to do with any type of perfection other than a purely logical one."[23]
The ideal-type is, instead, "the pure case, never actualized, uncluttered by
extraneous attributes and ambiguities."[24]

The second crucial element in Weber's methodology is his use of *Verstehen* (interpretive understanding) as the approach to understanding actions and ideas in their own time and context.[25] *Verstehen* is often
confused with Herder's and Dilthey's *Einfühlung* (empathetic understanding), which concerns intuitive and empathic comprehension of inner considerations. Instead, Weber's position is one between positivism
and hermeneutics. To Weber, *Verstehen* is an act of rational interpretation,
and he outlines the process in detail in a 1904 essay.[26]

The Role of Science

Science, according to Weber, is the affair of an intellectual aristocracy, and its quest the knowledge of the particular causes of social phenomena. It is not possible to analyze all social phenomena in their complete manifestation and causality, and Weber notes, further, that a description of even the smallest slice of reality can never be exhaustive. One can bring order to the complexity of reality only by concentrating on that part of reality that is interesting and significant in regard to cultural values and/or research questions.[27] Accordingly, a cultural social science necessarily involves some subjective presuppositions in regard to significance.[28]

It is clear that Weber sees a crucial role for values in the development of a cultural social science. Value discussions are important in the elaboration of value axioms as one attempts to discover general, irreducible evaluations. Value discussions are important in deducing the implications of value axioms. Value discussions are important in the determination of the factual consequences of alternative courses of action insofar as necessary means or unavoidable consequences are involved. Value discussions are important in providing problems for investigation by empirical research, particularly in Weber's cultural social science. Moreover, science itself is not free from suppositions of its own that may mask value orientations.[29] Science supposes both that the rules of logic and method are valid and that the knowledge yielded is worth knowing. These suppositions are based on faith, not proof.

Nonetheless, Weber argues strongly that science must eschew value judgments and seek "ethical neutrality." By value judgments, he means practical evaluations of the satisfactory or unsatisfactory character of the phenomena under consideration.[30] Weber asserts that there is no way to resolve conflicts about value judgments except by acceptance of a transcendental order of values such as those prescribed by ecclesiastical dogmas. Such an acceptance, he contends, is more an intellectual sacrifice than an assertion of science. Weber asserts that science cannot tell us what we shall do, it cannot tell us how we shall live, it cannot tell us whether the world has meaning or whether it makes sense to live in such a world.[31] These matters, however important, are simply beyond the legitimate purview of science.

In particular, Weber condemns those who "feel themselves competent to enunciate their evaluations on ultimate questions 'in the name of science' in governmentally privileged lecture halls in which they are neither controlled, checked by discussion, nor subject to contradiction."[32] He argues that it is one thing to state facts, to determine mathematical or logical relationships, or to reveal the internal structure of cultural values; it is another to take a stand on the value of culture itself. The task of the teacher is to serve students with knowledge and scientific experiment, not to imprint values or personal political views.[33] The teacher in the lecture hall should simply fulfill this given task in a workmanlike fashion— by recognizing facts and distinguishing them from personal evaluations, and repressing the impulse to exhibit personal tastes or other sentiments unnecessarily. Weber contends that those who seek something more than analysis and statements of fact in the classroom crave a leader, not a teacher.[34]

Processes of Rationalization

In moving from the method of sociology to its substance, Weber focuses on the concept of rationalization, which he considers to be the most general element in the philosophy of history and the constitutive element of modern Western society.[35] Weber contends that only in the contemporary West does science exist at a stage recognized as valid, that law is characterized by the strictly systematic forms of thought essential to rational jurisprudence, and that the trained official has become the pillar of both the modern state and economic life. He measures the degree of rationalization in society in two ways: by the extent to which ideas gain in systematic coherence and consistency, and by the displacement of magical elements of thought. Weber distinguishes between two basic types of rationality: value (*Wert Rationalität*) and purpose (*Zweck Rationalität*) rationality. Value rationality focuses on intrinsic value only and is oriented on the inner demands; it will consider the meaning of action only. Purpose rationality is focused on consequences or results of action. Both value and purpose rationality are subjective by nature—that is, in the eye of the beholder. As such, they must be distinguished from objective or objectified manifestations of rationality (such as economic organization, political order, legal system, religion, ethics, and science).[36]

A second and related emphasis in Weber's analysis is the concept of domination. Weber maintains that the emergence of rational societies is critically dependent on the way in which domination has been exercised. Domination, for Weber, is a subset of the broader phenomenon of power, which he defines as the possibility of imposing one's will on the behavior of other persons despite their resistance.[37] Domination is distinguished from other exercises of power on the basis of the perceived legitimacy of its exercise; that is, in the case of domination, it is believed that the ruler has the right to exercise power and the ruled have a duty to obey.[38] Weber describes two forms of domination: that based on constellations of interests and that based on authority.[39] Domination based on constellations of interests is found in religious and economic associations, whereas domination based on authority is found in legal and bureaucratic relationships.

Domination Based on Constellations of Interests

The first example of domination based on constellations of interests is religion. Weber's sociology of religion contains three major themes: an explanation of the distinguishing features of Western civilization; an analysis of the relationship between social stratification and religious ideas; and an examination of the effects of religious ideas on economic activities. Underlying all of this scrutiny is Weber's central theme of the rationalization of the processes of domination, which, for religion, comes in a movement from magicians to priests, who attempt to protect their positions by systematizing established beliefs. Within each religion, he identifies domination with a particular status group of religious leaders. For Confucianism, that status group is governmental officials with a literary education; for Hinduism, it is a hereditary caste of expert advisers (Brahmins); for Judaism, it is intellectuals trained in ritual and literature; and for Christianity, it is the urban bourgeoisie. Nevertheless, Weber did not argue that religion is simply a function of the ideal, material, or political interests of a particular status group. Instead, the church stands for a universalism of grace and for the ethical sufficiency of all who are enrolled under its institutional authority. Moreover, as is the case with all bureaucracies, there is a democratic tendency in religions as they become bureaucratized that fights against status privileges (an argument to which we will return in discussing bureaucratic organizations).[40]

Weber's analysis of Christianity focuses primarily on the Protestant sects and their relationship to capitalism.[41] His interest in the development of capitalism is derived both from his perception that capitalism has been a pervasive and unifying theme in modern history and from a desire to respond to Marx's concept of historical materialism. Weber's examination of the relationship between Protestantism and capitalism, and his assertion that causality flows in that direction, is an excellent example of both his emphasis on ideas, as opposed to material interests, and his historical, comparative approach to causal analysis. But Weber did not posit a simple cause-effect relationship between Protestantism and capitalism, nor did he consider the Protestant ethic to be the sole cause of capitalism. Instead, he emphasizes that social dynamics require a pluralistic analysis and that capitalism should be seen as the result of a specific combination of political, economic, and religious factors, not just the religious factor.

In discussing the relationship between Protestantism and capitalism, Weber employs a rather special perspective on modern capitalism—

which, he asserts, presupposes the existence of a number of conditions: that there is private ownership of the means of production; that formally free labor exists; that a limited government allows the market to operate relatively freely; and that a system of finances exists, particularly a money economy.[42] Modern capitalism is characterized by the following attributes:

1. The calculation of capital is made in terms of money.
2. Everything is done in terms of balances.
3. Calculation underlies every act of partners to a transaction.
4. Economic action is adapted to a comparison of money income with money expenses.[43]

Weber believes that capitalism represents the highest stage of rationality in economic behavior. By "rational," he means an economic system based not on custom or tradition, but on a systematic and deliberate adjustment of economic means to attain pecuniary profit.[44] The rationality of modern capitalism is of a special type, however. The rationality of capitalism is "formal" and is measured by the extent to which quantitative calculation is both technically possible and actually applied. In contrast, "substantive" economic rationality involves the adequacy of the provision of goods and services.[45] Weber asserts that the two concepts of economic rationality are always in conflict and that the formal rationality of money accounting and capitalism has no direct relationship to substantive considerations concerning the provision and distribution of goods and services.

A primary question for Weber, and one that joins his interests in religion and economics, is the source of the particular ethic of modern capitalism. His answer is Protestantism. Weber maintains that the Reformation did not mean the elimination of the church's control over everyday life. Instead, it meant a new form of control in which a religiously based secular ethic and a worldly asceticism replaced the otherworldly asceticism of Catholicism and its indifference toward the rewards of this life.[46] Protestantism gave positive spiritual and moral meaning to worldly activities and imparted an ethos of planning and self-control to economic activity.[47] The Protestant sects joined the idea that the gods bless with riches those who please them with a kind of religious conduct embodying the notion that honesty is the best policy. It thus delivered to capitalism its special ethos: the ethos of the modern bourgeois middle classes.[48]

The relationship between the Protestant ethic and the spirit of capitalism is most clearly illustrated in the doctrines of Calvinism and its emphasis on predestination. The doctrine of predestination holds that only a small proportion of men are chosen for eternal grace and that the meaning of individual destiny is hidden in impenetrable mystery. Furthermore, the elect do not differ visibly from the damned. Thus one cannot know his destiny. He must simply consider himself to be chosen and combat all doubts as temptations of the devil. The Calvinist creates his own salvation, or at least the conviction of his salvation, by the performance of deeds and in the service of a "calling." This independent salvation requires systematic and continuous self-control in the performance of each deed rather than an accumulation of deeds, as the Catholic Church had asserted.[49] In its emphasis on deeds, Calvinism rejected pure feelings and emotions and eliminated the idea that salvation could be granted by the church. Weber contends that whereas Catholics saw magic as the means to salvation with the priest as the magician, Calvinists demanded a life of good works that had no place for the Catholic cycle of sin, repentance, atonement, and release, followed by new sin. Calvinism sought to subject man to the dictates of a supreme will and to bring man's actions under constant self-control guided by ethical standards.[50]

Calvinism also sought to destroy spontaneous, impulsive enjoyment by insisting on ordered individual conduct and by transforming monastic asceticism into a worldly asceticism while adding the positive idea of proving oneself in worldly activity.[51] Protestant asceticism holds that it is morally objectionable to relax in the enjoyment of one's possessions; the individual needs hard, continuous bodily or mental labor. The acquisition of wealth in the performance of one's calling is encouraged, but consumption should be limited. The combined effect of limiting consumption and freeing acquisitive activity is a compulsion to save and accumulate capital.

Weber concludes that the religious roots of modern capitalism soon gave way to the tenets of worldly utilitarianism, which has resulted in an orgy of materialism. But the religious epoch gave to its utilitarian successor an amazingly good conscience about the acquisition of wealth and comforting assurance about the unequal distribution of worldly goods.[52] It also legitimated the exploitation of labor, since the employer's activity is also a "calling." But whereas the Puritan wanted to work because it was his "calling," modern man is forced to work in the "iron cage" of the new economic order, and the pursuit of material goods controls his life.[53]

Domination Based on Authority

Weber's second major form of domination is that based on authority. In systems of domination based on authority—as was the case with domination based on constellations of interests—obedience is dependent on the perception of legitimacy. The sources of legitimacy differ, however. Weber asserts that there are three sources of legitimacy for domination based on authority: charisma, tradition, and legality. These are pure, or ideal-types, while the bases of legitimacy usually occur in mixtures in their historical manifestations.

Charismatic Authority

Charismatic authority derives its legitimacy from the personal qualities of the leader. Weber defines charisma as the "quality of an individual personality by virtue of which he is set apart from ordinary men and treated as endowed with supernatural, superhuman, or at least specifically exceptional powers or qualities."[54] Accordingly, charismatic authority is a form of rule to which people submit because of their belief in the magical powers, revelations, or heroism of the leader.[55] Weber states that the pure type of charismatic authority appears only briefly, in contrast to the relatively more enduring structures of traditional and legal authority. Charismatic authority is a force for revolutionary change, and it is irrational in the sense that it is not bound by any intellectually analyzable rule.

The authority of the charismatic leader is constrained only by his personal judgment; he is not governed by any formal method of adjudication.[56] Disputes are settled by prophetic revelation or Solomonic arbitration. The relationship between the leader and the led under charismatic authority is typically unstable. Although the authority of the leader is not derived directly from the will of his followers (obedience, instead, is a duty or obligation), the charismatic leader still must constantly prove himself through victories and successes, since charisma disappears if proof is lacking. In sum, the charismatic leader knows only inner determination and inner restraint. He "seizes the task that is adequate for him and demands obedience ... by virtue of his mission."[57]

Administration under charismatic authority, according to Weber, is loose and unstable. The leader's disciples do not have regular occupations, and they reject the methodical and rational pursuit of monetary rewards as undignified. Whatever organization exists is composed of an aristocracy chosen on the basis of charismatic qualities. There is no procedure for appointment, promotion, or dismissal, and there are no career tracks. There is no continuing hierarchical assignment of tasks, since the leader can intervene at will in the performance of any task. Perhaps most important, there are no defined spheres of authority or competence to protect against arbitrary exercises of power, and no system of formal rules to ensure equal treatment and due process.[58]

Traditional Authority

Like charismatic authority, traditional authority involves personal rule, but unlike charismatic authority, it is not the product of crisis and enthusiasm. Rulers enjoy personal authority and followers are subjects, but the routine governs conduct. Traditional authority is based on respect for the eternal past, belief in the rightness and appropriateness of the traditional or customary ways of doing things. It rests on piety for what actually, allegedly, or presumably has always existed.[59]

Weber argues that administration under traditional authority tends to be irrational because the development of rational regulations is impeded; there is likely to be no staff with formal, technical training; and there is wide scope for the indulgence of personal whims. A person, not an order, is obeyed, as the leader claims the performance of unspecified obligations and services as his personal right. Traditional authority is a regime of favorites in which a shifting series of tasks and powers is commissioned and granted by a leader through arbitrary decisions.[60] Justice under traditional authority is a mixture of constraints and personal discretion. There is a system of traditional norms that are considered inviolable, but there is also a realm of arbitrariness and dependence on the favor of the ruler, who judges on the basis of personal relationships.[61]

Legal Authority

In legal authority, legitimacy is based on a belief in reason, and laws are obeyed because they have been enacted by proper procedures.[62] Thus, it is believed that persons exercising authority are acting in accordance with their duties as established by a code of rules and regulations.

In administration, the legitimacy of legal authority rests on rules that are rationally established. Submission to authority is based on an impersonal bond to a generally defined "duty of office," and official duty is fixed by rationally established norms.[63] Obedience constitutes deference to an impersonal order, not an individual, and even the giving of a command represents obedience to an organizational norm rather than the arbitrary act of the person giving the order. Thus, the official does not exercise power in his own right; he is only a "trustee" of an impersonal, compulsory institution. The organization of the administrative staff under legal authority is bureaucratic in form. The system of justice under legal authority is a balance between formal or procedural justice and substantive justice, but with relative emphasis on the formal aspects of justice.

In outlining the bases of legitimacy, Weber purposely eschews the notion of an evolutionary, linear progress from one form to another. Instead, he sees a general trend toward rationalization, which is punctuated by spontaneous and creative bursts of charisma. The victory of charisma over the rational and the routine is never complete, however, and, in the end, charisma itself is routinized.[64]

The basic problem of charismatic leadership is one of succession: what occurs when something happens to the charismatic leader? In coping with the problem of succession, the charismatic situation starts to yield to a "routinization of charisma."[65] Weber states that when the personal authority of the charismatic leader is displaced by mechanisms or rules for formally ascertaining the "divine will," a routinization of charisma has taken place.[66] In regard to succession, as established procedures used to select a successor come to govern the process, the forces of tradition and rationalization begin to take effect, and charisma is disassociated from a person and embedded in an objective institutional structure. In the process, an unstable structure of authority is transformed into a more permanent traditional or legal structure of authority. With routinization, discipline—in the form of consistently rationalized, trained, and exact execution of received orders—replaces individual action. The development of legal authority, either through the routinization of charisma or through the breakdown of the privileges of traditional authority, exerts a certain "leveling" influence, whereby the recognition of authority is treated as a *source* of legitimacy rather than as a *consequence* of authority. Thus, legitimacy in legal authority takes on some democratic overtones.[67]

Law. The two major examples of domination based on authority discussed by Weber are the legal structure and bureaucratic administration. Weber asserts that law grows out of the "usages" and "conventions" found in all societies.[68] Law is distinguished from mere usage and convention, however, by the presence of a staff, which may employ coercive power for its enforcement. Weber notes that not all legal orders are considered authoritative. Legal authority exists only when the legal order is implemented and obeyed in the belief that it is legitimate.

Weber says that there are two kinds of rationality associated with the creation of legal norms: substantive and formal. An act is substantively rational if it is guided by principles such as those embodied in religious or ethical thought. An act is formally rational when it is based on general rules. Conversely, an act is formally irrational if guided by means beyond the control of reason (such as prophetic revelation or ordeal) and substantively irrational if based on emotional evaluations of single cases.[69] Weber traces a developmental sequence in the rationalization of the law that begins with primitive procedures relying on a combination of magically conditioned formalism and revelation. Next comes a theocratic or patrimonial form of legal system, and, finally, from this stage there emerges an increasingly specialized and logically systematized body of law.[70] Although economic interests play a limited role in the systematization and rationalization of law, there is at least a parallel between economic systems and legal structures. Modern capitalism is the prototype of purposively rational behavior, and the formal rationality of legal thought is the counterpart of purposive rationality in economic conduct.

Legal Domination and the State. The concepts of *legal domination* and *state* are not coextensive for Weber, who holds that law is not exclusively a political phenomenon, but one that exists wherever coercive means are available. Conversely, the state has at its disposal means of greater effectiveness than coercive ones. Nonetheless, Weber defines the state in terms of the specific means peculiar to it—that is, the use of violent force. The state is a relationship of people dominating people, supported by means of the legitimate use of violence. It is a compulsory organization that structures domination and, in the modern state, concentrates the means of administration in the hands of the leaders.[71]

According to Weber, the state was originally created to protect interests, particularly economic interests, and it arose from the struggle between the estates and the prince—between the holders of privilege and the holders of power. This struggle resulted in an alliance between the monarchy and bourgeois interests that wanted to be free of administrative arbitrariness and the irrational disturbances of the privileged and to affirm the legally binding character of contracts. This stabilizing process eventuated in a legitimate legal order in the form of the modern state.[72] The modern state is characterized by a body of law, bureaucracy, compulsory jurisdiction over territory, and a monopoly over the legitimate use of force. Government administration in the modern state is bound by rules of law and is conducted in accord with generally formulated principles. The people who occupy positions of power are not rulers but superiors; they hold office temporarily and possess limited authority. The people, on their part, are citizens, not subjects.[73]

The rise of the modern state, based on systematized and rationalized law and administration, has produced a conflict between the formal justice embodied in that state and substantive justice. The difference is that whereas formal justice derives its premises from formal concepts, substantive justice derives its premises from the experience of life.[74] In traditional society, Weber says, judicial administration aims at substantive justice and sweeps away formal rules of evidence. This mode of proceeding may be rational in the sense of adherence to some general, fixed principles, but, Weber argues, not in the sense of logical rationality. Decisions in such a system may be based on considerations of equity, but they may equally well be made on the basis of expediency or politics.[75]

Bureaucracy. The second example of domination based on authority is bureaucracy. In addressing the topic of bureaucracy and its role in society, Weber makes one of his most influential contributions. Weber did not invent the term *bureaucracy*, nor was he the first to examine its role in society.[76] Nevertheless, Weber has given us one of the most famous descriptions of the characteristics of bureaucratic organizations and surely one of the most penetrating and controversial analyses of the bureaucratic phenomenon.

Weber's analysis of bureaucracy is logically tied to his interest in legal domination in the modern state. In fact, Weber considered bureaucracy to be a major element in the rationalization of the modern world and the most important of all social processes.[77] He asserts that domination both expresses itself and functions through administration. Organized domination calls for continuous administration and the control of a personal executive staff and the material implements of administration. Legal domination calls for an increasingly bureaucratic administration in which domination is based on systematic knowledge.

Weber defines an organization as an ordering of social relationships, the maintenance of which certain individuals take as their special task. The organization consists of members accustomed to obedience; an administrative staff that holds itself at the disposal of the masters; and the masters themselves, who hold a power to command not derived from a grant of power by others.[78] The orientation of human behavior to a set of rules is central to Weber's concept of the organization. Organizational rules regulate the possession and scope of authority in the organization.[79]

Weber identifies bureaucracy as the dominant organizational form in a legal-rational society. The development of bureaucracy is a product of the intensive and qualitative (as opposed to extensive and quantitative) enlargement of administrative tasks—in other words, complexity breeds bureaucracy. Weber defines bureaucracy by listing the features that are characteristic of a particular type of organization as well as those of a particular type of personnel system. The features of what he calls the "ideal-type" bureaucracy are as follows:

1. Administration is carried out on a continuous basis, not simply at the pleasure of the leader.

2. Tasks in the bureaucratic organization are divided into functionally distinct areas, each with the requisite authority and sanctions.

3. Offices are arranged in the form of a hierarchy.

4. The resources of the bureaucratic organization are distinct from those of the members as private individuals (that is, administrators do not own the means of administration). This characteristic derives from Weber's concept of office, in which the official role entails specific duties to be performed, but the resources to fulfill those duties are provided by someone other than the official.

5. The officeholder cannot appropriate the office (that is, the office cannot be sold by the official or passed on by heredity).

6. Administration is based on written documents.

7. Control in the bureaucratic organization is based on impersonally applied rational rules. Thus it is not simply the existence of rules but the quality and mode of application of those rules that distinguishes the bureaucratic organization.[80]

Weber also outlines the specific personnel system in the bureaucratic organization:

1. Officials are personally free and are appointed on the basis of a contract.
2. Officials are appointed, not elected. Weber argues that election modifies the strictness of hierarchical subordination.
3. Officials are appointed on the basis of professional qualifications.
4. Officials have a fixed money salary and pension rights.
5. The official's post is his sole or major occupation.
6. A career structure exists in which promotion is based on merit (though there may also be pressure to recognize seniority).
7. The official is subject to a unified control and disciplinary system in which the means of compulsion and its exercise are clearly defined.[81]

It is important to observe that the features of bureaucracy as an organizational system and as a personnel system are all internal to the organization and have been, since the 1950s, extensively investigated for their internal consistency. Time and again it appears that the correlation between these features of the ideal type of bureaucracy, as outlined above, is confirmed through empirical research.[82]

Weber states that the bureaucratic mechanisms described above exist only in the modern state and the most advanced institutions of capitalism. The ideal-type bureaucracy possesses rationally discussable grounds for every administrative act; it centralizes and concentrates the means of administration; it has a "leveling" effect in that it does away with plutocratic privilege and rests on equality in the eyes of the law and equal eligibility for office; and it creates permanent authority relationships.

Weber clearly believes bureaucracy to be the most rational and efficient organizational form devised by man. Bureaucracy is rational in that it involves control based on knowledge, has clearly defined spheres of competence, operates according to intellectually analyzable rules, and has calculability in its operations.[83] Bureaucracy is efficient because of its precision, speed, consistency, availability of records, continuity, potential for secrecy, unity, rigorous coordination, and minimization of interpersonal friction, personnel costs, and material costs.[84] In Weber's words,

Experience tends universally to show that the purely bureaucratic type of administrative organization—that is, the monocratic variety of bureaucracy—is, from a

purely technical point of view, capable of attaining the highest degree ⌐
ciency and is in this sense formally the most rational known means of carryin
imperative control over human beings. It is superior to any other form in ⌐ ⌐⌐⌐
sion, in stability, in the stringency of its discipline, and in its reliability.... It is finally superior both in intensive efficiency and in the scope of its operations, and is
formally capable of application to all kinds of administrative tasks.[85]

It is very important to emphasize that Weber argues *not* that bureaucracy
is the most efficient of all conceivable forms of organization, but that it is
merely more efficient than the known alternative forms of administration.[86] The alternatives, according to Weber, are collegial and avocational
administration, which, he contends, are inadequate beyond a certain size
limit or where functions require technical training or continuity of policy.[87] Weber is particularly determined in his opposition to democratic
administration, a form of collegial administration. He argues that even
simple forms of democratic administration are unstable and likely to fall
into the hands of the wealthy, since those who work do not have time to
govern. Moreover, as soon as mass administration is involved, democratic
administration falls prey to the technical superiority of those with training and experience and thus to domination by technical experts.[88] Weber
also has substantial reservations about the broader form of collegial administration. Collegiality, he argues, almost inevitably involves obstacles
to precise, clear, rapid decisions and divides personal responsibility. Collegial administration impairs promptness of decision, consistency of policy, the responsibility of the individual, the requisite ruthlessness toward
outsiders, and the maintenance of discipline within the group. Weber asserts that it is impossible for either the internal or the foreign policy of
great states to be carried out on a collegial basis. And, as is the case with
democratic administration, collegial administration will eventually give
way to the technical superiority of the hierarchical organization.[89]

Weber considers bureaucracy and capitalism to be mutually supportive social structures. The capitalist market demands what bureaucracy
provides—official business discharged precisely, unambiguously, continuously, with as much speed as possible, and according to calculable rules
that make bureaucratic behavior predictable.[90] Moreover, capitalism and
bureaucracy share an emphasis on formalistic impersonality in their relationships. In the market, acts of exchange are oriented toward the
commodity, and those acts, Weber asserts, constitute the most impersonal relationship into which humans can enter. Market ethics require
only that partners to a transaction behave legally and honor the inviola-
bility of a promise once given. The private enterprise system transforms
even personal relationships in the organization into objects of the labor
market and drains them of all normal sentiment.[91] The bureaucratic
organization, for its part, also offers the elements of calculability and

depersonalization. Bureaucratic organizations—that is, civil servants—operate *sine ira et studio* (without hatred or passion)[92] and thereby exclude irrational feelings and sentiments in favor of the detached—or "neutral"[93]—professional expert. By eliminating incalculable emotional elements, bureaucracy offers the attitudes demanded by the apparatus of modern culture, in general, and modern capitalism, in particular. The demand for legal equality and for guarantees against arbitrariness requires formal, rational objectivity in administration, not the personal choice of traditional authority, nor the emotional demands for substantive justice in a democracy.[94]

Although Weber admires the rationality and efficiency of bureaucratic organizations and respects the concept of justice embodied therein, he also associates bureaucracy with an oppressive routine that is adverse to personal freedom.[95] He observes that bureaucracy has penetrated all social institutions, public and private, and that bureaucracy limits individual freedom, renders the individual incapable of understanding his own activities in relation to the organization as a whole, and favors—in business, government, and education—the "crippled personality" of the specialist.[96] Indeed, Weber recognized the possibility that bureaucracy could become mankind's "iron cage," whose rigidity would easily snuff out human feelings and values.[97] The iron cage metaphor of bureaucracy is often interpreted as indicating a prison wherein the movement and activity of inmates is tightly controlled, but it can also be interpreted as pointing to an "essential scaffolding for thought," or a prerequisite structure of an entire body of thought. Finally, the iron cage can be regarded as a playground structure, where available apparatuses give structure to play but do not determine how the play is pursued or conducted. This iron cage as playground structure motif closely fits Weber's definition of bureaucracy as organization. Also, it is non-pejorative and thus nicely complements his definition of bureaucracy as a personnel system.[98]

Thus, though bureaucracy extends human capacities, it also increases the number of forces to which man is subject and may not even be just, since the propertyless masses may not be well-served by a doctrine of formal equality before the law.[99] Weber sees reversion to small-scale organizations as the only means of avoiding the dysfunctional consequences of bureaucratic organizations, but he realizes that such a reversion would deprive society of bureaucracy's benefits.[100]

Weber's Political Perspectives

Moving from Weber's sociological analysis to his political writings, we encounter some shifts in emphasis, if not changes in direction. Weber's political writings place more emphasis on class conflict and less on ideal interests, and they treat capitalism as an independent phenomenon, not just part of the processes of rationalization. Also, whereas Weber's sociology focuses on the achievements of bureaucracy, his political writings stress the limitations of bureaucracy and the likely future struggle between political leadership and bureaucracy.

Democracy, Power, and the Nation-State

The "state," according to Weber, represents the monopoly of the legitimate use of force over a given territory and is an "ultimate" in that it cannot be integrated into a more comprehensive whole.[101] The "nation," however, is more than coercive control over a territory; it is also a community of sentiment. A nation exists where there is some common factor among people that is regarded as a source of value and produces a feeling of solidarity. This solidarity can be expressed through a vibrant civil, associational society where citizens embrace contestation rather than apathy and where the feeling of solidarity finds expression in autonomous political institutions or at least creates a demand for such institutions.[102]

Culture is a complex of characteristics or values that constitute the individuality of a particular national community. Weber asserts that there is a reciprocally interdependent relationship between the state and its culture: the state can survive only if it can harness the solidary feelings of national community and culture in support of its power, while, conversely, the national community preserves its distinctive identity by the protection it receives from the state. Adhering to the position that nations and the cultures they incorporate should be preserved, Weber contends that the state should serve national and cultural values and that politics is the appropriate sphere for the pursuit of these nonmaterial values.[103] The ultimate value, he argues, is the power position of the nation in the world, which means that struggle and conflict are permanent features of social life. Even more, Weber believes that conflict should be encouraged, because the highest qualities of life—traits of independence engendered by struggles with the difficulties of life—can be developed only through conflict.[104] This encouragement extends even to the ultimate conflict, war, which, Weber contends, creates a sentiment of community and gives a consecrated meaning to death. Only in war can the individual believe that he is dying *for* something.

Weber supports democracy as a means of providing leadership for national ends, but his is a "democracy" of a special type, and even then his support is at best reluctant. He warns against viewing democracy as a panacea for society's ills, and he argues that democracy is inevitably governed by the "law of the small number"—that politics is controlled from the top by a small number of people. Democracy changes the rules for the selection of a leader, but leaders are still selected. Instead, Weber defends democracy as a postulate of practical reason. It is to be preferred simply because it is the only reasonable alternative to authoritarianism. Democracy permits mass involvement, but on an orderly and regular basis, and it is consistent with the requirements of modern institutions and their demands for equality of status.[105]

Nevertheless, Weber believes that democracy is not distinguished by direct mass involvement but by the use of demagogy, the regular use of the vote in choosing leaders, and organization by mass political parties. The influence of a democratic elite is viewed as not only inevitable but desirable. Warning against the evils of "leaderless" democracy, in which professional politicians who have no "calling" rule, Weber argues that democracy requires strong leadership. In his words,

> In a democracy the people choose a leader in whom they trust. Then the chosen leader says, "Now shut up and obey me." People and party are no longer free to interfere in his business.... Later the people can sit in judgment. If the leader has made a mistake—to the gallows with him![106]

Political leadership is required to ensure the supremacy of the political over the bureaucratic. Since Weber regarded bureaucratization of organization (and, in a way, the world) as inescapable, given the increasing complexities of economic, social, and political life, he expected that a caste of administrators would emerge—a new aristocracy, whose power was grounded in specialized skills.[107] Political leadership is also required to ensure the supremacy of the political over the economic by focusing on social unity in the face of the divisiveness of class and material interests.[108] Although Weber warned against leaderless democracy, he was also aware that democracy could lead to "Plebiscitary Caesarism" in the form of an individual carried to absolute power by the emotionalized masses.[109] What is needed is not just leadership but charismatic leadership, which requires more than popularity and it is different from Caesaristic rule. The charismatic leader is one who is truly destined to rule and is suited for his tasks by supernatural gifts.[110]

The importance of leadership to Weber is reflected in his discussion of the role and functions of the politician. The objective of politics, he tells us, is to share power or to influence the distribution of power, and politics itself is any kind of independent leadership in political associations.[111] Consequently, the politician must have a capacity for independent action, he should not sacrifice his personal judgment for official duties—that is, he should be willing to resign if it is necessary for him to do so in order to live up to the responsibilities of leadership—and he must have skill in the struggle for power.[112] The politician should combine passion and a feeling of responsibility with a sense of proportion—

passion in devotion to a cause and a sense of proportion developed by establishing some distance between himself and others.[113] He must fight vanity and avoid seeking power for power's sake. These attributes, Weber suggests, are most likely to be found among those whose economic position is sufficiently secure that they can "live for" politics, not have to "live off" it.[114] According to Weber, the prototypical modern politician is the lawyer who is both available for service and has the skills required for effective participation in the struggle for power.[115]

The functions of the politician are to give direction to policy in a continuing struggle with bureaucratic and party officials and to counter the influence of class conflict and material interests by giving expression to a common interest underlying the superficial perceptions of class interests. In regard to the latter function, Weber differs from Marx in believing that divisions of class can be overcome within the capitalist system and that workers and entrepreneurs have a common interest in the rationalization of industry. Nevertheless, he also recognizes that capitalism has led to the pursuit of material interests (a "dance around the golden calf"), has replaced personal relationships with impersonality, and has created conflict between those with property and the propertyless.[116] These negative effects have resulted in a degeneration of the national political outlook and the subordination of the true function of politics to sectional and class interests. Weber argues that politics should be neither merely the pursuit of power nor simply an extension of economic activity in the form of class or interest-group activity. Instead, political leadership should draw people to an awareness of common interests, including a common interest in the perpetuation of capitalism.

Weber further contends that the honor of the political leader lies in his exclusive personal responsibility for what he does. Unfortunately, the ethical bases for the assumption of personal responsibility are ambiguous. Weber distinguishes between two kinds of ethics: the ethic of ultimate ends and the ethic of responsibility. Under the ethic of ultimate ends, one feels responsible only for seeing that the "flame of pure intention" is not quenched and action is taken regardless of the consequences. Under the ethic of responsibility, one is held accountable for the foreseeable results of his actions.[117] The ambiguity stems from two sources. First, Weber argues, no ethic can tell us to what extent an ethically good purpose justifies an ethically dubious means. Second, one must face the reality that some of the tasks of politics can be performed only by the use of violence, an ethically dubious means. The ambiguity poses a paradox. On the one hand, everything that is striven for through political action employing violent means and following an ethic of responsibility endangers the salvation of the soul. On the other hand, if one pursues a goal following a pure ethic of ultimate ends, the goal itself may be discredited because responsibility for consequences is lacking. Weber admits that he cannot prescribe whether one should follow an ethic of ultimate ends or an ethic of responsibility, or when one should be followed and when the other. He does assert that only when the two supplement each other does one have a calling for politics.[118]

Weber's emphasis on political leadership was prompted, in large part, by his aversion to bureaucratic domination. He considered the ideologies of his day (primarily capitalism and socialism) to be of small consequence compared to what he perceived to be the nearly inexorable process of bureaucratization. Weber argues that bureaucrats will develop interests of their own and start to shape policy, increasing the attendant danger that the rule of law will be undermined, in the absence of effective political leadership.[119] Weber asserts that the official, according to his proper vocation, should not engage in politics; he should undertake only the impartial administration of his office.[120] The honor of the civil servant, Weber says, is vested in his ability to execute conscientiously the orders of superior authorities, "exactly as if the order agreed with his own convictions."[121] If the administrator receives orders with which he disagrees, he should make his views known to his superior; but if the superior insists, the administrator must comply to the best of his ability. In short, a sense of duty placed above personal opinion should be part of the administrator's ethic and is required for the rule of law.

The problem arises when the bureaucracy attempts to overstep its rightful functions and capabilities. Weber believes bureaucrats to be, like feudal lords, the primary exponents of power and prestige for their own political structure.[122] The aggrandizement of bureaucracy can subvert the rule of law, as the bureaucracy, which cannot be inspected and controlled, becomes a law unto itself. Moreover, Weber contends that the permanent official is more likely to get his way than is his nominal superior, who is not likely to be a specialist and thus may be at the mercy of his expert subordinate. Knowledge becomes an instrument of political power, and secrecy protects the bureaucrat's monopoly on information.

Weber considers the bureaucratic machine to be one of the hardest of social structures to destroy. Bureaucracy is *the* means for achieving rationally ordered societal action. Nevertheless, the bureaucrat is also part of a community of functionaries who have an interest in seeing that the bureaucratic mechanism continues to function. These officials may develop into a status group whose cohesion stems, not from economic interests, but from the prestige of a style of life that fosters the values of status, security, and order.[123] Even more, bureaucrats may become a privileged class and use their positions for personal advantage. As a power group, bureaucrats may develop a code of honor that includes not only a sense of duty but also a belief in the superiority of their own qualifications.[124] Indeed, Weber's bureaucrat is far removed from Hegel's civil servant as the guardian of the modern state. Once in power, the bureaucracy is difficult to dislodge because few among the governed can master the tasks performed by the bureaucracy. Democracy requires the prevention of a closed status group of officials from taking power and the minimization of the authority of officialdom. But the "leveling" consequences of democracy may occur only in regard to the governed rather than to their bureaucratic masters, in a process that Weber refers to as "passive democratization."[125]

What unites Weber's work and worldview is a deep-felt concern for how "individualistic life-conduct of the personality, inherited from the age of liberalism, may be preserved in our own highly bureaucratized and thoroughly rationalized Western culture."[126] The central political issue of balancing individualism with bureaucratization translates into the question of how to prevent bureaucracy from exceeding its functions or, conversely, how to maintain the supremacy of the politician. That is no simple matter. Collegial administration is slow and obscures responsibility; a structural separation of powers is inherently unstable, and one power is likely to become dominant; amateur administration does not provide the requisite expertise; direct democracy is possible only in small groups and also does not provide expertise; representative democracy must rely on political parties, which themselves are bureaucratized. Bureaucracy, Weber maintains, can be controlled only from the top. Charismatic leadership may be the solution, if there is one. It is, at least, the best hope. Politicians are the indispensable counterweight to bureaucracy, and both parliamentary and plebiscitary bases of leadership are necessary to prevent rule by a clique of political notables and governmental officials who will control the rule of law rather than be subject to it.[127]

Nor is the economic sphere immune from possible bureaucratic domination. Such domination, Weber argues, is as likely to be the result of the quest for the bureaucratic values of order and security as it is the result of a power drive by bureaucratic officials.[128] Weber sees the bureaucratic threat in the economic sphere as emanating from two sources: socialism, which seeks to replace capitalism with a bureaucratic order; and the possibility that the bourgeoisie itself will go "soft" and precipitate a decline in capitalist values. Weber argues that socialism will make autonomous economic action subject to the bureaucratic management of the state. Economic transactions accomplished by political manipulation will replace the rationality and individualism of a capitalist economy. He believes that a system of bureaucratic rule is inevitable, but socialism will accelerate the process of bureaucratization and thus lead to serfdom.[129] Capitalism also faces dangers from within. Ironically, capitalism is itself a prime reason for the bureaucratization that threatens to stifle individualism. In addition, capitalism has encouraged the pursuit of material goods and the desire for a secure subsistence, which, Weber contends, will result in a "vast army of state pensioners and an array of monopolistic privileges," and in the demise of the entrepreneurial spirit of capitalism.[130]

Despite an undeniably pessimistic strain, Weber avoids schemes involving inevitable social development or unavoidable historical cycles. There is the notion of a recurrent struggle between routinization and charisma. When the world becomes overly bureaucratized, the prophets and the Caesars return. The future is thus a field of strategy, not a repetition of, or unfolding of, the past. Social life is a "polytheism of values" among which choices are possible, and charisma, says Weber, is the metaphysical vehicle of human freedom.[131]

Conclusion

The main points of Weber's substantive sociology may be summarized as follows:

1. A fundamental dynamic of civilization has been the process of rationalization.

2. The process of rationalization is reflected in various forms of domination, or exercises of power perceived to be legitimate.

3. The two basic types of domination are domination based on constellations of interests and domination based on authority.

4. Domination based on constellations of interests is manifested in religious and economic associations.

5. Domination based on authority is manifested in the operations of the state and bureaucratic organizations.

6. The legitimacy of domination based on authority is derived from three sources: charisma, tradition, and legality.

7. There has been a general historical trend toward increasing rationality in social relationships, but that trend has not been unilinear. Instead, the advance of rationalization has been punctuated by outbursts of charisma and reversions to tradition.

8. Bureaucracy is the dominant organizational form in a legal-rational society and it derives its characteristics—predictability, calculability, and impersonality—as well as its sense of justice from the society in which it resides.

9. Whereas the past has been marked by a struggle between charisma and the forces of depersonalization, the future will see a struggle over who will enact the rules in a legal-rational society, a struggle that will pit the political leader against the professional bureaucrat.

Although Weber is held in an esteem that approaches reverence, he has not been without his critics. Indeed, scarcely a facet of Weber's work has not been the subject of careful scrutiny and, often, intense controversy. There is widespread agreement on one criticism. Weber's writing style is, at best, difficult, and the striking difference between the clarity of Weber's spoken word and the opaqueness of his written word is often noted.[132] Weber both defended and explained his sometimes tortured constructions by stating, "Personally I am of the opinion that nothing is too pedantic if it is useful in avoiding confusions."[133] It is not clear that Weber avoided confusion, but his writing certainly qualifies as oftentimes pedantic. Another general criticism of Weber's work is his tendency to rely more on assertion than on demonstration or proof. This imbalance was probably inevitable given the compass of Weber's interests and the sweep of his ideas. Nonetheless, his dismissal of important ideas is, at times, almost casual. For instance, Weber simply rules out some forms of democracy as being "impractical," and popular sovereignty is peremptorily reduced to the status of "popular fiction."[134]

But the bulk of the criticisms have focused on Weber's methodology, his historical analysis, and his analysis of bureaucracy. The critique of Weber's methodology centers on his use of the ideal-type construct. The ideal-type is intended to combine attributes in a logically consistent manner. It is to be based on, but not confined to, historical manifestations that approximate the ideal-type. There are several problems with Weber's use of the ideal-type construct. One is his occasional use of the construct in a self-serving manner. Consider, for instance, Weber's treatment of the concept of capitalism.[135] He defines a particular form of capitalism (an ideal-type, if you will) that has as its essence a "spirit" that emphasizes honest accumulation as a "calling," and he traces the causal roots of this brand of capitalism to ascetic Protestantism. Note that this form of capitalism need never have actually appeared in its "pure" condition in history—which means that an empirical test of the causal relationship is at least inappropriate and perhaps impossible. Note, too, that Weber is dealing with a narrowly defined economic phenomenon whose relationship to ascetic Protestantism may be more definitional than causal and which excludes other forms of economic activity generally considered to be "capitalistic." Nicos P. Mouzelis takes the critique of Weber's ideal-type a step further, arguing that Weber's "ideal characteristics are not always compatible with one another." In particular, Mouzelis contends that Weber's ideal-type bureaucracy is not necessarily rational and efficient, and, consequently, Weber's posited combination of bureaucratic characteristics may not be "objectively possible."[136] Finally, it is argued that the use of ideal-types alone does not accomplish Weber's theory-building objectives. To constitute a theory, it is held, the types should be "arranged and classified in a definite order of relationship."[137] This Weber failed to do.

Weber has also been criticized in regard to his historical analysis. Most of this criticism has been directed at his analysis of the causes of capitalism. Although Weber acknowledges the likelihood of causal pluralism, his own analysis is largely confined to the influence of religious ideas on economic activity. Moreover, while Weber sought to demonstrate that ideas preceded interests in the development of capitalism, he does not demonstrate that *both* Calvinism and capitalism were not the product of prior material interests.[138] Finally, it is argued that Weber failed to deal with the processes by which the religious ideas of a dominant status group actually became an everyday standard of behavior for the common man.[139] This omission leaves open the possibility that forces other than religious ideas may have been instrumental in giving rise to capitalism, and even to its particular "spirit."

Yet all of these criticisms pale in comparison to the reaction to Weber's formulation of the concept of bureaucracy.[140] It has been argued that bureaucracy is not necessarily rational, it may not be efficient, that other forms of organization may well be more efficient, and that bureaucracy, by virtue of its structural and procedural complexity, may permit, if not encourage, evasions of individual responsibility.[141] A particularly penetrating analysis is that of Robert Merton.[142] Merton accepts Weber's construction of the bureaucratic phenomenon, abides by Weber's ground rules on the intent and use of the ideal-type—that it must stand only the test of internal logical consistency or objective possibility—and goes to the heart of the Weberian bureaucracy (that is, the impersonal application of the rules) in formulating his critique.

For Merton, the problem of bureaucracy comes in the form of a paradox: the very organizational features that Weber thought to be associated with rationality and efficiency may instead be associated with irrationality and inefficiency. Merton cites as a case in point the consequences of the impersonal application of the rules in a bureaucratic organization. The impersonal application of the rules is intended to enhance organizational rationality and efficiency by encouraging a high degree of reliability and conformity in the behavior in the organization. Problems arise, however, when these traits (reliability and conformity) become exaggerated—which, Merton argues, is likely to be the case in bureaucratic organizations given a number of specified formal and informal dynamics. As rule enforcement assumes increasing significance, the organization develops what Merton refers to as a "punctilious adherence to formalized procedures"—more commonly known as "red tape." Eventually, the enforcement of rules becomes an end in itself, which results in a "displacement of goals" as an instrumental value (the enforcement of rules) is substituted for a terminal value (the accomplishment of organizational goals) as the purpose of organizational activity. Organizational rules become "sanctified," or imbued with a moral legitimacy of their own, and the organization develops rigor mortis and becomes unable to adapt to changing circumstances. In sum, Merton argues that bureaucracy contains "the seeds of its own destruction" in its emphasis on rules, and that the bureaucratic environment itself produces a mentality that encourages the enforcement of rules regardless of their consequences for the accomplishment of organizational objectives.

Still, Weber is likely to remain a subject of both respect and controversy. On matters administrative, his particular genius was to place administration in a broad historical context and to associate the processes of bureaucratization with the processes of rationalization in the Western world. Moreover, Weber associated the mechanisms of bureaucracy with familiar concepts of justice, such as due process and equal application of the law, thus lending bureaucratic organization a significance that transcends even considerations of rationality and efficiency.

NOTES

1. Thomas H. Kemple, "'Unfashionable Observations' on the Use and Abuse of Weber," essay review of five recent Weber studies, in *Minerva* 44 (2006): 325–326. See also a lengthy essay review by Isher-Paul Sahni in the September–October 2005 issue of *Canadian Journal of Sociology Online*, at www.cjsonline.ca/pdf/maxwebertoday (accessed March 27, 2007); and another by Gianfaranco Poggi, "Recent Work on Weber," *Political Theory* 26, no. 4 (1998): 583–590. Tracking the reception of Weber's work in the past half-century and considering its current relevance are Michael Lounsbury and Edward J. Carberry, "From King to Court Jester? Weber's Fall from Grace in Organization Theory," in *Organization Studies* 26, no. 4 (2005): 501–525.
2. H. Gerth and C. Wright Mills, *From Max Weber: Essays in Sociology* (New York: Oxford University Press, 1946), 6. Since the late 1980s, much more material on Max Weber's life and background has become available, together with publications of his letters and with translations of some of his quantitative-statistical studies. On this flurry of publication since the late 1980s, see Richard Swedberg, "The Changing Picture of Max Weber's Sociology," *Annual Review of Sociology* 23 (2003): 283–306. Indeed, one author observed in 1993 that Weber had too often been labeled an opponent of empirical work, but mainly because his quantitative-statistical work had never been translated; see Lynn McDonald, *The Early Origins of the Social Sciences* (Montreal/Kingston: McGill-Queen's University Press, 1993), 300. For an intellectual biography of Weber, see Fritz Ringer, *Max Weber: An Intellectual Biography* (Chicago: University of Chicago Press, 2004).
3. Gerth and Mills, *From Max Weber*, 8.
4. Reinhard Bendix, *Max Weber: An Intellectual Portrait* (Berkeley: University of California Press, 1960), 3.

5. Ibid., 3. Bendix states that Weber died of pneumonia.

6. Karl Loewenstein, *Max Weber's Political Ideas in the Perspective of Our Time* (Amherst: University of Massachusetts Press, 1966), 94, 98.

7. Gerth and Mills, *From Max Weber*, 26.

8. David Beetham, *Max Weber and the Theory of Modern Politics* (London: Allen & Unwin, 1974), 19.

9. Bendix, *Max Weber*, 8.

10. Gerth and Mills, *From Max Weber*, 39.

11. Donald G. MacRae, *Weber* (London: Fontana/Collins, 1974), 26.

12. Ibid., 39.

13. Max Rheinstein, *Max Weber on Law in Economy and Society* (New York: Simon and Schuster, 1954), xviii; and Gerth and Mills, *From Max Weber*, 49. The first complete translation of Weber's *Wirtschaft und Gesellschaft* did not appear until 1968: *Economy and Society: An Outline of Interpretive Sociology*, trans. Guenther Roth, Claus Wittich and others (New York: Bedminster Press, 1968).

14. MacRae, *Weber*, 20.

15. Max Weber, *The Theory of Social and Economic Organization*, trans. A.M. Henderson and Talcott Parsons (New York: Free Press of Glencoe, 1947), 92, 96.

16. Gerth and Mills, *From Max Weber*, 157.

17. Max Weber, *The Protestant Ethic and the Spirit of Capitalism* (New York: Scribner's, 1958), xiv.

18. Gerth and Mills, *From Max Weber*, 186–187.

19. Bendix, *Max Weber*, 259.

20. See Sven Eliassen, "Max Weber's Methodology: An Ideal-Type," *Journal of the History of the Behavioral Sciences* 36, no. 3 (2000): 250. Weber conducted, i.a., a survey among publishers and presses. See Wilhelm Hennis, *Max Weber: Essays in Reconstruction* (London: Allen & Unwin, 1988), 55.

21. Max Weber, *The Methodology of the Social Sciences*, trans. Edward A. Shils and Henry A. Finch (New York: Free Press, 1949), 94.

22. Rheinstein, *Max Weber on Law*, xxx.

23. Weber, *Methodology of the Social Sciences*, 98–99.

24. MacRae, *Weber*, 66. While Weber did his best to outline the nature of an ideal-type, several authors in the 1960s found it necessary to clarify further. E.g., A. Diamant, "The Bureaucratic Model: Max Weber Rejected, Rediscovered, Reformed," in *Papers in Comparative Public Administration*, ed. Ferrel Heady and Sybil L. Stokes (Ann Arbor: Institute of Public Administration, University of Michigan, 1962), 62–65; Seymour M. Lipset, *Political Man: The Social Bases of Politics* (Garden City, N.Y.: Anchor Books, 1963), 58–59; Renate Mayntz, "Max Weber's Idealtypus der Bürokartie und die Organisationssoziologie," *Kölner Zeitschrift für Soziologie und Sozialpsychologie* 17 (1965): 493–501; Nicos P. Mouzelis, *Organisation and Bureaucracy: An Analysis of Modern Theories* (Chicago: Aldine, 1967), 43–46. Such clarification continues to be necessary: for instance, Lloyd I. Rudolph and Susanne Hoeber Rudolph, in "Authority and Power in Bureaucratic and Patrimonial Administration: A Revisionist Interpretation of Weber on Bureaucracy," in *World Politics* 31, no. 2 (1979), write (p. 199) that Weber thought bureaucracies most effective "when they most closely approximate the ideal-typical . . . features he identified"; their conclusion, that Weber did not recognize the difference between power and authority

(p. 226), is equally wrong and is a simplistic distortion of Weber's—admittedly—complex thought. On Weber's careful distinction between authority and power, see also Norman Uphoff, "Distinguishing Power, Authority & Legitimacy: Taking Max Weber at His Word by Using Resources-Exchange Analysis," *Polity* 22, no. 2 (1989): 296.

25. See Max Weber, "Die 'Objektivität' sozialwissenschaftlicher und sozialpolitischer Erkenntnis" (1904), in Max Weber, *Gesammelte Aufsätze zur Wissenschaftslehre*, ed. J. Winchkelman (Tübingen: J.C.B. Mohr, 1985), 146–214.

26. Ibid.; see also Eliassen, "Weber's Methodology," 242–243, 249–250.

27. Considering various problems with and challenges to causal explanation, Weber sighs ". . . how is causal explanation of any individual fact at all possible? . . . The number and nature of causes that somehow influenced an individual event is, after all, always infinite." Author translation from Weber, *Wissenschaftslehre*, 177.

28. Weber, *Methodology of the Social Sciences*, 82.

29. Ibid., 20–21.

30. Ibid., 1. Joseph Agassi, "Bye-bye, Weber," in *Philosophy of the Social Sciences* 21, no. 1 (1991): 103, argues that the literature fails to distinguish two variants of value-free social science. The first is Weber's and "requires that every value stays put within a value system that justifies it so that only the ultimate values or the axioms of any value system should remain unjustified." The second variant, that of a readiness to give up individual preferences, is often thought of as from Weber, but it is not.

31. Gerth and Mills, *From Max Weber*, 143–144.

32. Weber, *Methodology of the Social Sciences*, 4.

33. Cf. Weber, *Wissenschaftslehre*, 151: "An empirical science should teach no one what they ought to, what they can and what they will do" (author's translation). This statement is reminiscent of Dwight Waldo's "I cannot and will not teach you what to think, I can teach you how to think" (Richard Stillman, verbal communication to author).

34. Gerth and Mills, *From Max Weber*, 149.

35. Beetham, *Max Weber and the Theory of Modern Politics*, 29.

36. On this distinction between subjective and more objective manifestations of rationality, see Mark R. Rutgers and Petra Schreurs, "The Morality of Value- and Purpose-Rationality: The Kantian Roots of Weber's Foundational Distinction," *Administration & Society* 38, no. 4 (2006): 403–421. For more on Weber's Kantian roots, see also Andrew M. Koch, "Rationality, Romanticism and the Individual: Max Weber's 'Modernism' and the Confrontation with 'Modernity,'" *Canadian Journal of Political Science* 26, no. 1 (1993): 1123–1144.

37. Gerth and Mills, *From Max Weber*, 180.

38. Mouzelis, *Organisation and Bureaucracy*, 15–16.

39. Rheinstein, *Max Weber on Law*, 324. Weber defines authority as a command of a definite content finding obedience on the part of specific individuals. See Martin Albrow, *Bureaucracy* (New York: Praeger, 1970), 39.

40. Gerth and Mills, *From Max Weber*, 288.

41. The first translation was that by Talcott Parsons: Max Weber, *The Protestant Ethic and the Spirit of Capitalism* (London: Unwin University Books, 1930). For further exploration of the link between capitalism and religion, see Volker Heins, "Weber's Ethic and the Spirit of Anti-Capitalism," *Political Studies* 16, no. 2 (1993): 269–283.

42. Weber, *Theory of Social and Economic Organization*, 42–50.

43. Weber, *Protestant Ethic*, 18–19.

44. Ibid., 1(e). Weber, for instance, considers capitalism to be more rational than centralized planning. Central planning, according to Weber, does not have the advantage of a price system, which reduces the scope of required decisions; it is limited by inadequate knowledge; planning authorities may serve only their own interests; planning decisions may be unenforceable; and it is likely to encounter difficulty in maintaining property rights and labor discipline. See Weber, *Theory of Social and Economic Organization*, 37–39.

45. Weber, *Theory of Social and Economic Organization*, 184–186.

46. Weber, *Protestant Ethic*, 40.

47. The same argument has been advanced by Richard J. Stillman, *Creating the American State: The Moral Reformers and the Modern Administrative World They Made* (Tuscaloosa: University of Alabama Press, 1998), 165–170. See also Heins, "Weber's Ethic and the Spirit of Anti-Capitalism," 272.

48. Gerth and Mills, *From Max Weber*, 313, 321.

49. Weber, *Protestant Ethic*, 103–115.

50. Ibid., 119.

51. Weber ascribes the following characteristics to Protestant asceticism: (1) inhibitions against immersion in the world; (2) a drive for mastery over worldly things so as to make the world over in a transcendental image; (3) an emphasis on rationality through the systematization of conduct according to practical norms; accordingly, the goal is not mere mastery, but *rational* mastery; (4) an ethical universalism in that all are treated by the same impersonal standards; (5) high functional differentiation in which each serves God's will in his own particular "calling." See Weber, *Theory of Social and Economic Organization*, 80–81.

52. Weber, *Protestant Ethic*, 177.

53. Ibid., 181.

54. Weber, *Theory of Social and Economic Organization*, 358.

55. Weber offers the concept of charisma as one from which value judgments about particular individuals perceived as having charisma have been excluded. Ibid., 359.

56. Bendix, *Max Weber*, 295–296.

57. Gerth and Mills, *From Max Weber*, 246.

58. Bendix, *Max Weber*, 302; and Weber, *Theory of Social and Economic Organization*, 360.

59. Gerth and Mills, *From Max Weber*, 296.

60. Weber, *Theory of Social and Economic Organization*, 343.

61. Gerth and Mills, *From Max Weber*, 296.

62. It is very common in the literature to speak of legal-rational authority. However, Weber only writes about legal authority, a usage followed by Gerth and Mills in their 1946 translation of parts of *Wirtschaft und Gesellschaft*; by Mouzelis in his *Organisation and Bureaucracy*; by Bendix in his *Max Weber: An Intellectual Portrait*; as well as by Starling in *Managing the Public Sector* (Boston: Thomson Wadsworth, 1998). For a discussion of Weber's legal authority in relation to rationality, see Jos C.N. Raadschelders and Richard J. Stillman, "Towards a New Conceptual Framework for Studying Administrative Authority," *Administrative Theory & Praxis* 29, no. 1 (2007): 17–18.

63. Ibid., 299.
64. Mouzelis, *Organisation and Bureaucracy*, 19–20.
65. Gerth and Mills, *From Max Weber*, 54.
66. Ibid., 250.
67. Weber, *Theory of Social and Economic Organization*, 73, 386.
68. A "usage" is a collective way of doing things that individuals perpetuate without being required by anyone to do so. A "convention" is a collective way of doing things that is perpetuated because failure to do so would provoke disapproval by persons in the environment. Convention is distinguished from mere usage in that it carries with it a sense of obligation or duty. Bendix, *Max Weber*, 389.
69. Rheinstein, *Max Weber on Law*, xl and xli.
70. Weber attributes the rationalization of legal systems in the West to several factors, including the rise of an economic system and other interests that were served by the systematization of the law; the concept of a higher or natural law, which led to the notion that general law should prevail over special law; and the influence of Roman law. Ibid., 304.
71. Gerth and Mills, *From Max Weber*, 78–83.
72. Rheinstein, *Max Weber on Law*, 345–348.
73. Bendix, *Max Weber*, 418–422.
74. Rheinstein, *Max Weber on Law*, xli and xlii.
75. Ibid., 264. Weber holds much the same opinion of the "popular justice" of the jury system. The jury system, he says, appeals only to the layman who feels annoyed whenever he encounters formalism and satisfies only the emotional demands of the underprivileged classes. Ibid., 318.
76. Martin Albrow, *Bureaucracy* (London: Pall Mall Press, 1970), 16, mentions that the first time the word *bureaucracy* appeared was in a letter by Baron de Grimm, who remembered that the late M. de Gournay, an *intendent* (high-ranking public official), used to say: "We have an illness in France which bids fair to play havoc with us; this illness is called 'bureaumania.' . . . Sometimes he used to invent a fourth or fifth form of government under the heading of bureaucracy." The major author briefly examining bureaucracy, or, more specifically, the civil servant's role in society, is Georg Hegel. See, especially, C. K. Y. Shaw, "Hegel's Theory of Modern Bureaucracy," *American Political Science Review* 86, no. 2 (1992): 381–389.
77. Albrow, *Bureaucracy*, 43.
78. Weber, *Theory of Social and Economic Organization*, 56; and Rheinstein, *Max Weber on Law*, 335.
79. Albrow, *Bureaucracy*, 38–39.
80. Weber, *Theory of Social and Economic Organization*, 330–332; Albrow, *Bureaucracy*, 43–44; Gerth and Mills, *From Max Weber*, 196–198.
81. Weber, *Theory of Social and Economic Organization*, 333–334; Albrow, *Bureaucracy*, 44–45; Gerth and Mills, *From Max Weber*, 198–204. For a more expanded listing of features of bureaucracy as organization and as personnel system, see Jos C. N. Raadschelders, *Government: A Public Administration Perspective* (Armonk, N.Y.: M. E. Sharpe, 2003), 211, 313.
82. See, especially, Eric J. Walton, "The Persistence of Bureaucracy: A Metaanalysis of Weber's Model of Bureaucratic Control," in *Organization Studies* 26, no. 4 (2005): 569–600.
83. Beetham, *Max Weber and the Theory of Modern Politics*, 69.
84. Rheinstein, *Max Weber on Law*, 349.

85. Weber, *Theory of Social and Economic Organization*, 337.
86. It is important to observe that mistranslation of Weber has often resulted in confusing rationality with efficiency. But Weber is very clear about the difference between these two concepts. See, e.g., Gyorgy Gajduschek, "Bureaucracy: Is It Efficient? Is It Not? Is That The Question? Uncertainty Reduction: An Ignored Element of Bureaucratic Rationality," *Administration & Society* 34, no. 6 (2006): 700–723. Gajduschek argues (716) that an advantage implicit in Weber's listing of why bureaucracy is more efficient than other forms of organization is "uncertainty reduction," which works both toward the future (predictability, calculability) and toward the past (reconstructing past outputs and procedures from written records).
87. Ibid., 415.
88. Rheinstein, *Max Weber on Law*, 331–334. The notion of domination by the wealthy or by technical experts under mass democracy is comparable to Michels's "iron law of oligarchy." See Roberto Michels, *Political Parties: A Sociological Study of the Oligarchical Tendencies of Modern Democracy* (1915; rpt. New York: Free Press, 1966), 342–356.
89. Weber, *Theory of Social and Economic Organization*, 397–402. On more specific devices, Weber does not like functional representation because it leads to mere compromise rather than to general agreement, and he does not like workers' councils because disagreements are settled on the basis of economic power, not spontaneous agreement.
90. Gerth and Mills, *From Max Weber*, 215.
91. Rheinstein, *Max Weber on Law*, 190–192.
92. While sometimes rendered as "sine ira ac studio" (e.g., the Gerth and Mills translation, p. 215), Weber writes "sine ira et studio" and follows this phrase with the German "ohne Haß und Leidenschaft," which translates as "without hatred or passion." Cf. *Wirtschaft und Gesellschaft*, 129.
93. See also Brian R. Fry and Lloyd Nigro, "Max Weber and U.S. Public Administration: The Administrator as Neutral Servant," *Journal of Management History* 2, no. 1 (1996): 37–46.
94. Rheinstein, *Max Weber on Law*, 351, 355.
95. Gerth and Mills, *From Max Weber*, 50.
96. Mouzelis, *Organisation and Bureaucracy*, 19.
97. Weber used the metaphor of the iron cage in *The Protestant Ethic*, but he spoke of *stahlhartes Gehäuse*, which translates better as "shell as hard as steel." The image of the iron cage originates with Parsons's translation; see Peter Baehr, "The 'Iron Cage' and the 'Shell as hard as steel': Parsons, Weber and the *stahlhartes Gehäuse* Metaphor in *The Protestant Ethic and the Spirit of Capitalism*," *History and Theory* 40 (2001): 153–169. The iron cage metaphor actually refers to the binding nature of the contemporary state, which includes bureaucracy.
98. For discussion of the "iron cage" as prisoner structure, as prerequisite structure, and as playground structure, see Jay Klagge, "Approaches to the Iron Cage: Reconstructing the Bars of Weber's Metaphor," *Administration & Society* 29, no. 1 (1997): 63–77. For bureaucracy as an essential scaffolding of thought, see Hunter Crowther-Heyck, *Herbert A. Simon: The Bounds of Reason in Modern America* (Baltimore: Johns Hopkins University Press, 2005), 117.
99. Gerth and Mills, *From Max Weber*, 221.

100. Weber, *Theory of Social and Economic Organization*, 338.
101. Gerth and Mills, *From Max Weber*, 48. Monopoly over the use of violence is central to Weber's concept of the state. Tilly's definition of the state contains four elements: control over a well-defined continuous territory; a relatively centralized administration; differentiation from other societal organizations (e.g., the church); and control over the use of violence. See Charles Tilly, *The Formation of National States in Western Europe* (Princeton: Princeton University Press, 1975), 27.
102. On the civil society element of Weber's thought, see Sung Ho Kom, "'In Affirming Them, He Affirms Himself': Max Weber's Politics of Civil Society," *Political Theory* 28, no. 2 (2000): 197–229, esp. 220–221. On the need for institutions, see Beetham, *Max Weber and the Theory of Modern Politics*, 122.
103. Beetham, *Max Weber and the Theory of Modern Politics*, 44.
104. Ibid., 39–42.
105. Ibid., 103–105. Democracy, in Weber's view, should incorporate features such as universal suffrage, popular representation, the initiative and the referendum, and the popular election of the head of state. See Loewenstein, *Weber's Political Ideas*, 25–26.
106. Gerth and Mills, *From Max Weber*, 42.
107. On this issue of the emergence of a new aristocracy, see also Regina F. Titunik, "The Continuation of History: Max Weber on the Advent of a New Aristocracy," in *Journal of Politics* 59, no. 3 (1997): 680–700.
108. Beetham, *Max Weber and the Theory of Modern Politics*, 217. See also Fry and Nigro, "Max Weber and U.S. Public Administration," 45, on this point.
109. Loewenstein, *Weber's Political Ideas*, 8, 26.
110. Ibid., 74–76.
111. Gerth and Mills, *From Max Weber*, 77.
112. Bendix, *Max Weber*, 441.
113. Gerth and Mills, *From Max Weber*, 115.
114. Beetham, *Max Weber and the Theory of Modern Politics*, 228.
115. Bendix, *Max Weber*, 442–443.
116. Beetham, *Max Weber and the Theory of Modern Politics*, 218–220.
117. Gerth and Mills, *From Max Weber*, 120–121.
118. Ibid., 127.
119. Bendix, *Max Weber*, 485.
120. Gerth and Mills, *From Max Weber*, 95.
121. Ibid.
122. Ibid., 160.
123. Beetham, *Max Weber and the Theory of Modern Politics*, 81.
124. Ibid., 73.
125. Gerth and Mills, *From Max Weber*, 226.
126. Wolfgang J. Mommsen, *The Political and Social Theory of Max Weber: Collected Essays* (London/Chicago: Polity Press/University of Chicago Press, 1989), x. See also the review of Mommsen's book by Robert J. Antonio, *Philosophy of the Social Sciences* 24, no. 1 (1994): 103–110.
127. Bendix, *Max Weber*, 457.
128. Ibid., 463.
129. Gerth and Mills, *From Max Weber*, 49–50.
130. Bendix, *Max Weber*, 461–462.
131. Gerth and Mills, *From Max Weber*, 72.

132. See, for instance, Albrow, *Bureaucracy*, 54; and Rheinstein, *Max Weber on Law*, vii.

133. Weber, *Methodology of the Social Sciences*, 20.

134. Beetham, *Max Weber and the Theory of Modern Politics*, 266.

135. Weber, *Protestant Ethic*, 7.

136. Mouzelis, *Organisation and Bureaucracy*, 47–48. However, in this particular section of an otherwise outstanding study, Mouzelis also writes (p. 47): ". . . one can argue that a perfectly rational-efficient organization having Weber's ideal characteristics is not objectively possible. . . ." This remark is puzzling when considering Mouzelis's clear discussion of ideal-types on pp. 43–46 (see also note 25 above), but it shows how difficult it is to escape the notion that an ideal-typical bureaucracy is possible.

137. Weber, *Theory of Social and Economic Organization*, 28.

138. Weber, *Protestant Ethic*, 7.

139. Bendix, *Max Weber*, 275.

140. See Albrow, *Bureaucracy*, 54–61, for a summary of these critiques.

141. On bureaucracy as a source of evil, see Guy B. Adams and Danny L. Balfour, *Unmasking Administrative Evil* (Armonk, N.Y.: M.E. Sharpe, 2004); and Guy B. Adams, Danny L. Balfour, and George E. Reed, "Abu Ghraib, Administrative Evil, and Moral Inversion: The Value of 'Putting Cruelty First,'" *Public Administration Review* 66, no. 5 (2006): 680–693.

142. Robert K. Merton, "Bureaucratic Structure and Personality," *Reader in Bureaucracy*, ed. Robert K. Merton et al. (New York: Free Press, 1952), 361–371.

Chapter 2

Frederick W. Taylor:
The Man, the Method, the Movement

A s was the case with the writings of Max Weber, a question likely to occur to the reader on first encountering the works of Frederick Taylor is why they should be included in a text on public administration. It would seem to be anomalous, at least on the surface, that an author who was almost exclusively concerned with private-sector management should be included in a volume dealing with the public sector.

The reason for doing so is that the definition of the field of public administration widely accepted in Taylor's day encouraged, indeed demanded, such an inclusion. That definition was founded on the premises that administration should be separated from political and policy concerns and that administrators should be limited to, in Woodrow Wilson's words, "the detailed and systematic execution of public law." It was argued that taking politics out of administration isolated a generic administrative function—namely, the appropriate ordering of means to given ends. Accordingly, it was permissible to search in the private sector, and even in other constitutional systems, for general administrative techniques that could be used to enhance efficiency in the operation of

American government and curtail the corruption and nepotism characteristic of the American public sector in the nineteenth century.

With this charge, attention naturally turned to the techniques of Scientific Management, which were directly concerned with the question of efficiency and had achieved a large measure of public notoriety, if not always acclaim. Scientific Management attracted the enthusiastic support of many in government who believed that those techniques could be applied in the public sector. Taylor himself thought the techniques of Scientific Management to be applicable to the public sector, since, in his judgment, the average public employee did little more than one-third to one-half of a good day's work.[1]

Thus, the reason for the inclusion of a review of Taylor's works in this volume is that Scientific Management was perceived as a way to achieve greater efficiency in the management of the public business. But this perception simply transforms an apparent anomaly into an irony. The irony is that a movement seen by most as a series of expedients to improve efficiency was regarded by its originator as primarily a mechanism for social reform. Taylor saw Scientific Management as a "mental revolution" in which a "scientific" approach could be brought to bear not only on the performance of physical tasks but on all social problems. Only the larger frame of social reform can explain the evangelical zeal of the adherents of Scientific Management and the passion of the opposition. Not only do Taylor's ideas continue to have appeal in business management and in public administration, but they actually have drawn increased scholarly attention in the past twenty years.[2]

In this chapter, Taylor as a man and Scientific Management as both a method and a movement are discussed. We pay more attention to Taylor's life than is the case for most authors in this volume because of the intimate relationships among the man, his methods, and the movement, as Taylor's virtues, and his vices, are reflected in Scientific Management. Indeed, it has been Taylor's fate to be stereotyped as an "obsessive, compulsive character, driven by a relentless need to tie down and master almost every aspect of his life."[3] This image, however, has been significantly amended in the past two decades.[4] On methods, we consider time-and-motion studies, wage-incentive schemes, and functional organization as three of the primary emphases in the techniques of Scientific Management. On the movement, we look at efforts to spread the gospel of Scientific Management and some of the controversy that surrounded those efforts.

Life

Frederick W. Taylor was born in Philadelphia on March 22, 1856, into a family with deep roots in American culture and a strong religious heritage. His father, Franklin, was a fourth-generation English Quaker and his mother, Emily, a sixth-generation English Puritan. Franklin earned an undergraduate and a master's degree from Princeton University and was an attorney in Philadelphia. He was something of a gentleman of leisure, however, and did not actively practice his profession, pursuing, instead, his interests in literature and history. He has been described as "devoid of aggressiveness and combativeness," and little of the father was to be found in the son.[5]

But Taylor's mother apparently exerted a powerful influence on her son. Emily Winslow Taylor's character reflected her Puritan background, which "fostered a bold sense of inquiry, dissatisfaction, revolt, a new vision, discipline, and a passion for making the new vision prevail."[6] All these attributes were to be found in Emily Taylor and later, even more decidedly, in her son Frederick. Emily was an expert linguist, an abolitionist, and a feminist whose home in Germantown became a salon for innovators and reformers. Whereas Franklin appears to have played a relatively minor role in the rearing of Frederick and his brother and sister, Emily was a major force, presiding over her children's education and running a household described as "a thing ruled regular."[7]

As a child, Frederick Taylor demonstrated little interest in his parents' social and philosophical concerns. The family lived in England, France, and Germany between 1868 and 1871, but the only apparent effects of this itinerant experience on Frederick were that he developed a lasting aversion to travel and a similarly lasting dislike for Germans.[8] Although the young Frederick was rather austere in his personal life, he had a love of games; this combination of control and playfulness was carried, in somewhat changing measure, throughout his lifetime. He was active in sports as a child and later participated in crew, baseball, skating, and gymnastics while at Exeter Academy. Taylor was also a member of the Young America Cricket Club and an avid tennis player, playing on the winning team in the U.S. Lawn Tennis Doubles Championship in 1881. In the late 1890s, he developed an interest in golf and played daily.

Sports were not Taylor's only extracurricular activity: he also sang tenor in the choral society and developed a reputation for his female impersonations on the stage.[9] Nonetheless, there was usually a sense of purposefulness to Taylor's play. His interest in mechanical inventions, for instance, was manifested in his sports activities. Among his inventions were a spoon-shaped handle for a tennis racket, a two-handled putter (later outlawed), and a method of tightening tennis nets with an iron socket.

As a student, Taylor proved to be more diligent than brilliant, but he achieved generally good results. At age sixteen, he entered Phillips Exeter Academy to prepare for the study of law, and, though demonstrating a rebellious spirit—evidenced by his being caught reading a book during chapel and cheating on an exam—he worked hard and earned good marks.[10] Near the end of his time at Exeter, however, Taylor suffered from a vision problem that his parents attributed to studying too much by kerosene lamp. The result was that, though he had planned to study law and had passed the Harvard University entrance examination with honors, he decided not to pursue that course. Instead, in an abrupt and curious change of direction, Taylor chose to become an apprentice machinist at the Enterprise Hydraulic Works, a small firm in Philadelphia where he spent four years. Thus, from a budding lawyer, a prospective engineer was born.

After serving his apprenticeship at Enterprise Hydraulic, Taylor assumed a position as an ordinary laborer at the Midvale Steel Works. The choice proved to be a fortunate one. Midvale, at that time, was owned by a friend of the Taylor family and run by William Sellers, an innovative engineer who took a personal interest in Taylor's development. At Midvale, Taylor progressed through the stages of an ordinary laborer's advancement, but at a pace seldom achieved by the ordinary laborer. He worked originally as a time clerk and machinist, became a gang boss after two months, and was chief engineer after only six years at Midvale.

It was at Midvale that the rudimentary concepts of Scientific Management began to form in Taylor's mind. As a laborer, he had identified with the workman and his mores, including sympathy for a practice Taylor would later resoundingly condemn: "systematic soldiering," or informal output restrictions imposed by the work group. When Taylor assumed managerial status, however, his outlook and identifications changed markedly. Affixing his primary loyalty to management, Taylor launched a concerted attack on systematic soldiering. His supervisory style was authoritarian in nature, and he became known as something of a "holy terror" in his relationships with his men—which at one point grew so touchy that Taylor exchanged physical threats with some members of his work group.[11]

Taylor's attempts to combat systematic soldiering led him to institute two important components of what was later to be known as Scientific Management: time-and-motion studies and a piecework incentive plan. Taylor reorganized the toolroom, standardized the tools, and created five positions that were the precursors of "functional foremen": an instruction card clerk, a time clerk, an inspector, a gang boss, and a shop disciplinarian. In addition, Taylor began his study of metal cutting, which would eventually consume twenty-five years of experimentation.

While at Midvale, Taylor also found time to take up the study of engineering. He negotiated a rather unusual arrangement with the Stevens Institute, at which he actually appeared only to take examinations.[12] He

received a degree in mechanical engineering from Stevens in 1883. Ironically, in light of his career interests, Taylor received little training in
mathematics or accounting; he later remedied these deficiencies by hiring competent mathematicians to assist him and by teaching himself the
basics of accounting. In 1886 Taylor joined the American Society for Mechanical Engineering, beginning a long and fruitful relationship that
would see the association serve as a public forum for the presentation of
most of Taylor's ideas on Scientific Management. Taylor would later serve
as president of the society.

In 1890 Taylor left a successful career at Midvale and entered into
what were probably the most difficult years of his life. While at Midvale,
Taylor had made some contacts with the navy, which led to an association
with a group called the Manufacturing Investment Company, a wood
pulp and paper manufacturing firm that held a patent on a process for
manufacturing wood pulp from lumber-mill by-products. His venture
into management was not entirely successful, for Taylor, as was his wont,
was apparently concerned more about improving productivity than about
advancing the financial position of the firm. What Taylor did develop
while he was with Manufacturing Investment was a deep distrust of big
business, which was to have a lasting impact, shaping his later programs
of social reform.[13]

Taylor left Manufacturing Investment in 1893 to become a consulting
engineer, introducing various aspects of his evolving management theories in a number of firms. This period of his life was marked less by success in consulting than by a coming together of most of the major
elements of Scientific Management. In 1895 Taylor presented his first report to the American Society of Mechanical Engineers, a paper entitled
"A Piece Rate System."[14] Although, as the title suggests, Taylor proposed
a new wage-incentive scheme, he was more concerned with the system of
management than with the scheme embedded in it. Also during this period, he made a series of investments that formed the basis of his personal wealth and subsequently enabled him to devote most of his time to
promoting Scientific Management.

In 1898 Taylor took a position with Bethlehem Steel Company, which
would prove to be a most productive association. While at Bethlehem,
Taylor installed a system of production management and functional supervision that incorporated many of the basic ideas of Scientific Management. He also collaborated on the invention of a high-speed tool steel,
later touted as the most important machine-tool invention of Taylor's lifetime.[15] The money received from the patent on this process was the
largest single increment to Taylor's personal fortune. After leaving Bethlehem in 1901, he spent the rest of his life basically as a publicist, educator, and social reformer in advancing the cause of Scientific Management,

and his attentions shifted, accordingly, from the technical aspects of Scientific Management to its social implications.

Over his lifetime, Taylor developed a philosophy of life, work, and society that shaped his approach to the development of a science of management. Although he himself scorned formal religion, his view of life reflected his Quaker and Puritan background. Taylor's grand aim was control—he believed that hard work yields morality and that weaknesses must be curbed by doing what is right.[16] Character is developed and reinforced by doing things that are tiresome, monotonous, and unpleasant.[17] This set of beliefs, plus Taylor's distrust of anything not based on provable facts, determined both the focus of his science of management and the methods he employed in elaborating it. This basic philosophy was also reflected in Taylor's disciplined lifestyle: he dressed only for utility; he did not drink alcohol, coffee, or tea; and even his approach to pastimes, as we have seen, was highly structured.[18] It has been said that the aesthetic was not in Taylor's blood; if he even had a concept of beauty, it was probably based on the elimination of the superfluous.[19]

Taylor's attitude toward life was also reflected in his attitude toward work. Though he reportedly had a strong personal distaste for manual labor, he described his years as an apprentice and the winter of 1895, which was spent cutting metal, as the happiest of his life.[20] Taylor was both celebrated and condemned for his often tactless and cold-blooded references to workingmen, but he had a respect for, and identification with, the workman. Indeed, Taylor purposely adopted the lifestyle and habits of the worker, including a penchant for swearing, which sometimes caused him difficulty in more formal circles.[21]

Taylor's approach to Scientific Management constituted a harsher critique of management than of the workers.[22] He felt that management was the basic cause of inefficiency, since it had not assumed its fair share of responsibility for the design and performance of work. Thus, workers "soldiered" because management had not performed its functions properly. Taylor's attitude toward the workman can perhaps be more appropriately characterized as one of noblesse oblige than as castigation. Comparing college professors to workingmen, he claimed, "We are all made of the same clay, and essentially of the same mental as well as physical fibre."[23] Taylor thought education as a gentleman demanded actual experience as well as respect both for a day's work and the men who do it. He ranked character, common sense, and education—in that order—as the elements of a good man.[24]

As a social reformer, Taylor is probably best described as a "conservative radical." He was surely inclined to the radical viewpoint, as evidenced by his distrust of big business, his scathing criticism of management practices, and his opposition to capitalism that was devoid of human consideration and characterized by financial privilege.[25] Yet Taylor rejected socialism, felt that labor unions had outlived their usefulness, and had little sympathy for what he called the "semiphilanthropic" gestures of the labor reformers of his day.[26] Though Taylor would later be identified with the Progressive movement, his direct concerns never extended much beyond the shop level, and his interest in the "labor problem" developed rather late in his career.

In assessing Frederick Taylor as a man, one derives a lasting impression of basic dualities and conflict. His passion for games versus his dedication to hard work and discipline, his tactless references to workmen versus his deliberate adoption of their lifestyle, his passion for order versus a personal habit of leaving things laying about, his plague of nightmares versus his preoccupation with control, his distaste for manual labor versus his reported pleasure in doing it, his dislike of clerical routines versus his praise of the monotonous grind, the incidents of rebellious behavior at Exeter versus his concern for character and integrity illustrate the dualities and suggest the conflicts. In sum, Taylor's personal life was characterized by tension and inner turmoil. Taylor has been described as a man marked by an excess of his virtues, but he was also a man apparently engaged in a struggle against a perceived inner weakness, in which a frenzy for order was a counterpart of the disorder within him.[27] And Taylor the man had an integral impact on Scientific Management as a method and as a movement.

The Method

Taylor identifies the basic social problem of his day as inefficiency. His objective is to increase efficiency by capitalizing on the difference between what can be done by a "first-class" man and by an ordinary worker, in the process, producing both higher wages for workers who choose to participate in the system and lower labor costs for management.

Taylor blames both management and the worker for inefficiency but reserves his sternest criticism for management, which, he contends, is responsible for nine-tenths of the problem.[28] Management, Taylor charges, is deficient both in terms of its lack of knowledge as to what constitutes a proper day's work and in its indifference to proper managerial practices. The worker contributes to the problem of inefficiency through systematic soldiering, or the purposeful and organized restriction of output.[29] But even here, Taylor lays the ultimate blame at the doorstep of management, whose ignorance and indifference encourage systematic soldiering on the part of the workmen.

Taylor argues that traditional styles of management, which employ a driving method of supervision (a combination of authoritarian rule and physical compulsion), and an incentive system (piecework) that discourages efficiency by lowering rates of compensation as productivity increases, combine to foster systematic soldiering. Even under the best of previous managerial practices—initiative and incentive management—Taylor contends that too much responsibility is placed on the worker and too little on management. Under initiative and incentive management, a worker is simply hired and sent out to perform specified tasks with little in the way of instruction or guidance from management; all too often, the result is inefficiency, since the worker is not likely to know how best to perform his assigned tasks. Taylor characterizes initiative and incentive management as a "lazy manager's philosophy," in which management has shirked its primary responsibilities in regard to job design.[30]

To correct these deficiencies, Taylor proposes an approach to management embodying a radically altered division of responsibilities between management and workers. Management is to assume a much larger portion of the burden and is to take primary responsibility for a scientific search for the best way of performing organizational tasks.

Taylor argues that there are two kinds of workmen: first-class and second-class. A first-class workman is both able and willing to do a task efficiently, and Taylor maintains that every man is a first-class workman at some kind of work. A second-class worker, in contrast, is physically able to perform a task but will not do so because he is lazy.[31] Taylor has little patience with, or sympathy for, a second-class workman—as he puts it, Scientific Management has no place for a bird who can sing, but won't.[32] It is management's responsibility to locate and/or develop first-class workmen, place them in positions suitable to their talents, provide them with good working conditions and appropriate implements, and give them detailed instructions on the best method of performing their tasks.[33]

All of this responsibility is to be based on the development of a science of management that is to replace rules of thumb passed on from workman to workman. Taylor's objective is to seek, coordinate, and systematize knowledge, and, by processes of observation, comparison, and abstraction, to deduce general laws of management.[34] This scientific endeavor is to concentrate on two kinds of experiments—the control and operation of machines and the standardization of human actions—with the intent of making man as predictable and efficient as the machines he tends.

Although Taylor believes it both advisable and necessary to utilize the knowledge of the workers in regard to the performance of their tasks, he does not consider them capable of developing a science of management themselves. Instead, Taylor charges management with the basic responsibility for developing the required science. In other words, management must first make itself efficient before expecting efficiency from the workers. Once the proper method—which includes identification of the most useful and efficient production procedures at the workfloor level—has been determined, workers are simply responsible for implementing it. Authority is to be exercised through an unveiling of scientific laws, not as an expression of arbitrary rule, but Scientific Management is to be implemented through enforced standardization of methods, enforced adoption of the best implements, and enforced cooperation between and among management and workers.[35]

Taylor summarizes this approach in his famous statement of the principles of Scientific Management, which are as follows:

1. The development of a science of management
2. The selection and training of the workman
3. Bringing science and the workman together
4. An equal division of work and responsibility between management and worker[36]

Thus, under Scientific Management, science would replace rules of thumb, harmony would replace discord, cooperation would replace individualism, maximum output would replace restricted output, and each workman would be developed to his greatest efficiency and prosperity.[37] In sum, Taylor's management approach was to be "founded on *commitment to science* and *friendly cooperation*."[38]

In pursuit of these objectives, Taylor devoted most of his productive lifetime to the quest for a science of management. In the course of this quest, Taylor discovered and/or implemented a series of innovations pertaining to the machinery of production, the organizational environment, and the people who used the machines and populated the organizations. While important, some of these developments—such as the invention of mechanical devices, the development of cost accounting techniques, machine-room layout and design, purchase and storage methods, tool standardization and toolroom reorganization, and mnemonic classification systems—fall beyond the purview of the present discussion, in which we concentrate instead on three central components of Taylor's Scientific Management: time-and-motion studies, wage-incentive systems, and functional organization.

Time-and-Motion Studies

As stated earlier, Taylor believed that the basic causes of inefficiency are management's ignorance about the proper time required to perform a task and the systematic soldiering by workmen that such ignorance encourages. Accordingly, a primary task for Scientific Management is to establish appropriate standards for task performance. These standards are to be based on scientific investigations of tasks performed using optimal methods rather than simple observations of actual performance in the workplace. The intent, thus, is not to measure the actual performance of the average workman but to determine what a first-class workman could do employing scientifically determined techniques.[39]

The primary tool of analysis in these investigations is the time-and-motion study, in which the general procedure is to break down physical activities into their component parts, specify the optimal routine for the performance of each component part, and discover the most efficient method for recombining the parts into the more complex task. More specifically, time-and-motion studies involve the following steps:

1. The worker is provided with the best implements, appropriately placed.

2. The task is analyzed and divided into elementary units.

3. Useless movements are discovered and discarded.

4. With the aid of a stopwatch, the analyst studies a skilled workman performing the task, in order to discover the quickest and best method for making each elementary movement. Such investigation is to be guided by a series of "principles" of physical activity—for example, the two hands should begin and complete their motions at the same time; the two hands should not be idle at the same time except during periods of rest; and the motions of the arms should be made in opposite and symmetrical directions and should be made simultaneously.

5. The elementary movements of the task are grouped in an appropriate sequence to maximize overall efficiency of task performance.

6. The proper method of task performance is described and recorded, and the time required to perform the task is determined.

7. An allowance is made for unavoidable delays. (Based on his investigations, Taylor asserts that 20–27 percent should be added to the actual working time to allow for unavoidable delays.)

8. Allowance should be made for the time it takes a new employee to learn the job.

9. Allowance should be made for rests and the intervals of rest required for a worker to recover from physical fatigue.[40]

The product of time-and-motion studies is thus a specification of the nature of a task, the best method of performing it, and the time required for the performance of the task, accounting for the capacity, speed, and durability of the worker. Since no two workmen work at exactly the same speed, performance standards should be set somewhere between the performance of a first-class man and the performance of an average man, and the standards should be gradually increased as the worker becomes more familiar with the system.

Once the basic time-and-motion study was performed, instruction cards containing the procedures derived were used in the training of other workers. The instructions contained on these cards were often set forth in exquisite detail. For instance, the instructions for the operation of a lathe consisted of 183 steps, all of which were to be accomplished in the manner specified and in the order listed.[41] Taylor's suggested procedure is to choose *one* man and allow him to work under the new system at a higher rate of pay. Other workers are expected to come voluntarily into the program as its attractions became apparent.

Although Taylor sought the "one best way" of performing various physical tasks, he never asserted that time-and-motion studies were an exact science. Instead, he felt that "laws" relating to human beings were subject to greater variability than those relating to physical things, and he reportedly could be content with "good enough" while still searching for the "best."[42] In this willingness to compromise, we can recognize a primitive version of Herbert Simon's bounded rationality. Thus, standards established through time-and-motion studies are to be accepted only conditionally, but they are not to be altered unless a new method of performing the task is discovered. This strict adherence is required to prevent arbitrary changes in standards as productivity increases. Taylor felt that such changes had served as a disincentive under previous managerial practices, as workers were penalized by lower marginal rates of compensation when productivity increased to unexpected levels.[43] The trick, of course, is to establish correct standards in the first place and then stick to them.

Wage-Incentive Systems

The distinguishing feature of Taylor's incentive system is the prior establishment of standards of work performance through time-and-motion studies. Consequently, Taylor felt that the actual method of reward—be it day work, piecework, task work with a bonus, or differential piecework—was a relatively unimportant part of the system. In his opinion, factors such as special incentives, higher wages, shorter working hours, better working conditions, and individual rewards for the worker based on performance would all overshadow the importance of the specific method of payment.

Taylor's basic approach to incentives is, first, to give each worker a definite task with detailed instructions and an exact time standard for the performance of each element of the task. When this task assignment process has been accomplished, the worker is to be paid extraordinary wages for performing the task in the allotted time but ordinary wages if the time allotment is exceeded. As noted, Taylor felt that the primary failing of previous incentive systems had been that they did not start with a sure knowledge of the time required to perform a task. Consequently, workers were encouraged to soldier either if standards were based on actual performance or, as was the case in some incentive schemes, if standards were increased as the workers produced more.

Taylor also objected to gain-sharing plans, such as those proposed by Towne and Halsey, which provided that, when work was done in a shorter time and at a reduced cost, the gain in profits was to be shared in a prescribed ratio between management and the workers.[44] Taylor argued that such plans shared a common failure in not establishing objective performance standards. In addition, he felt that these plans were deficient in that they did not recognize the personal contribution of each worker, and that the delay between performance and reward reduced the plan's ability to motivate the worker to produce more. Thus, he would have incentives based on prior standards of work performance, so that each worker would be rewarded on an individual basis and performance would be linked immediately (daily) to reward.

Although Taylor thinks the particular system of payment to be relatively unimportant, he generally supports the differential rate system he had devised while at Midvale. Under the differential rate system, the worker is assigned a clearly defined task, with a specified time allowed to perform the task. The task assignment, according to Taylor, should be made so difficult that it can be accomplished only by a first-class worker in the time specified. If the worker fails to perform the task in the required time, or if there are imperfections in the work performed, the pay rate is set at a level that is scarcely an ordinary day's pay. This base rate is to be determined by an analysis of payment for similar work in the relevant labor market.

If the worker accomplishes the task in the specified time without imperfections, a bonus of 30–100 percent of the base pay is earned, the specific amount of the bonus being dependent on the work involved: 30 percent of base pay for routine shop work; 50–60 percent for labor requiring severe bodily exertion and fatigue; 70–80 percent for jobs requiring special skill; and 80–100 percent for work involving both skill and physical exertion.[45] Taylor also advises against paying the worker too much, since this only results in demoralizing the worker, discouraging thrift, and encouraging the worker to look for the opportunity to work less.

Thus, under Taylor's incentive system, as in other pay schemes, success is rewarded by higher pay and failure is penalized by financial loss. Nevertheless, his system is distinguished from others because it is based on prior knowledge of what constitutes a good day's work. Given this knowledge, management is protected, since it is not likely to encounter unexpectedly high labor costs resulting from unanticipated increases in productivity, and the worker is protected—and thus not encouraged to soldier—since the work standards will not be changed in the absence of the discovery of a new way of doing the work.

Functional Organization

Taylor's prescriptions for organizational structure were a radical departure from previous practices. Previously, the military model of organization had prevailed, stressing unity of command at each level of the organization and culminating in a single executive body at the apex of an organizational pyramid. Under this arrangement, the foreman was responsible for a wide range of functions, including hiring, training, supervising, and firing his subordinates. Foremen were often hired on a contract basis and simply charged with getting the work done, with little direction from management.[46]

Taylor believed this arrangement to be deficient in two regards: first, it demanded an undue amount of technical expertise from top management; second, it expected too much from the foreman and, as a result, effectively precluded direct control by management over the workers. Consequently, he proposes both a decentralization of authority from general management and a centralization of authority from the foreman. The new locus of authority and responsibility is to be the planning department. In the process, Taylor divides the tasks previously performed by the foreman, allocating them to a number of "functional foremen."

The decentralizing aspect of Taylor's functional organization is the establishment of a cadre of technical experts in positions of power in the organization. This power is not to be fixed at the top level of the organization but in a planning department, and authority is to be exercised on the basis of knowledge, not mere position. The experts in the planning department are to be relatively free from bureaucratic controls exercised from above. Organizational executives are to limit themselves to handling problems that cannot be handled in the planning department. Top executives are to have a general knowledge of all the steps necessary in the accomplishment of organizational tasks, and they are to stay apprised of the character and fitness of important men working under them. But operational control for top executives is to be based on the "exception principle."[47] That is, the executive is to receive condensed reports of organizational activities and to concern himself only with exceptions from normal performance.

Functionalization also means centralization to the extent that some activities previously performed by the foreman are to be elevated to the planning department in order to establish management's central responsibilities in the areas of job design and planning and to institute direct managerial control over the workers. The planning department, consistent with its importance in Taylor's scheme of things, is assigned a wide range of functions, including performing time-and-motion studies, maintaining proper inventory levels, providing for the maintenance of equipment, analyzing orders for machines or work, and establishing a system of classification for materials and equipment. Although Taylor is not very precise on the point, the department is to be composed of a number of offices, such as a time-study office, a pay department, an information bureau, an employment bureau, and a rush-order department.[48]

Four of Taylor's functional foremen are to be assigned to the planning department: the route clerk, the instruction card man, the time clerk, and the disciplinarian.[49] The *route clerk* is to oversee the work flow, study specific jobs and decide the best method of doing them (both the required operations and the sequence of operations), indicate the tools to be used, make a chart showing the course of work through the shop, and determine the order in which various jobs are to be done. The *instruction card man* is to study the drawings and worksheet prepared by the route clerk, prepare detailed instructions for the performance of each operation, and indicate the length of time required for each operation. The *time clerk* is to be responsible for preparing pay and written reports, reviewing time cards to determine eligibility for bonuses, and allocating work costs to the proper accounts. The *disciplinarian* is to review trouble between workers and their bosses, hire and fire, and attend to other personnel matters.

The remaining four functional foremen are assigned to the shop and made responsible for the proper execution of the plan.[50] These foremen are called the gang boss, the speed boss, the inspection foreman, and the repair boss. The *gang boss* is to set up the job, organize and situate the required machinery, give instruction cards to the workers, and route the work through the shop. The *speed boss* is to see to it that machines are run at the proper speed and that the appropriate tools are used. In addition, the speed boss is to ensure that the job is performed in the prescribed fashion, and he is to instruct the worker on the use of machines. In case of failure, the speed boss is responsible for ascertaining the causes and demonstrating that the work could be done in the required time. The *inspection foreman* is to examine the products and ensure that they conform to standards. The *repair boss* is to be responsible for the adjustment, cleanliness, and general care of the machines, and he is to keep a record of repairs and maintenance.

Taylor's preferred style of supervision for these functional foremen is to hold a plum for the worker to reach for; crack the whip, with an occasional touch of the lash; and work shoulder-to-shoulder with the worker, pushing, teaching, guiding, and helping.[51] Though force is to remain available, it is to serve only as a supplement to appeals to self-interest. The worker is expected to do what he is told and, in effect, to become one in a complex train of "gear wheels" constituting the overall organization.

It should be noted that in abandoning the military style of organization, with its emphasis on unity of command, Taylor is making the worker directly responsible to eight foremen—four from the planning department and four on the workfloor. This arrangement, which combines a normal hierarchical organization with features of a project organization, was never really implemented. Nowadays, it is more commonly known as a matrix organization, wherein an employee has two bosses, one responsible for substance of work and another for productivity. To avoid conflict, Taylor requires that the duties of the various foremen be precisely defined so that none interferes with others. More important, Taylor argues that an effective unity of command is retained in the organization, since knowledge is to be enshrined as the single master.[52] The organizational hierarchy is to be based on abilities, as each individual is encouraged to rise to his highest level of competence. This progress is to include the movement from worker to managerial status; and Taylor countenances, indeed encourages, a higher ratio of what he calls "brain workers" to "hand workers."

At this point, it is important to observe how radical Taylor's functional organization was and how (perhaps uniquely) American it was in its fragmentation of authority along functional lines. Theories can be advanced as if they were universal, though in reality they may very well be specific to and characteristic of a particular culture. For instance, in his discussion of Taylor's functional organization, the French engineer Henri Fayol observed that unity of command was an inviolable principle and that Taylor's system most likely had to be translated into hierarchical terms before it could be considered acceptable to and useful in France. Fayol was baffled by the fact that Taylor must have been a successful manager even though he was violating the unity of command principle. Geert Hofstede and Gert Jan Hofstede point out that Blaise Pascal (1623–1662) had the answer: "There are truths in one country that are falsehoods in another."[53]

These three components—time-and-motion studies, wage-incentive systems, and functional organization—constitute the core of Taylor's Scientific Management. But Taylor would object to the notion that these, or any other listing of procedures and techniques, capture the essence of Scientific Management. For him, Scientific Management is more than a "series of expedients to increase efficiency." Instead, it requires a "mental revolution" on the part of both management and workers, as science replaces rules of thumb, and mutual confidence between management and workers replaces "suspicious watchfulness."[54] It was in pursuit of this mental revolution that Taylor embarked on a campaign to promote the spread of Scientific Management in the early 1900s.

The Movement

In his early efforts, Taylor's interests were largely technical, and his objective that of efficiency. Not until 1899, in a speech to Bethlehem managers, did he even suggest that Scientific Management could be reduced to a body of principles.[55] In 1901, however, Taylor abruptly changed course, and the inventor and engineer became an educator and social reformer. In so doing, Taylor turned his attention from the technical aspects of Scientific Management to its social consequences, with particular emphasis on the "labor problem."

At the turn of the century, the labor force was in a virtually permanent state of turmoil and unrest, reflecting a high level of antagonism between management and the workers. Taylor believed that the application of the techniques of Scientific Management could address the causes of this conflict by defining a proper day's work, by providing just compensation for the worker, and by giving management a good rate of return on its investment. In this way, attention could be diverted from contention over division of what Taylor calls "the surplus" to increasing that surplus and, in the process, serving the interests of both management and the workers.[56] That is, management could get what it wants (lower labor costs) and the workers could get what they want (higher wages) by increasing efficiency.

Taylor's concept of the organization under Scientific Management is thus one in which harmony would replace discord and cooperation would replace conflict, as an underlying compatibility of interests between management and the workers was exposed through the application of Scientific Management techniques. As Taylor puts it,

The majority of men believe that the fundamental interests of employees and employers are necessarily antagonistic. Scientific Management, on the contrary, has for its very foundation the firm conviction that the interests of the two are one and the same; that prosperity for the employer cannot exist through a long period of years unless it is accompanied by prosperity for the employee and vice versa.[57]

Indeed, Taylor identifies "close and intimate cooperation" between management and the worker as integral to the mental revolution embodied in the doctrines of Scientific Management.

Although Taylor stresses cooperation in the workplace, authority is not to be shared equally by management and the workers. Taylor's approach can probably be better described as a form of benevolent paternalism in which hierarchy is to remain the primary mechanism of control and coordination in the organization. Nevertheless, Taylor contends that management is to be as severely disciplined as the workers under Scientific Management. The exercise of authority is to be based on the mandate of right reason resting on scientific laws, and those laws are to be as binding on management as hierarchical authority is to be on the worker. Management is thus to be a senior partner—deriving its authority from superior competence—in a scientific enterprise in which knowledge is to be enshrined as the ultimate master. Taylor simply believes the worker to be less competent and thus unable to construct the required science of management. Accordingly,

in almost all of the mechanic arts the science which underlies each act of each workman is so great and amounts to so much that the workman who is best suited to actually doing the work is incapable of fully understanding this science without the guidance and help of those who are working with him or over him, either through lack of education or through insufficient mental capacity.[58]

Indeed, Taylor contended that an "intelligent gorilla" would be at least as useful as the Eastern European immigrants he found working at Bethlehem.[59]

Taylor sees the organization under Scientific Management as constituting a mutually beneficial exchange, by which significant rewards accrue to both management and the workers. The benefits to management are an increase in output and lower labor costs. Taylor estimated that the application of the principles of Scientific Management would result in a doubling of output per man and per machine, and he reported that those companies already employing the techniques of Scientific Management were more prosperous than ever before.[60]

Benefits to the workers would come in a variety of forms. Most obviously, the worker would receive higher compensation under Scientific Management. Though he would generally not recover the full benefits of increased productivity (because of the cost of developing new techniques and implements), he would receive significantly higher wages. Moreover, Taylor claimed that the 30–100 percent higher wages received under Scientific Management had proven to be satisfactory, leaving no contention over the distribution of the surplus.[61] More indirectly, the worker would benefit from the lower consumer prices made possible by lower labor costs. But Taylor felt that the primary benefit to the worker was more intangible in nature: the development of a better character. He contended that training under Scientific Management would aid the worker in general intellectual and moral development. Under Scientific Management, workers would be given more interesting work that would more fully develop their talents. Moreover, Scientific Management would produce not only a better worker but also a person who would be able to live better, save money, and become more sober.[62]

In terms of the social reform movements of the day, Scientific Management would fall among those Haber calls "systemizers."[63] This movement, comprised basically of engineers, looked to technological expertise, hierarchy, and discipline for a solution to the labor problem. Taylor's particular interests took him from mechanical efficiency to the interface between man and the machine. He believed that far from ignoring the human factor, as his critics charged, he alone was meaningfully addressing the labor problem, and he had little brief for the other reform movements of his day.

The Industrial Betterment movement was dismissed by Taylor as a collection of "semi-philanthropic aids," which were of "distinctly secondary importance." Industrial Betterment, a forerunner of the later Human Relations movement, argued that human happiness was a business asset, that well-being for the worker would yield hard work and greater productivity, and that the natural goodness of man would flourish if nurtured in a benevolent environment.[64] In order to achieve a higher level of human happiness, the Industrial Betterment movement supported a variety of reforms, such as comfortable lavatories, lunchrooms, kindergartens, athletic grounds, night schools, safety training, and free lectures. Although not entirely discounting such reforms, Taylor's approach to the labor problem was based on a contrasting set of premises. Whereas Industrial Betterment assumed that morality and well-being would yield hard work, Taylor argued that hard work would yield morality and well-being. Whereas Industrial Betterment thought better working conditions would bring out man's "natural goodness," Taylor asserted that the natural weaknesses in man must be curbed by insisting that he do what is right through hierarchical controls.

Taylor was similarly disdainful of the union movement. Though he believed that unions can play a useful role in relieving the worker of the worst excesses of previous managerial practices, he felt that they had outlived their usefulness. Unions, Taylor argued, foster the restriction of output by making the work of the least efficient the standard of performance. In addition, Taylor accused unions of employing abhorrent tactics. In his words, "The boycott, the use of force or intimidation, and oppression of nonunion workmen by labor unions are damnable; these acts of tyranny are thoroughly un-American and will not be tolerated by the American people."[65] Taylor hoped to avoid the tendency toward unionization through "systematic individualization," in which individuals rather than positions are rewarded, and rewards are based on scientific assessments of productivity. Taylor tempered his position, however, by stating that Scientific Management should not be implemented unless it was agreeable to both management and the workers, and he even suggested that there was no reason why a joint commission of employers and workers could not be established to set daily tasks.[66]

Scientific Management's intended reach transcended even this concern with the labor problem. Harlow Person, a president of the Taylor

Society, expressed this broader intent in stating the hope that "we may discover that the philosophy, principles, and techniques [of Scientific Management] are applicable to conservation problems of entire nations, and perhaps of an entire world." [67] Even further, Person asserted: "The very survival of democratic institutions may depend on a lifting of productivity to new degrees of adequacy which will rapidly eliminate starvation, establish a feeling of greater economic security, and destroy impulses to follow false leaders along paths of violence toward a totalitarian world." [68] For Taylor, the diffusion of character was the essence of democracy, and that character was to be instilled by adopting both the mentality and the techniques of Scientific Management.

After leaving Bethlehem in 1901, Taylor largely withdrew from direct contact with the technical work of Scientific Management and became increasingly concerned with promoting the cause. His primary vehicle for this effort was a series of publications; his platform, at least initially, was the American Society of Mechanical Engineers (ASME), which he had joined in the 1880s while he was still at Midvale. During 1902 and 1903, Taylor worked on the manuscript for *Shop Management*, a report on the progress of Scientific Management, in which his emphasis began to shift from efficiency to the social implications of the movement.[69] *Shop Management* was presented as a paper to the ASME in 1903 and subsequently published in book form by the society.

In 1906 Taylor presented "On the Art of Cutting Metals" to the ASME as his presidential address.[70] Although largely technical in nature, the paper signaled Taylor's most significant mechanical invention—high-speed tool steel—which represented the culmination of some twenty-five years of research. In June of 1907, he began a new series of lectures on differences between existing systems of management and his own system of "task management." These lectures expanded into his most famous book.[71]

In 1909 Taylor completed his best-known and most controversial work, *The Principles of Scientific Management*, effecting a transition in which the social implications of Scientific Management were emphasized almost to the exclusion of technical matters.[72] He submitted this manuscript, as he had all his writings, to the ASME for consideration for publication, but the society balked at its publication, given the publicity then attendant on Scientific Management and Taylor's stress on nontechnical material.[73] When the paper had been held by the ASME for nearly a year without action, Taylor withdrew the manuscript and had it published at his own expense for distribution to ASME members.[74] *Principles* was subsequently serialized by *American Magazine* and published by Harper and Brothers in 1911. Thus Taylor's most famous work did not bear the imprimatur of the ASME, and a rift was created within the society between those who believed an engineer to be simply a technician and those who supported a broader role of social responsibility. This rift would grow in the years following, eventuating in the formation of separate organizations by Taylor and his associates to promote Scientific Management.

Taylor's publications gained him some notoriety, but the Scientific Management movement acquired widespread public attention through hearings on railway rates, conducted by the Interstate Commerce Commission (ICC) in 1910. The hearings became a forum for a confrontation between the railroads, which were seeking higher rates, and the Progressives, represented by Louis Brandeis, who argued that a rate increase would not be necessary if the railroads were simply operated more efficiently.[75] Brandeis's concern for efficiency brought him into contact with exponents of Scientific Management, from whom he solicited testimony. Interestingly, in view of the fact that the hearings served as a springboard to public fame for the Scientific Management movement, Taylor himself did not testify.[76] Instead, testimony was received from three prominent Taylor associates: H.L. Gantt, Frank Gilbreth, and Harrington Emerson. Once Taylor realized the significance of the hearings, however, he worked closely with Brandeis.[77]

The ICC hearings precipitated a period of intense public scrutiny of the techniques and philosophy of Scientific Management. In 1912 Congress launched an investigation into whether or not Scientific Management should be forbidden in government agencies. This time, Taylor did testify, and he was subjected to extensive, and often hostile, questioning by members of the House Investigating Committee.[78] These hearings were the beginning of a five-year congressional examination and debate over the desirability of employing the techniques of Scientific Management in the federal government; they ended in legislation prohibiting it.[79]

Although his availability was limited by his wife's ill health, Taylor pursued a number of other activities designed to promote the cause of Scientific Management. Between 1901 and 1914, he lectured annually at the Harvard Graduate School of Business Administration; he participated, on a limited basis, in the application of Scientific Management techniques at federal arsenals; and, at his home in Philadelphia, he entertained a steady stream of visitors who came to learn about Scientific Management from the master.

Meanwhile, the practice of Scientific Management was spreading through business and government. Although by 1910 Taylor conceded that no single firm had adopted Scientific Management in its entirety, he estimated that 50,000 workmen were employed under some form of Scientific Management.[80] In government, there was a great deal of enthusiasm for, and some limited attempts to apply, the principles of Scientific Management—probably the most extensive efforts being those made at federal shipyards and arsenals. Between 1906 and 1908, the Mare Island Shipyards near San Francisco became the first "scientifically managed" government plant.[81] By 1908, the Watertown Arsenal in Massachusetts had become a model plant, achieving a 50 percent decrease in material cost and a doubling of output per man.[82]

At the local level, which was the bastion of progressive reform at the turn of the century, Scientific Management evinced a great deal of interest. The most thorough applications were effected in New York and Chicago.[83] Members of New York City's Bureau of Municipal Research, a leader in the reform movement, occasionally entertained Taylor in their offices and became enthusiastic advocates of Scientific Management. In Philadelphia, Taylor's home city, a director of Public Works was appointed to institute Scientific Management procedures.

Interest in Scientific Management also spread abroad. *The Principles of Scientific Management* was translated into nine languages: French, German, Dutch, Swedish, Russian, Lettish, Italian, Spanish, Japanese, and Chinese.[84] Taylor's work influenced a variety of areas, such as accounting, education, consulting, library science, architecture, health, the military, public administration, industrial and organizational psychology, and gender studies.[85] But his influence was not uniform. In countries where courses in industrial architecture and new technologies were taught—including France, Germany, Italy, and Russia—Scientific Management caught on very quickly. Consider the enthusiastic reception of Scientific Management among modernist European architects such as Walter Gropius and Le Corbusier. It was not so readily accepted in Spain, though, where industrial architecture was not part of an engineering curriculum until the late 1900s, or in the United Kingdom, where none of the most influential architects had studied engineering or technical subjects.[86]

Interest in Scientific Management eventually boomed in England, and Georges Clemenceau ordered that its principles be applied in all French military plants.[87] Later, the movement was endorsed, albeit on a qualified basis, even in the Soviet Union, where Lenin had once characterized it as a form of cruel bourgeois exploitation. Beguiled by its scientific attainments, however, Lenin later urged its adoption as part of a policy to centralize authority and as a necessary step on the road to socialism.[88]

Taylor himself was rather conservative in his approach to social reform, but Scientific Management quickly became identified with broader social movements in the United States, such as the Progressive movement and a larger campaign against waste and inefficiency. The Progressive movement preached the gospel of efficiency in the name of a democracy that was to be led by an elite cadre of experts. Efficiency became the watchword of the day, as the Taft Committee on Economy and Efficiency was established at the federal level and a host of efficiency commissions sprang up at state and local levels of government. Scientific Management was even embraced by the women workers' movement, despite Taylor's assertion that women were less efficient than men and less regular in their attendance, and so should look forward to getting married.[89] In more recent times, several of Taylor's management approaches to job design, selection, motivation and incentive systems, job performance criteria, performance appraisal, organizational development and change, and employee attitudes found their way into such organizational theories as Total Quality Management.[90]

Within the Scientific Management Movement itself, the Society to Promote Scientific Management (later to be called the Taylor Society) was formed in 1911. Its membership included, among others, a future Supreme Court justice, Louis Brandeis, and Mary Parker Follett.[91] In addition, a group of Taylor's associates struck out in a number of directions, not all of them to Taylor's taste. Among the most prominent were H. L. Gantt and Frank Gilbreth. Gantt's technical concern was production-control techniques, but he also adhered to a technocratic social philosophy in which an expert elite was to put down the rule of the mob. He advocated an economic system that was to transform industries into public-service corporations run by committees of producers, distributors, and consumers. In 1916 Gantt formed the New Machine, an organization designed to acquire political and economic power.[92] Taylor would castigate Gantt for straying too far from his technical concerns.

Frank Gilbreth was most closely identified with time-and-motion studies, and he developed a photographic method of conducting those studies. Gilbreth, whose life was later popularized in the book and subsequent movie entitled *Cheaper by the Dozen,* has been described as a "talented technician, a flamboyant personality, and an aggressive and occasionally unscrupulous promoter."[93] Gilbreth formed the Taylor Society, but he later broke with Taylor, who considered him to be overly preoccupied with time-and-motion studies to the exclusion of other elements of Scientific Management.

As Scientific Management received greater public attention, it also attracted significant opposition, led by labor unions, particularly the metal trades unions, which protested its application at the Watertown Arsenal.[94] Union protests against Scientific Management led to the aforementioned congressional inquiry that ended in legislation prohibiting the use of its techniques in federal agencies. Socialists, following Lenin's line, denounced Scientific Management as a form of capitalist exploitation.[95] Even in the ASME, long a forum for Taylor's ideas, opposition developed. In 1912 the society appointed a committee to investigate Scientific Management.[96] Although the results of the investigation were inconclusive, Taylor and his associates chose to work largely outside the ASME thereafter.

Following Taylor's death in 1915, the Scientific Management movement continued, but in altered form. Splits among Taylor's disciples diluted the impact of their efforts, and, eventually, compromises with the forces of the opposition—along with changing social, political, and economic conditions—altered the course of reform. By the 1920s, unions had reached a compromise with advocates of Scientific Management by which the unions accepted time-and-motion studies in return for the movement's acceptance of collective bargaining.[97] The exponents of Scientific Management even incorporated elements of industrial democracy in their doctrines, and unions became supporters of "humanized" Scientific Management. The result of the compromises was less controversy, but also a substantial loss of distinctiveness and fervor in pursuit of the cause. By the 1920s, the Scientific Management movement had largely retreated from comprehensive strategies of social reform and returned to its initial concentration on technical matters.

Conclusion

In developing Scientific Management, Taylor made undoubted contributions to the understanding of, and prescriptions for, the management of organizations. Yet, he is probably better characterized as a synthesizer than as an innovator—that is, his contribution was less the introduction of new ideas than the integration of existing ideas into a coherent system. The man-machine interface was the primary focus of Taylor's efforts, and his synthesis of managerial concepts in this area extended the perspectives of both the engineers (from machines to men) and the industrial reformers (from men to machines). In addition, Taylor advanced the cause of systematic investigation by the precision of his measurements, which replaced the prior reliance on rules of thumb. Scientific Management was clearly a movement that was right for its time, and its impact is still evident, particularly in industrial engineering.

Scientific Management also suggested the importance of cooperation in the workplace and called for an end to the arbitrary exercise of managerial authority. Taylor was hardly a humanist, but he did recognize the interests of the workers, at least to the extent that they shared with management a stake in higher productivity. Thus suspicion and mutual distrust were to be replaced by a joint pursuit of shared objectives—a goal that would be emphasized even more by Elton Mayo and associates (see chapter 5).

Despite these contributions, Scientific Management is limited both in its scope and in its scientific accomplishments. Its scope neglects the impact of factors external to the organization and considers only some of the factors that are internal to the organization. Taylor never extended his technical studies much beyond the shop level; the broader financial aspects of the firm were of little concern to him. His sole venture into the broader areas of management at Manufacturing Investment Corporation was something less than a stunning success, and he developed a reputation among those who employed him as having a talent for "making money fly."[98] Taylor gave the impression that he would pursue efficiency regardless of the cost, and his techniques, like the man, tended to suffer from an excess of their virtues.

Taylor has been most roundly, and perhaps unfairly, condemned for an alleged neglect of the human factor in the organization. Indeed, in the course of the twentieth century, Taylor's work was increasingly stereotyped as grounded in a mechanistic conception of organizations and its workers, in contrast to the attention Mayo and Barnard gave to the human element.[99] Especially in the past two decades, though, appreciation for the subtleties of Taylor's work has steadily been growing.[100] It is probably fairer to state that Taylor operated on the basis of a limited set of assumptions about the nature of man and his relationship to the organization. He assumed, at least implicitly, that the ordinary worker was only segmentally involved in the organization—that is, he had interests other than work—and that he was seeking instrumental rewards from his organizational involvement—rewards that would allow him to acquire his primary gratifications elsewhere. In addition, Taylor assumed that the worker would rationally pursue his self-interest, relatively undistracted by his feelings, attitudes, and private goals. Given this image of man and his relationship to the organization, Taylor believed that behavior could be rendered predictable by the proper manipulation of monetary incentives. This view is not so much wrong as it is partial: subsequent research has indicated that individual behavior in the organization is influenced by a considerably broader range of variables, including a host of social and psychological factors that Taylor adjudged irrelevant to productivity.

Finally, Taylor was not entirely successful in achieving his scientific objectives. Although he claimed that Scientific Management is "a true science resting upon clearly defined laws, rules, and principles," the claim is of dubious validity.[101] The claim to scientific status is subject to interpretation. Taylor defined science simply as "classified or organized knowledge," and Scientific Management would seem to qualify by that rather loose definition.[102] The claim of having arrived at clearly defined laws, rules, and principles is more difficult to support. Taylor admitted that laws relating to human behavior are subject to greater variability than are those relating to physical phenomena, and he believed that time-and-motion studies, a central component of Scientific Management, could not be reduced to an exact science.[103] Indeed, as we have seen, the latter point led to a falling-out between Taylor and Frank Gilbreth, one of Taylor's leading disciples.

Perhaps even more critically, Taylor never arrived at scientifically determined standards of work performance or rates of compensation. Performance standards did not reflect the "one best way" of performing a job. Instead, the prescribed methods were "state-of-the-art" solutions that were subject to change on the discovery of a better method. The choice of a "first-class workman" to perform the task and establish the standards was largely arbitrary and dependent on self-selection through a volunteer process. The choice of an actual standard by which to evaluate work performance was similarly arbitrary. Since no two workers proceed at exactly the same pace, work standards were to be set at some unspecified point between the performance of the observed first-class workman and that of the average workman. Rates of basic compensation and the size of the bonus that was to be a function of that basic wage were to be established by two criteria, neither of which was entirely objective in nature. First, the base wage was to be barely sufficient to allow the worker to sustain himself. Second, the base wage was to be comparable to wages received by workers performing similar tasks in a relevant labor market. Thus, the matter of an appropriate division of rewards was left unsettled, and it remained a major point of contention between Taylor and his critics, particularly the labor unions.

Scientific Management was truly a creature of its inventor and, as such, shared both his virtues and his shortcomings. It embodied a work ethic and social morality that transcended a scientific and technical enterprise. If Taylor failed in his scientific ambitions, he succeeded far beyond his original intentions in capturing the public's imagination and altering some traditional concepts of management.

NOTES

1. Perhaps there is something distinctly American about Scientific Management. Suspecting that his lumberjacks/carpenters were somewhat slow or lazy, George Washington one day rode out early, told them which piece of land to clear, sat down and observed for the remainder of the day, making notes, how many feet of timber four men could hew in a certain amount of time; see Henry Wiencek, *An Imperfect God: George Washington, His Slaves, and the Creation of America* (New York: Farrar, Straus and Giroux, 2003), 92–93. On the other hand, this managerial zeal may reflect a more universal bent toward precision and efficiency. For instance, in his 1555 *De re metallica*, Agricola notes precise times of shifts for mining operations; see G. T. Whitrow, *Time in History: Views of Time from Prehistory to the Present Day* (New York: Barnes & Noble Books, 1988), 113.

2. Some years ago, a four-volume anthology was published containing reprints of publications (articles and chapters) by and about Taylor from 1912 to 2000. See *F. W. Taylor: Critical Evaluations in Business and Management*, ed. John C. Wood and Michael C. Wood (London/New York: Routledge, 2002).

3. Cf. Gareth Morgan, *Images of Organization* (Thousand Oaks, Calif.: Sage Publications, 2006), 212–213. Obviously, it serves Morgan's purpose to depict Taylor as such in a chapter where the organizational metaphor of a psychic prison is explored. However, research in the past two decades has resulted in a much more nuanced, and actually quite human, image of Taylor. See, e.g., Robert Kanigel, *One Best Way: Frederick Winslow Taylor and the Enigma of Efficiency* (Cambridge, Mass.: MIT Press, 2005). Indeed, it has been observed that Morgan pays no attention to the specific life situations in which Taylor's ideas were formulated; see Michael Roper, "Masculinity and the Biographical Meanings of Management Theory: Lyndall Urwick and the Making of Scientific Management in Inter-war Britain," *Gender, Work and Organization* 8, no. 2 (2001): 184.

4. See, e.g., Stephanie C. Payne, Satoris S. Youngcourt, and Kristen M. Watrous, "Portrayals of F. W. Taylor across Textbooks," *Journal of Management History* 12, no. 4 (2006): 385–407.

5. Frank Barkley Copley, *Frederick W. Taylor: Father of Scientific Management*, vol. 1 (New York: American Society of Mechanical Engineers, 1923), 45. For more recent studies on Taylor's life and work, see Hindy Lauer Schachter, *Frederick Taylor and the Public Administration Community: A Reevaluation* (Albany: State University of New York Press, 1989); C.D. Wrege and R.G. Greenwood, *Frederick W. Taylor, the Father of Scientific Management: Myth and Reality* (Homewood, Ill.: Business One Irwin, 1991); and Daniel Nelson, ed., *A Mental Revolution: Scientific Management since Taylor* (Columbus: Ohio State University Press, 1992).

6. Quotation from Stuart P. Sherman, "What Is a Puritan?" in Copley, *Frederick W. Taylor*, 28.

7. Ibid., 53.

8. Ibid., 66.

9. This penchant was later carried to a curious extreme when Taylor would try out his wife's horses by donning her skirts and riding sidesaddle through town. Ibid., 374.

10. Daniel Nelson, *Frederick W. Taylor and the Rise of Scientific Management* (Madison: University of Wisconsin Press, 1980), 25.

11. Copley, *Frederick W. Taylor*, 153.

12. Ibid., 127.

13. Nelson, *Frederick W. Taylor and the Rise of Scientific Management*, 53–54.

14. Frederick W. Taylor, "A Piece Rate System," in *Scientific Management*, ed. Clarence Bertrand Thompson (Easton, Pa.: Hive Publishing, 1972), 636–683.

15. Nelson, *Frederick W. Taylor and the Rise of Scientific Management*, 86. It has been convincingly argued that the credit for developing high-speed tool steel should be equally shared between Taylor and J. Maunsell White III. See Christopher P. Neck and Arthur G. Bedeian, "Frederick W. Taylor, J. Maunsell White III, and the Matthew Effect: The Rest of the Story," *Journal of Management History* 2, no. 2 (1996): 20–25. Part of Taylor's work at

Bethlehem involved the development of new ways to load pig iron, and he used the story of the pig-iron experiments numerous times in lectures by way of illustrating principles of Scientific Management. Charles D. Wrege and Richard M. Hodgetts, in "Frederick W. Taylor's 1899 Pig Iron Observations: Examining Fact, Fictions, and Lessons for the New Millennium," *Academy of Management Journal* 43, no. 6 (2000): 1283–1291, point out that the content of this story changed over time and so Taylor's account is not a reliable source of what really happened. On the other hand, Jill R. Hough and Margaret A. White, in "Using Stories to Create Change: The Object Lesson of Frederick Taylor's 'Pig Tale,'" *Journal of Management* 27 (2001): 585–601, argue that this changing content should not draw attention away from the major object lesson of the story.

16. Samuel Haber, *Efficiency and Uplift: Scientific Management in the Progressive Era, 1890–1920* (Chicago: University of Chicago Press, 1964), 20.
17. Ibid., 7.
18. Copley, *Frederick W. Taylor*, 83.
19. Ibid., 110.
20. Taylor, "Testimony" (before the special House committee), in Frederick W. Taylor, *Scientific Management* (New York: Harper & Brothers, 1911), 125.
21. Copley, *Frederick W. Taylor*, 89.
22. This particular element of Taylor's work—critique of management—is part of the re-evaluation of Taylor since the late 1980s. See, i.e., Sigmund Wagner-Tsukamoto, "An Institutional Economic Reconstruction of Scientific Management: On the Lost Theoretical Logic of Taylorism," *Academy of Management Review* 32, no. 1 (2007): 105–117, esp. 111.
23. Copley, *Frederick W. Taylor*, 188.
24. Ibid., 126.
25. Ibid., 387.
26. F. W. Taylor, *Shop Management* (New York: Harper & Brothers, 1947), 200.
27. Haber, *Efficiency and Uplift*, 5.
28. Copley, *Frederick W. Taylor*, 292.
29. Cognitive mapping of Taylor's ideas showed that "soldiering" was the most important concept in terms of both the number of direct links to other concepts and the centrality score (i.e., how central is a concept to the overall theory?). See Pierre Cossette, "Analysing the Thinking of F.W. Taylor Using Cognitive Mapping," *Journal of Management History* 40, no. 2 (2002): 168–182, esp. 173–174.
30. Copley, *Frederick W. Taylor*, 241.
31. Several authors observed that Taylor's ideas foreshadow the distinction made by Douglas McGregor in 1960 (theory X and Y). They also note, though, that Taylor sits between McGregor's extremes, since Taylor believes that many workmen require no discipline, but that it is human instinct to be lazy. See Louis W. Fry, "The Maligned F.W. Taylor: A Reply to His Many Critics" (1976), in Wood and Wood, *F. W. Taylor*, 94; Hindy Lauer Schachter, "Morris Cooke: A Link between Taylor and Public Administration" (1989), in ibid., 126; and Wagner-Tsukamoto, "An Institutional Economic Reconstruction of Scientific Management," 111.
32. Taylor, "Testimony," 175.
33. It is important to point out that Taylor favored individual work above group work because he believed that rewards work best when allocated on

the basis of individual performance. One author suggested that this idea has gained influence. For instance, Irving Janis suggested in 1972 that when groups become too cohesive, they are susceptible to groupthink— i.e., rational thinking is sacrificed in the name of unanimity. See Edwin A. Locke, "The Ideas of Frederick W. Taylor" (1982), in Wood and Wood, *F. W. Taylor*, 143.

34. Copley, *Frederick W. Taylor*, xxiv.
35. Frederick W. Taylor, *The Principles of Scientific Management* (New York: Harper & Brothers, 1919), 83.
36. Ibid., 36–37.
37. Ibid., 140.
38. See Chris Nyland, "Taylorism, John R. Commons, and the Hoxie Report," *Journal of Economic Issues* 30, no. 4 (1996): 987 (italics in original).
39. Taylor, *Scientific Management*, 25.
40. Copley, *Frederick W. Taylor*, 227. On the point of rest, see also Chris Nyland, "Taylorism and Hours of Work," *Journal of Management History* 1, no. 2 (1996): 8–25.
41. James March and Herbert Simon, *Organizations* (New York: Wiley, 1958), 14.
42. Copley, *Frederick W. Taylor*, 265.
43. Ibid., 211.
44. Nelson, *Frederick W. Taylor and the Rise of Scientific Management*, 14–16.
45. Frederick Taylor, "Shop Management," in Taylor, *Shop Management*, 26.
46. Nelson, *Frederick W. Taylor and the Rise of Scientific Management*, 7.
47. Copley, *Frederick W. Taylor*, 302.
48. Taylor, "Shop Management," 111.
49. Copley, *Frederick W. Taylor*, 324–325.
50. Ibid.
51. Ibid., 321–322.
52. Ibid., 290.
53. See Lee D. Parker and Philip Ritson, "Fads, Stereotypes and Management Gurus: Fayol and Follett Today," *Management Decision* 43, no. 10 (2005): 1351; see also Geert Hofstede and Gert Jan Hofstede, *Cultures and Organizations: Software of the Mind* (New York: McGraw Hill, 2005), 249–250.
54. Copley, *Frederick W. Taylor*, 10.
55. Nelson, *Frederick W. Taylor and the Rise of Scientific Management*, 90.
56. Taylor, "Testimony," 30.
57. Taylor, *Principles of Scientific Management*, 10.
58. Ibid., 41.
59. Nelson, *Frederick W. Taylor and the Rise of Scientific Management*, 91.
60. Taylor, *Principles of Scientific Management*, 28.
61. Taylor, "Testimony," 147.
62. Taylor, *Principles of Scientific Management*, 74. Taylor's favorite example was "Schmidt" (actually Henry Noll), who was taught to load pig iron under the techniques of Scientific Management. Noll, unfortunately, later lost his job and his home because of excessive drinking. See Nelson, *Frederick W. Taylor of Scientific Management*, 98.
63. Haber, *Efficiency and Uplift*, 19.
64. Ibid., 20.
65. Taylor, "Shop Management," 191.
66. Taylor, "Testimony," 145.
67. Harlow Person, Foreword to Taylor, *Scientific Management*, xvi.

68. Ibid.
69. Taylor, "Shop Management."
70. Taylor, "On the Art of Cutting Metals," in Thompson, *Scientific Management*, 242–267.
71. A reprint of the complete lecture can be found in "Report of a Lecture by and Questions put to Mr. F.W. Taylor: A Transcript," *Journal of Management History* 1, no. 1 (1995): 8–32; see also an introduction to this lecture by Charles D. Wrege, "F.W. Taylor's Lecture on Management, 4 June 1907: An Introduction," *Journal of Management History* 1, no. 1 (1995): 4–7. It has been noted that Taylor included some writing of one of his associates, Morris Cooke. Charles D. Wrege and Anne Marie Stotka, "Cooke Creates a Classic: The Story behind F.W. Taylor's *Principles of Scientific Management*," in Wood and Wood, *F.W. Taylor*, 99–116. See also Fry, "Maligned F.W. Taylor," 96; and Schachter, "Morris Cooke," 117–137.
72. Taylor, *Principles of Scientific Management*.
73. Nelson, *Frederick W. Taylor and the Rise of Scientific Management*, 174.
74. See Carol Carlson Dean, "*The Principles of Scientific Management* by Frederick W. Taylor: The Private Printing," *Journal of Management History* 3, no. 1 (1997): 18–30.
75. Nelson, *Frederick W. Taylor and the Rise of Scientific Management*.
76. He was, though, present at the hearing where Edith Wyatt, co-author of *Making Both Ends Meet: The Income and Outlay of New York Working Girls* (1911), testified before the congressional committee. See Chris Nyland, "An Early Account of Scientific Management as Applied to Women's Work, with comment by Frederick W. Taylor," *Journal of Management History* 6, no. 6 (2000): 250.
77. Brandeis has been described as someone ". . . who more than anyone else popularized the term 'scientific management' and promoted its virtues to a wider public"; see Richard P. Adelstein, "'Islands of Conscious Power': Louis Brandeis and the Modern Corporation," *Business History Review* 63, no. 3 (1989): 648.
78. Taylor, "Testimony." See also Nelson, *Mental Revolution*, 5.
79. Haber, *Efficiency and Uplift*, 69.
80. Taylor, *Principles of Scientific Management*, 28.
81. Nelson, *Frederick W. Taylor and the Rise of Scientific Management*, 155.
82. Ibid., 166.
83. Haber, *Efficiency and Uplift*, 110–111.
84. Copley, *Frederick W. Taylor*, xx.
85. See Wood and Wood, Introduction to *F.W. Taylor*, 9. For more about his influence on accounting, see, e.g., Richard K. Fleischman, "Completing the Triangle: Taylorism and the Paradigms," *Accounting, Auditing & Accountability Journal* 13, no. 5 (2000): 597–623.
86. See Mauro F. Guillén, "Scientific Management's Lost Aesthetic: Architecture, Organization, and the Taylorized Beauty of the Mechanical," *Administrative Science Quarterly* 42 (1997): 704–706, 714–715.
87. Haber, *Efficiency and Uplift*, 120.
88. Ibid., 129.
89. Copley, *Frederick W. Taylor*, 464.
90. Payne, Youngcourt, and Watrous, "Portrayals of F.W. Taylor across Textbooks," 389–392; see also Daniel Martin, "From Mechanical Engineering

to Re-engineering: Would Taylor Be Pleased with Modern Management?" *Journal of Management History* 1, no. 2 (1995): 38–51.

91. See Chris Nyland, "Taylorism and the Mutual-Gains Strategy," *Industrial Relations* 37, no. 4 (1998): 529; and Nyland, "An Early Account of Scientific Management as Applied to Women's Work," 249.

92. Haber, *Efficiency and Uplift*, 44.

93. Nelson, *Frederick W. Taylor and the Rise of Scientific Management*, 131.

94. Haber, *Efficiency and Uplift*, 68.

95. Ibid., 65. However, the socialists were also beguiled, as was Lenin, by the potential benefits of the application of Scientific Management.

96. Nelson, *Frederick W. Taylor and the Rise of Scientific Management*, 182.

97. Ibid., 202.

98. Haber, *Efficiency and Uplift*, 16.

99. For a recent example of such stereotyping, see Satyuanarayana Parayitam, Margaret A. White, and Jill R. Hough, "Juxtaposition of Chester I. Barnard and Frederick W. Taylor: Forerunners of Management," *Management Decision* 40, no.10 (2002): 1011. But there was resistance to Scientific Management back in the 1930s. For instance, Peter Drucker, *The End of Economic Man: A Study of the New Totalitarianism* (London: William Heinemann, 1939), characterized economic man as a manager who treats people as a factor of production and fails to meet social responsibilities. Drucker developed Management by Objectives, which aggregates organizational objectives on the basis of unit and individual objective setting, as an antidote to Taylor's emphasis on specialization and organizational fragmentation. See Nelson, *Mental Revolution*, 31, 209.

100. See Schachter, *Frederick Taylor and the Public Administration Community*, and "Morris Cooke." See also Oliver E. Williamson, Introduction to *Organization Theory: From Chester Barnard to the Present and Beyond*, ed. Oliver E. Williamson (New York: Oxford University Press, 1990), 4.

101. Taylor, *Principles of Scientific Management*, 7.

102. Taylor, "Testimony," 41.

103. Copley, *Frederick W. Taylor*, 234.

Chapter 3

Luther H. Gulick:
The Integrated Executive

Whereas the works of both Max Weber and Frederick Taylor would appear, at first blush, to be related only tangentially to the study and practice of public administration, Luther Gulick and his writings are directly and obviously central to those concerns. If there is a single person who personifies public administration in the United States, it is Luther Gulick. Indeed, his status in the field is such that he is sometimes referred to as the "Dean of Public Administration." [1] That title is well earned, for Gulick's work spans most of the period of the conscious study of public administration. Very few, if any, scholars and practitioners can say that their publication record extends over seventy years. Gulick's first publication (a book-length version of his doctoral dissertation) appeared in 1920, and his last (an article in *Public Administration Review*) in 1990.[2] His ideas, evolving over time, mirror both many of the changes in the field and some enduring themes that underlie those changes; and his record of public service is perhaps unparalleled in the field—or, at least, matched by very few.

The enduring themes are the most germane to our interests here, and we use the works of Luther Gulick as indicative of a line of thought that has had, and continues to have, substantial impact on the conduct of public administration in the United States. Gulick's work reflects many of the emphases of the reform movement of the early twentieth century as it applied to public-sector organization and management. He adopts Wilson's theme that a science of administration should be constructed, and that it should be founded on basic principles applicable in both the public and private sectors. The common objective is to achieve greater efficiency in public-sector operations. These themes are elaborated with Gulick's particular stress on structural reform in the name of consolidation and integration, centralization to enhance executive power, professionalization to improve the quality of personnel in the public sector, and the rationalization of decision-making and management processes to assure greater effectiveness and efficiency in service delivery.

Perhaps the strongest of Gulick's emphases is the enhancement of executive power, both within organizations and among the organizations of the executive branch. A strong executive is required to coordinate properly the fragmented activities performed in individual public organizations and in the public sector as a whole. Unified and concentrated leadership is necessary to rationalize operations and to locate responsibility at the apex of the organizational pyramid. In the relationship between branches of government, the executive should plan, propose, and implement public policies and programs, while the legislature should be restricted to review and approval.

In one regard, Gulick differs significantly from many of his contemporaries: his stance on the politics/policy vs. administration dichotomy. Rejecting the common contention that the two domains can be, or should be, separate and distinct, Gulick argues that such a separation is impractical, impossible, and undesirable.[3] Instead, we should develop a system that allows the fullest use of the expertise of the public administrator, including expertise on matters of public policy.

One gets from Gulick the overall sense that government has an important and useful role in society and that the administrator plays a vital part in the performance of necessary governmental functions. In this way, too, Gulick reflects both the temperament of the time and the sense of mission so characteristic of the reform movement. Gulick's passion for his mission is clearly evidenced in his writings and, even more powerfully, in his administrative career.

Life

Luther Halsey Gulick was born in Osaka, Japan, on January 17, 1892.[4] The middle of three children of missionary parents, he was the third Gulick to bear the name Luther Halsey, sharing it with an uncle who was the coinventor (along with James Naismith) of basketball. The Gulick family was of Dutch descent, tracing its American roots to 1653, and numbered among its members a long line of scholars, doctors, teachers, scientists, authors, missionaries, and pastors. Gulick's father, Sidney Lewis Gulick, was an astronomer and mathematician as well as a theologian. His mother, Cara May (Fisher), the daughter of a California banker and ranch owner, was a professionally trained nurse.

Gulick lived in Japan for the first twelve years of his life. He describes himself as being full of mischievous adventure (having once almost burned down his house while trying to make gunpowder), hot-tempered, active, and spoiled—characteristics that prompted a mission elder to comment, on his father's departure from Japan, "Yes, we were sorry to have Dr. Gulick leave us; but after all he did take Luther with him." The Gulick family returned to the United States in 1904, later spending a winter in Germany, where Luther studied at a local technical high school and learned to speak German.[5] In 1906 he moved to Oakland, California, to stay with his maternal grandmother and attend high school. Apparently an industrious youth, Gulick worked at a bookstore and delivered newspapers, finding his most dependable customers to be saloon keepers and the madams of two brothels. His schoolwork went well in Oakland, but he reports that he made few friends.

In 1907 Gulick was awarded a scholarship by Hotchkiss, a boarding school in Lakeville, Connecticut, where he spent his next three years. His studies there focused on Greek, Latin, and mathematics; he participated in debate, joined the literary society, and ran on the school track team until he broke an ankle, which ended his athletic endeavors. After a shaky start, and despite some problems with spelling, Gulick performed well at Hotchkiss, achieving honor-roll status and the top rank in his class. He also developed, however, what he describes as an "overly competitive nature," which was manifested, for instance, in a tenacity in debate that was considered ungentlemanly and would soon cause him difficulty.

During the summer of 1910, Gulick traveled to England as a deckhand on a cattle boat and then bicycled across the British Isles. On his return to the United States, he learned that his scholarship at Hotchkiss had been terminated because he was a "disturbing factor." Since he had placed well on national examinations, Gulick decided not to return to Hotchkiss but to apply instead for admission to Oberlin College in Ohio. Accepted there on a provisional basis, he soon gained full admission by making the dean's list in his first semester. Gulick earned his keep while at Oberlin by washing dishes, scrubbing floors, and beating rugs at a boardinghouse for missionary children; cutting lawns; selling magazines; and promoting lectures and concerts. During the summers, he worked as a section hand for a railroad, sold aluminum pots and pans, worked on a farm, poured cement for a mausoleum, and served as a swimming instructor at a girl's camp in New Hampshire. He also made his first entry into politics in 1912 by managing a local campaign for Theodore Roosevelt's Bull Moosers.

Gulick received a BA with honors in political science from Oberlin and membership in Phi Beta Kappa in 1914.[6] On graduation, he entered Oberlin's Theological Seminary, with the intent of following his father in missionary work. Though he earned a master's degree in philosophy in 1915, Gulick found himself beset by what he calls "agnostic uncertainties," which resulted in a major change in direction in his career plans. Coming to believe that the essence of spiritual life is not in the formal elements of religion but in the basic values of "fundamental honesty, individual human dignity, justice and human rights, the opportunity for creative fulfillment, social responsibility, 'charity' as defined by St. Paul, selfless devotion to noble causes, and deep emotional participation in the Universe," he maintained his parents' commitment to the advancement of humankind but decided that his best contribution could be made through social work and government rather than as a missionary.

Consequently, Gulick applied to Columbia University, which he entered in the fall of 1915 as a doctoral candidate with a fellowship in political science and public law. Even more important, he came into contact with the New York Bureau of Municipal Research, attending courses at the bureau's Training School for Public Service and commencing what was to be a lifelong association. Gulick specialized in administration and budgeting and, in 1917, secured a position as secretary of the Joint Special Committee on Finance and Budget Procedure of the Massachusetts General Court (legislature). This experience produced the material for his doctoral dissertation, which was published in 1920 as *Evolution of the Budget in Massachusetts*, although he did not receive his PhD in law from Columbia until 1921.[7] After a year's stint in the army, where Gulick served as a captain and staff member of the Statistics Branch of the General Staff, he was appointed director of the Training School for Public Service and secretary of the Board of the Bureau, thus embarking on what was to be a singularly distinctive career in the public service.

During the 1920s, he was appointed director of the Bureau of Municipal Research, which was reconstituted as the National Institute of Public Administration (later to be called simply the Institute of Public Administration); he would serve in that capacity until 1962. Under Gulick's leadership, and with an expanded mandate, the institute undertook administrative studies in several states over the following twenty years.[8] In addition to performing his duties as director of the institute, Gulick served as chairman of the Governmental Research Association, as director of research for the New York Taxation and Retrenchment Commission, and as a member of the National Tax Association's Committee on a Model Tax Law. In 1931 he was promoted to Eaton Professor of Municipal Science and Administration at Columbia University, a position that he held until 1942. During the thirties, Gulick's interests expanded to include the state and federal levels: in 1933 he was appointed secretary and director of the Social Science Research Council's Commission of Inquiry on Public Service Personnel, and from 1933 through 1936, he was director of the Regent's Inquiry into the Character and Cost of Public Education in the State of New York.

Between 1936 and 1937, Gulick served as a member of the President's Committee on Administrative Management and coedited the famous *Papers on the Science of Administration,* to which he contributed two papers.[9] It is this latter effort for which he is best known. What is less well-known, though amply documented, is that Herbert Brownlow, Charles Merriam, and Gulick had already, in late 1933, agreed that a discussion of the administrative role of the chief executive would be necessary. Two years later they reiterated this call, and the Public Administration Committee approved in October 1935 a study of the overall management of the executive. In order to increase support for such a study, the three main members agreed that the president himself ought to be approached. On their behalf, Merriam drafted a letter in late January 1936, and President Roosevelt decided by early March to assign such an inquiry a committee appointed and funded by the White House.[10]

With the coming of the 1940s and the onset of World War II, Gulick went to Washington, serving in a wide array of capacities. He acted as a consultant to both the Treasury Department and the secretary of war. In addition, Gulick served as chief of the Bureau of Organization and Planning and of the War Production Board between 1941 and 1945; worked with the Bureau of the Budget; took charge of the technical aspects of the reorganization of the Smaller Plants Corporation; organized and acted as chairman of the Advisory Committee on Education in the office of the Coordinator for Inter-American Affairs; and served as a member of the Census Advisory Committee of the Department of Commerce.

A central concern for Gulick during the war years was postwar plans and operations.[11] He served as coordinator of postwar programs in the National Resources Planning Board, as a member of the staff of the Office of Foreign Relief and Rehabilitations Operations, and as acting chief of the Secretariat of the United Nations' Relief and Rehabilitation Administration. While working for a year (1945–1946) as an aide for administrative matters on the White House staff, Gulick became a member of the U.S. Reparations Mission Staff and, in that capacity, traveled to Brussels, Manila, Moscow, Nuremberg, Paris, Potsdam, Tokyo, and Vienna.[12]

Returning to New York after the war, Gulick resumed his activities with the Institute of Public Administration. Between 1950 and 1953, he was executive director of the Mayor's Committee on the Management Survey of the City of New York. He was then appointed the first city administrator of New York, a position he filled until 1956. In 1959 Gulick was appointed to the New York City Commission on Government Operations. In addition, he served as a consultant to the United Nations and to a variety of countries (Egypt, England, France, Germany, Greece, India, Italy, Iran, Iraq, Japan, Korea, Peru, the Philippines, and Taiwan).[13]

As Gulick moved into his seventies and eighties, his level of activity continued almost unabated. In 1962 he was made chairman of the board of the Institute of Public Administration. He also served as a member of the New York City Charter Revision Commission; as cochairman of a New York City zoning committee; a member of the Mayor's Committee on Professional, Technical, and Managerial Manpower; chairman of a commission on a model-city charter; a member of the Mayor's Committee on the Transition (1965–1966); a member of the Board of Trustees of the National Recreation and Park Association; and consultant to various foreign countries and international organizations. In 1982, at the age of ninety, Gulick was appointed chairman emeritus of the Institute of Public Administration.

Gulick received a host of awards in recognition of his distinguished record of public service. Among the most prominent of them were the Distinguished Citizen Award of the National Municipal League, the Twenty-Fifth Anniversary Citation and the Dwight Waldo Award of the American Society for Public Administration, the Distinguished Service Award of the National Academy of Public Administration, the National Planning Award of the Regional Planning Association, and the Gruenberg Award of the Governmental Research Association. He died on January 10, 1993.

The Role of Government in Society

Gulick had few pretensions about his abilities as a theorist. In his words, "I shall leave to the political historians and philosophers the comprehensive and systematic interpretation of the world, as I am neither historian nor philosopher. My interests and experience are rather in getting things done through administrative and civic action."[14] Nonetheless, one can derive from his writings at least a general orientation concerning the role and functions of government in society. Gulick asserts that man is a social animal with facile hands, a restless curiosity, and an inventive and retentive mind. Man's nature calls for social contact and his limitations for a specialization of "knowledge, skill, taste, art, and emotion."[15]

Government, according to Gulick, is the means by which willful, strong, and selfish human beings can live together cooperatively. The necessity of governmental activity arises when private actions based on self-interest and guided by the "unseen hand" of the market prove to be inadequate. Government functions to control conduct in the name of maximum freedom and to provide cooperative community services— that is, those that can be performed better, more economically, or more satisfactorily on a cooperative basis. In all of this activity, government should manifest a "decent human sympathy for the weak."[16]

Although government must act, Gulick does not believe that it should act unilaterally. He maintains that "in a pluralistic society, there is no place for an exclusive pursuit by the central government of national goals and programs embracing public and private activities."[17] Presaging a similar emphasis in the 1970s and 1980s, Gulick asserted that the public and private sectors should become partners in a cooperative enterprise serving the common good, and he believed planning to be a vital ingredient in this cooperative venture. Recognizing that it will inevitably be based on value judgments, Gulick argues that planning should be multidisciplinary in character, involving all relevant disciplines and soliciting the views of special-interest groups as well as the opinions of the "ordinary public."[18] Since limits on knowledge limit the precision of planning, he asserts that planning should deal in the marginal value of incremental change rather than fixing absolute priorities, and that it should function as a general guide, not an immutable blueprint, for change.[19]

Gulick identifies market failure as a primary justification for governmental action, but he does not consider it to be the sole cause of the growth of government. Enlargement of the role of the public sector, he argues, may also be attributed to pressure from "enthusiasts, bureaucrats, and politicians for enlarged budgets," and he maintains that there is no evidence of "survival of the fittest" among governmental agencies.[20] Survival, according to Gulick, may well be as much a tribute to inertia as to adaptability. Therefore, extensions of governmental activity should be preceded by careful examination of the consequences of such action for society, and attempts to make the state omnipotent should be resisted.[21]

The role of the state should be limited because of uncertainty about the future; lack of wisdom, experience, knowledge, and character among leaders; lack of administrative skill and technique; the vast number of variables involved in comprehensive action; and the absence of orderly methods of developing new ideas and programs in a totalitarian state.[22] Democratic government in a pluralistic society, according to Gulick, is superior to totalitarian government in its ability to generate new ideas, in the presence of the corrective effect of free criticism, and in the requirement of the common man's appraisal of the end product. Although he acknowledges that totalitarian governments have little difficulty in regimenting attitudes and thus securing the consent of the governed, he feels them to be prone to a "hardening of the arteries" without sufficient channels of communication for proposing or assessing change.[23] Gulick concedes that there are no fixed limits on the role of government. Nevertheless, he argues that the state should not, and is not likely to, encompass all human activity.

In order for government to perform properly its required duties, a substantial reordering of functions is required. Gulick asserts that neither the public nor the legislature is capable of the planning needed by an effective government. The public, according to Gulick, cannot deal with the intricacies of planning. Thus the responsibility for planning must be delegated by the public and discharged by the governmental system.[24] The legislature, for its part, has no central focus of responsibility and cannot act in an expeditious and coherent fashion. Gulick maintains that we should be less concerned with checks and balances in executive-legislative relationships than with the distinction between policy planning and execution on the one side and policy adoption or veto on the other.[25] His ideal government is one in which the chief executive, supported by a special staff, draws the plans; the legislature accepts or rejects proposed policies; the executive carries out the adopted plan; and the public exercises general control through participation in political parties and pressure groups. This allocation of functions, Gulick believes, would produce the unified management necessary not only for efficiency and effectiveness but also for meaningful democratic control as responsibilities are more clearly defined and assigned.

Gulick also calls for a redefinition of responsibilities in the federal system. He contends that national legislators too often enact policies that ignore the necessities of state and local governments, while state and local governments sometimes take action as though there were no federal government or national problems.[26] In contrast to his recommendation of a functional allocation of duties between the executive and legislative branches, Gulick argues that it is not possible to achieve a clear separation of functions in the federal system. Instead, he supports "pragmatic solutions" in which functions are divided into their local, state, and federal "aspects," and responsibilities assigned accordingly. These assignments should be flexible and subject to change based on continuing planning and cooperation among authorities at each level of government.[27]

Gulick's own notions about the proper responsibilities of the several levels of government changed over time, although he generally advocated a major role for the federal government. During the Great Depression, Gulick argued for the assumption of substantial new powers by the federal government, including control over the entire field of business, transportation, banking, and taxation, as well as "basic control" in the areas of wages, hours, working conditions, prices, distribution, profits and finance, and general trade practices.[28] He later tempered this sweeping pronouncement by maintaining that where divergence and local adaptation are required, responsibilities should be decentralized, so that the smallest unit capable of embracing the geographical extent of a problem and able to command the appropriate professional service would assume responsibility.[29] Even where national policies are required, grassroots administration is still desirable if clear standards of delegation are established to ensure uniform enforcement of policy and adequate protection of individual rights.

The Role of Administration in Government

The dominant theme during much of the time in which Gulick wrote was that politics and policy considerations should be separated from administrative matters. Gulick's own position was that it is impractical, impossible, and undesirable to make such strict separations. According to Gulick, administration involves the determination of major policy; the development and adoption of specific programs; the creation of the organization; provision of personnel; authorization of finances; administrative supervision, coordination, and control of activities; and the audit and review of results.[30] Under this broad definition, he maintains that administration is necessarily involved in both politics and the policy process.

Gulick attributes two meanings to the word *politics.* In its vulgar sense, the word means seeking selfish advantage or advancement through the control of rulers, but its true sense points to the actions by which rulers control.[31] The problem is that there is no objective way of distinguishing between vulgar and true politics, since the distinction lies in the motivation of the actor rather than in the action itself. Therefore, attempts to control the vulgar aspects of politics in administration run the danger of denying the true political function of administration. Furthermore, efforts to keep politics in its vulgar sense out of administration have proven to be impractical. Prohibition of political activity in a system of checks and balances, Gulick contends, results in a virtually powerless government that "can't go wrong because it can't go at all." Efforts to eliminate politics from administration by setting up independent public agencies only frustrate efforts to establish an integrated government that is capable of planning.[32] In sum, Gulick maintains that the old dichotomy between politics and administration has broken down, and he argues that a new doctrine should be developed that permits "the fullest possible use of the expert in an appropriate framework of political and professional responsibility."[33]

Gulick's own formulation is a rather tenuous accommodation of politics, policy, and administration. He distinguishes among the roles of politicians, political appointees, administrators, and technicians in determining degrees of political and policy involvement. The role of the politician is to maintain equilibrium in the overall system by monitoring and adjusting the relationships among the experts, bureaucrats, and interest groups. Political appointees are to act as intermediaries, explaining the experts to the public and the public to the experts.[34] The administrator's role is to understand and coordinate public policy and to interpret policy directives to the operating services, but with unquestioned loyalty to the decisions of elected officials. The administrator differs from the political executive in that the administrator does not make final decisions on policy, does not advocate policies before the public, and does not succeed or fail on policy positions. Finally, the technician generally should be limited to the consideration of "technical matters."[35]

Though the roles ascribed to these several actors indicate, in rough fashion, the relative degree of involvement in policy and political activity, Gulick concedes that the acts of all public officials are a "seamless web of discretion and action" and that discretion is likely to involve the official in policy considerations.[36] The amount of discretion decreases as one moves from the elected official to the technician. Nevertheless, not all policy matters are referred to the top, and, consequently, much discretion inevitably resides at the bottom, where "public servants touch the public." Moreover, any particular decision is political, not technical, if the public deems it to be such.[37] Therefore, the differences among the roles in regard to policy and political involvement are differences in degree rather than differences in kind; the successful administrator must understand, and be able to deal with, the strategic dimensions of the politico-administrative system in which he must operate.[38] Effective administration rests on singleness of purpose, clarity of policy, and public support. Gulick's charge to administrators is to fuse knowledge and skills with public desires, political forces, and common sense; evolve a course of remedial, structured action; and take steps to secure the authority to act.[39] This mode of proceeding entails "political" activity in its true sense and injects the administrator into the policy process.

Science and Administration

The policy/politics-administration dichotomy had been the basis on which early authors in the field had hoped to construct a science of administration. By separating administration from policy and politics, it was argued, administration could be defined as a value-free endeavor and thus the legitimate subject of scientific analysis.

Although Gulick rejects the policy/politics-administration dichotomy, he too aspires to the application of scientific methods to administrative matters. According to Gulick, "Through science and the scientific spirit man has freed himself, at least in his material existence, from the complete domination of habit."[40] He believes that the same methods and spirit can be applied to investigations of human behavior and, indeed, thinks it "inevitable that there should be in every field of human endeavor an effort to reduce experience and phenomena to measurable terms."[41] In regard to public administration, Gulick sees the scientific method as a way to "substitute for ignorance, competence; for the amateur, the professional; for the jack-of-all-trades, the expert; for superficial facility, increasing differentiation and specialization; and for the untutored novitiate, the trained executive."[42] To be sure, Gulick does not blindly advocate some kind of "natural science" approach to matters of public administration. Indeed, in the second of his two papers for the Brownlow report, he expresses frustration with any suggestion that public administration, or the social sciences at-large for that matter, should follow the research standards of the natural sciences, which had—in Gulick's words, the "simple and easy task of understanding the mechanistic and mathematical relationships of the physical world."[43] Instead, Gulick advocated vigorously for the application of Scientific Management.[44]

Gulick argues that we must move beyond the mere collection of easily accessible facts, law, and practices and even beyond problem-oriented applied research to a scientific pursuit of solutions to the problems of modern government. These problems range from the details of management to the philosophy of society. A science of administration would embody "a system of knowledge whereby men may understand relationships, predict results, and influence outcomes in any situation where men are organized at work together for a common purpose."[45] The scientific pursuit entails intellectual examination and classification of phenomena, testing hypotheses by experiment and exploration, and the application of discovered truths to the world of nature with continuous questioning of results.[46] The objective is the discovery of "principles" or "immutable laws of administration," which can be distilled and simplified for practical application to administrative matters.[47]

Having rejected the politics/policy-administration dichotomy, Gulick is faced with the problem of the role of values in administration and a redefinition of an appropriate domain for scientific analysis. Anticipating a position later taken by Simon, he states that values are concerned with the assessment of the desirability of ends, and he acknowledges that values, so defined, are inevitably involved in administration and are not amenable to scientific investigation. Consequently, science cannot embrace the entirety of administrative activity. He contends, however, that values are not involved in statements of "variations and interrelation-ships"—scientific analysis can reveal what, under certain conditions, is likely to occur. Thus, the appropriate domain for a science of administration is the investigation of relationships between actions and outcomes. Gulick contends that the only value endemic to the scientific endeavor itself is efficiency, although, in application, efficiency must be accommodated to other social and political values.[48]

Gulick is aware of the problems in developing a science of administration. The social sciences have an elusive subject matter, since human beings are dynamic and, to some unknown extent, unpredictable.[49] Furthermore, the study of human behavior raises the problem of establishing appropriate controls for scientific experimentation. Nonetheless, Gulick considers scientific research to be a necessity and "a powerful ally, if not an indispensable adjunct of efficient democracy."[50]

Gulick is also aware of the potential dangers of scientific "expertise." He notes that we are confronted by specialists who know more and more about less and less, that experts may assume that they know better than the people what the people need, and that experts may assert knowledge and authority in fields in which they have no competence. These dangers are significant because, as Gulick observes, "a government program which relies upon a professional group of experts will, within a generation, come under the leadership and direction of that profession."[51]

The answer to the dangers of technocracy, according to Gulick, is a sense of professionalism that imposes responsible self-discipline and recognizes that final action cannot be taken by experts. In a democracy, the common man must be the ultimate judge of what is good for him. This does not mean that the expert is unnecessary. Rather, the requirements of democracy impose on the expert and the administrator an obligation to communicate better with both political leaders and the common man and to educate them about the conditions conducive to effective administration. As Gulick puts it, "To move democracy, you must not only develop the facts through research but you must develop also the vocabulary of the leaders and the support of the masses."[52]

Administrative Organization

Gulick agrees with the objectives of the early reform movement in the United States, but he differs on the appropriate strategy for reform. The original "good government" movement concentrated on specific abuses and sought reform through the electoral process. What is needed, Gulick contends, is reform of the basic structure and underlying processes of administration. Functions must be defined, work divided, structures and relationships formalized, staffs professionalized, and activities rationalized.[53]

This strategy entails reforms such as a short ballot, a strong executive branch, consolidation of agencies, and the adoption of more "businesslike" practices in government. On the last point, Gulick suggests that public administration and private administration belong to a single broad science despite their different objectives and emphases. Both deal with groups of men working toward specified goals with a division of labor; both arrive at policy decisions through planning; both coordinate, direct, and hold accountable; both seek to maximize results through incentives and the best use of men, materials, and time; both must be sensitive to public opinion and to the continuity of the enterprise in a changing environment.[54]

Gulick asserts that administrative reform should be guided by a new set of "principles." American government was originally based on principles derived from an aversion to executive power and a desire for representativeness. These principles were as follows: many governmental officials should be elected (the long ballot); elections should be held frequently; a system of checks and balances should be constructed to contain executive power; many heads are better than one (that is, a preference for committee leadership); and anyone is competent to hold any governmental position.[55] Experience, says Gulick, has demonstrated the defects of these principles. The election of many officials and frequent elections have produced neither good government nor democratic government; the system of checks and balances has resulted in "more brakes than driving power"; multiheaded agencies have deprived the system of responsible and energetic leadership; and inexperienced men have proven to be incapable of handling important executive and technical work.[56]

What is needed, Gulick maintains, is an administrative branch that is capable of planning and implementing democratic policies. He advises that administrative reform be guided by the following principles:

1. Related work should be administered as a unit.
2. All agencies should be consolidated into a few departments.
3. Each unit of administrative work should be placed under a single, responsible official selected on the basis of proven ability, technical knowledge, and experience.[57]
4. The power of the department head should be commensurate with his responsibility.
5. Each head of a large department should have a staff for performance evaluation.
6. Responsibility for each function should be vested in a specific official.
7. The number of elected officials should be reduced.

8. Boards or commissions should not be used for administrative work. They should be limited to quasi-legislative and quasi-judicial functions.

9. All administrative work should be headed up under a single chief executive, who should be directly elected by, and responsible to, the voters or their representatives.

10. The chief executive should have the power to appoint and discharge department heads and to direct their work.

11. The chief executive should have a research staff to report on the work of the departments and search for improved methods of operation.[58]

In short, the administrative branch should be integrated and placed under the leadership of strong and competent executives, with a powerful chief executive overseeing the entire process.

Reform also requires both a rational division of work and subsequent integration *within* each organization as part of an integrated executive branch. According to Gulick, the division of work and the integrated organization are "the bootstraps by which mankind lifts itself in the process of civilization."[59] Division of work is necessary because men differ in nature, capacity, and skill; because one man cannot be in two places at the same time; because one man cannot do two things at the same time; and because man is limited in his range of knowledge. Integration is required to provide central coordination among the "unit tasks" defined by the division of work in the organization. Accordingly, the theory of organizations is concerned with the structure of coordination imposed on the divided work of the organization.

One ingredient of integration is the grouping of similar tasks in the organization. Gulick identifies four bases on which the unit tasks of an organization may be grouped:

1. Purpose: tasks grouped by the service rendered—such as departments of Health and Human Services.

2. Process: tasks grouped by the skill or technology employed—such as the United States Bureau of the Census.

3. Clientele or materiel—such as the Department of Agriculture specifically servicing farmers.

4. Place: any deconcentrated unit or field agency as an extension of an administrative headquarters—such as the regional offices of the Internal Revenue Service, the Federal Emergency Management Agency, the Central Intelligence Agency, and so forth.

Although Gulick emphasizes the importance of purpose in coordinating efforts in the organization, he notes that the selection of any particular base will depend on the stage of organizational development, technological changes, the size of the organization, and the specific advantages and disadvantages attached to the use of a particular base in a given organization.[60]

The concentration on division of work and grouping of unit tasks in the organization is what Gulick calls a "bottom-up" perspective on the organization. This perspective properly emphasizes the "principle of homogeneity," or the grouping of similar tasks. Nevertheless, the bottom-up view, if taken alone, ignores the necessities of control and coordination in the organization. Therefore, Gulick also advises a "top-down" view, noting that if subdivision and specialization in the organization are inevitable, coordination is a necessity.[61] He identifies two primary mechanisms of control and coordination in the organization: the structure of authority, and ideas or singleness of purpose.[62]

Coordination through the structure of authority is, of course, a central mechanism of control. It requires a single overall directing executive authority, the provision of a supervisor for each job, and the determination of the unit tasks into which the overall job will have to be divided.[63] In establishing the structure of authority, Gulick warns, the effective span of control at each level of the organization is limited by the knowledge, time, and energy of the supervisor. The span of control can be extended, however, where work is routine, repetitive, measurable, and homogeneous in character.[64]

Leadership is also a vital element of coordination through authority. Gulick asserts that the principle of unitary, concentrated leadership is almost universal, and he advises that leaders be given both power and, with particular reference to the public sector, the time to use it. Gulick assigns to the executive a wide range of functions that are summed up in the acronym, POSDCORB—Planning, Organizing, Staffing, Directing, Coordinating, Reporting, and Budgeting. The executive organization should be structured around these functions, and, according to Gulick, none of the functions should be performed outside the executive office.[65] Gulick attaches special importance to the planning function. Planning is the means by which purpose is translated into programs; it involves the identification of key controllable items that are to be manipulated to achieve organizational objectives.[66] Gulick asserts that planning should be performed by specialists, but he advises that those in charge of planning should also be in charge of operations to ensure both a proper correlation between plans and operations and the effective implementation of the plans.

Although Gulick stresses the structure of authority and the role of leadership as coordinating mechanisms in the organization, he acknowledges that reliance on hierarchy alone is not sufficient to produce an integrated organization. The organization must also employ *coordination by ideas*, thereby developing the desire and will to work together with a singleness of purpose.[67] This means that the tasks of the administrator must be accomplished more by persuasion than by coercion and discipline. Gulick states that "the way to solve problems is by personal negotiation, with all of the cards on the table, not by inconsiderate, independent, and precipitate action."[68] Coordination through ideas, according to Gulick, can render the absurdities of hierarchy "sweet and reasonable," and he considers a clear statement of purpose to be the best guarantee of effective administration.[69]

An integrated executive structure in government, according to Gulick, provides not only coordination but also a single focus of leadership and political responsibility that is more amenable to democratic control than a series of autonomous units.[70] He cautions that we should also be cognizant of the limits of integration imposed by constraints on effective knowledge, decision-making capability, and management technique.[71] Thus, a balance must be struck between the desire for integration and the limits of its applicability.

From Principles to Particulars

As noted previously, Gulick considered himself to be a man of action, and much of his career was devoted to the application of the ideas and principles just reviewed. In discussing these applications, it is useful to start with a brief look at the Institute of Public Administration, which was both a source of many of Gulick's beliefs and an instrument for their implementation.

The institute, called the New York Bureau of Municipal Research when it was founded in 1906, became an integral part of the efficiency movement in America.[72] Although they were concerned with economy and efficiency, the leaders of the bureau were also driven by a "profound devotion to democracy" manifested in their call for responsible and responsive government and the education of the citizenry.[73] The founders of the bureau sought the expansion of governmental functions in order to make democracy "a living, vital thing."[74] Thus, the bureau's mission was not simply to achieve efficiency, but to encourage a more positive role for government, as well as to create the enlightened citizenry that was considered necessary for true democracy.

The bureau, described by Gulick as "a power house and idea factory" for the efficiency movement, was centrally involved in the pursuit of administrative principles and their practical application.[75] The aims were to promote efficient and economical government; to promote the adoption of scientific methods of accounting and the reporting of municipal business; to secure constructive publicity; and to collect, classify, analyze, correlate, interpret, and publish the facts.[76] Basic emphasis was placed on the concentration of executive responsibility and the development of appropriate planning, coordinating, budgeting, and personnel practices.[77]

The bureau—and later the Institute of Public Administration—pursued its objectives through two major mechanisms: the governmental survey and the Training School for the Public Service. The governmental survey, which was the bureau's primary instrument of analysis, entailed the grouping of administrative activities into major functions, the assignment of an investigator to each function, the analysis of statutory and constitutional provisions regarding each function, and an investigation of the actual organization and operation of the agencies involved.[78] Recommendations were then developed with the objective of better unifying, standardizing, clarifying, coordinating, and controlling governmental activities. These recommendations were discussed with agency executives for possible implementation, and reports were issued to the public in accord with the bureau's mission of civic education.

The second major mechanism was the bureau's Training School for the Public Service, established in 1911. The school's purpose was to "train men and women for administrative responsibility, for unofficial public service, and for governmental research."[79] The program encompassed one year of study plus a three-month internship. The staff of the bureau served as instructors and the city as a laboratory, as students were assigned to bureau studies to develop their skills.[80]

Gulick's personal interests, bred of his experience with the bureau and shaped by his leadership of that organization, were largely in the fields of public finance, personnel, and metropolitan government. While still a student at the Training School for Public Service, Gulick was appointed secretary of the Joint Special Committee on Finance and Budget Procedure of the Massachusetts state legislature. The experience produced a lasting interest in public finance and shaped many of his ideas about budgetary reform. Gulick generally supported increased executive responsibility in financial matters and a correspondingly reduced role for the legislature, both of which were intended to free the purposeful executive from legislative indecision.[81] He also advocated "functionalized," or program, budgeting, which employs performance indicators for review and evaluation. Finally, Gulick prescribed a substantial measure of centralization of financial responsibility within the states. He urged that the state have jurisdiction over the administration of all taxes except the property tax, local taxes levied for purposes other than regulation, and a few other taxes that can "naturally be administered by local units."[82]

Gulick's second major area of interest was personnel. Here, he supported a "positive career service" in the public sector, which, he argued, would place politics on a higher plane of issues and men, not jobs and special privileges, and would secure the effective personnel necessary for a democracy to carry out the decisions and desires of the people.[83] Gulick's proposed formula was "pick 'em young, tell 'em everything, and treat 'em rough, but fairly."[84] In other words, public employees should be recruited early, they should have an apprentice period to learn the job, and "weak sisters" should be left behind.

Gulick's proposed career system would extend to all nonpolitical top positions in government and would consist of five career classifications: unskilled services, skills and trades service, clerical service, professional and technical service, and administrative service. There should be competitive examinations for all career classifications, based on the particular skills required for each classification. A probationary period should be served by all public employees, and strict controls should be placed on temporary appointments to avoid circumvention of the competitive examination requirement. Advancement in the career service should be based on merit, and good salaries and adequate retirement benefits should be offered to attract and retain qualified employees. Safeguards should be built into the system to protect employees from arbitrary dismissal.[85]

As one would expect, given his lifelong association with the Institute of Public Administration and New York City government, Gulick also was centrally concerned with the problems of metropolitan government. His ideas on metropolitan government were generally consistent with his concept of federalism discussed earlier—that is, assignment of responsibilities to the various levels of government according to "aspects" of functions, and reliance on the smallest unit of government capable of dealing with a problem. There were some equivocations on the matters of executive versus legislative powers and the centralization of fiscal responsibilities.

As did the reform movement in general, Gulick attached great importance to the city. He stated that the city "offers the masses democratically the opportunity for the highest culture and it schools men in freedom, self-control, and social adaptation to change."[86] Nevertheless, Gulick recognized that urban life poses problems as well as opportunities. Cities suffer from congestion, concentrations of minorities and the poor, the necessity of providing services to people who do not live there, and a lack of fiscal resources. The problems of the city, Gulick argued, are not due solely to size, for the costs of scale are at least partially mitigated by the economies of scale, and Gulick contended that no "laws" limit the size of metropolitan government.[87] Instead, the metropolitan problem is one of bad political engineering and inadequate management devices. Gulick asserted that government has failed to act in many areas and suffers from fractionalization in those functions that have been undertaken. An inadequate revenue base coupled with an unbalanced population and a lack of political resources and clearheaded leadership, he argued, have rendered metropolitan governments unequal to the tasks they face.

Gulick identified several alternative approaches to the solution of metropolitan problems: the creation of limited-purpose agencies for the metropolitan area, transfer of fractionated activities to the next higher level of government, the creation of local multiple-purpose agencies, solving problems serially by intergovernmental contracts, establishing a department of local affairs at the state level, the reconstruction of the county, and the creation of a new layer of government for the metropolitan area. Whatever its particular form, the essential elements of metropolitan governance are flexibility and political viability in establishing boundaries; geographical, social, and economic comprehensiveness; joint action on interrelated activities; a representative body drawn from the area as a whole; the protection of local communities in their continuing responsibility for local functions; and an adequate fiscal structure.[88] Gulick's preferred solution, despite his general insistence on executive control and his suspicion of legislative bodies, was the creation of a Metropolitan Council that would rely on voluntary cooperation among the responsible political executives and community leaders of the existing jurisdictions.[89] The council would be a legislative body composed of the chief elected officials in the metropolitan area as well as directly elected members.

Although metropolitan governance is important, federal support is also required. According to Gulick, the ultimate solution to metropolitan problems requires action at all levels of government, featuring central involvement by the federal government and leadership by the president.[90] Each level of government should deal with aspects of functions that fall within its domain in a fiscal system that combines intergovernmental payments and the delegation of independent taxing power to appropriate state and local units.[91]

Conclusion

The major components of Gulick's approach to government and administration may be summarized as follows:

1. Government should play a positive role in society by acting when private efforts prove to be inadequate in serving the common good. Wherever possible, cooperative arrangements between the public and private sectors should be established, and planning should be an essential element of all public endeavors.

2. The executive branch at all levels of government should propose and implement policies, while the legislative branch should be limited to the approval or rejection of executive proposals.

3. Within the executive branch, the chief executive should be strengthened through more powerful hierarchical controls, improvement in staff support, consolidation of executive departments, and, at the state and local levels, reduction in the number of elected officials.

4. Collaborative relationships among federal, state, and local governments should be developed, and "aspects" of functions allocated to the appropriate levels of government. In particular, the federal government should acknowledge the national aspects of problems at the state and local levels and assume a leadership role in addressing those problems.

5. Administrators are necessarily involved in political and policy matters, and administrative theory should be reformulated to accommodate the use of professional expertise in a full range of administrative functions.

6. Scientific methods should be employed to discover general principles of administration that can be applied to achieve greater efficiency and effectiveness in governmental operations.

7. Executive-branch organizations should be internally integrated by arranging for top leadership to coordinate activities through the structure of authority and by developing a unity of purpose within the organization.

In short, Gulick's recipe for administrative reform entails the assumption of new functions by government; more efficiency in the functions undertaken; centralization within executive agencies and within the executive branch as a whole; and governance by experts who are subject to direct control by an elected chief executive, veto by the legislature, and general oversight by the public.

Assessing Gulick's ideas is rather difficult because many of his ideas changed, or at least moderated, over the course of his lengthy career. Moreover, he often seemed to be led more by his passion for reform than by the findings of systematic research. As a result, his thoughts are sometimes marked by unresolved tensions, and his pronouncements often lack empirical support.

At points, Gulick's ideas seem inconsistent. For instance, although Gulick is renowned for his advocacy of integrated structures, he is willing to tolerate a federal system in which there is no unity of command, no definition of functional responsibility, and no clear chain of command, and in which authority is not commensurate with fiscal responsibility. More often, the tension is evidenced in opposing considerations. Thus Gulick suggests a large role for the state, but asserts that there are limits to the role the state can, and should, play; he supports planning, but says there are limits to the degree to which planning can be effectively performed;

he argues for integration, but recognizes that there are limits on the extent to which integration is possible; he supports a career civil service with protection from political interference, but he also wants to strengthen the political chief executive in relationships with executive agencies; he would enlarge the role of the expert, but acknowledges the problem of controlling the expert in a democratic society. The problem is not so much that there are opposing considerations on all these matters—that is probably inevitable. The problem lies in determining where the balances should be struck and/or under what conditions a particular course of action should be pursued. Gulick provides no clear guidance on these critical issues.

A similar problem arises in regard to some of the principles of administration that Gulick espouses. Consider, for instance, the principles of homogeneity and integration. The principle of homogeneity states that similar tasks should be grouped in the organization. But all activities cannot be grouped along a single dimension, nor is there a dominant alternative. Instead, the combination of methods used in grouping tasks should be determined by examining the advantages and disadvantages of the various bases for grouping organizational tasks. Gulick fails to provide concrete criteria for choosing among the bases, however, and he offers little more than informed speculation about the probable consequences of any particular selection. On the principle of integration, Gulick argues that an integrated organization will produce efficient and effective administration, automatic coordination through clearly specified channels of communication, and clear assignments of responsibility that make democratic control more effective. This outcome is certainly plausible, but an equally plausible case can be made that "red tape" is a more likely result than effectiveness and efficiency in the integrated organization, that integration will discourage communication by virtue of elongated channels of communication and organizational formality, that responsibility will be obfuscated rather than clarified in the labyrinth of bureaucracy, and that an integrated executive branch headed by a powerful chief executive may result in tyrannical government.

Gulick's emphasis upon unity of command and efficiency as two of the core principles of organization sprang from a deep-felt desire to develop a science of administration. His ideas, though, met with criticism almost as soon as they appeared in print. Thus, Charles Hyneman of Louisiana State University criticized the overall scientific claims in 1939, and one year later, Edwin O. Stene wrote that Gulick's principles "... can hardly be called anything but opinions."[92]

Unresolved tension also characterizes Gulick's approach to organizational management. He would rely primarily on the hierarchical structure of authority to achieve control and coordination in the organization.

Even "coordination through ideas" is seen by Gulick as a method of hierarchical control and a way to make that control seem reasonable. The question is whether hierarchically integrated organizations are sufficiently attentive to the wide range of needs that have been found to motivate people in organizations. Gulick is sensitive to this issue. He asserts, for instance, that our primary task should be to "release the hidden energy in human nature" and that "nothing must take second place to our effort to understand the patterns of human awareness and how men who are working together in teams can find release for their full energies."[93]

But Gulick fails to address the potential incompatibilities between hierarchically integrated organizations and the satisfaction of human needs in the organization. For instance, the hierarchically integrated organization would have a limited span of control to ensure close and direct supervision. Yet it has been argued that close supervision dampens morale and inhibits the assumption of individual responsibility on the part of subordinates. Hierarchical integration is commonly associated with an elaborate division of labor to capitalize on the economies of specialization, whereas job enlargement (that is, less specialization), it is argued, promotes a greater sense of identification with the overall mission of the organization and a greater sense of individual achievement in task performance. The hierarchically integrated organization requires centralized decision-making procedures, but decentralized and participatory decision procedures have been supported as a way of giving the individual a greater sense of involvement in the organization and increasing the likelihood of individual acceptance of organizational decisions.

Finally, some of Gulick's positions appear to be more value commitments than "scientific" statements. His support for a strengthened and integrated executive branch is a case in point. Gulick contends that executive leadership will lead to more efficient and effective administration and will result in a higher degree of democratic control, but he provides little evidence in support of this contention. Moreover, his acceptance of the value of executive leadership conflicts with other values, such as representativeness and neutral competence.[94] The conflict with representativeness is that a powerful executive branch may escape both meaningful electoral controls (witness the oft-heard charge of an "imperial presidency") and the controls provided by the "checks and balances" of the legislative branch—a problem that would be exacerbated by Gulick's proposal to limit severely the powers of the legislature. The conflict with neutral competence is that executive leadership requires more control by political officials over appointed officials and so puts the administrator in a position of potential conflict between professional standards and hierarchical directives.

These problems should not diminish an appreciation of the significance of Gulick's contributions to the study and practice of public administration. Ideas such as those expressed by Gulick are deeply engrained in both spheres. The ideas that the study of public administration should be integrally related to the practice of public administration, that citizen enlightenment is required for effective democracy, that businesslike techniques should be adopted to improve the efficiency of governmental operations, that executive leadership is required for effective administration, that professionalism should be encouraged in the public service, and that government should be made more responsive and responsible defined the focus of public administration for a generation of scholars, and they remain central themes in the discipline. It should also be noted that the very normative emphasis that frustrates Gulick's search for a science of administration also accounts, in large measure, for the lasting impact of his ideas.

Moreover, Gulick's contributions to public administration should be assessed at least as much in terms of what he did as in regard to what he said. His long service with the Institute of Public Administration, his involvement with the President's Committee on Administrative Management, his administrative record during the war, his varied activities in the administration of New York City, as well as the awards and honors associated with his activities, stand as elegant testimony to Gulick's distinguished status in the discipline.

NOTES

1. We are not sure when was the first time that Gulick was accorded this title, but the usage can be found in Stephen K. Blumberg, "Seven Decades of Public Administration: A Tribute to Luther Gulick," *Public Administration Review* 41, no. 2 (1981): 245–248.
2. While Gulick's complete publication list includes 20 books, reports, or studies, more than 160 articles, well over 250 sets of notes, texts or drafts, and a large body of correspondence, it is not accessible for lack of a bibliography. See Paul P. Van Riper, "The Literary Gulick: A Bibliographical Application," *Public Administration Review* 50 no. 6 (1990): 609–614. As of May 2007, Van Riper was in the process of completing a book-length manuscript on the political and administrative thought of Luther Gulick, whose last article was titled "Reflections on Public Administration: Past and Present" and also appeared in *Public Administration Review* 50, no. 6 (1990): 599–603.
3. On Gulick as one of the first to debunk the dichotomy, see Michael M. Harmon, *Public Administration's Final Exam: A Pragmatist Restructuring of the Profession and the Discipline* (Tuscaloosa: University of Alabama Press, 2006), 12.
4. In the preparation of the first edition of this volume, information on Gulick's early life was taken from autobiographical notes provided by Pro-

fessor Paul Van Riper of Texas A&M University and drawn from material provided directly by Dr. Gulick. See also Lyle C. Fitch, "Luther Gulick," *Public Administration Review* 50, no. 6 (1990): 604–608; as well as Lyle C. Fitch, "Making Democracy Work: Luther Gulick" (working paper 91-25, Institute of Governmental Studies, University of California, Berkeley, 1991).

5. Gulick's early, largely informal, schoolwork went badly until it was discovered that he had poor eyesight (he eventually lost sight in one eye). He remained a slow reader throughout his life and did not read for pleasure until after his retirement.

6. He became engaged to Helen McKelvey Swift, whom he later married, in the same year.

7. Luther Gulick, *Evolution of the Budget in Massachusetts* (New York: Macmillan, 1920). On the publication of Gulick's study and the year he received his PhD, see James D. Carroll, "Luther Halsey Gulick," *PS: Political Science and Politics* 26, no. 3 (1993): 578–579.

8. The states included Massachusetts, New York, Virginia, South Dakota, Delaware, Tennessee, New Jersey, Michigan, and Maine.

9. Luther Gulick, "Notes on the Theory of Organization," in *Papers on the Science of Administration*, ed. Luther Gulick and L. Urwick (New York: Institute of Public Administration, 1937), 3–45; and "Science, Values, and Public Administration," in ibid., 191–195.

10. See Alasdair Roberts, "Demonstrating Neutrality: The Rockefeller Philanthropies and the Evolution of Public Administration, 1927–1936," *Public Administration Review* 54, no. 3 (1994): 226; Alasdair Roberts, "The Brownlow-Brookings Feud: The Politics of Dissent with the Academic Community," *Journal of Policy History* 7, no. 3 (1995): 314; Alasdair Roberts, "Why the Brownlow Committee Failed: Neutrality and Partisanship in the Early Years of Public Administration," *Administration & Society* 28, no. 1 (1996): 17–18 (especially on Merriam's invitation to the president); and Alasdair Roberts, "The Unassailable Principle: Why Luther Gulick Searched for a Science of Administration," *International Journal of Public Administration* 21, nos. 2–4 (1998): 250–251.

11. Gulick reflected upon his wartime experiences in his *Administrative Reflections from World War II* (University: University of Alabama Press, 1948).

12. He also attended the Potsdam Conference in 1945 and the meeting of the foreign ministers in Paris in 1946.

13. This listing of postwar positions and consulting activities is taken from Carroll, "Luther Halsey Gulick," 579; for a listing of other activities, see Stephen K. Blumberg, "Seven Decades of Public Administration," 245.

14. Luther Gulick, *The Metropolitan Problem and American Ideas* (New York: Knopf, 1962), 4.

15. Luther Gulick, "What the City Does for and to Its Citizens," *Public Management Journal* 21, no. 12 (December 1939): 335.

16. Gulick, *Metropolitan Problem and American Ideas*, 14.

17. Gerhard Colm and Luther Gulick, *Program Planning for National Goals*, Planning Pamphlet no. 125 (Washington, D.C.: National Planning Association, 1968), 5.

18. Luther Gulick, "The Concept of Regional Planning," *Public Policy* 12 (1963): 108.

19. Ibid., 102.
20. Luther Gulick and Charles F. Aufderhar, "The Increasing Cost of City Government," *American City Magazine* 31, no. 1 (July 1924): 15; and Gulick, "Notes on the Theory of Organization," 43.
21. Luther Gulick, *American Foreign Policy* (New York: Institute of Public Administration, 1951), 229.
22. Gulick, "Notes on the Theory of Organization," 40.
23. Gulick, *Administrative Reflections from World War II*, 127.
24. Luther Gulick, "Politics, Administration, and the 'New Deal,'" *Annals* 169 (September 1933): 58.
25. Ibid., 66.
26. Luther Gulick, "Planning and Cooperation," *State Government* 20, no. 3 (March 1947): 87.
27. Ibid., 86.
28. Gulick, "Politics, Administration, and the 'New Deal,'" 64.
29. Gulick, *American Foreign Policy*, 181–182.
30. Ibid., 57.
31. Luther Gulick, "Politics, Administration, and the 'New Deal,'" 59–60.
32. Ibid., 55–57.
33. Luther Gulick, "Next Steps in Public Administration," *Public Administration Review* 15, no. 2 (Spring 1955): 76.
34. Gulick, *American Foreign Policy*, 217–218.
35. Commission of Inquiry on Public Service Personnel, *Better Government Personnel* (New York: McGraw-Hill, 1935), 20–35.
36. Gulick, "Politics, Administration, and the 'New Deal,'" 61.
37. Ibid., 62.
38. Luther Gulick, "The Twenty-Fifth Anniversary of the American Society for Public Administration," *Public Administration Review* 25, no. 1 (March 1965): 4.
39. Ibid., 2.
40. Luther Gulick, *The National Institute of Public Administration* (New York: National Institute of Public Administration, 1928), 101.
41. Luther Gulick, "Wanted: A Measuring Stick for School Systems," *National Municipal Review* 18, no. 1 (January 1929): 3.
42. Gulick, *National Institute of Public Administration*, 52.
43. As quoted in Roberts, "Unassailable Principle," 249.
44. See Gulick's presentation entitled "Public Administration: A Field in Urgent Need of Scientific Management," delivered before the Taylor Society on December 4, 1931, and published in the *Bulletin of the Taylor Society* 17 (1932). Parts of this speech can be found in Paul P. Van Riper, "Luther Gulick on Frederick Taylor and Scientific Management," *Journal of Management History* 1, no. 2 (1995): 6–7.
45. Gulick, "Science, Values, and Public Administration," 191. The same argument was recently made by Kenneth J. Meier, "Public Administration and the Myth of Positivism: The AntiChrist's View," *Administrative Theory & Praxis* 27, no. 4 (2005): 650–668.
46. Luther Gulick, "The Scientific Approach to the Problems of Society and Government," *University of Buffalo Studies* 15, no. 2 (March 1938): 29.
47. Luther Gulick, "Principles of Administration," *National Municipal Review* 14, no. 7 (July 1925): 400.
48. Gulick, "Science, Values, and Public Administration," 192–193.

49. Gulick, "Scientific Approach to the Problems of Society and Government," 31.
50. Gulick, *National Institute of Public Administration*, 45.
51. Gulick, *American Foreign Policy*, 216.
52. Luther Gulick, "The Recent Movement for Better Government Personnel," *American Political Science Review* 31, no. 2 (April 1937): 301.
53. Luther Gulick, "Metropolitan Organization," *Annals* 314 (November 1957): 57.
54. Gulick, "Twenty-Fifth Anniversary of the American Society for Public Administration," 1; and "Next Steps in Public Administration," 74. Perhaps a bit of a stretch, but this observation by Gulick is comparable to *probing*, the "broad, diffuse, open-ended, mistake-making social or interactive process, both cognitive and political." See Charles E. Lindblom, *Inquiry and Change: The Troubled Attempt to Understand & Shape Society* (New Haven, Conn.: Yale University Press, 1990), 7.
55. *Proceedings of the Sixteenth Annual Conference on Taxation under the Auspices of the National Tax Association* (New York: National Tax Association, 1924), 265.
56. Ibid., 266.
57. Thomas Hammond, "In Defence of Luther Gulick's 'Notes on the Theory of Organization,'" *Public Administration* 68, no. 2 (1990): 143–173, observes that Gulick had criticized Taylor's functional foremanship as violating the principle of unity of command. However, Hammond shows that Taylor did recognize the potential for conflict between foremen and he quotes Taylor's 1911 study *Shop Management*. Indeed, while Taylor advocated functional division of labor between first-level supervisors, he did recognize the need for some hierarchy of authority to facilitate conflict resolution; see especially pp. 159–160.
58. Ibid., 266–267; and Gulick, "Principles of Administration," 401.
59. Gulick, "Notes on the Theory of Organization," 4.
60. Ibid., 15, 21–30. Gulick's four methods of departmentalization are still considered useful in capturing the complexity or organizational redesign. Hammond, analyzing the redesign of the intelligence community, makes extensive use of Gulick. See Thomas H. Hammond, "Why Is the Intelligence Community So Difficult to Redesign? Smart Practices, Conflicting Goals, and the Creation of Purpose-Based Organizations," *Governance: An International Journal of Policy, Administration, and Institution* 20, no. 3 (2007): 401–422.
61. Ibid., 11, 6.
62. Ibid., 6. He also mentions habit or routine as a coordinating mechanism, but does not elaborate on the point.
63. Ibid., 7.
64. Ibid. In his critique upon the principle of restricted span of control, Herbert Simon argued that this could lead to excessive red tape, while a large span of control might lead to lack of supervisory control; see Herbert Simon, *Administrative Behavior: A Study of Decision-making Process in Administrative Organization* (New York/London: Free Press/Collier-Macmillan, 1957), 26–28. Recently, Meier and Bohte argued that both Gulick and Simon had a point, since the "correct" span of control varies with level of organization. See Kenneth J. Meier and John Bohte, "Ode to Luther Gulick: Span of Control and Organizational Performance," *Administration*

& Society 32, no. 2 (2000): 115–137; and Kenneth J. Meier and John Bohte, "Span of Control and Public Organizations: Implementing Luther Gulick's Research Design," *Public Administration Review* 63, no. 1 (2003): 61–70.

65. Ibid., 13–14.

66. Gulick, *Administrative Reflections from World War II*, 80.

67. Hammond, "In Defence of Luther Gulick's 'Notes on the Theory of Organization,'" 158, asserts that Gulick's emphasis on the importance of ideas foreshadowed Chester Barnard's claim that "the inculcation of belief in the real existence of a common purpose is an essential executive function." See also Barnard, *The Functions of the Executive* (Cambridge, Mass.: Harvard University Press, 1938), 87; Philip Selznick, *Leadership in Administration: A Sociological Interpretation* (Evanston, Ill.: Row, Peterson, 1957); and T. J. Peters and R. H. Waterman, *In Search of Excellence* (New York: Warner Books, 1982).

68. Gulick, "Planning and Cooperation," 86.

69. Gulick, "Notes on the Theory of Organization," 39; and *Administrative Reflections from World War II*, 77.

70. Gulick, *Metropolitan Problem and American Ideas*, 81–82.

71. Ibid., 85–89.

72. For reviews of the history of the institute, see Gulick, *National Institute of Public Administration*; Jane S. Dahlberg, *The New York Bureau of Municipal Research* (New York: New York University Press, 1966); and Camilla Stivers, *Bureau Men, Settlement Women: Constructing Public Administration in the Progressive Era* (Lawrence: University Press of Kansas, 2000).

73. Dahlberg, *New York Bureau of Municipal Research*, v.

74. Ibid., 32.

75. Luther Gulick, "Perspectives in Public Administration: Past, Present, and Future" (paper delivered at C.W. Post Center, Long Island University, Greenvale, New York, December 19, 1979).

76. Dahlberg, *New York Bureau of Municipal Research*, 20–21.

77. Ibid., 174–227. These practices involved procedures such as executive budgeting, cost accounting, audit procedures independent of the executive branch, central control and standardization of governmental purchases, central control and compensation equalization in personnel, revenue control and improved methods of tax collection and property assessment, in-service training programs, and establishing standards for drawing organization charts.

78. Gulick, *National Institute of Public Administration*, 36–40.

79. Ibid., 55.

80. Ibid., 73. This apprentice system later gave way to more structured lecture and discussion courses in charters and municipal corporations, municipal organization, budgeting, public accounting and financial reporting, purchasing and storing of materials, civil service and personnel, taxation and revenues, public debt, engineering administration, police and fire administration, public welfare, education, governmental research, and the relationship between the administrators and the citizen. Frederick Taylor's *Scientific Management* was required reading. See Dahlberg, *New York Bureau of Municipal Research*, 129. Initially, the school had an arrangement with Columbia University whereby its students could acquire general advanced training in government and administration. Later, under Gulick's leader-

ship, the school moved away from basic graduate instruction and began accepting only advanced, experienced students for training.

81. For instance, Gulick cites, with tacit approval, Cleveland's budget reform proposal to the committee, consisting of the following procedures: (1) the governor should submit budget estimates to the legislature; (2) the governor should appear before the legislature to explain the estimates; (3) a legislative committee of the whole, meeting in joint session, should consider the governor's estimates; (4) the legislature should vote separately on the requests of each organizational unit; (5) members of the legislature should only be able to propose reductions in the governor's estimates; (6) the governor should submit a final budget to the legislature containing the actual and estimated revenues and expenditures for the two previous years and a statement of current assets, liabilities, and surplus or deficit; (7) if differences remain between the governor and the legislature, a public referendum should be held on the budget. See Gulick, *Evolution of the Budget in Massachusetts*, 131–133; and Dahlberg, *New York Bureau of Municipal Research*, 174.

82. *Proceedings of the Sixteenth Annual Conference on Taxation*, 267–268.

83. Commission of Inquiry on Public Service Personnel, *Better Government Personnel*, 81.

84. Luther Gulick, "Toward a Municipal Career Service," *Public Management Journal* 17, no. 11 (November 1935): 332.

85. Commission of Inquiry on Public Service Personnel, *Better Government Personnel*, 4–8.

86. Gulick, "What the City Does for and to Its Citizens," 356.

87. Gulick, "Metropolitan Organization," 58.

88. Gulick, *Metropolitan Problem and American Ideas*, 60.

89. Gulick, "Metropolitan Organization," 63–65.

90. Gulick, *Metropolitan Problem and American Ideas*, 129.

91. Gulick, "Planning and Cooperation," 87.

92. See Hammond, "In Defence of Luther Gulick's 'Notes on the Theory of Organization,'" 260. Edwin O. Stene, "Public Administration," *American Political Science Review* 34, no. 6 (1940): 1124.

93. Gulick, "Next Steps in Public Administration," 75.

94. Herbert Kaufman, "Emerging Conflicts in the Doctrines of Administration," *American Political Science Review* 50, no. 4 (December 1956): 1057–1073.

Chapter 4

Mary Parker Follett:
The Group Process

Mary Parker Follett was an innovative thinker who offered ideas that were not to gain major acceptance until some time after her death. Perhaps the distinguishing feature of Follett's work is her treatment of the role of social conflict. Follett argues that conflict itself is neither good nor bad, but simply inevitable. Whether the consequences of conflict are good or bad depends on the uses to which conflict is put. If it is used to produce an interpenetration of ideas and integrative solutions, it is good. If it results in domination by one side or compromise in which both sides simply yield something, the results will be unsatisfactory. In other words, Follett argues that we can use conflict to produce harmony, not simply victory or accommodation.

This view of conflict is novel, particularly in the literature on organizations, where the dominant paradigm has been one of the organization as a cooperative social system—even among authors, such as Taylor, who support hierarchical organizational structures. Follett also desires cooperation in the organization, but, for her, cooperation is a process and an outcome, not a precondition. Indeed, cooperation is likely to be the result of a merging of differences in pursuit of the interest of the whole.

The preceding point is related to another of Follett's central themes: the importance of the group process. Follett contends that individuals achieve their true expression in group relationships, wherein individual activities realize increased range and enhanced significance. She considers the state to be both a logical extension of the group process and its highest expression; both the group and the state serve a purpose greater than individual interests. Here, Follett offers a most provocative definition of the *general interest* as not simply the product of individual interests but the product of individual interests in social relationships; it is represented by the *social* interests defined in the group process. Interestingly, Follett has reservations about the ability of "ballot-box democracy" to produce the general interest so defined. Ballot-box democracy, to Follett, is likely to yield only the consent of the many to the rule by the few, when what is required is the creative interaction of all.

Follett's innovative thinking extends to questions of organizational management and is clearly related to her view of more general social processes. Swimming against the tide of ideas of her time, Follett urges horizontal flows of communication as opposed to the view that communication should follow the formal chain of command; she argues that control in the organization is pluralistic and cumulative (that is, it arises from below), as opposed to the conventional view that control should be concentrated in the apex of the organizational pyramid and cascade downward; she contends that authority should flow from the "law of the situation" (that is, the objective demands of the work situation) rather than being based on personal imposition; and she maintains that leadership is the ability to create functional unity in the organization through the proper correlation of controls, rather than personal power to command based on position.

These, then, are a few of Follett's seminal ideas, and her forte was the presentation of a few important ideas in a logically compelling fashion. Her writing has not only a logical flow, however, but also a certain rhythm. The aim of the following exposition is to capture both the flow and the rhythm of Follett's ideas and logic.

Life

Mary Parker Follett was born on September 3, 1868, in Quincy, Massachusetts.[1] Her family was of English-Scottish-Welsh extraction, and Mary was the older of the two children of Charles Allen and Elizabeth Curtis (Baxter) Follett. Her father, a machinist in a local shoe factory, developed a drinking problem, but in 1872 he took a temperance pledge and found a steady job again. Nonetheless, the family had to take in boarders to make ends meet, and finally, they all went to live with Mary's grandfather. Both he and her father died in 1885, the grandfather leaving her an inheritance that allowed her to live independently for the rest of her life.[2] Because her mother, the daughter of a prosperous banker, suffered from ill health, Follett was deprived of a childhood, as she had the responsibility for taking care of an invalid mother and a younger brother.

Follett's early education was acquired at the Thayer Academy in Braintree, Massachusetts, from which she graduated in 1884 at the age of fifteen. In 1888 Follett entered what was to become Radcliffe College, where she studied English, political economy, and history for two years before traveling to England to study at Cambridge University in 1890 and 1891. She performed well at Cambridge, delivering a paper on the U.S. House of Representatives that was to form the basis for her first book, and she developed a lasting interest in English life. Her studies were cut short by her mother's illness, however, and she was forced to return home before she could sit for examinations. Returning to Radcliffe, Follett attended intermittently until 1898, when she received her AB degree, graduating summa cum laude at the age of twenty-nine. Her book, *The Speaker of the House of Representatives*, had been published two years earlier.[3] About this book, President Theodore Roosevelt observed that Follett "understood the operation of Congress a great deal better than Woodrow Wilson," whose *Congressional Government* had been published in 1885.[4]

On leaving Radcliffe, Follett embarked on a career in social work, supported by her inheritance. She was primarily involved with community centers in Boston, where she pioneered in the development of evening programs in the public schools and vocational guidance programs. In 1918 Follett published her second book, *The New State*.[5] Originally intended as a report on her work with the community centers, the book blossomed into a major critique of American political theory and institutions in which Follett built on her knowledge of political science and added a new dimension—group dynamics—that was to be her central focus for the rest of her career. Follett's third book, *Creative Experience*, followed in 1924.[6] Probably her most important statement, *Creative Experience* elaborated on some of the themes introduced in *The New State* and focused even more centrally on the group experience.

In 1925 Follett shifted direction, becoming a lecturer on industrial management—an area she believed to be among the most critical and promising in terms of human relations. In 1929 she moved to England, where she continued her study of industrial conditions and lectured extensively. After her death, these lectures were collected and published by Henry Metcalf and her close friend Lyndall Urwick, under the title *Dynamic Administration: The Collected Papers of Mary Parker Follett*.[7] Urwick edited another selection of papers that was published in 1949 under the title *Freedom & Co-ordination: Lectures in Business Organization.*[8]

Mary Parker Follett was soft-spoken and unassuming in manner, reportedly having little taste for power or prestige. She did have a gift for making friends and a facility for winning confidence and esteem. Although she never managed a business, she developed a number of close relationships with leading industrialists on both sides of the Atlantic. Follett read Latin, Greek, French, and German, and she was interested in music, painting, nature, and travel. Never married, Follett lived with Isobel L. Briggs in Boston in the latter half of the 1890s, and with Dame Katharine Furse in London from 1928 until her death. In the fall of 1933, Follett went to Boston to check into her investments and her health, and during an operation there on December 16, doctors discovered invasive cancer. She passed away two days later at Boston's Deaconess Hospital.[9]

Follett's early intellectual orientation was toward Hegelian philosophical idealism, and evidence of that influence crops up throughout her writings.[10] Later becoming interested in the "new psychology," with its emphasis on group dynamics, she vacillated between this idealism and a pragmatic view that training people to become efficient instruments of organizational ends was an integral part of administration.[11] Follett believed that the study of institutions alone is not sufficient. What is needed, she argues, is the objective study of how people behave together, which requires empirical studies of human relations and social situations based on both participant observation and experimentation.[12] Of these two approaches, Follett chose participant observation, arguing that one cannot see experience without being a part of it, for life never stops long enough to be tested, and one cannot get outside life to view it.[13] Social life is in a constant state of flux and constitutes a complex unity built of mutual interrelationships and an interweaving of experience. One must be a part of life, either to observe it or to know it.

Accordingly, Follett employed intimate knowledge based on personal observation to construct an approach to social life and industrial management that anticipated by half a generation the observations of others in the field. Especially since the 1980s, Follett's work has been enjoying greater popularity. By way of example, her work on interconnectedness and cooperation is said to be very similar to contemporary stakeholder theory.[14] Her administrative theories in general appear to have commonalities with modern feminist theory.[15] Finally, Follett's collectivist/individualist synthesis has echoes in Amitai Etzioni's I&We paradigm.[16]

That appreciation for her work is increasing in recent years and that it is quite evenly divided among several disciplines—business, psychology, sociology, public administration, political science, and a variety of interdisciplinary studies[17]—begs the question, though, why she gradually disappeared from view. During her lifetime, the quality of her work was highly regarded. She was a member of the Taylor Society, which made some classify her later as belonging to the Scientific Management movement. In both the United States and Britain she developed close ties with a variety of scholars. Her U.S. contacts included Henry Metcalf (who had established the Bureau of Personnel Administration in New York), Ordway Tead (who coauthored with Metcalf the first personnel management study, in 1920), Herbert Croly, and Luther Gulick.[18] The quality of her thinking was, in Gulick's eyes, good enough that he included her essay, "The Process of Control," in the *Papers on the Science of Administration,* which he coedited with Lyndall Urwick in 1937.[19] In fact, Urwick developed a close emotional and intellectual relationship with Follett (who was his mother's age) and admired her thinking greatly.[20]

It has been suggested that she fell off the radar screen because she was classified as part of the Scientific Management school, because her ideas about management styles resonated less well at the time than those of Mayo (see chapter 5, on simple, paternalistic, rational, and authority-based management), and because she lacked the institutional academic base from which some of her contemporaries worked. Perhaps her impact in the 1930s was limited simply because she was a woman in the male-dominated world of business and government management.[21] It is also possible that her diminished visibility was due to ideological objections to her declaration that the state is the ultimate group—this assertion could have had dangerous implications in an era that saw the rise of totalitarian governments in Europe.

Approach to Social Science and Methodology

In the introduction to *Creative Experience* (xvi), Follett writes that "the social sciences are in some respects in the state of the physical sciences before Newton," who showed, she argued, how quantitative and qualitative analysis complement one another. But her idea of social science is not one that emulates the epistemology and methodology of the natural sciences, because "we must face the fact, that it is seldom possible to 'observe' a social situation as one watches a chemical experiment; the presence of the observer usually changes the situation" (xi). As with anything in Follett's work, her ideas about social science are informed by both pragmatism and idealism.

Her membership in the Taylor Society appears to contrast with the more idealistic elements of her thought. How did she balance the demand for objective analysis, on the one hand, with the need for personal observation, on the other? Follett leaves no doubt about her answer to that quandary: in the introduction to *Creative Experience,* she writes that researchers should not rely exclusively on quantitative or qualitative methods but, instead, should try to "understand the relation between quantitative and qualitative analysis."[22] More specifically, in her view, nonlinear social dynamics—the concept that social interaction cannot be predicted—and logical positivism were not antithetical but antinomial paradoxes. Carefully controlled experiments and observations were needed in the social sciences, but the researcher should be aware of the nonlinearity in human and organizational systems. Follett emphasized the necessary connection between quantitative and qualitative methods in the hope that it would "make human interplay productive" and would assist in the moral and social progress of the community.[23]

She also deplored the habit of severing object (dependent variable) from subject (independent variable). In her own words, "... the subjective idealists have overemphasized the subject, and the realists, the object."[24] To Follett, the reality of organizational behavior cannot be captured in subject or object alone, but must be seen in the interaction between subject and object, since each is a function of the other.[25] This epistemological and methodological point of view leads straight into one of the core concepts in her thought: *circular response*—the reciprocal influence between subject and object.

The Group Process

Follett argues that the individual is a social being who finds both identity and a sense of fulfillment in a group experience. The group itself is more than a mob, a herd, or a mere aggregation of members.[26] Instead, the group is a cohesive and coherent entity whose processes can lead to changes in individual ideas and actions that produce mutual compatibility and harmony among its members. Thus, the potential for social unity lies in the group process, which involves an intermingling of differences and the emergence of a composite of ideas representing what is best for all.[27]

According to Follett, society can be understood only by a study of the flux of group relationships, which leads to unity.[28] In this setting, there are neither individuals independent of society nor a society independent of individuals. Instead, there is a reciprocal relationship in which the individual both shapes society and is shaped by it. Social unity is, in Follett's phrase, a "whole a-making" in the interweaving of individual activities as the individual and the society evolve together.[29]

For Follett, the core of the group process is creating, and her central concern is the processes by which groups can create something that individuals working separately could not have created. The group process is guided by the "law of interpenetration" and the "doctrine of the wholes." Under the former, members of a group are reciprocally conditioning forces, as human interaction evokes new forms through the synthesis of differences.[30] The process of interpenetration and the emergence of synthesis results in a "whole," which, though not greater than the sum of its parts, is different from its parts.[31] Follett's doctrine of the wholes maintains that the whole cannot be understood by an analysis of its constituent parts. The whole is a dynamic entity produced by human interaction, in which the interests of the whole are the interests of individuals in *social relationships*.[32] The interests of the whole emerge from a group process of the interpenetration and synthesis of ideas, actions, and feelings. The group purpose is not preexistent. Instead, it evolves from interaction and is embodied in the unification of differences as the group process gives rise to a feeling of "sympathy," by which the individual finds his or her own interests in the group's interest.[33]

Conflict and Its Resolution

The group process does not rest on the assumption of an a priori identity of interests. On the contrary, Follett asserts that differing interests—and conflict among them—are inevitable. Conflict as continuing, unintegrated differences may be pathological, but the conflict itself is neither good nor bad. Furthermore, since conflict cannot be avoided, it should be used, much as a violin uses friction to make music.[34] The task of society is to produce harmony and unity from dissonance and conflict, as diversity is assimilated into the larger whole through the interpenetration and interweaving of ideas and actions.[35]

Follett identifies three primary means for the resolution of social conflict: domination, compromise, and integration.[36] *Domination*, which encompasses coercion, persuasion, imitation, and voluntary submission, is inherently flawed because it ends in the victory of one side to a dispute. As a result, domination is not creative, since it involves no interpenetration of ideas or interweaving of activities and is likely to produce antagonism in the defeated party.

Compromise is a similarly unsatisfactory method for the resolution of social conflict. Compromise, according to Follett, rests on the principle of "reciprocal abandonments" and the false assumption that, by some system of magic, subtraction (that is, each party yielding something) may somehow become a process of addition.[37] In compromise, Follett argues, there is no qualitative change, only the vain hope that the truth lies somewhere between the competing sides. Compromise is "temporary and futile," and the partisanship on which it is based starves the cooperative nature of man.[38]

Integration is Follett's preferred method for the resolution of social conflict. She argues that when conflicting interests meet, they need not oppose, but may simply confront.[39] What should be sought in this confrontation of differing interests is an integration that gives all sides what they really want. Integration is thus the emergence of a creative synthesis produced by the interaction of differing interests that represents a harmonious marriage of those differences (like the nut and the screw).[40] Integration is neither solely cooperative nor solely competitive in nature. It is a synthesis of competition and cooperation that yields creative solutions.[41] Integration is not a permanent condition, but a dynamic equilibrium in which succeeding disruptions are but moments in new integrations. Integration should be reflected not only on the intellectual level but also in concrete activities, as conflicts are assimilated into the larger whole and actual control over behavior is established.[42]

Circular response is the process by which integration is achieved. Follett maintains that social interactions are not characterized by simple cause-effect relationships, in which a stimulus is the cause and a response the effect. Instead, social interactions are reciprocal, or circular, relationships in which the individual both affects, and is affected by, the social environment. Moreover, individual reactions are "always to a relating." As Follett puts it, "I never react to you, but ... it is I-plus-you reacting to you-plus-me."[43] To complicate things further, every situation is a relating of things that vary—which means that the relating itself must vary. In sum, social situations are in a state of flux, for each member of society exists in a condition of mutual interdependence with all others, as all of us create each other all the time.

Evocation is the means by which each of us "calls out" something from others, thus activating circular response, which involves the interpenetration of ideas and activities and leads to integration. Evocation, according to Follett, "releases something, frees something, opens the way for the expression of latent capacities and possibilities."[44] Thus it leads to creative adjustment of differing interests and the discovery of what Follett calls "plus-values," or values that represent creative responses to social conflict.[45]

Follett maintains that there is no result of the process of circular response, evocation, and integration, only moments in the process. Progress is an "infinite advance toward the infinitely receding goal of infinite perfection" and is determined by the capacity for cooperation.[46] Objectives are not preexistent but emerge from the evolving situation as experience generates will and purpose. Integration, represented by agreement, comes from the uniting of experience, and its significance is derived not from the fact that values are held in common but from the fact that they are created in common.[47] The collective will embodied in the integrative solution expresses agreements on ends larger than individual ends, but the collective will is based on the concrete claims of individuals, and the social interests defined are simply individual interests generalized.[48]

Conditions for Effective Integration

Follett concedes that not all disputes can be settled by integration.[49] Some differences may be irreconcilable. Moreover, integration may be discouraged by such factors as the relative ease of fighting, the enjoyment of domination, manipulation of the process by leaders, and lack of skill in the techniques of integration.[50] Nevertheless, Follett contends that the opportunities for integration are likely more numerous than might be expected and that we should be alert to those opportunities. Successful integration requires that opportunities be recognized, that differences be brought into the open, that significant rather than simply dramatic issues be the central focus, that broader issues be broken into parts that can be dealt with separately, and that interacting of different interests be encouraged.[51] The failure to integrate is likely to result in a loss of the expression of individual potentialities, a diminution of the power of the social unit, and a level of tension that is conducive to crowd manipulation.[52] Both *The New State* and *Creative Experience* focus on formal and concrete individuals and groups, while, for instance, Etzioni also directed attention to the influence of abstract groups formed around such issues as race or ethnicity.[53]

The Group and Individualism

Follett argues that her concept of the group does not deny the concept of individualism. On the contrary, she asserts that the group permits the truest expression of individuality. According to Follett, there is no separate ego. Instead, individuals are created by reciprocal activity, and "individuality" is not uniqueness, but the capacity for union or the ability to find one's place in the whole.[54] The power of relating makes the individual of value, and the act of relating allows the individual to offer more to the group.

Furthermore, the group process does not result in a loss of individuality through either domination by others or domination by the whole.[55] The individual is not dominated by others because the group process involves the intermingling and the interpenetration of the ideas of all. The individual is not dominated by the whole because the individual is part of the whole. Thus, the group process represents a synthesis of individualism and collective control in the form of collective self-control. There are not individual rights, only group rights; and the group does not protect rights, it creates them. The duty of the individual is neither to himself or herself nor to others, but to the group, and the group serves the true and long-term interests of the individual.[56]

The Group and Freedom

Nor, Follett maintains, does the concept of the group deny the concept of freedom. For Follett, freedom is the "harmonious, unimpeded working of one's own nature," which is social in character, and "liberation from the tyranny of particularistic impulses."[57] Thus, freedom is achieved through social relationships as the range and significance of individual activity is increased. From this perspective, the individual is not free simply when making "undetermined" decisions. Determinism is an inevitability, as the individual is simultaneously determined and determining in social relationships. Instead, the individual is free when creating new opportunities, which is best done in a group setting governed by the law of interpenetration and the doctrine of the wholes. In Follett's words, they are free who "*win* their freedom through fellowship."[58] The group process seeks the freedom of all by means of the authority of the whole and the function and contribution of each of its members.

Circular Response, Power, and Control

Just as the law of interpenetration and the doctrine of the wholes do not deny the concepts of individualism and freedom, the quest for integration through circular response, Follett contends, does not deny the reality of power and the existence of control. Follett asserts that the desire for power is a predominant feature of life and acknowledges that power will always be unequally distributed.[59] Rather than abolishing power, integration through circular response both transforms power and increases it. Power is transformed from "power-over" to "power-with," and it is increased as greater power accrues to the whole, and thus to the individual, by virtue of the group's ability to satisfy a wider range of individual needs.

Power is a capacity that cannot be delegated; it is "a self-generating, self-sufficing, all-including activity."[60] Follett defines power as "the ability to make things happen, to be a causal agent."[61] She contends that the only genuine basis of power is the interweaving of experience produced by circular response. Consequently, power is jointly developed and it is coactive, not coercive.[62] Integration reduces the necessity of exercising power-over, and increases the possibility of exercising power-with, by reducing areas of irreconcilable difference in which the arbitrary exercise of power is required. The coactiveness of power stands in close relation to the notion that "we have power over ourselves together ... together we will control *ourselves*."[63] In an organizational setting, this concept means that managers "should give workers a chance to grow capacity or power for themselves."[64] In contemporary parlance, this coaction is called empowerment, and it is an integral element of TQM and other comparable management approaches.

Whereas power is the capacity to make things happen, Follett defines control as "the application of power as a means toward a specific end."[65] She argues that control is impossible without unity and that the degree of control depends on how far the ideas and concrete activities of people can be united. Interaction in circular response *is* control, not simply a process by which it is established, and control is implemented as mutual interaction creates new situations.

The State and Social Life

According to Follett, the state is a logical extension of the group process and the highest expression of social life. She asserts that man joins groups to give expression to his multiple natures (the Law of Multiples) and that only the state can express the compounding and multiple compounding of natures involved in social life.[66] As the group will is an expression of the individual will at a higher level of purpose, so too is the state an expression of individual and group will at an even higher level of purpose. The true state gives rise to the great group that is unified by common ends, its sovereignty resting on the group process and the principle of integration.[67] As such, the state cannot leave us alone, it cannot regulate us, it can only express us.[68] The state is a fulfillment of the individual; in Follett's words, "The home of my soul is in the state."[69]

The Role of Law

The supreme function of the state is the moral ordering of social relationships.[70] Nevertheless, laws that govern those relationships cannot be based entirely on fixed principles. Follett contends that there is no private conscience, only a socially conditioned conscience, and, as a result, we do not follow right but create it.[71] Accordingly, law must be embedded in the social process, and it should not be a restraining force to protect interests but a positive force to broaden and deepen interests.

Follett maintains that the old idea of law was based on the concept of "contract" and particularistic interests and that it incorporated the notion that man could do what he wanted with his own.[72] This individualistic concept, she argues, has given way to the idea that law derives its authority from the fact that it was produced by the community and that the administration of justice should be a vital part of the social process. Nevertheless, Follett does not believe that the system of jurisprudence should be entirely pragmatic in character.[73] Instead, law should be a blend of principle and precedent, both of which should be interpreted in the light of present experience.[74]

Planning

The prescribed positive role of the state is illustrated by Follett's support for national planning. She contends that large-scale planning is imperative and that such planning is the only alternative to chaos.[75] Planning, like law, should be an intrinsic part of the social process, however. Follett argues that coordination, not coercion, should be substituted for laissez-faire. That coordination should be in the form of the correlation of multiple controls at lower levels rather than superimposed state control. The state should act as a facilitator in the national planning process by providing for direct and voluntary contact among the heads of industry for the purpose of the self-coordination of their own activities.[76]

Ballot-Box Democracy

How can the "true state" be realized? Though Follett espouses democracy, she had little faith in existing democratic methods, which she referred to as "ballot-box" democracy, nor did she have much hope for the major reform proposals of her day. According to Follett, democracy was born of the pursuit of individualism and has been dominated by particularistic interests. First, party domination and, then, a marriage of business and politics have inhibited individual participation in the political process and served parochial interests while seeking justification under the guise of majority rule.[77]

Ballot-box democracy, Follett argues, is not real democracy. Ballot-box democracy relies on brute numbers rather than on a genuine union of interests; it is based on the "law of the crowd," which employs suggestion or persuasion as its primary technique. Ballot-box democracy rests on the "doctrine of consent," which asserts that the few should decide while the many assent. This doctrine, according to Follett, is simply a rationalization for the arbitrary exercise of power. Mere acquiescence is not sufficient. Different kinds of information are required in the political process; fact situations change, which necessitates the continuing input of all interests, and the activities of the people are integral to that changing situation.[78] In short, consent does not capitalize on the potential contributions of the many. The tragedy of democracy, Follett alleges, is not that we have no public opinion but that we think we do.[79] In fact, there is no genuine confronting of real differences in ballot-box democracy and thus no creativity in producing a collective will. What is needed is not consent, but coaction.

Follett was similarly wary of the major reform proposals of her day, regarding them as inadequate to the task of achieving the true state. Progressives, she argues, continue to emphasize the voter, not the man, by concentrating on the extension of suffrage.[80] Though Follett believed socialism to be the logical next step in industrial development, she charges that socialists seek a shortcut to the true state. Socialization of property must be preceded by socialization of the will.[81] The group theory of politics, or political pluralism, makes a contribution by recognizing the importance of group life. But pluralism fosters particularistic interests and relies on the balance of power theory. Pluralism thus frustrates attempts at integration because, by the time the balancing groups meet, it is likely to be too late to reach agreement. In their opposition to the monistic state, Follett argues, the pluralists have simply pitted the group against the state and run the danger of substituting group tyranny for state tyranny.[82]

Real Democracy

Follett asserts that we have not yet tried "real democracy" to achieve the true state. Perfection of the mechanisms of representation, reliance on majority rule, dependence on party organization, and submission to the law of the crowd are insufficient. Indeed, they are counterproductive. Democracy should not simply register opinions; it should attempt to create unity. This effort will require that new principles of interpersonal association be discovered and that minds be trained to work together constructively in the pursuit of the collective will. Follett's concept of real democracy rests on substantive participation by the many and a federalist political structure.

Participation

Follett maintains that the illusion of consent should be replaced by substantive participation to open the way for creative interpersonal relationships. An active and responsible citizenry will allow democracy to develop power from the interplay of daily concrete activities and inspire creativity through the interpenetration of ideas. Substantive participation and a mentality receptive to integrative solutions, in turn, will lead to the formulation of the collective will and its realization in the concrete activities of everyday life. Such participation *qua* empowerment will actually improve performance.[83]

Although emphasizing participation, Follett disavows any "mystic faith in the native rightness of public opinion."[84] Instead, she places her faith in the ability of collective thought, evolved through the group process, to inspire creativity and integration, rather than simply degenerating into collective mediocrity.

Federalism

Follett asserts that substantive participation should take place in a federal political structure if it is to produce effective representation. For Follett, the small group is the core of democracy, and the "democratic soul is born in the group" as individuals learn to be part of the social whole.[85] Small groups are thus a vital stage on the path toward a more complete whole.

Follett argues that the fundamental social group is the neighborhood group.[86] The neighborhood group facilitates understanding through acquaintance, provides regular and constant interaction, and involves more varied contact than do self-selected groups. The neighborhood group should assume responsibility for functions of its own in order to foster better citizenship, imbue its members with a creative attitude by encouraging constructive interpersonal relationships in "experience meetings," and act as a building-block for broader systems of representation.[87]

The process of representation should be cumulative, as members of the smaller group select representatives for the next larger group—in a progress from neighborhood groups to district councils to city councils, to state governments, to the national government.[88] Representatives, for their part, should be responsible not merely for winning victories but for reaching agreement. This dual responsibility requires that representatives be allowed to exercise their own best judgment as to what is right rather than simply reflecting the expressed interests of their particular constituencies. Yet the representative should not be an entirely free agent. The representative should maintain a reciprocal relationship with both the represented and the representative group and make the represented group aware of the activities of the representative group.[89]

Follett acknowledges that there may be problems with this system of representation. People from the same group may have different interests, and it may not be possible for one individual to act for another. Nevertheless, the general thrust of the federal structure should be to get ideas represented and to provide an appropriate forum for the integration of differences.

Follett maintains that there is an important role for leadership in the real democracy. Indeed, she contends that democracy is not opposed to aristocratic leadership, and that the democratic process itself is a breeding ground for a new aristocracy as leaders emerge from neighborhood groups.[90] The function of leadership is transformed in real democracy, however. The leader is not to control the group but to express it by assisting the group in finding integrative solutions. The leader should also anticipate what public opinion will be and establish conditions for constructive change. In short, the leader's role is to release the energy of the group, to unite energies to carry out purposes, and to aid in creating new purposes.[91] In modern language, the leader in the group allows deutero-learning. Groups in any organization should be raised into a mode of lifelong learning, which includes not only formal education but also experience and training throughout life.[92]

The Role of the Expert

As there is a role for leadership, so too is there a place for the expert in Follett's democracy of inequalities and complementary contributions.

Democracy is not simply the people consenting to the rule of the expert, however, and Follett decries what she calls the "pernicious tendency" to make the opinions of the expert prevail by crowd methods.[93] Accurate information is required in the policy process, but there are limitations on the advice of the expert. In the first place, there is no *ante facto* will on which the expert can construct a policy. Instead, purpose and will emerge from a continuous process of mutual adjustment and integration. Moreover, the "facts" on which the expert is to base advice cannot be accepted at face value. Full and accurate information is often difficult to secure and, even if information is available, some things do not lend themselves readily to precise measurement. The facts themselves are not static and must be evaluated in the light of changing circumstances. The expert may choose which facts to present, and different facts may be elicited by different observers. Experts do not simply gather information; they condense and interpret it, raising the possibility that personal biases and preferences may contaminate the "facts."[94]

Consequently, Follett argues that the findings of the expert must be balanced against the ideas of others, as one form of experience is united with another, and that the expert (whether a subject specialist or a generalist manager) must take his cue from the situation at hand. One cannot and ought not to generalize experience too quickly to a new situation.[95] Democracy thus requires both expert advice and an active electorate, as well as a government of popular control and centralized responsibility.[96] The expert should be more than on tap, but not on top.

Group Processes and the Industrial Organization

Although Follett was primarily interested in human relations and group processes in general, much of her later, and best-known, work focused on industrial organizations. She believed the basic principles of human behavior—interacting, evoking, integrating, and emerging—to be the same in business as in other group settings, and her analysis of business organizations is based on these fundamental concepts. Follett chose to concentrate specifically on industrial organizations for a number of reasons. First, she had access to business organizations, having established contact with several prominent businessmen during her career. Second, she thought that the business setting offered original and interesting material for analysis, and she was attracted by the businessman's action-oriented approach to problems. Finally, and most important, Follett viewed the business organization as a social agency performing vital social functions.

The greatest service business provides to society is work itself. Through work, business furnishes the opportunity for personal development and the occasion for the interweaving of activities from which "spiritual values" are created.[97] As such, business serves a broader social purpose than mere profit-making; it offers a place for pioneering in human relations. In business, technical knowledge could be combined with scientific investigations of cooperative human behavior to discover basic principles of organized activity. It is organized activity, Follett contends, that separates mediocre from high endeavor; in the knowledge of organized activity lies the potential solution to world problems.[98]

Coordination

From Follett's perspective, the primary task of the organization is the coordination of efforts, which transforms a collection of individuals into a working unit. Coordination, the reciprocal relating of all factors in the situation, results in the integrative unity of the organization. It is best accomplished by "cross-functioning," or the direct contact of persons and departments responsible for related activities.[99] Accordingly, communication and authority should flow horizontally, as well as vertically, in the organization. Furthermore, coordination should be a continuous process encompassing both planning and execution, and each department should base its actions on what is good for the company as viewed from that department.

Control and Authority

Follett contends that control and authority flow from proper coordination—not, as is often assumed, coordination from control and authority. As noted previously, Follett defines power as the ability to make things happen, and control as "power exercised as a means toward a specific end." In other words, power is a capacity, while control is the exercise of power, or a process. Attaining control is a function of the ability to see the field of control as a complex whole and the ability to pass from one field of control to another, not simply predicting, but creating new situations.[100]

Follett notes two emergent aspects of control. First, control is coming to mean more the correlation of many controls—that is, control is cumulative—rather than the superimposition of control by a central authority. Second, control is becoming more "fact control" than "man control."[101] That is, control is being exercised more on the basis of the demands of the situation as established by scientific investigation and less on the basis of personal and arbitrary mandate.

These characteristics of control are manifested in the exercise of authority (which Follett defines as "vested control") in the organization.[102] Follett describes the organization as an interweaving of functions, in which authority derives from the unifying process of coordination. Accordingly, organizational authority is not "supreme," nor is it delegated.

Instead, authority is pluralistic and cumulative (that is, it arises from below), and it is based on function rather than on position. As such, authority is the outcome of interlocking activities, accruing to those with knowledge and experience and the skills to apply that knowledge and experience.[103]

Follett argues that we have been misled by "the illusion of final authority."[104] Authority is a process, not the final moment of decision.[105] Authority is actually held by those with knowledge, not by the person at the top, and it involves a long series of interrelated activities prior to the act of decision. This is not to say that there is no final authority. Follett acknowledges that some questions have to be decided at the top of the organization.[106] Nevertheless, authority does not merely flow from the top of the organization. It is a reciprocally conditioning relationship based on circular response, in which functional knowledge and skill become the ultimate master.

As with control, Follett contends that the arbitrary exercise of organizational authority is diminishing. There are a number of drawbacks to the arbitrary exercise of authority: we lose what might be learned from the subordinate, friction is created, pride in work is destroyed, and the sense of individual responsibility is lessened.[107] Instead of exercising authority "over" subordinates, organizations have begun to develop "power-with" all members of the organization in response to what Follett refers to as "the law of the situation," which requires sensitivity to "the interweaving, reciprocal responses and evolving changes that constitute the situation." Authority is determined by the objective demands of the work situation rather than by personal imposition.[108] Thus, orders come from the work, not work from orders, and orders do not derive their validity from either the position of the superior or the consent of the subordinate but from the mutual contributions of the order-giver and the order-receiver.[109] In sum, authority resides in a function, is derived from the demands of the situation, and is the result of circular behavior.

The arbitrary exercise of authority can be avoided by assuring that all members know the purposes of the organization, giving reasons for an order whenever possible, not being disagreeable in giving orders, knowing the principles of work activity, mutually deciding which principles to apply, creating attitudes conducive to the carrying out of orders, and providing proper incentives in the organization.[110] Authority can be "depersonalized" by developing standard practices and habit patterns so that activity can be governed by technique rather than by direct command. As the arbitrary and personal exercise of authority is reduced, a sense of functional unity is created, pride of craft is restored, and a sense of responsibility is engendered among all members of the organization.

Leadership

Follett's conceptions of authority and control do not eliminate the requirement of effective leadership in the organization. But a different kind of leadership is required that follows the general pattern she outlined for leadership in society. According to Follett, the old theory of leadership was based on the power of personality: a good leader was considered to be "one who has a compelling personality, who wields power, who constrains others to his will."[111] Actually, Follett contends, there are three kinds of leadership—leadership of position, leadership of personality, and leadership of function—and, of these, leadership of function is the most important.[112] Leadership of position is ineffective without functional capability. Position and function should coincide, but this is not always the case. Leadership of personality may only be an attempt to dominate by "masterful or persuasive" traits. Follett does not disregard personal qualities, but she does believe that they have been overemphasized. For Follett, organizing ability is more important than ascendancy traits, and learning the job is more important than the ability to exploit one's personality.[113]

In Follett's view, effective leadership is based not on position or personality but on the ability to create functional unity in the organization. The basic task of the leader is to organize and integrate experience—that is, to practice facilitative leadership. In that sense, her leader is comparable to the one described by Chester Barnard (see chapter 6) but differs from Barnard's in that she emphasizes "horizontal rather than vertical authority."[114]

Somewhat more concretely, Follett identifies three leadership functions: coordination, definition of purpose, and anticipation.[115] Coordination involves educating and training individuals so that each can give what he or she is capable of giving, providing an opportunity for participation, and unifying the various contributions. In Follett's words, the executive is responsible for "making the organization chart a going affair."[116] Definition of purpose is required so that all may feel that they are working for a common end. Anticipation entails understanding the long-term good of the greater community and creating situations in which that good can be achieved. In order to perform these functions, the leader must have a thorough knowledge of the job, an ability to grasp the total situation, the capacity to create as well as direct power, the talent to see future directions, and a pioneer's sense of adventure.[117]

Although much of her discussion centers on the role and functions of the top executive, Follett believes that the future will depend on more widely diffused leadership in the organization.[118] The need for leadership exists at many points in the organization, and each person should be prepared to answer the challenge of leadership of his or her own job. This diffusion of leadership does not mean that responsibility is likewise diffused. Centralization and decentralization can be accomplished simultaneously, as the top executive retains responsibility for the whole, while each individual assumes responsibility for his or her own function in the whole.[119] In this way, the leader neither abandons responsibilities nor takes responsibility from others. Instead, the leader makes each feel his or her own responsibility. Contrary to the popular conception of the leader as a boss, Follett argues that the mark of a good leader is how little bossing he has to do.[120] The effective leader shows others what to do to meet their own responsibilities. The relationship between leaders and followers should be reciprocal, as leaders guide and followers keep their leaders in control by making suggestions, taking wrong orders back for correction, and keeping the faith in a common purpose.[121]

A relationship of particular concern to Follett is that between the executive and the expert. She notes that there is a trend toward specialization in the organization, and that, as a result, most decisions are made by those with special expertise. Thus, the exercise of authority more often represents the consent of the governors than the consent of the governed.[122] This trend toward specialization creates an apparent dilemma. On the one hand, the executive cannot abdicate his decision-making responsibilities. On the other hand, he may not have the specific knowledge requisite to effective decision making. Follett's solution is to deny the dilemma. She counsels that the knowledge of the expert be joined with the knowledge of the executive. The opinion of the expert should not coerce, but should enter into the decision process by means of circular response and integration.[123]

Worker Participation

Much of Follett's work emphasizes participation, which fosters circular response and thus encourages integration of differences. Nonetheless, she gives only a qualified endorsement to full worker participation in the management of the organization. Follett believes that workers and management should share in joint control, but in a limited fashion. Participation, to Follett, means "everyone taking part, according to his capacity, in a unit composed of related activities."[124] The qualifying phrase suggests that worker participation does not necessarily mean industrial democracy. Follett does not believe, for instance, that workers should be allowed to elect their supervisors.[125] She feels that workers need not be consulted on all issues, only those on which they are competent to have some opinion.[126] More generally, Follett states that the worker should not be given a vote on something he does not know about, and, she contends, the worker cannot vote intelligently on how a business should be run.[127]

Instead of industrial democracy, employee participation should be an application of "functional power." This means that labor should expect only the degree of control that goes with its function.[128] The purpose of participation should be to join the capacities of workers and management so that labor can assist management, not by sharing existing power, but by developing joint power and thus creating new power.

The effectiveness of such participation requires that both management and labor learn the secret of the group process. Worker participation is not merely a procedure for collective bargaining, which Follett views as a "temporary expedient" that neither gives labor a direct share in industrial control nor fosters the cooperative attitude required for circular response, evocation, and integration. Worker participation is not simply a means for forestalling trouble; indeed, participation is likely to make things harder on management, not easier. Worker participation is not merely a medium for the exchange of information, which should be united, not exchanged, by a cooperative study to get at the facts. Worker participation is not simply a means to gain consent, for what is needed is cooperation, not consent. Worker participation is not merely a recognition of the "rights" of labor, since jobs, not rights, should be the focus of participation. Worker participation is not simply a way for management to avoid responsibility, for that only passes the problem on.[129]

Worker participation, according to Follett, is a way to increase collective responsibility through the recognition of an identity of interests, an awareness of interdependence, an interpenetration of activity, and an integration of differing perspectives. The recognition of a reciprocal responsibility between management and workers establishes the interweaving of experience as the only legitimate "boss" in the organization.[130]

Conclusion

Follett's work is distinguished more by the originality of her ideas than by their number. She is a process-theorist *avant la lettre*.[131] The central thread of her analysis may be summarized as follows:

1. The group is the core of the social process and the means by which the individual achieves fulfillment. When, however, individuals are treated unjustly, this sense of fulfillment is in jeopardy. When emotions take over, productivity declines.[132]

2. The state is an extension of the group process at a higher level of objective and is the highest expression of social life. The true state is best achieved in a democracy featuring full participation and a federal structure based on neighborhood groups.

3. The organization is a group distinguished by the structured nature of its activities.

4. The primary task of the organization is the coordination of its activities to produce functional unity.

5. Functional unity in the organization, as in all groups, is best achieved through the interaction of related activities and the interpenetration of ideas in a pattern of circular response, evocation, and integration. This pattern requires the participation of all members of the organization, as each member contributes that which he or she is able to contribute.

6. In this context, organizational control and authority are derived from the process of functional relating and are based on knowledge and the law of the situation rather than on position.

7. Organizational leadership performs the functions of providing the opportunity for participation and guiding individual endeavors in the pursuit of common purposes.

The main problem with Follett's work is that her idealism is showing. That idealism is perhaps most vividly reflected in her aversion to what she considers to be false contrasts. Thus, Follett argues that we can have collectivism as well as individualism and freedom, circular response as well as power and control, aristocracy as well as democracy, executive control as well as the supremacy of expert knowledge, centralization as well as decentralization. Even integration is defined as a solution to conflict in which everyone gets what he or she wants. In short, Follett has a tendency to say, in effect, that we can have everything at once. One need not question the possibility of combinations of these contrasting concepts to doubt the possibility of achieving all of them simultaneously.

Follett's idealism would not be a significant problem except that she claims to be dealing, not with what should be, but with "what perhaps may be."[133] Although it is not entirely clear what Follett means by this statement, it would seem to indicate that she intended to construct, not an ideal world, but a possible world. Accordingly, her construction must stand the test of achievability, not just desirability.

Follett's case rests on two fundamental assumptions: that attitudes can be changed and that interests are so structured as to permit integrative reconciliation. Attitudinal change is required for the integrative process to work properly. Individuals must develop a cooperative attitude that fosters a search for integrative solutions to conflict, and they must aspire only to exercise "power-with" rather than grasping for "power-over." Follett was not blind to the baser side of human nature. Having dealt with the subject of political power in her book on the Speakers of the House, she acknowledges a human desire to exercise power-over.[134] Instead,

Follett would appear to be engaging in "best-case" hypothesizing in assuming that those baser instincts can be overcome and human behavior can be what she would have it.[135] Whether such a change is possible is debatable. Follett offers little in support of her stand other than a hope that education can alter attitudes and an implicit belief in the malleability of human nature and the will to change.[136]

Follett's second assumption is that interests are so structured as to permit integrative reconciliation—which, of course, need not be the case. Consider the following possible configurations of interests:

1. A commonality of interests exists. In this case, there is no occasion for integration, since no differences exist. The appropriate mechanism of choice is not integration, but unanimity.

2. Interests are separate and unrelated. In this case, since there are no related differences, there is no occasion for integration. The mechanism of choice depends on the circumstances. Under a condition of unlimited resources, the likely mechanism of choice is mutual accommodation. Under a condition of limited resources, the likely mechanisms of choice are compromise or domination.

3. Interests are separate but related. This configuration of interests presents the possibility of integration, but only if the interests are compatible. If the interests are inherently in conflict, the likely mechanism of choice is, again, compromise or domination.

In short, the possibility of integration depends on a particular configuration of interests, and the relative frequency of occurrence of that configuration is unknown. Furthermore, even if interests are in the appropriate configuration, disagreement over objectives and/or the means to achieve those objectives may remain as an impediment to integrative solutions.

One is driven to the conclusion that Follett's analysis of society and organization is only partial and remains largely untested. Nevertheless, she performs a substantial service by calling attention to the importance of integration and alerting us to the possibility of its use in resolving social conflict. Moreover, the ideas Follett presented and the dynamics she revealed anticipated later developments in such organizational topics as organizational behavior, participative leadership and empowerment, organizational integration and differentiation, contingency-based management, stakeholder theory, strategic alliances, network organization structures, TQM, corporate social responsibility, lifelong learning, the learning organization, organizational justice theory, and nonlinear dynamics.[137] Her work is enormously popular in business management, and it has attracted increased attention in public administration. Beyond these fields, her work is also relevant to social work,[138] political science, organizational sociology, and psychology. Truly a person ahead of her time, Follett's actual contribution to the understanding of organizational life may not yet be fully recognized, and her potential contribution not yet fully realized.

NOTES

1. Material on Follett's life is taken from the *Dictionary of American Biography*, Supplement 1 (New York: Scribner's, 1944), 308–309; *Notable American Women*, 1607–1950 (Cambridge, Mass.: Belknap Press of Harvard University Press, 1971), 639–641; and L. Urwick, ed., *The Golden Book of Management* (London: Newman Neame, 1956), 132–137. Additional biographical information can be found in Albie M. Davis, "An Interview with Mary Parker Follett," *Negotiation Journal* (July 1989), 223–235; Pauline Graham, ed., *Mary Parker Follett: Prophet of Management* (Boston: Harvard Business School Press, 1994); Albie M. Davis, "Liquid Leadership: The Wisdom of Mary Parker Follett," 1997, at http://sunsite.utk.edu/FINS/Mary_Parker _Follett/Fins-MPF-03 (accessed March 26, 2007). For a full biography, see Joan C. Tonn, *Mary P. Follett: Creating Democracy, Transforming Management* (New Haven, Conn.: Yale University Press, 2003).
2. Tonn, *Mary P. Follett*, 13–18, 31–32; see also Davis, "Interview with Mary Parker Follett," 232.
3. Mary Parker Follett, *The Speaker of the House of Representatives* (New York: Longman, Green, 1896).
4. As quoted in Davis, "Interview with Mary Parker Follett," 232.
5. Mary Parker Follett, *The New State: Group Organization, the Solution of Popular Government* (New York: Longman, Green, 1918).
6. Mary Parker Follett, *Creative Experience* (New York: Longman, Green, 1924).
7. The first English edition of *Dynamic Administration* appeared in 1941, published by Management Publication Trust in Bath. The first American edition, also edited by Metcalf and Urwick, was published in 1942 by Harper and Brothers in New York. The second edition was edited by Elliot M. Fox and L. Urwick and published by Hippocrene Press in New York in 1977. On a side note, it is interesting that Urwick stated how much Ordway Tead's help had aided in securing the publication of Follett's collected papers. On this, see Ellen S. O'Connor, "Integrating Follett: History, Philosophy, and Management," *Journal of Management History* 6, no. 4 (2000): 173–174. O'Connor takes her information from A. I. Cohen, "Mary Parker Follett: Spokesman for Democracy, Philosopher for Social Group Work, 1918–1933" (unpublished Dissertation, Tulane University School of Social Work, New Orleans, 1971). While O'Connor lists the first edition of *Dynamic Administration* as published in 1940, it really appeared in 1941. See, among other sources, Lee D. Parker and Philip Ritson, "Fads, Stereotypes and Management Gurus: Fayol and Follett Today," *Management Decision* 43, no. 10 (2005): 1342.
8. This collection was published by the Management Publication Trust in London (which had moved from Bath; see note 7). A reprint was issued by Garland Publishing in New York in 1989.

9. Davis, "Interview with Mary Parker Follett," 234. Briggs was 20 years older than Follett, while Furse was about the same age; see Tonn, *Mary P. Follett,* 101.

10. See O'Connor, "Integrating Follett," 168.

11. See James A. Stever, "Mary Parker Follett and the Quest for Pragmatic Administration," *Administration & Society* 18, no. 2 (1986): 170.

12. Follett, *Creative Experience,* xi, xii.

13. Ibid., 134–135.

14. See Melissa A. Schilling, "Decades Ahead of Her Time: Advancing Stakeholder Theory through the Ideas of Mary Parker Follett," *Journal of Management History* 6, no. 5 (2000): 224.

15. See Noel O'R. Morton and Stefanie A. Lindquist, "Revealing the Feminist in Mary Parker Follett," *Administration & Society* 29, no. 3 (1997): 348–371.

16. See Lori Verstegen Ryan and Matthew A. Rutherford, "Mary Parker Follett: Individualist or Collectivist? Or Both?" *Journal of Management History* 6, no. 5 (2000): 219.

17. As reported by Brian R. Fry and Lotte L. Thomas, "Mary Parker Follett: Assessing the Contribution and Impact of Her Writings," *Journal of Management History* 2, no. 2 (1996): 11–19.

18. See O'Connor, "Integrating Follett," 173–174. In the Introduction to *Creative Experience* (xix), Follett explicitly thanks Herbert Croly for enlarging her vision of the development of democracy and the meaning of citizenship.

19. See Camilla Stivers, "Integrating Mary Parker Follett and Public Administration" (book review of Tonn, *Mary P. Follett*), *Public Administration Review* 66, no. 3 (2006): 475.

20. See Michael Roper, "Masculinity and the Biographical Meanings of Management Theory: Lyndall Urwick and the Making of Scientific Management in Inter-war Britain," *Gender, Work and Organization* 8, no. 2 (2001): 198–199.

21. See Parker and Ritson, "Fads, Stereotypes and Management Gurus," 1344.

22. See Follett, *Creative Experience,* xvi. See also Laurie J. Barclay, "Following in the Footsteps of Mary Parker Follett: Exploring How Insights from the Past Can Advance Organizational Justice Theory and Research," *Management Decision* 43, no. 5 (2005): 750–751.

23. See Follett, *Creative Experience,* xi; see also Mark E. Mendenhall, James H. Macomber, and Marc Cutright, "Mary Parker Follett: Prophet of Chaos and Complexity," *Journal of Management History* 6, no. 4 (2000): 201–203.

24. See Follett, *Creative Experience,* 54.

25. Ibid., 54–57, 59–61.

26. Follett, *New State,* 89.

27. Ibid., 25.

28. Ibid., 76.

29. Fox and Urwick, *Dynamic Administration,* 160; Mendenhall et al., "Mary Parker Follett," passim.

30. Follett, *New State,* 23; and idem, *Creative Experience,* 303.

31. Follett, *Creative Experience,* 98.

32. Ibid., 47.

33. Follett, *New State,* 44–45.

34. Fox and Urwick, *Dynamic Administration,* 1–2.

35. Follett is nowadays most frequently cited in the conflict resolution litera-ture. See, e.g., Fry and Thomas, "Mary Parker Follett," 15; Davis, "Inter-view with Mary Parker Follett"; and Deborah M. Kolb, "The Love for Three Oranges, or: What Did We Miss about Ms. Follett in the Library?" *Negotiation Journal* (October 1996): 339–348, esp. 340.

36. Ibid., 2. For another discussion of these three conflict resolution mecha-nisms, see Domènec Melé, "Ethics in Management: Exploring the Contri-bution of Mary Parker Follett" (working paper no. 618), IESE Business School, University of Navarre, Spain, March 2006.

37. Follett, *Creative Experience*, xiv.

38. Ibid., 156, 163. On the point that, in compromise, neither party will be fully satisfied, see also Schilling, "Decades Ahead of Her Time," 232.

39. Ibid., 156.

40. From Introduction, by Fox and Urwick, to *Dynamic Administration*, xxv.

41. Follett, *New State*, 112.

42. Follett, *Creative Experience*, 150.

43. Ibid., 62.

44. Fox and Urwick, *Dynamic Administration*, 162.

45. Ibid., 165.

46. Follett, *New State*, 51.

47. Ibid., 34.

48. Ibid., 48.

49. Follett, *Creative Experience*, 163.

50. Fox and Urwick, *Dynamic Administration*, 16–19.

51. Ibid., 7–16.

52. From Introduction, by Fox and Urwick, to *Dynamic Administration*, xxx.

53. This point is made by Ryan and Rutherford, "Mary Parker Follett," 219.

54. Follett, *New State*, 62, 65.

55. Ibid., 70.

56. Ibid., 52. See also Mendenhall et al., "Mary Parker Follett," 197–199. In the context of the public realm, one could argue that collective self-con-trol amounts to self-government, and in that sense Follett's work fore-shadows that of Vincent Ostrom.

57. Ibid., 69.

58. Ibid., 72.

59. Follett, *Creative Experience*, 180, 189.

60. Ibid., 185.

61. Fox and Urwick, *Dynamic Administration*, 70.

62. Ibid., 72.

63. Follett, *Creative Experience*, 186, 187. Italics in original.

64. Ibid., 109. On these elements of power as capacity, as empowerment, and as co-active behavior, see also David M. Boje and Grace Ann Rosile, "Where's the Power in Empowerment? Answers from Follett and Clegg," *Journal of Applied Behavioral Science* 37, no. 1 (2001): 102.

65. Ibid., 70.

66. Follett, *New State*, 296–297.

67. Follett does not shrink from the extension of this logic to the interna-tional level. She contends that organized cooperation should be the basis for international relations and should reflect the interpenetration of the "rich content of widely varying characteristic and experience." See ibid., 345.

68. Ibid., 183.
69. Ibid., 312.
70. Ibid., 333.
71. Ibid., 52.
72. Ibid., 126.
73. On this point, see also Stever, "Mary Parker Follett and the Quest for Pragmatic Administration," 169–170.
74. Follett, *Creative Experience*, 278.
75. Fox and Urwick, *Dynamic Administration*, 260.
76. Ibid., 261–263.
77. Follett, *New State*, 165–167.
78. Follett, *Creative Experience*, 28.
79. Follett, *New State*, 220.
80. Ibid., 168.
81. Ibid., 74.
82. Follett, *Creative Experience*, 230.
83. On this point, see Schilling, "Decades Ahead of Her Time," 237–238.
84. Ibid., 216.
85. Follett, *New State*, 160.
86. Though emphasizing neighborhood groups, Follett would not deny a role for other groups, such as occupational groups; see ibid., 320.
87. Follett, *Creative Experience*, 212.
88. However, Follett proposes that the Senate might be composed of experts or representatives of occupational groups; see *New State*, 246.
89. Follett, *Creative Experience*, 253–254.
90. Follett, *New State*, 228.
91. Fox and Urwick, *Dynamic Administration*, 233.
92. See Manjulah S. Salimath and David J. Lemak, "Mary P. Follett: Translating Philosophy into a Paradigm of Lifelong Learning," *Management Decision* 42, no. 10 (2004): 1289; and Leslie Delapena Wheelock and Jamie L. Callahan, "Mary Parker Follett: A Rediscovered Voice Informing the Field of Human Resource Development," *Human Resource Development Review* 5, no. 2 (2006): 267–268.
93. Follett, *Creative Experience*, 21.
94. Ibid., 10–18.
95. Ibid., 136; see also Morton and Lindquist, "Revealing the Feminist in Mary Parker Follett," 360.
96. Follett, *New State*, 175.
97. Fox and Urwick, *Dynamic Administration*, 112.
98. Ibid., 115.
99. Urwick, *Freedom and Coordination*, 63.
100. Fox and Urwick, *Dynamic Administration*, 172–173.
101. Ibid., 260.
102. Ibid., 70.
103. Urwick, *Freedom and Coordination*, 45–46.
104. Fox and Urwick, *Dynamic Administration*, 117.
105. As far as we know, Mary Parker Follett was the first to regard authority as a process. This aspect of her work has been gaining influence over the past 15–20 years, although it is not always acknowledged; see, e.g., Jos C. N. Raadschelders and Richard J. Stillman, "Towards a New Conceptual Framework for Studying Administrative Authority," *Administrative Theory & Praxis* 29, no. 1 (2007): 4–40, esp. 26–29.

106. Urwick, *Freedom and Coordination*, 43.
107. Ibid., 19–22.
108. From Introduction, by Fox and Urwick, to *Dynamic Administration*, xxvi, 29–30.
109. Urwick, *Freedom and Coordination*, 31.
110. Fox and Urwick, *Dynamic Administration*, 23–24; and Urwick, *Freedom and Coordination*, 24.
111. Fox and Urwick, *Dynamic Administration*, 235.
112. Urwick, *Freedom and Coordination*, 58.
113. Fox and Urwick, *Dynamic Administration*, 249.
114. As quoted in Wheelock and Callahan, "Mary Parker Follett," 265; see also Parker and Ritson, "Fads, Stereotypes and Management Gurus," 1342; and C. McLarney and Shelley Rhyno, "Mary Parker Follett: Visionary Leadership and Strategic Management," *Women in Management Review* 14, no. 7 (1999): 292–302.
115. Ibid., 225–228.
116. Ibid., 225.
117. Urwick, *Freedom and Coordination*, 50–54.
118. Ibid., 59.
119. Fox and Urwick, *Dynamic Administration*, 51.
120. Urwick, *Freedom and Coordination*, 49.
121. Ibid., 54–55.
122. Fox and Urwick, *Dynamic Administration*, 176.
123. Urwick, *Freedom and Coordination*, 70.
124. Fox and Urwick, *Dynamic Administration*, 178.
125. Ibid., 38.
126. Urwick, *Freedom and Coordination*, 83.
127. Follett, *Creative Experience*, 20.
128. Fox and Urwick, *Dynamic Administration*, 139.
129. Ibid., 132–137.
130. Ibid., 79–80. See also Dafna Eylon, "Understanding Empowerment and Resolving Its Paradox: Lessons from Mary Parker Follett," *Journal of Management History* 4, no. 1 (1998): 16–28; and Schilling, "Decades Ahead of Her Time" and Melé, "Ethics in Management."
131. Michael Harmon, in *Public Administration's Final Exam: A Pragmatist Restructuring of the Profession and the Discipline* (Tuscaloosa: University of Alabama Press, 2006), 94, called her public administration's first and greatest process theorist. Her work greatly influenced, for instance, Charles Lindblom's partisan mutual adjustment (see chapter 8) and O. C. McSwite's notion of iterative and collaborative experimentation; see McSwite, *Legitimacy and Public Administration: A Discourse Analysis* (Thousand Oaks, Calif.: Sage, 1997), 149–150.
132. On this specific topic of emotionality of injustice, see Barclay, "Following in the Footsteps of Mary Parker Follett," 745–746.
133. Ibid., 5.
134. Follett, *Creative Experience*, 180.
135. This approach might be contrasted with that of economics, which has been called "the dismal science" because of its "worst-case" assumptions about human nature (i.e., that man is motivated only by primitive self-interest) and its dire predictions.
136. Follett, *New State*, 363.

137. In fact, even a longer list is possible. See, e.g., Parker and Ritson, "Fads, Stereotypes and Management Gurus," 1345–1346; and Salimath and Lemak, "Mary P. Follett," 1294–1295.
138. See, e.g., Katherine Selber and David M. Austin, "Mary Parker Follett: Epilogue to or Return of a Social Work Management Pioneer?" *Administration in Social Work* 21, no. 1 (1997): 1–15.

Chapter 5

Elton Mayo:
The Human Relations Approach

In the work of Mary Parker Follett, we have seen the beginning of a dissent from the Classical view of the organization. Elton Mayo's work adds new dimensions and lends some empirical support to that dissenting view.

Mayo echoes two of Follett's basic themes: the importance of the group process and the cumulative nature of authority in the organization. The group process is central to the analyses of both Follett and Mayo, for both see man as a social animal who finds a sense of identification and function in the group. Accordingly, individual behavior is largely determined by the group process and cannot be properly understood outside that process. The two also agree on the cumulative nature of authority in the organization, although Mayo does not emphasize this facet of the organization as much as Follett did. For Mayo, the cumulative nature of authority is implied in the recognition that the needs of subordinates must be satisfied if they are to become productive members of the organization and in the perception that the voluntary cooperation of all members of the organization must be secured if the organization is to be successful in achieving its objectives. Both Follett and Mayo temper their pronouncements on authority by acknowledging that elite leadership will be required, although the role of the elite is to establish the basis for proper group interaction, not to lead in an authoritarian manner.

Mayo extends Follett's perspective by adding a more general (and rather gloomy) sociological interpretation and by elaborating on the role of the small group within the organization. The more general sociological perspective is Mayo's assertion that the social disorganization attendant on the transition from a traditional to a modern society has led to personal disorganization. The linkage to organizational behavior comes in his contention that the problem of personal disorganization is exacerbated in the industrial setting. In industry, work has been reduced to a monotonous routine, and the highly specialized procedures adopted have deprived work of a sense of social function. Routine and monotonous work, in turn, leads to a state of "reverie," in which obsessions impair work performance.

Follett's analysis is extended inward by Mayo's focus on the importance of the work group inside the organization. The texture of the small-group experience, according to Mayo, largely determines individual behavior in the organization. Whether that texture is such that it produces spontaneous cooperation or generates hostility depends on the steps management takes to secure a spirit of cooperation and teamwork. A key actor in this scenario is the supervisor, who, operating at the point of human interface in the organization, is most likely to know of, and be able to respond to, the human needs of his or her subordinates.

Mayo also adds the important dimension of empirical research to his analysis. Although there is substantial controversy about the quality of his empirical analysis, Mayo's work did signal the importance of systematic investigation focusing on small groups within the organization. Indeed, the Western Electric research spurred a veritable deluge of empirical analyses, conducted under the general rubric of the Human Relations approach, which focused on the relationships among changes in the organization, worker satisfaction, and productivity.

There are also some points of disagreement between Follett and Mayo. A fundamental difference lies in the role of conflict in group interactions. Follett holds that conflict should be recognized and used for productive purposes, while Mayo contends that conflict is pathological and should be avoided. In his view, spontaneous cooperation, not conflict, is the proper basis for relationships in the organization, and it is up to an elite to create the conditions for the emergence of spontaneous cooperation. Another point of difference is on the role of the state. Follett regards the state as a logical extension of the group process and, thus, as the ultimate expression of the individual. Mayo, in contrast, sees the state as a potential instrument of tyranny, and he argues that its role should be subordinate to that of "peripheral" groups whose activities are crucial to social growth.

Elton Mayo may appear at first blush to be the most controversial author included in this volume—though he perhaps shares that distinction with Frederick Taylor. However, the frequency with which Mayo is discussed (if often in a stereotypical manner) in the public administration literature justifies his inclusion. Much of the controversy swirls around the Western Electric research and, more particularly, around Mayo's interpretation of that research. The controversy has shaped the structure of this chapter in three ways. First, Mayo's general sociological and political perspectives are examined in some detail, since it has been argued that these perspectives influenced his interpretation of the Western Electric study. Second, the series of experiments at Western Electric is itself reviewed; with apologies to those already familiar with that research, we thought it best to provide a summary, since some knowledge is necessary to make sense of critiques of that work. Third, critiques of the Western Electric researches are reviewed in order to give the reader a taste of the nature of the controversy. We believe this systematic overview to be important because the research at Western Electric and its critics raise some fundamental questions about the nature of the organization and about the relationship between the organization and its members.

Life

George Elton Mayo was born on December 26, 1880, in Adelaide, Australia—the second child and the oldest son of seven children.[1] His father was an engineer by training who had a very successful career as an estate agent, and several generations of the family had been prominent in the fields of medicine and law.

Mayo had something of a checkered educational experience. His early education was acquired at home. At age twelve, he entered Queen's College and, at age fourteen, St. Peter's College, where he apparently performed capably, winning the Westminster Scholarship in 1895. In 1897 Mayo enrolled at the University of Adelaide to study medicine, but he soon became bored with the routine of medical studies. Mayo's parents then sent him to medical school, first in Edinburgh (1902) and then in London (1903), but no interest in medicine was ever truly kindled, and he eventually left school. In the succeeding years, the restless Mayo sought to define his career interests, trying his hand at journalism and lecturing at the Working Men's College before returning to Australia in 1905 to become a partner in a printing firm. Still not satisfied, Mayo reentered the University of Adelaide in 1907, studying philosophy and psychology. This time, his interests crystallized, and Mayo went on to obtain both BA and MA degrees. On graduation in 1910, he taught logic, ethics, and psychology—first at the University of Adelaide and then at the University of Queensland. He married Dorothea McConnel in 1913; thereafter, when absent, he would write to her every day, and these letters provide valuable information about Mayo's work and self-appraisal.

In the succeeding years, Mayo developed an interest in the relationship between society and individual problems, and he became involved in the psychotherapeutic treatment of shell-shocked soldiers during World War I. The ideas and the experience he acquired during this period, as well as the bitter class divisions and labor strife in Australia at that time,[2] were to significantly influence Mayo's subsequent work. The end of the decade saw the publication of his first book, *Democracy and Social Freedom*,[3] and his appointment to a newly created chair of philosophy at the University of Queensland.[4]

In 1922 Mayo emigrated to the United States, attracted by the opportunity to continue his studies of social and industrial problems. He gained an appointment as a research associate at the Wharton School of Finance and Commerce of the University of Pennsylvania and received a grant from the Laura Spelman Rockefeller Foundation to study industrial problems. While at the University of Pennsylvania, Mayo did a study of a Philadelphia textile mill and published a series of articles in the *Personnel Journal* and in *Harper's Magazine*. The latter caught the eye of Wallace B. Donham, dean of the Harvard Business School, and in 1926 both Mayo and his Rockefeller grant moved to Harvard, where Mayo was appointed associate professor of industrial research and director of the Department of Industrial Research.[5] Mayo's work, focused on the psychological, social, and organizational aspects of industry, served as a complement to the physiological studies of Harvard's Fatigue Laboratory.

In 1927 a chance encounter and a casual conversation produced a collaboration that was to have a dramatic influence on the study of organizations. While in New York to speak at a meeting of the National Industrial Conference Board, Mayo met George A. Pennock, an engineer at the Hawthorne Plant of the Western Electric Company.[6] On the basis of their conversation, Pennock invited Mayo to come to the plant to look over the puzzling results of a lighting experiment that the Western Electric engineers had been conducting. This visit was to eventuate in five years of experimentation, which have become known as "the Western Electric researches" or "the Hawthorne studies." Much of Mayo's effort during the 1930s was devoted to the conduct of that research and to a series of speeches and publications elaborating on the results of the investigations and extending Mayo's interpretation of their psychological and sociological import. In 1933 he published *The Human Problems of an In-*

dustrial Civilization, which constituted both a preliminary report on the Western Electric researches and a considerably broader interpretation of their implications.[7]

At this point in his career, Mayo experienced some difficulty. In 1934 his daughters were sent to school in England, and his wife decided to join them; he would cross the Atlantic every summer. Apparently, he liked the trans-Atlantic lifestyle but thoroughly dreaded the separation. It has been argued that in Lyndall Urwick's work, the emphasis on structure over emotion was influenced by the fact that he lived in a close-knit family situation. Mayo, on the other hand, when separated from his family for long periods of time, became much more nostalgic in his theorizing and "drawn towards study of the worker's emotional life."[8] This frequent separation would continue until 1939, the year that the main publication to come out of the Hawthorne studies, *Management and the Worker*—coauthored by Mayo's associates, F.J. Roethlisberger and W.J. Dickson—was published by Harvard University Press. In his autobiography, Roethlisberger indicated that he was involved in writing this book in order to assure that Mayo had something to show for himself, but other literature seems to suggest that without Mayo the whole project would never have been completed. Indeed, Mayo would have written the study himself had not glaucoma prevented him from doing so.[9]

In the early 1940s, Mayo participated in a study of absenteeism and turnover in the aircraft industry in Southern California that echoed many of the findings of the Western Electric researches. In 1945 Mayo published his best-known and perhaps most controversial book, *The Social Problems of an Industrial Civilization*, in which he attempted to synthesize the findings of his major empirical investigations and to weave them into the broad tapestry of an analysis and critique of modern industrial society.[10] In 1947 he delivered two final lectures at Harvard, which were later published as a monograph, *The Political Problems of an Industrial Civilization*.[11] Mayo retired from Harvard in the same year and returned to England, where he resided until his death in 1949.

An abundance of restless energy fueled Mayo's particular talent, which was in providing intellectual stimulation for, and integrating the activities of, a research team or working group. Described by Roethlisberger as a "blithe spirit" and "an adventurer in the realm of ideas,"[12] Mayo was less a systematic thinker than a sower of "seeds to be cultivated."[13] His blithe spirit was manifested in something of a nonconformist attitude. During his association with the Western Electric Company, for instance, Mayo would arrive at the offices in mid-morning and, instead of taking lunch with company executives, would frequent "joints" on Cicero Avenue near the plant. He reportedly treated the authorities at the Rockefeller Foundation as casually as those at Western Electric.[14]

As a scientific investigator, Mayo stressed "intimate, habitual, intuitive familiarity" with the subject of investigation rather than quantitative measurement and controlled experimentation.[15] Mayo believed that the investigator should have a "knowledge-of-acquaintance" concerning human and social phenomena, not merely "knowledge about" those phenomena.[16] Accordingly, his methods were more those of clinical observation than those of laboratory experimentation. On a more general level, Mayo believed that philosophy is a good subject to engage in at the beginning and end of one's life, but, in the middle years, one should live it.[17] His own career offered at least a rough approximation of that belief: early on, Mayo was primarily concerned with general social, political, and philosophical questions; in the middle years, he engaged in scientific investigation based on direct observation; and, in his later years, he returned to his broader concerns, now conditioned by his observations and experience. He is, perhaps, best described as an applied social scientist.[18]

Mayo's Social, Political, and Philosophical Perspectives

Mayo's base assumption is that man is a social animal.[19] As such, he has a fundamental instinct for association with other humans and achieves a sense of meaning, purpose, and personal security in cooperative relationships. Society itself constitutes a cooperative system, and a civilized society is one in which cooperation is based on understanding and the will to work, rather than on force.[20] Thus, civilization is based on the spontaneous and voluntary cooperation of its members and is an "adventure in freedom" involving a struggle for both material control and individual expression.[21]

Although civilization is an adventure in freedom, Mayo also maintains that the "free life" must be based on social conditioning. Without the learned routines of social behavior, confusion would prevail.[22] Consequently, the intelligent development of civilization depends on "semi-automatic" routines of behavior, learned in personal associations, that make social collaboration both possible and effective. Logic and the immediate material interests of the individual are important, but they can be effective only in an existing social organization that is founded on established routines of social interaction. Mayo asserts that if the routines of society are disrupted, society will disintegrate into a "horde of individuals" seeking only self-preservation.[23] He maintains that in a traditional society with established social routines, everyone understands economic activities and the social functions performed. The individual recognizes his or her social function and achieves adaptation when identified with that function.[24]

The Social Malaise

Mayo contends that modern society suffers from a breakdown of the social routines of traditional society. The breakdown began in the sixteenth century when the church lost authority.[25] Since then, there has been a progressive descent from "real civilization" toward mere cultures that change and pass. According to Mayo, we are now experiencing a condition of social disorganization. Modern society, with its specialized logic and increased tempo of scientific and technological change, has destroyed the social routines that fostered a sense of unity and the spirit of collaboration in traditional societies. The church has lost its authority. Work has been organized according to the dictates of mass production, with the result that occupation has been divorced from social function. Ethnic diversity and geographical mobility have sundered personal ties. Even the family has become isolated and insignificant in the turbulent milieu of modern society.

Mayo asserts that the problem of social disorganization has been exacerbated by an economic theory that emphasizes competition in the pursuit of individual self-interest and by a political system that heightens the level of social conflict by playing to the fears of the masses. Economic theory, based on the nineteenth-century concept of individualism, considers society to be a collection of unrelated individuals motivated by hedonistic interests.[26] Society is only a rabble of individuals competing for scarce resources; the worker is simply a cost of production; and economic logic produces a sense of human isolation and defeat. This general disintegration results in the formulation of a social code at a lower level in opposition to economic logic.[27]

Politics, instead of being a solution to the problem of social disorganization, has become part of the problem. Politics has succeeded only in dividing society into hostile camps, thereby rendering united action impossible and thwarting society's efforts to preserve its unity. This problem is most clearly evidenced, paradoxically, in democratic governments. Mayo contends that political parties were established to educate the public and thus give form to public opinion.[28] In actuality, however, they have become mere devices for winning elections, as politicians appeal to the fears and hatreds of the masses. This devolution has resulted in the debasement of the political function and a trend toward collective mediocrity.[29] In the process, the ideal of political liberty has been translated into the reality of "servitude to all that is intellectually futile and emotionally base."[30] The party system, based on class consciousness and the obsessions of hate and fear, has created a rift in the foundations of society and has exaggerated, rather than alleviated, the problem of social disorganization.

Social Disorganization and the Individual

Mayo argues that social disorganization leads to personal disorganization, since social disorganization deprives the individual of the traditional sense of social understanding and support.[31] Mayo contends that in modern society socialization has been subordinated to logic, but the logic developed has been inadequate to the task of promoting effective social relationships. Moreover, when an individual faces problems for which logic is inadequate and for which a code or tradition no longer exists, the likely response is irrationality.[32] The resort to irrationality is even more likely when the social situation is characterized by rivalry and complicated by mental obsessions.

As a result of these conditions of social and personal disorganization, Mayo asserts that individuals in modern society exist in a state of anomie, or planless living, having been deprived of their sense of social function.[33] In this state of anomie, the individual is apt to be beset by reverie, or undirected thinking, which determines the individual's attitude toward life. According to Mayo, reverie normally illuminates and informs concentration, and the ability to shift rapidly back and forth from concentration to reverie is the achievement of the trained mind.[34] But reverie can also lead to the dominance of pessimism or melancholy, which may become virtually uncontrollable. These unacknowledged reveries are then manifested in strange ideas and eccentric behavior. Mayo asserts that no one is entirely free from the unreason produced by reverie and that the mentality of the average individual suggests a mild form of manic-depressive psychosis characterized by solitude and pessimism.[35] The search for amusement to avoid this reflective mood is merely an escape, as the individual seeks comfort in "artificial beauty, promiscuous adventure, or narcotic phantasies."[36] Long trains of unacknowledged reveries lead, in turn, to compulsions or obsessions, in which individuals "overthink" situations and attribute their ills to a hostile environment. This obsessive state produces an incapacity to respond to present situations, especially social situations.

Mayo contends that there is a mutual interaction between social disorganization and personal obsessions. Consequently, the problems of social maladjustment and psychoneurosis cannot be separated. On the one hand, sociology has demonstrated a relationship between social and personal disorganization that breeds a tendency toward obsession.[37] From the sociological perspective, these morbid preoccupations are caused by a defective relationship between the family and the surrounding community. Thus, sociologists maintain that psychoneurosis is a social rather than an individual phenomenon and results from the undue isolation of the family unit.

Psychologists, on the other hand, have shown that obsessive ills may be created by defective individual social conditioning.[38] Mayo argues that at the back of the infant mind is a repetition of primitive attitudes and beliefs. The infant feels impotent and afraid and, like the primitive, resorts to "magic" in the form of superstitions or taboos to reduce the feelings of impotence, fear, and ignorance.[39] To the extent that these attitudes and beliefs escape the synthesis of adolescence, they can reappear and dominate the life of an adult as childhood fears develop into adult obsessions. Alternatively, exercises of parental discipline may drive youths to obsessive conflict between the extremes of total acceptance and total rejection of authority.[40] Thus, the psychological perspective suggests that social hostilities and obsessive behavior may be primarily not social, but individual, ills. Social ills may exacerbate individual ills, but Mayo contends that if the problem is attacked solely from the social end, the effort will be to no avail.[41]

Whatever the source, obsessions prevent fixed attention, and failure provokes a crisis of reverie in which victims of obsessional ideas are unable to rouse themselves from their evil dreams. These obsessions complicate individual and social situations by permitting the intrusion of irrational motivations and delusions in human behavior. The irrational motives are not inherited or instinctual, but the product of defective social learning. Irrationality engendered by obsession makes the burden of decision the burden of possible sin, and, according to Mayo, life may be "made wretched and brought to nothing by irrationalities developed during a lifetime."[42]

Industry and Social Disorganization

Mayo asserts that the technological and scientific advances that contribute to social disorganization are most dramatically evidenced in industry, and that conflict and class consciousness are magnified in the industrial setting. He considers the industrial organization to be a fundamental social unit. The individual's sense of meaning comes primarily from a trade or profession that gives the individual worker the feeling that his or her work is socially necessary.[43] Yet in modern society, Mayo contends, occupation has become separated from social function, and social conflict has embittered relationships within industry.[44]

Some blame for this bitterness can be assigned to both major parties to the dispute: management and labor. On management's part, a clear understanding of the technical and economic aspects of the organization is coupled with only rough guesswork about the human aspect of the organization. Work is so organized that it tends to lose, rather than gain, in interest as the imposition of highly systematized procedures destroys the traditions of work and craftsmanship. Mayo contends that the "great stupidity" of modern society is its disregard of the fact that the machine shop is a "potent agent of repression" and a "perversion of human energy."[45]

On labor's part, the response to changing industrial conditions has been unionization, which only increases the level of conflict. Mayo considers unions to be a reactionary attempt to conserve human values by "stalling" and thus resisting change.[46] Collective bargaining is similarly dismissed as a primitive squabble raised to a pseudoscientific level that only perpetuates class conflict.[47]

Industry and Personal Disorganization

Just as social disorganization is magnified in the industrial setting, so too is the condition of personal disorganization further complicated in the industrial setting. Machine production is monotonous and demands minimal concentration. As a result, work is likely to be performed in a mood of reverie, and personal ills are likely to inhibit work performance.

Mayo notes that this problem is often diagnosed as one of fatigue. Yet studies have indicated that fatigue, in a physiological sense, does not seem to be the problem.[48] The "fatigue" observed is not gradual in its onset, it is not related to a depletion of "fuel reserves," it is not associated with "oxygen debt," and it occurs long before the muscular system is exhausted. In short, the concept of physiological fatigue appears to be complicated by "mental fatigue" in the factory setting. Work continued after the appearance of mental fatigue is accompanied by an "oscillation of attention" and by pessimistic reflection or reverie,[49] and it accentuates the individual's tendency to irrational thinking. This problem is most pronounced in the case of work that is unskilled and for workers who are uneducated.[50]

Mayo contends that the alternative to these fatigue disabilities is the achievement of a "steady state" condition of equilibrium.[51] Without such an equilibrium, the worker will be unable to continue to perform effectively. Thus, the strategic problem is to discover the sources of interference in the individual's state of equilibrium, which may be a function of the kind of work done and the intelligence of the worker. The temperament of the worker and social factors in the workplace are of at least equal importance, however. The individual reacts to a composite situation, although different individuals may react differently to the same situation.

The social setting of work is of particular importance to Mayo. He argues that work done in isolation becomes monotonous. Conversely, work gains in interest and dignity as an essential part of a social function.[52] Thus, work is an exercise of skill best done in social surroundings. Furthermore, Mayo contends that informal relationships, communications, and cooperation among people in the workplace are more important than technical logic and the immediate material interests of the individual.[53] Logic and incentives can work, but they are effective only in a supportive social organization.[54] If the social environment is not supportive, the interpersonal situation can produce "interferences" resulting in shifts in the individual's equilibrium and in impaired performance.

Mayo argues that monotonous work, inadequate social conditions, and personal disorganization have combined to yield discontent in industry. Reveries born of imperfect adjustment to industrial conditions make the individual dissatisfied, restless, and unhappy, and they encourage pessimistic thinking. Irrationalities produced by such thinking resemble the unreason demonstrated by the shell-shock victims Mayo treated during World War I. Dominated by reveries, the individual is afraid to think out problems and thereby get rid of the fears. As a result, production suffers, and the individual becomes easy prey to the appeals of the politician and of amusement promoters, which only worsens the situation.[55]

Mayo's argument, to this point, can be summarized as follows:

1. Civilization has moved from a society of established customs, an individual sense of social function, and accepted routines of personal interrelationships to a society marked by disruptive social, scientific, and technological change.

2. These changes have resulted in a condition of social disorganization in which logical responses to change have not been developed and irrational responses have been substituted for previous traditions.

3. The problem of social disorganization has been accentuated by an economic theory that promotes competition in the pursuit of self-interest and a political system that panders to the fears and superstitions of the body politic. Consequently, society has degenerated into class warfare, and there is a pervasive sense of anomie among individuals in society.

4. The social malaise is manifested in individual behavior in the form of uncontrolled reveries and irrational obsessions, which prevent proper adaptation to changing social conditions.

5. The problems are most acute in industry, where technological change has robbed work of its social meaning and where uncontrolled reveries and obsessions have resulted in strained interpersonal relationships, labor unrest, and diminished work effectiveness.

The Solution

What is Mayo's solution to these maladies? It is perhaps instructive to start with what he believes are *not* the solutions. Socialism, according to Mayo, is not the solution, since all the socialists can propose is a return to the "evil regime" from which laissez-faire theorists delivered us.[56] In addition, socialism gives rise to class consciousness and fosters the belief that society is composed of classes whose interests are naturally opposed. Mayo argues that this belief is both scientifically false and politically dangerous.[57] The issue, Mayo asserts, is not the ownership of property per se, but the social use of property; he contends that, if property is confiscated, all personal responsibility for its use will disappear.[58]

In a series of five articles in 1922, published in the *Industrial Australian and Mining Standard* and written before his departure to the United States, Mayo clearly identifies himself as an enemy of socialism. For instance, in the third article, on the mind of the agitator, he observes: "To any working psychologist, it is at once evident that the general theories of Socialism, Guild Socialism, Anarchism and the like are very largely the phantasy constructions of the neurotic.... In the Middle Ages it was religion that supplied phantasies of heaven; in our time it is some variant of Socialism." In the fourth article, on the will of the people, he observes: "The worker, dimly aware of his loss of authority and prestige, has been encouraged to expect that this loss would be more than compensated by his political enfranchisement.... What is Socialism but an endeavour to regain a lost sense of significance in the scheme of things. A great part of Socialistic literature challenges comparison with the fairy tales of a primitive people."[59] His contempt for socialism remained part of Mayo's psychology until the end of his life. Shortly before his death, he registered disenchantment with both the English weather and "this Socialist-ridden country."[60]

Nor are trade unions the solution to society's ills. Trade unions create the belief that there can be no harmony of interests between the employer and the employee—a belief that Mayo brands as "definitely obsessive."[61] Thus, collective bargaining served no other purpose than fanning a class war, "in which the antagonists lost sight of their social character and function."[62] For Mayo, the appropriate response to unionization is to anticipate its development and make it unnecessary. Earlier, we mentioned that the Rockefeller Foundation financed Mayo's work because his interests and concerns matched those of the Foundation, which fostered a clear anti–trade union attitude.[63] It has been suggested that Mayo's early work attracted the attention of Dean Donham, who, since the early 1920s, had wanted to point the Harvard Business School in the direction of industrial psychology so as to become a leadership training institute with the objective of protecting the existing order, capitalism, and even Western civilization.[64]

Industrial democracy is not the cure, since neither the employer nor the employee knows what is wrong. Workers' democracy would only result in placing power in the hands of those least likely to be able to know what to do—the least skilled workers.[65] Indeed, "... in all matters of social skill the widest knowledge and the highest skill should be sovereign rather than the opinion of 'collective mediocrity.'"[66]

Popular palliatives—such as revised incentive schemes, vocational adjustment, and new personnel systems—are also likely to be ineffective.[67] Such remedies are merely ad hoc responses to particular situations and fail to address the underlying problems. Indeed, Mayo argues that the demand for increased wages, for instance, may be simply a symptom of unrest, not its cause.[68]

Nor can improved family life or the better use of leisure time effectively address the basic social problems. A happy family life is not enough; social discipline beyond the family is required if individuals are to develop a capacity for fitting into a social situation and functioning properly in that situation.[69] Leisure time may be used to develop new stable relationships with other people, but seeking compensation in the "rose garden" cannot ease the sense of defeat at work.[70] Mayo argues that the right use of leisure is, and must be, subordinate to work actually done for the community.

Mayo's solution to the problems of social and personal disorganization lies in a combination of a restricted role for the state, the return of control to "peripheral" organizations, the creation of an administrative elite, the acquisition of scientific knowledge, and the development of an educational process appropriate to society's needs and problems. Mayo argues that the state is a subsidiary function of society whose first duty is to conserve the freedom of growth in the community. As such, the state cannot rightly do more than reflect social growth by recording the achievements of society, criticizing existing social relationships, and forbidding any contravention of established morality.[71] The state is simply an expedient to recognize social change. It cannot take the lead in creating change.

The problem with democratic government is that, in assuming that all authority derives from the state, it is likely to become tyrannical. Democracy must recognize that growth is a characteristic of social life, not the state, and that government should not exceed its moral function by undertaking social direction.[72] Democracy involves two phases: critical control from the top, and spontaneous and cooperative control from below. In emergencies, central control is required. After the emergency has passed, however, control must be transferred to peripheral groups such as informal groups in the workplace. Mayo contends that it is this transfer that distinguishes democracies from absolutist governments.[73] Continuation of central control inhibits the development of extrapolitical social activities, which are crucial to social growth.

If the peripheral organizations are to function properly, Mayo argues that knowledge of human nature must be expanded, an informed administrative elite must be created, and the system of education must be improved. According to Mayo, societies suffer and die from ignorance. The particular ignorance of modern society is its ignorance of human nature.[74] The tasks of modern society are to substitute intelligent understanding for the integrative religious feelings of medieval times and to exorcise the current sense of social futility and hopelessness. Such understanding can come only from scientific analysis of the human situation based on direct observation. That is, we must initially develop what Mayo calls "knowledge-of-acquaintance," coming from direct experience, rather than mere "knowledge about," which relies on reflective and abstract thinking. Only then can we proceed to the development of appropriate skills, experimentation, and logic in the scientific quest.[75] Most critically, the industrial situation must be better understood. Industrial research must be concerned not only with the physiological and biochemical but also with the psychological and social factors of industry.[76]

The second requirement for effective democratic development, in its broader sense, is the creation of an informed administrative elite. Mayo contends that democracy has given too much attention to Rousseau and too little to Machiavelli. Rousseau relied too much on the "pious hope" that desires inimical to the general welfare would somehow be canceled in general discussion, whereas Machiavelli recognized that administrators must set themselves to the task of understanding human motives, cultivating desirable social movements, and checking the undesirable.[77] Mayo asserts that civilization breaks down because of problems in administration and that democracy, in particular, has failed to realize the importance of administrative knowledge and skill. On morality, every individual must be judged equally. Scientific questions should be determined by skilled investigators, however, and the widest knowledge and the highest skills should be sovereign in these matters, not the opinion of "collective mediocrity."[78] Once again, the critical arena for the identification and development of an informed administrative elite is industry, which should be guided by administrators who recognize the importance of the human factor and who can learn ways of adapting workers to the new industrial system by creating conditions that prevent an emergence of obsessive reverie.[79]

The final requirement for effective democratic development is to improve the system of education. Mayo asserts that the prime duty of education is to emancipate people from fear through understanding.[80] Education is a prelude to adventure and should light up the imagination of youth. Mayo contends that morbid adolescents of forty have had too much to say in the instruction of youth.[81] Youth scorns "dull compromises," and that refractory spirit is the essence of civilization and morality.

The primary focus of education should be to develop a critical control of reverie thinking—to get the subjects of education into the reveries of students. This process will eliminate dangerous reveries and demonstrate both the right use of reverie and the right relationship between reverie and concentration. Mayo argues that one can eliminate the eccentric from industry, but it is far better to eliminate eccentricities from otherwise normal persons in industry by better education.[82] In this way, we can reach the "nightmind" of the child and the savage surviving in the civilized adult, thereby freeing humanity from the bonds of irrationality and superstition.

Mayo recognizes that we cannot return to the simplicity of traditional society.[83] Technical advance is required to establish the better standards of living that are vital to effective democracy. Nevertheless, securing collaboration in an industrial society cannot be left to chance. The state can play a role, but it is a necessarily limited role because compulsion has never succeeded in rousing eager and spontaneous cooperation. Mayo's vision is an "adaptive society" characterized by control from below by persons with skills in social relationships and communication.[84] The adaptive society should be based on an attitude of spontaneous cooperation, and it should be free from irrationality and obsession. The path to the adaptive society is built on new knowledge and powers derived from scientific investigation. With this knowledge will come personal freedom, an end to industrial unrest, and the possibility of world peace as societies learn to cooperate in the tasks of civilization.[85]

Mayo's Empirical Studies

Mayo's belief that society is not merely a horde of individuals, his conviction that knowledge of the human situation is vital to civilization, and his insistence on direct observation as a first step in the acquisition of that knowledge led him to a series of empirical studies designed to start the process of accumulating "knowledge-of-acquaintance" in the industrial setting.

The Philadelphia Textile Mill

In 1923, while Mayo was still at the University of Pennsylvania, he was asked to undertake a study of turnover and morale in the spinning department of a Philadelphia textile mill.[86] The department was experiencing a turnover rate of 250 percent and the workers had a generally low level of morale. Previous experiments with a variety of incentive schemes had not been successful in either reducing turnover or improving morale.

The company itself was, according to Mayo, well-organized, and its management was both enlightened and humane. The president of the company was well-regarded and generally inspired loyalty in his workers. Paradoxically, conditions in the spinning department were not noticeably inferior to those in the rest of the mill. But the work in the department was repetitive and demanded constant vigilance, as piecers walked up and down work alleys twisting together broken threads; and the work was essentially solitary. Mayo found workers in the department to be possessed of reveries that were "monotonously and uniformly pessimistic."[87]

Mayo decided to test the effects of rest periods on work attitudes and performance, and to adopt a research procedure that he was to employ throughout his empirical investigations. This approach combined direct observation of the work and working conditions with interviews that were designed to evoke the attitudes of workers about their work. Mayo was not original in recognizing the importance of rest periods, for we know that Taylor had done so twenty years earlier. However, we suspect that Mayo was among the first to systematically explore the effects of rest periods on performance and attitude.

The rest pauses produced beneficial results almost immediately. Labor turnover in the department was effectively eliminated, productivity increased, workers felt less fatigued, and melancholic reveries disappeared. And when, shortly thereafter, under heavy demands for increased production, rest periods were abandoned, the effects were a drop in productivity and a return of pessimistic reveries. Rest periods were then reinstituted, but this time they were to be "earned" according to level of production rather than regularly scheduled. During this time, productivity increased but did not attain the levels reached in the original rest-pause experiment. Spurred by these results, the president of the company ordered the reestablishment of regularly scheduled rest periods, which resulted in a 10 percent increase in production. Finally, rest periods were alternated among work groups in the department, and the groups themselves were allowed to determine the method of alternation. Again, the results were positive: morale improved, fatigue was diminished, absenteeism decreased, and there was no labor turnover.

Mayo summarized his findings as follows:

1. Spinning produces postural fatigue and induces pessimistic reverie.

2. Rest pauses relieve these conditions and increase productivity by restoring normal circulation, relieving postural fatigue, and interrupting pessimistic reverie.

3. Rest pauses are more effective when they are regular and the workers have received instruction in the techniques of relaxation.

4. The life of the worker outside the mill is improved as workers become more interested in their families and more sober.[88]

More generally, Mayo interprets these findings in a manner consistent with his broader perspectives on the industrial environment. He argues that the attitudes of workers in the spinning department were of paramount importance. The problem of turnover was not the result of an organic reaction to working conditions, but the result of the workers' emotional response to the work performed. Furthermore, the problem was not monotony per se, but repetitive work done under a social condition of isolation that led to abnormal preoccupations.[89] Solitary and repetitive work done on a daily basis intensifies the tendency toward pessimistic or paranoid meditation, and this tendency, Mayo argues, is the single most important factor in productive efficiency.[90] Thus unrest, manifested here in high rates of turnover and absenteeism, is a symptom of disturbances to the equilibrium between the worker and his work, accompanied by pessimistic preoccupations that determine the individual's attitude toward work.

Mayo asserts that the results of the institution of rest periods was as much a product of the mental interruption of obsessive reveries as of the elimination of physical fatigue.[91] His explanation for the increase in work effectiveness goes beyond the rest periods themselves, however. He asserts that several changes had been introduced that combined to change the human atmosphere in the department, making it more "social" and lending dignity to the work performed.[92] Social interrelationships improved; workers welcomed the opportunity to express themselves freely to a trained interviewer; the experiment itself demonstrated management's interest in the workers; and the president of the company had helped to transform a "horde of solitaries" into a social group by giving the workers control over their rest periods.[93]

The Western Electric Researches

Mayo's next major involvement in direct observation was in the famed Western Electric researches, conducted at the company's Hawthorne Plant, near Chicago, beginning in 1927.[94] The work of Mayo and his associates had been preceded by a series of experiments by engineers at Western Electric concerning the effect of the degree of illumination on worker productivity.[95] In the first of these experiments, three departments were exposed to different levels of lighting. The results were inconsistent: in one department, output fluctuated with no direct relationship to the intensity of illumination; in the second department, output remained relatively stable over the period of the experiment; in the third department, output increased as the level of lighting increased but failed to decline when the level of lighting was decreased.

Subsequent investigations did little to resolve these inconsistencies. In a second experiment, a test group and a control group were subjected to different levels of lighting. Output in the test group increased, as was expected; however, output also increased in the control group, where the level of lighting was held constant. A third experiment involved just the use of artificial lighting to afford greater control over the degree of illumination. In this case, output suffered under decreased lighting only when the workers complained that they could barely see. Further informal experimentation served only to add to the confusion, as two operators maintained their level of productivity even when the degree of illumination was reduced to the approximate level of moonlight.

Confounded by these results, company officials sought the advice of Mayo and his associates at Harvard, who suggested that human response had defeated the purpose of the lighting experiments. The Harvard group argued that the workers had reacted to the experiments themselves, not to the level of lighting, and speculated that the implicit expression of management's concern in merely conducting the experiments had been a determining factor. This reaction was to become known as the "Hawthorne Effect."

At the outset, Mayo's involvement in the Western Electric researches was minimal. Indeed, he never participated directly in the collection of data at the Hawthorne Plant.[96] Mayo became more prominently involved later in the experiments, when problems arose with the interpretation of the results.[97] From that point on, he visited the plant frequently, assisted in training interviewers, and participated in the interpretation of the results.[98]

Rest-Pause Experiments. The Harvard group's initial interest was in the effects of fatigue and monotony on work performance. Accordingly, the researchers decided to test for the effects of rest periods, and of variations in the length of the workday and workweek. Since it was believed that the illumination studies had suffered from inadequate experimental controls, a small group was selected and separated from the rest of the plant. Given the interest in monotony and fatigue, a repetitive task was decided on: the assembly of telephone relays. Two female relay assembly operators were chosen on the basis of their experience and cooperative attitude; they then were allowed to choose three other participants. These five subjects were informed about the nature of the experiment and were told specifically that its purpose was not to increase productivity—it was expected only that they work at a normal pace.

An observer was assigned to the test room with responsibility for maintaining a friendly atmosphere in the room and for keeping records of conversations and group relationships. In addition, data were collected on such items as the quantity of output (recorded unobtrusively by a mechanical device), quality of output, reasons for temporary stops, time spent in bed every night, the medical condition of the operators, room temperature, outside temperature, and relative humidity. Finally, all the operators were periodically interviewed on a separate and individual basis.

Despite the researchers' efforts to establish rigorous experimental controls and the elaborate array of statistics collected, a number of changes in the relay assembly test room escaped control and went unmeasured. These changes, as we shall see, loomed large in the eventual interpretation of the experiment's results. Most critically, the payment system, the style of supervision, and the social environment were changed in the test room. Incentives in the test room were based on that group's productivity. Rewards were thus more closely linked to individual performance in the test room than in the larger group working in the regular plant. The method of supervision in the test room was also different, as the observer took over some supervisory functions and became responsible for maintaining a friendly climate. Finally, the social environment changed as the operators became members of a small group and were allowed to talk more freely than at their previous stations.[99]

There were five major periods in this study, which lasted from 1927 through 1932.[100] In the first period, productivity records were established while the operators were still in their regular department. In the second period, the workers were moved to the test room to become familiar with their new surroundings, but no other changes were made. The third period involved the introduction of an incentive plan based on the productivity of the test group itself. The fourth and fifth periods were the central focus of the experiment, as rest periods of varying duration and frequency were instituted in period 4 and the length of the workday and workweek were manipulated in period 5.

In a pattern that was to be characteristic of most of this research, the study of the relay assembly test room produced unexpected results and, as a consequence, raised more questions than it answered. In the rest-pause experiments, output generally increased regardless of the frequency and duration of the pauses. A problem did arise in regard to the amount of talking going on in the room. This resulted in a reprimand from the supervisor, an attempt to get the women to pay more attention to their work by requiring that they call out difficulties, and the return of two of the operators to the regular department because of the talking problem and "behavior approaching gross insubordination."[101] Variations in the length of the workday and workweek produced similar results. Only when the length of the working day was reduced by a full hour did output suffer. Of particular interest was a period in which the work group was ostensibly returned to its original working conditions. Output did diminish, but it did not fall back to its original level.

Several possible explanations for the increase in productivity in the re-lay assembly test room were considered by the research group. The in-crease could be attributed to improved materials and methods of work, fatigue reduction, the reduction of monotony, the small-group incentive plan, the changed method of supervision, or the altered social situation in the test room. Improved materials and methods of work were dis-missed as being relatively insignificant.[102] The idea of fatigue reduction was examined more closely, but found wanting. This conclusion was based primarily on the finding that when conditions were supposedly re-turned to their initial state, production did not fall back to the pre-exper-imental level.[103] In addition, physiological tests indicated that the operators were working well within their physical capacities, and output did not follow the pattern predicted by a hypothetical "fatigue curve."[104] The monotony hypothesis was also rejected, though somewhat more equivocally. Output, again, did not follow the predicted "monotony curve," but it was felt that monotony might not be fully reflected in out-put measures.[105]

Thus, the list of possible factors involved in the increased productivity in the relay assembly test room was reduced to the incentive system, meth-ods of supervision, and a changed social environment. To measure the possible effects of the incentive system, two more experiments were un-dertaken. In one, a second relay assembly test room, *only* the method of incentives was changed—that is, pay was based on small-group output.[106] In the other, involving the task of splitting sheets of mica into thinner strips, the conditions were to be the same as in the first relay assembly test room *with the exception* of the small-group incentive plan.[107] Comparisons of these two groups, it was believed, would permit an assessment of the relative impact of incentives versus other working conditions on output.

For the second relay assembly test room, five women were selected by the supervisor and paid separately from the rest of the department. The result was a 12.6 percent increase in output, followed by a decline in pro-ductivity when the experiment ended. Thus, the findings seemingly sub-stantiated the incentive hypothesis. But the researchers believed that a rivalry between the first and second relay assembly test rooms had also contributed to the increase in productivity.[108]

The mica-room experiment was designed to replicate the conditions of the first relay assembly test room except for the incentive system. Two operators were selected by the research team, and those two chose the remaining three participants.[109] As in the first relay assembly test room, rest pauses and the length of the working day and week were varied.[110] The results were a moderate decline in output when the workers were first moved into the test room, a modest increase in output when rest pauses were introduced, a moderate decline after that point, and constant output over the final stages of the experiment. Thus, instead of a continuous increase, productivity showed little consistent relationship to the rest pauses and increased only after the initial introduction of the rest pauses. Undismayed, the researchers proceeded to explain away these seemingly perverse results. The decline in output after the introduction of the rest pauses was attributed to anxiety about possible cutbacks in employment, which constituted "interfering preoccupations."[111] Furthermore, the researchers concluded that the mica-room experiment was only a "story of individuals" without an incentive system designed to promote group solidarity.[112]

Based on these findings, it was concluded that incentives were not the sole explanation for the observed increases in productivity. The negative evidence of the mica-room experiment regarding manipulation of working conditions other than incentives was suspect because it fell short of experimental requirements. The positive findings on the relationship between incentives and productivity in the second relay assembly test room were attributed to a rivalry between the test rooms rather than to the incentive system itself. Finally, it was observed that, though productivity had increased in the second relay assembly test room, the increase had not been as great as the 30 percent increase in the first relay assembly test room. This discrepancy further reinforced the conclusion that something more than incentives was involved in the increase in productivity in the first relay assembly test room. In addition, the research group felt that whatever the effect of incentives may have been, that effect was dependent on other social factors.[113]

Thus, by a process of elimination, it was decided that the combination of a changed method of supervision and an altered social situation had been the primary factors in increasing output in the first relay assembly test room. Paradoxically, neither change had been intentionally introduced in the experiment itself. The new method of supervision had been the unplanned result of the research group's assuming some of the functions of the regular supervisor. The new method of supervision was not necessarily less strict, but it had a different quality: sympathetic listening replaced the giving of orders and personal criticism, and the operators felt that their new "supervisors" had a personal interest in their well-being. Also, the work group was consulted about possible changes, it was not pushed to achieve higher output, and social conversation was permitted within the group. It was argued that these changes in the quality of supervision, as well as the segregation of the work group and the small-group incentive plan, had produced a new social situation in which the individual workers had become part of a "work team," with a sense of comradeship among its members. A sense of social solidarity had thus been created that led to improved morale, relationships of confidence and friendliness, and enhanced work effectiveness. To Mayo, this meant that the supportive social structure had strengthened the "temperamental inner equilibrium" of the workers and allowed them to achieve a mental state that "offered a high resistance to a variety of external conditions."[114] In other words, the workers had developed a high and stable level of work effectiveness and were relatively unaffected by changes in working conditions, such as rest pauses and hours worked.

The Interviews. Given the importance attached to supervisory style and social conditions in the relay assembly test room, the next stage of the research began to focus more directly on those factors. This stage involved an interview program that started in 1936 with a handful of counselors. By 1941, there were 55 counselors who covered 21,000 of the 40,000 employees at the Hawthorne plant. The interviews were conducted in rooms with floor lamps, an end table, and two cushioned chairs so that interviewees could sit back and relax. And so they did. As one employee observed: "Counseling is a good idea. I'll take an easy chair and an extra cigarette anytime."[115] The interviews were originally designed to improve supervisory methods by gathering data on working conditions and workers' responses to supervision. That intention soon succumbed to the unanticipated consequences of the interviews themselves.

As a device for learning about conditions in the plant, the interviews were a notable failure. The comments on physical conditions expressed in the interviews were found to bear little relationship to the facts of the situation, criticisms addressed to persons or company policies were difficult to assess, and the interviewers had a hard time keeping the respondents to subjects the research team had intended to examine. Consequently, the interview format was changed to allow the respondents to comment on subjects of their own choosing. Under this revised format, it was soon learned that the interviews revealed more about personalities than about the objective work situation and that the comments expressed in the interviews could be understood only in a context of the expectations and moods of the workers. This discovery led to a focus on the emotional significance of events and objects, as preoccupations or "obsessions" became a matter of central concern. Moreover, it was found that the interviews had a cathartic effect on the subjects and were thus of considerable therapeutic value. The welcomed opportunity to express themselves freely assisted the workers in getting rid of useless emotional complications, easing the sense of personal futility, learning to associate with others, and developing a desire to work better with management.[116]

The personal preoccupations revealed in the interviews were found to be partly a product of personal background and family environment. In a significant departure from Mayo's previous position, however, it was found that the obsessional preoccupations were also the result of the social environment in the workplace.[117] Individual attitudes were shaped by group sentiments, and those sentiments had a direct impact on work performance. This impact was often manifested in the form of a group concept of a "fair day's work" that was typically lower than management's expectations.[118] Thus, it was concluded that the major difficulty in the work situation is not one of external influences or errors in supervision, but something more intimately human that is a product of group experience. Based on this conclusion, the focus of the research shifted once again—this time to an examination of the effect of informal social groups in the organization.

The Bank-Wiring Observation Room. The final stage of the Western Electric researches, conducted from November 1931 to May 1932, was designed to extend and confirm the observations of the interview program. In this stage, telephone bank–wiring operators were observed to study a shop situation from a sociological perspective. Fourteen men were selected for the experiment—nine wiremen, three soldermen, and two inspectors. The purpose of the experiment was explained to the men, and output records were kept prior to the beginning of the experiment. The workers were then moved to a separate room and an observer was assigned to act as a "disinterested spectator," looking for evidence of an informal group and attempting to understand the functions of such a group in regard to its members.[119] In addition, an outside interviewer was attached to the group to investigate individual attitudes. The group was considered a separate unit for payment purposes, and the incentive system was designed to tie individual earnings to group output.

The results of the experiment, in this case, conformed to the expectations of the research team. Group output remained at a constant level, and each individual in the group restricted his output in accordance with the group's concept of a fair day's work. In general, the social relationships within the informal group frustrated the pursuit of organizational interests as the group adopted its own performance standards and enforced them by social sanctions such as name-calling ("ratebusters," "chiselers," and "squealers") and "binging," or hitting a violator on the shoulder.[120]

The researchers concluded that the informal group had created fear about management's intentions and that the group performed the function of protecting its members from outside interference and internal indiscretions.[121] In that process, social considerations came to outweigh logical and economic considerations. Given the structure of the incentive scheme, logical and economic considerations should have led to an increase in output, but, instead, group norms took precedence over considerations of individual self-interest. Conformity to group norms determined whether the operator was accepted by the group, and individual performance was a function of group status rather than ability.[122] According to Mayo, the informal group in the bank-wiring room was a means of resisting rapid changes in the environment, which deprived work of its social meaning and over which the group had little control.[123] Thus, protection of the group became more important than spontaneous cooperation in the service of organizational objectives.

The Southern California Aircraft Industry

Mayo's final venture in direct observation was another study of absenteeism and turnover, this time in the Southern California aircraft industry during World War II.[124] Adopting a somewhat broader sociological perspective, Mayo and his associates first examined the community environment to look for possible causes of high rates of absenteeism and turnover in the industry. They concluded that the basic problem was not the restless population movement characteristic of the area at that time, but the fact that the military draft had withdrawn workers who had previously held work teams together. There had been similar occurrences elsewhere, however, and Mayo asserts that such external forces will have a major impact only when management has not been sufficiently attentive to the development of cohesive working groups in their organizations.[125]

Consequently, as had been the case at Western Electric, the study focused on social factors internal to the organization as probable determinants of absenteeism and turnover. The study also had a progressively narrowing perspective, moving from an industrywide focus to an examination of a single company and then of selected departments within that company, and, finally, to a detailed analysis of a single work center that had a low rate of absenteeism.

The findings pretty much followed those of the Western Electric researches. It was found that the rate of absenteeism and turnover was a function of the formation of work teams. Absenteeism and turnover were lower when these teams created a condition of "active cooperation" with the company's policies and purposes.[126] Furthermore, team formation was found to be largely dependent on the quality of supervision and leadership—both formal and informal—in the work group. Successful supervisors were those who had been trained in the techniques of handling human relations; had assistants to take care of routine and technical problems, thus freeing the supervisor to respond to human problems; and allowed the workers to participate in the determination of working conditions.[127] Informal leadership was also found to be important. In one successful work center, the work was actually in charge of a "lead-man," and the foreman rarely visited the center. The leadman, a college-educated worker with considerable experience in the industry, facilitated the work of others by giving technical, personal, and social help to individual workers; seeing that adequate work materials were available; and handling contacts with the rest of the company.[128]

These findings were corroborated in interviews with workers who were irregular in their attendance. The "irregulars" were characterized by a condition of personal disorganization and discontent. Many left the job because their work had never become an integral part of their total lives. This condition was traced to supervisors who were inconsiderate and showed "irritable impatience" rather than personal consideration and understanding.[129] As a result, the irregulars were simply a collection of unrelated individuals, not members of a cohesive group or team.

Mayo views the results of this study as being consistent with the findings of his previous investigations. The desire for association, he maintains, is deeply rooted, and informal social groups will inevitably exist. The only question is whether the attitude of the group will be one of hostility and wariness or one of wholehearted cooperation and friendliness.[130] The development of the social group should not be left to chance. Instead, management must be sensitive to the need for a meaningful social-group experience and must create the conditions under which that need can be fulfilled in a manner compatible with effectiveness in the achievement of organizational objectives.

The Impact of Direct Observation on Mayo's Perspectives

Most of Mayo's thoughts about the nature of the "industrial problem" were pretty much in place before his empirical investigations. A consistent theme in his writings is that the problem is the maladjusted individual who is besieged by evil reveries, dominated by obsessive preoccupations, and afflicted by irrational behavior. But whereas Mayo had earlier viewed the problem in terms of personal history and a broader malaise of social disorganization, his empirical research led him to concentrate on the role of the social group within the organization in determining the individual's attitude toward work. These groups can either assist the organization in achieving its goals or can thwart those efforts.

Mayo argues that there are three persistent problems of management: the application of science and technical skill, the systematic ordering of operations, and the organization of teamwork or sustained cooperation.[131] Management, he charges, has paid too much attention to the first two elements and too little to the third. In particular, management has failed to perceive the importance of informal social groups, which, Mayo argues, are a response to a basic human need. Without a supportive social environment, workers become preoccupied by their personal situations and irrational in their behavior. This personal isolation results in a sense of exasperation and futility and the likelihood of conflict between loyalty to the company and loyalty to the social group.

Accordingly, management must assume responsibility for creating conditions conducive to the development of a cooperative team spirit. Appeals to technical and economic logic are not sufficient. Technological change must be conditioned by an awareness of the limitations of, and consequences for, social change. Economic incentives can help to promote greater work effectiveness, but only in an otherwise healthy social situation. In short, management must learn to appeal to individual and social emotions and attitudes in a more intimately human way. Psychotherapeutic techniques can help individuals get rid of their obsessive preoccupations. Such techniques, however, must be coupled with a conscious effort to improve the social climate in the organization. A key ingredient in this effort is the supervisor, who, operating at the point of human interface in the organization, can play an important role in fostering supportive interpersonal relationships and team morale.

Mayo's Critics

Mayo's research, and more particularly his interpretation of that research, has raised a virtual firestorm of criticism. The criticism has been directed at both Mayo's philosophical values and his methodology and has centered on the most famous of his enterprises, the Western Electric researches.[132]

The ideological critiques have taken exception to Mayo's neglect of conflict in the organization and to what is perceived as a bias in favor of management. The critics charge that Mayo, blinded by his assumption of a natural harmony of interests in the workplace and by his single-minded pursuit of spontaneous cooperation, failed to recognize the inevitability—indeed, desirability—of social conflict. It is argued that workers and management are fundamentally in conflict and that spontaneous cooperation and unanimity of purpose are, therefore, impossible.[133] Thus, industrial research should be directed at developing means for accommodating conflict rather than disregarding it. Central to this concern is the role of unions. Mayo, as we have seen, had little regard for unions and collective bargaining, and he conducted his research in organizations that had no unions. On this basis, Mayo is castigated for neglecting a major mechanism for conflict resolution, both by virtue of his personal bias and in his choice of research location.[134]

Furthermore, it is argued that where Mayo did observe conflict, he attributed it to workers' sentiments and attitudes rather than to objective working and social conditions. For instance, in the bank-wiring observation room experiment at Western Electric, Mayo stresses group sentiments and status as the determinants of output restriction, rather than hostility to management bred of more concrete considerations, such as disputes over money, power, and control. The critics maintain that it is at least equally plausible to interpret the group's restriction of output as a *collective* defense of economic interests, in which the motivating impulse was resistance to change adversely affecting those interests, as to see them simply as a primitive urge to form a tribal society in miniature.[135] Viewed in this light, worker resistance could even reflect worker solidarity that transcends individual psychological distinctions and immediate financial gain. In other words, industrial conflict, instead of being an irrational reaction to evil reveries, may well be the product of conflicts in values arising from the socioeconomic structure. As such, industrial conflict represents a power struggle between management and the workers over the division of the joint product and goes beyond the factory gate to a more general condition of class conflict.[136]

The critics also charge Mayo with a pro-management bias produced, in part, by his abhorrence of conflict. Mayo, it is argued, assumes that happiness and personal security are found in the subordination of the individual to a common purpose and rests his hopes on a managerial elite to rescue society from the ravages of personal independence. Thus, the critics contend that Mayo's goal is, in fact, a static society in which workers are to be manipulated by a benevolent leadership that requires workers not only to do the work but to like it as well.[137] From this perspective, the organization is taken as a given, and the individual is expected to change. Little consideration is given to the possibility that management's orientation, not that of the worker, may be "defective."[138] Hence, the management techniques proposed by Mayo simply amount to new methods of social control designed to manipulate the worker's emotional and mental processes in order to build a harmonious organization. Exercises of managerial authority are simply disguised by the vocabulary of "human relations."[139]

Mayo's bias in favor of management is also said to be revealed in his emphasis on the skills of cooperation without reference to the aims of that cooperation. Although Mayo claims to be interested only in the efficiency of work performance, the concept of efficiency, it is argued, is empty without some notion of social value; and in the absence of an explicit statement of other social values, efficiency will be oriented toward the goals of management.[140] Thus, Mayo sees workers as "cooperating" only when they accept the goals of management.[141] It has been said that the Human Relations approach provided the managers "with a more subtle yet powerful means of exercising authority in the workplace which could challenge the democratic approach of elements of the Scientific Management community who sought to enable workers to become active participants in the management of the labour process."[142] Mayo was not the only one, and likely not the first to express concerns about the manager's authority. Indeed, Henry Dennison—a paper-products manufacturer in Boston, president of the Taylor Society between 1919 and 1921, member of several presidential committees under Wilson and Harding, and, like Chester Barnard, a practitioner with an eye for theory—wrote a series of studies on social or organizational engineering in the 1920s, "surveying most, if not all, of the territory later formally mapped out by Mayo and his colleagues."[143]

Finally, Mayo is charged not only with neglecting the inevitability of conflict but also with ignoring its desirability. Mayo's critics contend that a plurality of social relationships in which individuals are members of groups both within and outside the workplace produces divided loyalties, which are admittedly conducive to conflict but also vital to freedom of choice.[144] This freedom is necessary to resist the totalitarian demands of any single organization; conflict, within the rules of the game, protects the rights of the individual vis-à-vis the organization.

Mayo's work has also been subjected to substantial empirical criticism. Two of the more prominent empirical critiques are those by Alex Carey and by Richard H. Franke and Paul D. Kaul.[145] Both critiques concern the rest-pause experiments in the Western Electric study.

Carey challenges Mayo's interpretation of the results of the experiments in the two relay assembly test rooms and the mica-splitting room. He contends that Mayo and his associates understated the role of financial incentives and distorted the findings on supervisory style. On incentives, Carey notes that in the second relay assembly test room, where only the method of payment was changed, output increased while the incentive system was in force and decreased thereafter. This pattern, Carey argues, would normally be taken as evidence of a direct and favorable influence of incentives on output, but Mayo chose to disregard this possibility and, instead, attributed the increase in output to an alleged rivalry between the first and second relay assembly groups. In addition, in the mica-splitting room, where there was no change in the incentive system, individual rates of output increased, but total group output declined because of a shortening of the workweek. Mayo suggests that "friendly supervision" led to an increase in productivity, while Carey contends that the individual increase may have been due simply to fatigue reduction

from a shorter workweek. Moreover, there was a *decline* in group productivity, thus casting doubt on the importance of new modes of supervision.
Furthermore, since a combination of incentives and friendly supervision
in the first relay assembly test room led to a substantial increase in total
output but friendly supervision alone led to no increase in total output in
the mica-splitting room, Carey maintains that all of the increase in output
in the first relay assembly test room could logically be attributed to financial incentives alone.

Carey also challenges Mayo's interpretation of the role of supervisory
style in the first relay assembly test room, arguing that the supervision was
not as consistently "friendly" as Mayo suggests. Operators were required
to call out their mistakes as a means of keeping their minds on their jobs,
were subjected to numerous reprimands for talking too much, and were
warned about the loss of their free snacks if their performance did not
improve. These threats culminated in the dismissal of two operators from
the test room for insubordination. Carey maintains that there were actually three phases of the experiment, identified by the kind of supervision
exercised in each phase. In the first phase, supervision was generally
friendly, casual, and low-pressure; there was no substantial increase in
productivity in this phase. The second phase was marked by increasingly
stern and close supervision, with no change in output. In phase 3, which
followed the replacement of the two operators, supervision again became
free and friendly, and output increased sharply. Carey suggests that the
increase in output in phase 3 may have been the result of an exercise of
supervisory discipline in phase 2 (the dismissal of the operators) and the
higher productivity of, and leadership roles assumed by, the replacement
operators. In addition, the relaxation of supervisory control in phase 3
may have been the *result* of higher productivity, not its cause.

Carey asserts that the Western Electric researches were characterized
by "gross error and incompetence."[146] The researchers misinterpreted
the data, failed to establish sample groups representative of some larger
population, ignored the systematic use of control groups, and rested
their conclusions on the statistically unreliable findings of a study of only
five operators. As a result, Carey contends, "the limitations of the
Hawthorne studies clearly render them incapable of yielding serious support for any sort of generalization whatever."[147]

Franke and Kaul offer a somewhat more dispassionate and systematic
critique than that of Carey. These critics focus on the measured variables
of the first relay assembly test room—rest pauses, hours of the working
days, days in the working week, and the small-group incentive plan—as
well as the inadvertent changes caused by the replacement of two operators (conceptualized à la Carey as an exercise of managerial discipline)
and the onset of the Great Depression. These variables are used in time-

series regression analysis to determine their explanatory power regarding the quantity and quality of work for both the group and individual members of the group.

For group productivity, the variables listed account for 97 percent of the variance in hourly and weekly output, and the exercise of managerial discipline bears the strongest relationship to both measures of group output. For the quality of group output, a measure of the quality of the materials provided to the work group was added, and the resulting equation accounted for 92 percent of the variance. Similar results were found for individuals, in which case, the percentage of variance explained ranged from 66 to 90 percent for hourly output, from 89 to 95 percent for weekly output, and from 56 to 98 percent for quality of output.

The authors conclude that managerial discipline, the depression, and the rest pauses account for most of the variance in the quantity and quality of output in the first relay assembly test room.[148] These equations, the authors argue, are so strong that the impact of other factors, such as the social conditions emphasized but not measured by the Western Electric researchers, was likely to have been negligible.[149] Indeed, the findings suggest that it was not a relaxation of oppressive supervision but its reassertion that was the primary factor in improving the performance of the workers.[150]

To summarize, the critics charge that the research at Western Electric was superficial, missed the point, originated in the personal biases of the researchers, was deliberately formulated to favor one group over another, and was methodologically naive.[151]

Conclusion

These critiques constitute a potentially devastating attack on Mayo's work. Nevertheless, the critiques themselves are not definitive, and rejoinders are both possible and appropriate.

In regard to the ideological critiques, it is clear that Mayo assumed a harmony of interests in the community and in the organization. His critics merely propose an alternative assumption—an inevitable conflict of interests—rather than presenting evidence to contradict Mayo's assumption. Mayo may have been unfair in branding the assumption of a conflict of interest as "obsessive." Indeed, his own stance, and the tenacity with which he maintained it, would appear to be no less obsessive. But the burden of proof regarding this critical assumption is as great for his critics as it is for Mayo.

Mayo would also deny that he had a bias in favor of management. He repeatedly stated that he had no intrinsic interest in increased productivity.[152] Productivity is only a measure of the worker's capacity to sustain interest in work under a variety of conditions and an indicator of the performance of the human organism. Thus, Mayo's concern was human behavior in general, not its particular manifestation in productivity.

Turning to the empirical critiques, the critics first argue that Mayo understates the role of financial incentives in motivating behavior. But Mayo did not claim that financial incentives were unimportant. He did say that such incentives will have the expected effect only when acting on an appropriate social situation. The differing results in the first relay assembly test room and in the bank-wiring room would seem to support this assertion: in the former setting, financial incentives were associated with higher output in a supportive social environment, while in the latter, incentives failed to elicit higher productivity without supportive social norms. In addition, subsequent research supports Mayo's position that the effect of financial incentives is mediated by psychological and social "filtering" processes.[153] Finally, it should be noted that Franke and Kaul failed to find evidence of a substantial independent influence for incentives on performance in the relay assembly test room.[154]

The empirical critique related to supervisory style is more troublesome. It is apparent that supervision in the relay assembly test room was not as benign as Mayo and his associates suggested. Yet Mayo was more concerned with the broader social environment of the work than with supervision per se. This broader scope is evidenced, for instance, by the fact that the Western Electric researches shifted in emphasis from supervision to the social group in the interview period and maintained that focus in the bank-wiring room study. Nor is Franke and Kaul's assertion that the explanatory power of their "measured" variables precludes a role for other social factors convincing. If the regression model is insufficiently specified and excludes variables closely related to the variables included, the observed relationships may be spurious, or the variables examined may simply be "intervening" variables—that is, they are effective only on prior conditions. In short, Mayo may have been wrong about supervision in this particular instance, but right on the effects of supportive social conditions, which he thought could be created by friendly and sympathetic supervision.

The more general empirical critique of Mayo's work is that it did not fulfill the requirements of controlled experimentation. This criticism must be considered in the broader context of Mayo's approach to scientific investigation and his objectives in the investigations he conducted. Mayo considered his work, including the research at Western Electric, to be exploratory in nature.[155] In addition, his approach was more one of "clinical observation" than of laboratory experimentation. Experiment and logic, according to Mayo, must follow, not precede, observation—by which one acquires the appropriate "knowledge-of-acquaintance."

The effort at controlled experimentation in the Western Electric researches was abandoned during the rest-pause experiments at about the time that Mayo became more involved in the studies. From that point on, the research no longer focused on single variables but moved to the broader constellation of social factors in the work environment. The investigations lost some precision in the process, but Mayo believed this loss to be inevitable. Discussing his later study in Southern California, he stated: "Our concern was with significant approximations rather than complete accuracy; complete accuracy can be had only in mathematics; in factual determination an approximation is the best that can be achieved." [156] Placing his emphasis on "habitual, intuitive familiarity with the data," Mayo was impatient with what he considered to be a vain pursuit of quantification and experimental controls. In Mayo's words, "the poor observer … continues dogmatically onward with his original thesis, lost in a maze of correlations, long after the facts have shrieked in protest against the interpretation put upon them." [157] In short, Mayo was prepared, when necessary, to sacrifice illusory precision for real understanding.

Nevertheless, the foregoing considerations do not entirely absolve Mayo of his scientific responsibilities. The weaknesses in the research design and methodology employed by Mayo throughout his empirical investigations make his work subject to question and his speculative interpretations of that work subject to controversy. [158] The Western Electric researches, in particular, embodied a progression of unanticipated outcomes and interpretations based on mere surmise as to why the expected did not occur. What ended up being the primary concern in the investigations—conditions in the social group—were never systematically examined.

These methodological ambiguities, in turn, leave Mayo open to the charge that he merely discovered what he was looking for in his empirical studies, based on previously held beliefs. Thus Mayo may have fallen prey to his own criticism of the "crowd psychologists," of whom he wrote: "Their opinion of humanity is determined before the discussion begins; they seek only indications that fortify or 'rationalize' their preconceived ideas." [159]

Mayo also remains vulnerable to the charge that his work has a pro-management bias, regardless of his intentions. Although Mayo's emphasis changes from the individual to the social group in his empirical investigations, the "maladjusted" individual remains the source of the industrial problem. Thus, it is the individual who is to be "cured" under the benevolent and informed guidance of a managerial and administrative elite. No wonder that Taylorism, which did pay attention to the "human factor in industry," was eclipsed by Mayo's Human Relations movement.[160] Managers did not care for sharing authority and liked much better the idea that their authority was strengthened through seemingly nonauthoritarian means.

Mayo's story of an encounter with a young radical is, perhaps, instructive in regard to the nature of the cure. The radical "suffered" from resistance to authority, which was the product of an unhappy relationship with his drunken father. After therapeutic counseling, the young man lost interest in his radical activities, abandoned his former associates, took a clerical position, and kept it.[161] In short, the cure was an accommodation to authority, which some might consider obeisance. One is reminded of Clark Kerr's protest that management should buy the labor power of the worker and leave his psyche alone.[162]

For Mayo, the question is not who is to control, but whether control will be exercised on a rational basis.[163] But this pronouncement simply evades a fundamental issue and admits the possibility of the manipulation of the individual to serve the purposes of management. Mayo's primary concern may not have been improved productivity, but the techniques he offers have a substantial manipulative potential, whether for ill or for good.

Despite these reservations, Mayo's ideas have had an undeniable impact on the study of organizations, and his work has been translated into Arabic, German, Italian, Japanese, and Spanish. Mayo's attention to defining his underlying assumptions and exploring the broader implications of his studies is refreshing in a field that has become dismayingly bereft of such considerations. One does not have to agree with Mayo's position to appreciate the fact that critical issues are raised and examined in his works. Moreover, Mayo's work was largely responsible for a major shift in the study of organizations. His concern with the attitudes and sentiments of the worker, the importance he attached to the social group in determining individual behavior, and his search for "knowledge-of-acquaintance" based on direct observation, all served as inspiration for a succeeding generation of scholars. Especially from the 1960s on, Mayo's attention to group leadership, informal relations, and so forth, resurfaces in the study of organizational culture and climate.

NOTES

1. Information on Mayo's life, except where otherwise noted, is taken from George F. F. Lombard, "George Elton Mayo," *Dictionary of American Biography*, supplement 4, 1946–50 (New York: Scribner's, 1974), 564–566. More biographical information can be found in Richard C. S. Trahair, *The Humanist Temper: The Life and Work of Elton Mayo* (New Brunswick, N.J.: Transaction, 1984); and J. H. Smith, "The Enduring Legacy of Elton Mayo," *Human Relations* 51 no. 3 (1998): 221–249.

2. See James Hoopes, "Managing a Riot: Chester Barnard and Social Unrest," *Management Decision* 40, no. 10 (2002): 1014.

3. Elton Mayo, *Democracy and Freedom: An Essay in Social Logic* (Melbourne, Australia: Macmillan, 1919).

4. It may appear odd that Mayo was appointed chair of philosophy when he did not have a PhD. However, it was then possible in England and Australia to occupy such a position without a doctoral degree as long as a sufficient body of work justified the appointment. The custom of not requiring a PhD for career advancement reflected the fact that research productivity was considered more important. Indeed, it would have seemed improper to have mid-career people who were academically and professionally well-established submitting their work for external judgment by a (sometimes whimsical) doctoral committee.

5. It is intriguing to note that Harvard's president, A.L. Lowell, had resisted Mayo's appointment for over a year, and that he was initially hired for a four-year term on the condition that he be supported by corporate grants. For almost twenty years, Mayo was supported by grants from the Rockefeller Foundation. See Ellen S. O'Connor, "The Politics of Management Thought: A Case Study of the Harvard Business School and the Human Relations School," *Academy of Management Review* 24, no. 1 (1999): 122–123.

6. "The Fruitful Errors of Elton Mayo," *Fortune* 34, no. 5 (November 1946): 181.

7. Elton Mayo, *The Human Problems of an Industrial Civilization* (New York: Viking, 1960).

8. See Michael Roper, "Masculinity and the Biographical Meanings of Management Theory: Lyndall Urwick and the Making of Scientific Management in Britain," *Gender, Work and Organization* 8, no. 2 (2001): 200. See also Smith, "Enduring Legacy of Elton Mayo," 238.

9. See F.J. Roethlisberger, *The Elusive Phenomena: An Autobiographical Account of My Work in the Field of Organizational Behavior at the Harvard Business School* (Boston: Division of Research, Graduate School of Business Administration, Harvard University; distributed by Harvard University Press, 1977). See also Kevin T. Mahoney and David B. Baker, "Elton Mayo and the Carl Rogers: A Tale of Two Techniques," *Journal of Vocational Behavior* 60 (2002): 442; J.H. Smith, "Elton Mayo and the Hidden Hawthorne," *Work, Employment & Society* 1, no. 1 (1987): 111; and Smith, "Enduring Legacy of Elton Mayo," 236.

10. Elton Mayo, *The Social Problems of an Industrial Civilization* (Boston: Graduate School of Business Administration, Harvard University, 1945).

11. Elton Mayo, *The Political Problems of an Industrial Civilization* (two lectures delivered at a conference on Human Relations and Administration, Harvard University Graduate School of Business Administration, May 10–11, 1947).

12. Roethlisberger, *Elusive Phenomenon*, 50, 51.

13. Mayo, *Human Problems*, ix.

14. Roethlisberger, *Elusive Phenomenon*, 50–52.

15. Ibid., 30.

16. Mayo, *Social Problems*, 16.

17. Roethlisberger, *Elusive Phenomenon*, 36.

18. See Smith, "Enduring Legacy of Elton Mayo," 246.

19. Elton Mayo, "The Great Stupidity," *Harper's Magazine* 151 (July 1925): 230–231.

20. Mayo, *Political Problems*, 6.

21. Elton Mayo, "Civilization—The Perilous Adventure," *Harper's Magazine* 149 (October 1924): 590.

22. Elton Mayo, "Routine Interaction and the Problem of Collaboration," *American Sociological Review* 4, no. 3 (June 1939): 335.

23. Mayo, *Social Problems*, 41.

24. Elton Mayo, "The Maladjustment of the Industrial Worker," in *Wertheim Lectures on Industrial Relations, 1928* (Cambridge, Mass.: Harvard University Press, 1929), 172.

25. Mayo, *Political Problems*, 20.

26. Mayo, *Democracy and Freedom*, 5.

27. Mayo, *Human Problems*, 116.

28. Mayo, *Democracy and Freedom*, 65.

29. Ibid., 20.

30. Ibid., 27.

31. Mayo, *Human Problems*, 123–124.

32. Ibid., 158.

33. Ibid., 125.

34. Elton Mayo, "Irrationality and Revery," *Personnel Journal* 1, no. 10 (1923): 481.

35. Mayo, "Great Stupidity," 230.

36. Ibid., 233.

37. Elton Mayo, "Psychiatry and Sociology in Relation to Social Disorganization," *American Journal of Sociology* 42 (May 1937): 830.

38. Ibid.

39. Mayo, "Civilization," 594.

40. Elton Mayo, "Sin with a Capital 'S,'" *Harper's Magazine* 154 (April 1927): 544.

41. Elton Mayo, "Civilized Unreason," *Harper's Magazine* 148 (March 1924): 530.

42. Ibid.

43. Mayo, *Democracy and Freedom*, 37.

44. Obviously, Mayo was not original in claiming this anomie. Indeed, the notion of "social man," while often attributed to Mayo, was well-established in the sociological literature since Durkheim. See James C. Dingley, "Durkheim, Mayo, Morality and Management," *Journal of Business Ethics* 16 (1997): 1118.

45. Mayo, "Great Stupidity," 231.

46. Mayo, *Human Problems*, 174.

47. Mayo, "Civilization," 591.

48. Mayo, "Maladjustment of the Industrial Worker," 170; and *Human Problems*, 162.

49. Mayo, "Maladjustment of the Industrial Worker," 171.

50. Ibid., 194.

51. Mayo, *Human Problems*, 162.

52. Elton Mayo, "What Every Village Knows," *Survey Graphic* 26, no. 12 (December 1937): 696.

53. See James L. Garnett, "Trends and Gaps in the Treatment of Communication in Organization and Management Theory," in *Handbook of Adminis-*

trative Communication, ed. James L. Garnett and Alexander Kouzmin (New York: Marcel Dekker, 1997), 34; Pasi Pyöriä, "Information Technology, Human Relations and Knowledge Work Teams," *Team Performance Management* 11, nos. 3–4 (2005): 105; and O'Connor, "Politics of Management Thought," 128.

54. Mayo, "What Every Village Knows," 697.
55. Mayo, "Great Stupidity," 233.
56. Mayo, *Democracy and Freedom*, 47.
57. Ibid., 38.
58. Ibid., 12.
59. Both quotations in O'Connor, "Politics of Management Thought," 127, referencing Elton Mayo, "Industrial Peace and Psychological Research, III: The Mind of the Agitator," 111, and "Industrial Peace and Psychological Research, IV: The Will of the People," 159–160, *Industrial Australian and Mining Standard* 67 (1922).
60. As quoted in Smith, "Enduring Legacy of Elton Mayo," 223.
61. Mayo, "Maladjustment of the Industrial Worker," 167.
62. O'Connor, "Politics of Management Thought," 125, referencing Mayo's *Democracy and Freedom*, 19.
63. Manfred Moldaschl and Wolfgang G. Weber, "The 'Three Waves' of Industrial Group Work: Historical Reflections on Current Research on Group Work," *Human Relations* 51, no. 3 (1998): 354.
64. O'Connor, "Politics of Management Thought," 124–125.
65. Mayo, *Democracy and Freedom*, 58; and "Great Stupidity," 229, 231.
66. O'Connor, "Politics of Management Thought," 125, referencing Mayo's *Democracy and Freedom*, 57.
67. Mayo, "Great Stupidity," 231.
68. Mayo, "Irrationality and Revery," 481.
69. Mayo, "Psychiatry and Sociology," 829.
70. Mayo, "Great Stupidity," 230.
71. Mayo, *Democracy and Freedom*, 73.
72. Ibid.
73. Elton Mayo, "Research in Human Relations," *Personnel* 16, no. 4 (1941): 267–268.
74. Mayo, "Civilization," 590–591.
75. Mayo, "Social Problems," 19.
76. Mayo, "Maladjustment of the Industrial Worker," 191.
77. Mayo, "Great Stupidity," 226.
78. Mayo, *Democracy and Freedom*, 57.
79. Mayo, "Maladjustment of the Industrial Worker," 195.
80. Mayo, "Civilization," 593.
81. Mayo, "Sin with a Capital 'S,'" 545.
82. Mayo, "Irrationality and Revery," 483.
83. Mayo, *Social Problems*, 9.
84. Ibid., 11.
85. Mayo, *Democracy and Freedom*, 70.
86. This research is reported in Elton Mayo, "Revery and Industrial Fatigue," *Personnel Journal* 3, no. 8 (December 1924): 273–281.
87. Ibid., 274.
88. Ibid., 281; Mayo, "Maladjustment of the Industrial Worker," 184.
89. Mayo, "Revery and Industrial Fatigue," 280.

90. Ibid., 279.
91. Ibid., 281.
92. Mayo, "What Every Village Knows," 696.
93. Mayo, *Social Problems*, 67.
94. For a comprehensive report of this study, see F.J. Roethlisberger and William J. Dickson, *Management and the Worker* (Cambridge, Mass.: Harvard University Press, 1939). For a more recent study, see Richard Gillespie, *Manufacturing Knowledge: A History of the Hawthorne Experiments* (New York: Cambridge University Press, 1991).
95. Roethlisberger and Dickson, *Management and the Worker*, 14–18. See also Frank Merrett, "Reflections on the Hawthorne Effect," *Educational Psychology* 26, no. 1 (2006): 143–146, regarding the early illumination experiments.
96. Roethlisberger, *Elusive Phenomenon*, 48, 49.
97. Ibid., 48.
98. This association was never very formal. True to Mayo's personal predilections, the collaboration was spontaneous, with no formal contracts or agreements. See ibid.
99. Ibid., 39.
100. For another detailed description of the relay assembly test room and the bank-wiring observation room experiments, see George C. Homans, "The Western Electric Researches," in *Readings on Modern Organizations*, ed. Amitai Etzioni (Englewood Cliffs, N.J.: Prentice-Hall, 1969), 99–114. It is interesting to note that Homans worked for Mayo prior to the war.
101. Roethlisberger, *Elusive Phenomenon*, 54.
102. Ibid., 87.
103. Ibid.
104. Ibid., 127, 117.
105. Ibid.
106. Ibid., 129–134.
107. Ibid., 134–158.
108. Ibid., 158.
109. In this case, random selection of the participants was attempted. However, only two of those selected wished to participate in the experiment. Ibid., 136.
110. The interpretation of the results of this experiment was complicated by the fact that the operators were also required to work overtime. Ibid., 134.
111. Ibid., 153.
112. Ibid., 156.
113. Ibid., 160.
114. Mayo, *Human Problems*, 92.
115. Ibid., 83. Usually, the appreciation and condemnation of the Hawthorne research is based on the relay assembly test room experiments. Much less attention, if any at all, is given to these interviews aimed at developing better understanding of industrial conflict in relation to better understanding of human nature—that is, insight into the "total situation" of workers, including their emotions, private lives, values, and so on. Indeed, Mayo's *Management and the Worker* was primarily focused on that topic, and not on the early experiments. Note that Taylor also had observed the importance of knowing an employee's personal life in relation

to productivity. See also Augustine Brannigan and William Zwerman, "The Real 'Hawthorne Effect,'" *Society* (January–February 2001): 55–60. For more detail on the interviews by counselors, see Scott Highhouse, "The Brief History of Personnel Counseling in Industrial-Organizational Psychology," *Journal of Vocational Behavior* 55 (1999): 318–336; the quote from the employee is at 323.

116. Mayo, *Social Problems*, 84.
117. Roethlisberger and Dickson, *Management and the Worker*, 314.
118. Ibid., 379.
119. Ibid., 390.
120. Ibid., 522.
121. Ibid., 523.
122. Ibid., 520.
123. L.J. Henderson, T.N. Whitehead, and Elton Mayo, "The Effects of Social Environment," in *Papers on the Science of Administration*, ed. Luther Gulick and L. Urwick (New York: Institute of Public Administration, 1937), 156.
124. This research is reported in Elton Mayo and George F. F. Lombard, *Teamwork and Labor Turnover in the Aircraft Industry of Southern California*, vol. 31, no. 6, Business Research Studies no. 32 (Boston: Harvard University Graduate School of Business, Bureau of Business Research, October 1944).
125. Ibid., 6.
126. Ibid., 17.
127. Mayo, *Social Problems*, 100–101.
128. Mayo and Lombard, *Teamwork and Labor Turnover*, 19.
129. Ibid., 24.
130. Ibid., 28.
131. Ibid., 1.
132. For an extensive review of these critiques, see Henry A. Landsberger, *Hawthorne Revisited: Management and the Worker, Its Critics, and Developments in Human Relations in Industry* (Ithaca: New York State School of Industrial and Labor Relations, 1958).
133. See, for instance, Herbert Blumer, "Sociological Theory in Industrial Relations," *American Sociological Review* 12, no. 3 (June 1947): 273; and Reinhard Bendix and Lloyd H. Fisher, "The Perspectives of Elton Mayo," *Review of Economics and Statistics* 31 (1949): 318.
134. Landsberger, *Hawthorne Revisited*, 43–46, 51.
135. Georges Friedmann, "Philosophy Underlying the Hawthorne Investigation," *Social Forces* 28, no. 2 (December 1949): 208.
136. Landsberger, *Hawthorne Revisited*, 63.
137. Clark Kerr, "What Became of the Independent Spirit?" *Fortune* 48 (July 1953): 111.
138. W.A. Koivisto, "Value, Theory, and Fact in Industrial Psychology," *American Journal of Sociology* 58, no. 6 (May 1953): 570.
139. Bendix and Fisher, "Perspectives of Elton Mayo," 317.
140. Koivisto, "Value, Theory, and Fact in Industrial Psychology," 567.
141. Bendix and Fisher, "Perspectives of Elton Mayo," 316.
142. Kyle Bruce, "Henry S. Dennison, Elton Mayo, and Human Relations Historiography," *Management and Organizational History* 1, no. 2 (2006): 193.
143. Ibid., 177.
144. Clark Kerr, "What Became of the Independent Spirit?" 134.

145. Alex Carey, "The Hawthorne Studies: A Radical Criticism," *American Sociological Review* 32, no. 3 (June 1967): 403–416; and Richard Herbert Franke and James D. Kaul, "The Hawthorne Experiments: First Statistical Interpretation," *American Sociological Review* 43, no. 5 (October 1978): 623–643.

146. Carey, "Hawthorne Studies," 416.

147. Ibid.

148. Franke and Kaul, "Hawthorne Experiments," 636.

149. Ibid., 636–637.

150. Ibid., 636.

151. Adapted from Landsberger, *Hawthorne Revisited*, 46. The methodological quality of the Hawthorne experiments has also been questioned by Jones, who found that worker productivity levels were interdependent. See Stephen R.G. Jones, "Worker Interdependence and Output: The Hawthorne Studies Reevaluated," *American Sociological Review* 55, no. 2 (1990): 176–190; and idem, "Was There a Hawthorne Effect?" *American Journal of Sociology* 98, no. 3 (1992): 451–468.

152. See, for instance, Mayo, "Revery and Industrial Fatigue," 275–276; Henderson, Whitehead, and Mayo, "Effects of Social Environment," 146; and Elton Mayo, "Changing Methods in Industry," *Personnel Journal* 8, no. 5 (1939): 327.

153. Jon M. Shepard, "On Alex Carey's Radical Criticism of the Hawthorne Studies," *Academy of Management Journal* 14, no. 1 (March 1971): 30.

154. Franke and Kaul, "Hawthorne Experiments," 636. See also Jones, "Worker Interdependence and Output" and "Was There a Hawthorne Effect?"

155. Mayo, *Social Problems*, 128.

156. Ibid., 91.

157. Ibid., 116.

158. Bruce, "Henry S. Dennison, Elton Mayo, and Human Relations Historiography," 193.

159. Mayo, "Civilized Unreason," 529.

160. See the comparison between Dennison and Mayo in Bruce, "Henry S. Dennison, Elton Mayo, and Human Relations Historiography," 2006.

161. Mayo, "Routine Interaction and Problem of Collaboration," 337–338.

162. Kerr, "What Became of the Independent Spirit?" 136.

163. Mayo, *Human Problems*, 174.

Chapter 6

Chester Barnard:
Organizations as Systems of Exchange

In the works of Chester Barnard, we reach the culmination of the trend, noted in the writings of Follett and Mayo, toward considering authority to be cumulative in nature—that is, arising from below rather than emanating from the apex of the organizational pyramid. At the same time, Barnard provides a conceptual justification for Mayo's assertion that the organization must learn to respond to the needs of subordinates as they perceive them if it is to be effective in accomplishing its objectives. Both considerations are rooted in Barnard's conceptualization of the organization as a system of exchange.

Taking these propositions in reverse order, we can trace the idea that subordinates' needs must be satisfied as they perceive them to Barnard's view that the relationship between the individual and the organization constitutes a free contractual arrangement. The terms of the contract are expressed in an implicit or explicit agreement about what the organization will offer in the form of inducements and what will be expected of the individual in the form of contributions. This contract is subject to termination by either party if it believes that the terms of the contract are not being fulfilled. On the individual's side, participation will continue only as long as he (or she) perceives that he is receiving more from the organization than he is required to contribute. Moreover, the balance of inducements and contributions is a matter of personal and subjective evaluation by the individual. From this perspective, it is clear that the organization must respond to individuals' needs as they perceive them. Otherwise, the individual will refuse to participate further in the organization.

The assertion that authority is cumulative in nature is similarly derived from Barnard's conceptualization of the organization as a system of exchange. Barnard takes the argument a step further by asserting that the individual's response to organizational directives is a function of incentives in the organization. In brief, he asserts that the greater the perceived balance of inducements over required contributions, the more likely it is that the individual will accept organizational directives. And, once again, that balance is a matter of personal and subjective evaluation. This consideration, in turn, leads Barnard to define authority as "the character of a communication (order) in a formal organization by virtue of which it is accepted by a contributor to, or member of, the organization as governing the action he contributes." This definition suggests that authority resides not in a position but in a relationship between a superior and a subordinate, and that authority is exercised not on issuance of a command but on its acceptance. Thus, authority ultimately arises from the bottom; it does not descend from the top. This formulation helped to establish one of the basic items on the research agenda of the Behavioral approach: the problem of securing compliance to organizational authority.

Barnard made at least two other major contributions to the study of organizations. One is his assertion that organizations are, by their nature, cooperative social systems. As we shall see, Barnard derives this proposition from a series of assumptions about human nature and the reasons for association in formal organizations. A second contribution is Barnard's specification of the functions of the leader. In a literature in which leadership would soon come to be defined as little more than supervision, Barnard charges the leader with responsibilities of more heroic dimensions. Among them is the responsibility for establishing and observing a moral code in the organization and adjudicating disputes arising therefrom.

Even these groundbreaking theories fail to exhaust the list of Barnard's contributions to the study of organizations. Others include the systems concept of the organization, the focus on informal organizations, the emphasis on decision making, the attention given to nonlogical thought processes, and the focus on executive organization as a communication system.[1] This is, indeed, an impressive list, and it helps to explain why Barnard's works remain among the most widely cited in the literature.

Life

Chester Irving Barnard was born in Malden, Massachusetts, on November 7, 1886.[2] His family was one of modest means, and the home environment was "frugal but intellectual." Barnard's father, a machinist, raised young Chester and his brother after the death of his wife. Barnard had little formal religious training—the family was only loosely associated with the Congregational Church—but they often engaged in philosophical discussions, and Barnard was imbued with a New England mentality stressing "independence of mind, pragmatism, respect for the individual, and industriousness." These traits would later be reflected both in Barnard's career and in his writings.

Barnard was born nearsighted, and he had poor balance. Consequently, his involvement in the usual boyhood sports and other physical activities was limited. Instead, Barnard became a voracious reader and an accomplished pianist, and he was generally something of a loner. Because of limited family finances, Barnard was forced to go to work after completing grammar school, and he continued to work throughout his school years. While awaiting enrollment at Mount Hermon prep school,[3] Barnard worked at the school's farm; later, he supported his studies at Harvard by conducting a dance orchestra and typing theses. At Harvard, Barnard completed three years of study, majoring in economics, but his efforts fell short of a degree because of his lack of training in science and his consequent inability to master chemistry. Although Barnard never had an "earned" degree in higher education, he was eventually awarded honorary degrees by such prestigious universities as Brown, Princeton, Pennsylvania, and Rutgers.

In 1909 Barnard left Harvard to embark on what would prove to be a long and distinguished career with the Bell Telephone Company. He began in the statistics department, translating from German, French, and Italian sources to enable studies of foreign rate systems, and he soon became an expert on rate systems. In 1922 Barnard moved to Pennsylvania to become assistant to the vice president and general manager of the Bell Telephone Company of Pennsylvania; he was promoted to vice president after four years. In 1928, at the age of forty-one, he became president of the Bell Telephone Company of New Jersey.[4] Barnard left the Bell System in 1948 to assume the position of president of the Rockefeller Foundation, where he served until he reached the mandatory retirement age in 1952.[5] Barnard subsequently served as chairman of the National Science Foundation and in a variety of other public capacities, before his death on June 7, 1961.

While pursuing his main career interests, Barnard also compiled an impressive record of public service. He was the founding director of the

New Jersey Emergency Relief Fund in 1931–1932, and he filled that position again in 1935. Only days into his second term, he was forced to handle a crowd of about 2,000 people expressing anger at the state's treatment of the unemployed. At some point, the police started attacking the crowd, and what Barnard initially described as an overreaction by the police became the "riot of the unemployed"—the title he used for a lecture at Harvard University in the spring of 1938. It is alleged that this and other lectures cemented Barnard's reputation as a seminal thinker in his early years. His ideas fitted perfectly with those being developed by Mayo and colleagues at the Harvard Business School, such as the assertion that group identity and social recognition are more important organizational forces than power and money.[6]

During World War II, Barnard served as president of the United Service Organization, as director of the National War Fund, and as a member of the Naval Manpower Survey Committee. He was also assistant to the secretary of the Treasury, a consultant to the director of the Federal Office of Science Research and Development, a member of the Atomic Energy Committee, and a consultant to the American representative to the United Nations' Atomic Energy Committee. In addition, Barnard was a founder of the Bach Society of New Jersey, a participant in various youth activities, a member of the boards of several companies, and director of the National Bureau of Economic Research. He maintained memberships in the American Association for the Advancement of Arts and Sciences, the American Academy of Arts and Science, the American Philosophical Society, and the Institute of World Affairs. He also served on the first (1949) and second (1955) Hoover Committees, which were charged with studying the reorganization of the executive branch and the civil service.[7]

Barnard has been described as reserved, dignified, and somewhat awe-inspiring.[8] Unlike several of the authors discussed in this volume, he never acquired a circle of personal devotees, for he believed service, which requires "fortitude" and "adherence to principles," to be more important than popularity.[9] Barnard's record at New Jersey Bell brought only mixed reviews from his contemporaries.[10] Although he accepted several honorary degrees, he turned down a number of others, deeming them empty distinctions. Overall, one gets the impression of a somewhat distant and aloof man with a strong sense of propriety and dedication to his work. As we shall see, these are some of the attributes Barnard ascribed to the effective executive.

Considering Barnard's level of activity in other areas, it is not surprising that his publications were somewhat limited in number. He began writing in the 1920s and, over the course of his lifetime, produced some thirty-seven published articles and two books—of which, the 1938 *The*

Functions of the Executive is the most renowned.[11] It is in that study that Barnard made his most important contribution to the understanding of organizations.

The genesis of *Functions of the Executive* was somewhat ironic, given its subsequent importance. Barnard had no original intention of writing a book; the manuscript was drawn from a series of eight lectures he gave at the Lowell Institute at Harvard. Publication apparently came about as a result of the desire of Harvard University Press to do something with the Lowell lecture series, rather than because of the content of Barnard's lectures.[12] At the request of the press, Barnard undertook the arduous task of producing a publishable manuscript, attacking the problem with characteristic care and vigor. He ended up writing sixteen drafts of the manuscript and later claimed that there is "scarcely a word that has not been thoroughly weighed."[13] At the same time, he acknowledged that "the doctrine is difficult ... labored, abstract, and abstruse."[14]

Barnard disclaimed any specific intellectual heritage for the ideas and concepts in *Functions of the Executive*, stating that he did not draw ideas directly from his extensive readings nor make an attempt to put together a collection of his personal observations. In particular, he denied the intriguing possibility that there was some connection between that book and Elton Mayo's work at Western Electric. Despite some apparent links—Barnard and Mayo were acquaintances at Harvard, and Barnard worked at Bell Telephone Company while Mayo did his research at one of Bell's subsidiaries—as well as some strong parallels between Barnard's ideas and those of Mayo, Barnard said that he knew nothing of the Western Electric researches.[15]

Whatever the source of his ideas, the lasting impact of *Functions of the Executive* is indisputable. The book is one of the most widely cited in the literature on organizations and continues to have substantial influence.[16]

The Origins and Development of Organizations

Although Barnard's book is entitled *The Functions of the Executive*, his objectives in writing the book were far broader than that phrase would imply. In fact, Barnard sought to join the theory of the state and the theory of organizations and to elaborate a theory of human behavior that would go beyond its economic aspects.[17] Accordingly, he starts with some fundamental observations about society (and in a separate memo addresses how it should be studied), the nature of human behavior, and the genesis and nature of organizations in society that provide the context for his discussion of the role and functions of the executive in the organization.

Society and How to Study It

Barnard describes society as a "complex of informal organizations" in which a network of formal organizations is embedded.[18] Human beings need association, and that need calls for local activity and interaction—without which we are emotionally lost. The prime outlet for our logical or scientific faculties is purposive cooperation, which satisfies our intellectual needs. Barnard then writes, "Either small enduring informal organizations or large collectivities seem always to possess a considerable number of formal organizations. *These are the definite structural material of a society.*"[19]

Given that social reality is so complex and that studying it involves self-aware human beings, Barnard holds that the social sciences should not model themselves on the natural sciences. Even though he wrote that the social sciences had bootlegged their epistemology from the natural sciences, he believed that social scientists should focus on the generalizability (external validity) of their findings rather than on uncovering causal relations (internal validity). Indeed, he regarded the potential contribution of positivism to be limited, arguing that practitioners of the social sciences had been so enamored of natural science epistemology that they had forgotten to look for facts regarding behavior that were useful in practical management situations, including people's state of mind, attitudes, intuitions, purposes, interactions, and thoughts.[20]

Human Nature

Barnard begins with some fundamental assumptions about the nature of human beings. In his view, human beings are physically and biologically limited, social, active, and purposeful, and they possess a limited degree of free will. The first three characteristics lead to cooperative behavior in organizations: physical and biological limitations raise the necessity of cooperation if individuals are to achieve purposes beyond their own capacities, while the social nature of the human being leads to cooperation with other persons to achieve those purposes. Indeed, Barnard argues that human organisms are incapable of functioning except in conjunction with other human organisms.[21] Finally, he asserts that passive associations among humans are not durable—that they are impelled to do something. This need for purposeful activity leads to the organization of cooperative activities to achieve joint purposes. In short, given these assumptions, Barnard argues that organizations are, *by their nature*, cooperative endeavors.

Barnard's characterization of human beings as possessing free will shapes his conception of the relationship between the individual and the organization. Although Barnard assumes that humans have the power of choice, he recognizes that that power is limited. Indeed, the *limitations* on choice make choice possible, since the individual would likely be overwhelmed if confronted by a large number of alternatives.[22] Consequently, the processes of choice are, in part, techniques for narrowing the range of alternatives. The limitations on choice are imposed by physical, biological, and social factors. For instance, some alternatives may be excluded because they are simply physically impossible; others may be excluded by psychological conditioning; yet others may be excluded because of social constraints.

It is important to underline the fact that Barnard, like Simon after him, considers two major classes of limitations: those existing because of "the biological faculties or capacities of individuals *and* [those reflecting] the physical factors of the environment."[23] When discussing "limited choice," Barnard pays attention to both sets of factors—individual and environmental constraints—while Simon later increasingly focuses on modeling the bounded rationality of the individual only. A major limiting factor in the organizational setting is the definition of the organization's purpose, which helps to identify relevant alternatives. Such limitations are necessary to choice in that they describe an area in which choice can take place. Nevertheless, an irreducible minimum of free will still exists, and this characteristic makes human behavior something more than merely conditioned response.[24]

The organization attempts to influence individual behavior either by narrowing the limitations on choice or by expanding the opportunities for choice. In the first instance, the individual is regarded as an object to be manipulated; in the second, as a subject to be persuaded.[25] In either case, the individual's response is not totally predetermined. Instead, the individual has an area of choice that both grants him a degree of freedom and imposes a measure of responsibility for his actions. As we shall see, both implications are integral to Barnard's formulation of the organization and the individual's role in it.

Cooperative Activity

Based on these assumptions about the nature of human beings, Barnard traces the development of cooperative activity in organizations. In his view, cooperation originates in the need to accomplish purposes that cannot be accomplished individually. Cooperation is thus a means of overcoming limitations imposed by the physical environment or by the biological characteristics of the individual, depending on one's perspective.[26] These limitations can be overcome by cooperation, or the joining of an individual's efforts with those of others in order to accomplish a purpose. In short, cooperation arises from the existence of a purpose and the experience of limitations, and the limiting or strategic factor to be overcome is physical or biological in nature.

Once cooperation has been decided on, the limiting factor is social relationships. To survive, the system must be not only effective in achieving the cooperative purpose but also efficient in satisfying individual motives. In addition, the satisfactions received by each individual must be greater than the burdens imposed by the cooperative effort. The balancing of satisfactions and burdens is the method by which the system induces cooperative social relationships. Barnard notes that successful cooperation is not the normal situation—few cooperative ventures have withstood the ravages of time, and, at any given point in time, only a small minority of society is willing to partake in a particular cooperative enterprise.[27]

Informal Organization

The next stage in the development of an organization is the informal organization.[28] Barnard describes informal organizations as transitory in character, rather structureless in form, and involving interactions that occur without any specific joint purpose. He contends that informal organizations serve an important function, however, by establishing general understandings, customs, habits, and institutions, thus creating conditions favorable to the rise of formal organizations.[29] Furthermore, since informal organizations are essentially passive associations, and since Barnard maintains that human beings are by nature active and purposive, informal organization virtually compels some amount of formal organization.

Formal Organization

Formal organizations are distinguished from informal organizations in that cooperative efforts are conscious, deliberate, and purposeful. Barnard therefore defines the formal organization as "a system of consciously coordinated activities or forces of two or more persons."[30] It should be noted that Barnard defines formal organizations in terms of "activities" or "forces" rather than in terms of people. He reasons that since no individual is vital to the organization—that is, one person may be freely substituted for another as long as the activity is maintained—the organization is not a group of people but a series of actions designed to achieve a goal or goals. Furthermore, the activities constituting the organization are not limited to those of employees. Instead, the activities also include those of investors, customers, clients, and suppliers. Barnard does reserve the term "organization" for that part of the cooperative system from which the physical environment and the broader social environment have been excluded. Nevertheless, social elements *within* the organization are included, and, he asserts, these elements are the strategic factor in the formal organization.[31]

Complex Formal Organization

The final stage of organizational development is the complex formal organization. Barnard maintains that complex organizations grow out of simple formal organizations whose size is restricted by limits on communication.[32] Growth requires the creation of new units, but overall purpose serves as the unifying element in the complex organization. The limits of communication shape the structure of the complex organization by requiring that the subunits be specialized and relatively autonomous. The necessity of coordinated communication in a complex organization requires the location of executive functions in a single body that directs the activities of those relatively autonomous subunits by acting as a communication center. Consequently, although relatively autonomous, organizational subunits must act within the limits imposed by the larger organization.

Barnard ascribes five basic characteristics to complex formal organizations: they are systems, they are depersonalized, they are specialized, they contain informal organizations, and they make use of an environment-oriented decision process. As *systems*, complex formal organizations possess a number of significant properties. They are composed of subsidiary or partial systems and are themselves part of a larger social system that creates a series of mutual interdependencies. The organization qua system is also dynamic because of changes in the environment and the evolution of new purposes. Finally, it is vital to Barnard's analysis to note that the organization as a system is more than simply a sum of its parts.[33] This point is important for two reasons. First, the posited distinction between the system and its component parts allows Barnard to distinguish between the objectives of the cooperative system as a whole and the "motives" of individuals in the system. The distinction is also important because Barnard argues that each participant in the organization must receive more in inducements (rewards) than is given in contributions to the organization. Since individual contributions are the source of organizational inducements, each individual can receive more than is contributed only if something additional is created by the operation of the system per se. This additional element is the result of cooperative activity in the organization.

A second characteristic of complex formal organizations is that organizational activities are *depersonalized*. As noted earlier, Barnard claims that the significance of any given individual to the organization is limited, which leads him to define organizations in terms of forces or activities rather than persons. Barnard acknowledges that, outside the organization, a person is a unique individual. On joining a cooperative system, however, a person's efforts are depersonalized in the sense that the individual's activities must be determined by the needs of the system, not by individual motives.[34] Persons are thus agents, but their actions are not personal. Instead, organizational activities are guided by an acquired organizational personality, and individual motives are satisfied by the distribution of rewards in the organization.

A third characteristic of complex formal organizations is that they are *specialized*. Barnard's categorization of the bases of specialization is similar to Gulick's listing of purpose, process, clientele (materiel), and place (geography) as the bases for organizational specialization (see chapter 3). Barnard adds time and persons to Gulick's list and cautions that the several bases of specialization are mutually interdependent. Specialization by person—or "associational specialization," as Barnard calls it—is the most important addition from Barnard's perspective, given his emphasis on the social factors in organizational behavior. Barnard argues that specialized units should be composed of socially compatible persons in order to foster cooperation and minimize conflict.[35]

Nonetheless, Barnard felt that purpose is the primary aspect of specialization. Specialization by purpose involves the progressive breakdown of the overall organizational purpose or purposes into intermediate or more detailed objectives that actually constitute means of achieving the ultimate objectives of the organization. The intermediate objectives serve as a basis for organizational specialization as they are assigned to subunits and become the purpose of those subunits. Barnard contends that it is important that each member of an organizational subunit understand the purpose of that unit in order to be properly motivated. It is not necessary that each individual understand the purpose of the overall organization, however, since a requirement of intellectual understanding may be divisive.[36] It is only necessary that each individual in the organization have a belief in the ultimate purpose of the organization.[37]

A fourth characteristic of complex formal organizations is that they *contain informal organizations*. Barnard states that informal organizations always exist within formal organizations and describes them as "areas of special density" for interactions that occur without any specific joint purpose.[38] According to Barnard, informal organizations should not be viewed as simply an unavoidable evil. On the contrary, he claims that if informal organizations did not exist, they would probably have to be created, since they perform a number of functions for the organization. Informal organizations assist communication, help to maintain cohesion in the formal organization, and foster a feeling of personal integrity in the largely depersonalized environment of the formal organization.[39] In addition, informal groups create and maintain the "fiction of superior authority"—that is, the belief that authority comes from the top of the organization. By employing the word *fiction*, Barnard does not mean to imply that hierarchical authority is not real. Instead, he uses the term in the sense of an explanation for overt acts; the fiction is a belief fostered by informal group processes. The fiction of superior authority both serves as a justification for delegating organizational decisions upward and signals that the good of the organization is at stake in the exercise of authority.[40]

A fifth characteristic of complex organizations is "a technique of decision, an organizational process of thinking, which may not be analogous to that of the individual."[41] Barnard argues that organizational acts are dominated by organizational, not personal, objectives and that, consequently, *any decision has to take the objective environment into account.* This process includes attention to organizational purpose, because only an explicated point of view—one that becomes apparent through purpose or objective—will make the larger environment intelligible. It also requires attention to the external environment, which "consist[s] of atoms and molecules, agglomerations of things in motion, alive; of men and emotions; of physical laws and social laws; social ideas, norms of action, of forces and resistances."[42] This environment is constantly in flux. The decision maker constantly balances the objective environment (physical and biological limitations) with the subjective environment (perceived economic, social, and emotional factors).[43]

Barnard's Fundamental Assumptions

To summarize, Barnard makes the following points regarding the nature of the individual, the genesis of complex formal organizations, and the characteristics of complex formal organizations:

1. Humans are, by nature, physically and biologically limited, social, active, and purposeful in their behavior, and they possess an irreducible minimum of free will.

2. The existence of a purpose and the experience of individual limitations leads to cooperative activity.

3. When cooperative activity is undertaken, the strategic or limiting factor to be overcome is social in nature.

4. To survive, the cooperative system must be both effective in accomplishing its purposes and efficient in satisfying individual motives.

5. Initially, cooperation may be informal. Given the individual's active and purposeful nature, however, formal organizations are likely to arise in which cooperative activity is deliberate, conscious, and purposeful rather than spontaneous.

6. Complex formal organizations are created from simple formal organizations; the simple organizations constitute the relatively autonomous component parts of the complex formal organization.

7. Complex formal organizations are characterized by their systemic nature, depersonalized activity, specialization, the existence of informal groups, and an environment-oriented decision process.

This formulation serves as a prelude to the heart of Barnard's creative contribution to the theory of organizations: the dynamics of organizational behavior.

Organizational Dynamics

Barnard identifies three basic organizational activities: inducing a willingness to cooperate on the part of organizational participants, establishing and defining organizational purpose, and communication.[44] Inducing a willingness to cooperate involves the system of incentives within the organization and is a function of inducements offered by the organization and contributions required of the participants; its result is deference to organizational authority. Purpose is divided into two elements: first, what Barnard calls the "cooperative aspect," which is concerned with the interests of the organization as a whole; and second, the "subjective aspect," which involves individual motives.[45] Accordingly, the subjective aspect of purpose is related to the incentive system, while the cooperative aspect is related to organizational decision making. Communication, the third essential element of organizational activity, is important both in conveying the purpose of the organization and in the exercise of authority.

In the following examination of Barnard's theory of organizational dynamics, willingness to cooperate is discussed under the headings of incentives and authority; establishing and defining purpose are discussed under the headings of decision making (objective aspect) and incentives (subjective aspect); and communication is discussed under the heading of authority and in the section on executive functions.

The Incentive System

Barnard conceives of the organization as a system of exchange between the organization and each of its participants. The decision by any individual to participate in the organization involves an immediate cost: the loss of control over one's personal actions. As Barnard puts it: "The ethical ideal upon which cooperation depends requires the general diffusion of a willingness to subordinate immediate personal interests for both the ultimate personal interest and the general good."[46] Consequently, willingness to cooperate involves a personal cost-benefit calculation that is dependent on individual purposes, desires, and impulses of the moment (Barnard calls these factors "motives"). Participation in the organization is a function of the net inducements (inducements minus costs) offered by the organization compared to the net inducements afforded by alternative activities. Evaluations of inducements and costs are personal and subjective for each individual and are based on the "egotistical" motives of self-preservation and self-satisfaction.[47] Furthermore, Barnard argues that these evaluations are seldom a matter of logical thought. Having made the decision to participate in the organization, the individual's willingness to cooperate is contingent on the continuing perception of a net positive balance of inducements over required contributions. The organization is in equilibrium when all participants perceive that they are receiving more from the organization in the form of inducements than they are required to contribute.

Incentives are related to personal motives and are thus associated with personal efficiency and effectiveness and with organizational efficiency as defined by Barnard. Personal efficiency is achieved when the unsought consequences of personal behavior are unimportant or trivial—that is, when the behavior satisfies the motives of the behavior. Personal behavior is effective when a specific desired end is accomplished.[48] In either case, behavior is evaluated in terms of personal purposes and motives. Organizational efficiency, which is also defined in terms of individual motives, is achieved when the motives of individuals in the organization are fulfilled; it is a function of the capacity of an organization to offer inducements in sufficient quantity to maintain the system. Organizational effectiveness, in contrast, is not related to personal motives; it is the degree to which the purposes of the organization have been fulfilled and, as such, has no direct relevance to personal motives.[49] This definition of organizational effectiveness is predicated on Barnard's position that organizational activities are depersonalized and, consequently, that the purpose of those activities is "removed" from the individual.

Barnard's listing of inducements or incentives is quite broad and includes a number of nonmaterial incentives that he felt had previously received too little attention. Barnard divides incentives into two categories: objective incentives, which he calls the "method of incentives"; and subjective incentives, which he calls the "method of persuasion." Objective incentives may be specific or general in character. Specific objective incentives include material incentives, personal incentives, nonmaterial opportunities, physical working conditions, and "ideal benefactions," or the capacity of individuals to satisfy personal ideals such as pride of workmanship or altruistic service. General objective incentives include associational attractiveness (that is, the avoidance of personal aversions based on nationality, color, or class); adaptation of working conditions to habitual methods and attitudes; the opportunity of enlarged participation (that is, a feeling of greater participation in the course of events, or a sense of mission); and a "condition of communion," or a feeling of solidarity, social integration, and comradeship.[50]

Barnard notes that different individuals are likely to be motivated by different incentives. Consequently, organizations are never able to offer all of the objective incentives and are usually unable to offer sufficient levels of incentives even among those they command. One possible organizational response is growth, which allows the organization to increase its range and level of incentives, and Barnard identifies the desire to increase available incentives as the primary cause of growth. Another response is persuasion—Barnard argues, in effect, that if the organization does not have what the participants want, it should try to make them want what it has.[51] The subjective aspect of incentives, persuasion, is, once again, divided into a number of categories. Somewhat anomalously, Barnard includes the creation of coercive conditions among the methods of persuasion. Nevertheless, he maintains that no complex organization can operate for any length of time on the basis of coercion. A second method of persuasion is propaganda, which may entail general justifications for the organization as a whole or specific appeals in recruiting. The final method of persuasion is what Barnard terms the "inculcation of motives," by which the organization directly attempts to condition the motives of individuals and their emotional response to organizational incentives.

One aspect of the incentive system that Barnard singles out for special attention is the status system.[52] Barnard asserts that a hierarchy of positions with a gradation of honors and privileges is an important nonmaterial incentive in the organization. He defines status as "that condition of the individual that is defined by a statement of his rights, privileges, immunities, duties, and obligations in the organization and, obversely, by a statement of the restrictions, limitations, and prohibitions governing his behavior."[53] Barnard sees status systems as arising from differences in individual abilities, difficulties in performing jobs, the importance of the job performed, credentialing, and the need for the protection of the integrity of the individual. Status may be of two kinds: functional status, which is based on competence in the job performed; and scalar status, which is based on position in the organization.

Recognizing the disruptive tendencies of status systems, Barnard acknowledges that they may lead to distorted evaluations of individuals, restrict the circulation of elites because of a reluctance to deprive a person of existing status, distort the system of distributive justice by according some more than their due measure of perquisites, exaggerate the importance of administrative matters over leadership, exalt the symbolic function of status, and generally limit the adaptability of the organization. But Barnard emphasizes the positive functions that the status system can perform for the organization. Not only a form of incentive in the organization, the status system can also encourage a sense of responsibility and assist organizational communications by establishing that they are authentic (that is, they are organizationally approved), authoritative (they came from an appropriate source), and intelligible (they employ language suitable to the status of the individual addressed).

Authority

If incentives provide the basis for the willingness to cooperate, authority is its expression. It is in regard to the concept of authority that Barnard makes perhaps his most significant contribution. As noted earlier, Barnard defines authority as "the character of a communication (order) in a formal organization by virtue of which it is accepted by a contributor to, or 'member' of, the organization as governing the action he contributes; that is, as determining what he does or is not to do so far as the organization is concerned."[54] In other words, authority resides in a relationship between a superior and a subordinate, not in a position; and it is effectively exercised only when accepted, not on issuance of a command. This definition of authority springs directly from Barnard's conceptualization of the organization as a system of exchange. Since continuing participation is contingent on the assessment of a net positive balance of inducements over required contributions, the participant has the alternative of refusing to accede to organizational authority, based either on the threat of withdrawal or on actual withdrawal from the organization. As Barnard puts it: "The existence of a net inducement is the only reason for accepting *any* order as having authority."[55]

Barnard posits four conditions for the effective exercise of organizational authority, all of which emphasize the role of the subordinate in the authority relationship and the importance of effective communication.[56] First, the subordinate must understand the directive. Second, at the time of the decision regarding whether or not to accept authority, the subordinate must believe the directive to be consistent with the purpose of the organization. Third, the subordinate must believe the directive to be consistent with his or her personal interests as a whole. Fourth, the subordinate must be mentally and physically capable of complying with the directive. Given this emphasis on subordinate perception, communication will perform a key role in the exercise of authority. Added to these four conditions is the idea that authority will have to be established time and again; it is not a static property that can be wielded once invested in an "office" (that is, a particular, well-defined position in a Weberian sense).[57]

Barnard's assertions that acceptance is the critical act in the exercise of authority and that it is contingent on net inducements, as well as his listing of the conditions for the effective exercise of authority, emphasize the subjective nature of the exercise of authority and underline the possibility that authority may not be accepted. Indeed, Barnard notes that attempted exercises of authority are often ineffective and that disobedience under certain conditions may well be a moral responsibility. All of this reasoning suggests that the subordinate's response to organizational directives is not predetermined. Instead, Barnard indicates that the subordinate's response may take any of three forms: acceptance of a directive without consideration of its merits, acceptance only after consideration of the merits, and rejection.[58]

The first of these potential responses reflects what Barnard calls the "zone of indifference" and is of particular importance to the organization. Involving acceptance without consideration of merits, the zone of indifference thus constitutes an area in which orders are automatically obeyed. That is, the subordinate does not pause to examine whether the directive satisfies the conditions stated for the effective exercise of authority. Instead, directives falling within the zone of indifference involve activities that reside in a domain described by the individual's "contractual agreement" with the organization and therefore will be performed without hesitation. Barnard argues that a sizable zone of indifference among subordinates is necessary to facilitate the smooth operation of the organization.

Although Barnard emphasizes the subjective aspect of authority and admits the possibility that orders may be—and in some cases should be—disobeyed, he does not gainsay the importance of the objective aspect of authority, and he acknowledges that organizational authority is usually effective. Objective authority, or authority based on position or competence, is both present and important in the organization; and when authority of position is combined with authority of competence, it can be a very effective force. There are several reasons why organizational authority is usually effective.[59] First, the organization can increase the size of the zone of indifference and the overall zone of acceptance (and correspondingly reduce the zone of rejection) by judiciously manipulating organizational incentives and employing persuasive techniques. Second, to the extent that directives fall within the range of duties anticipated at the time the individual joined the organization, those directives are likely to be in the individual's zone of indifference and perceived as a "contractual obligation." Third, orders are not usually given unless they conform to the four conditions outlined by Barnard. Finally, informal group attitudes tend to buttress the exercise of organizational authority. Since authority is necessary to organizational survival, Barnard argues that all participants have a stake in preserving organizational authority. Consequently, informal group influences are likely to maintain and stabilize the individual's zone of indifference. In addition, informal group attitudes foster the previously mentioned "fiction of superior authority," or the belief that authority comes down from above.

Decision Making

Decision making is an integral function in the organization, being both the means by which the purpose of the organization is related to the organization's environment and the means by which purpose is translated into organizational action. Barnard defines decisions as "acts of individuals ... which are the result of deliberation, calculation, and thought ... involving the ordering of means to ends."[60]

According to Barnard, there are two major categories of decisions: personal decisions and organizational decisions. Personal decisions are decisions about whether or not to participate in the organization; they have already been discussed in reference to the incentive system.[61] Barnard says personal decisions are made outside the organization and cannot be delegated, since they are subjective in nature. Furthermore, as indicated earlier, personal decisions are not likely to be the product of logical thought.

Organizational decisions, in contrast, are decisions that are dominated by organizational purpose, not personal considerations, and are developed as a logical sequence of events.[62] As such, Barnard argues that organizational decisions can, and should, be delegated. Organizational decisions are best made at communication centers by executives who specialize in organizational decision making. This process assures both that requisite information is brought to bear on the decision and that organizational decisions are appropriately coordinated. Organizational decisions, in contrast to personal decisions, are also the product of logical thought. This does not mean that organizational decisions are necessarily correct, for factual premises and reasoning may be faulty. But Barnard argues that the logical processes of discrimination, analysis, and choice are required. Indeed, Barnard maintains that the deliberate adaptation of means to ends is the essence of formal organization.[63]

Organizational decisions consist of two elements: the organization's purpose, or the "moral" element; and the "opportunistic" element, which involves finding what circumstances are significant with reference to the organization's purpose. Barnard takes the moral element or purpose of the organization as given at the time of the decision.[64] As such, organizational purpose is part of the "environment" of decision making, which also includes the physical world, the social world, external objects and forces, and circumstances of the moment. Organizational decisions are intended to adjust the purpose of the organization to the other aspects of the decision environment; purpose enables the decision maker to discriminate between the relevant and irrelevant elements of the decision environment.

The relevant elements of the decision environment consist of strategic factors and complementary factors. The identification of these factors constitutes the opportunistic element of organizational decision making. Strategic factors (or limiting factors) are those conditions of the environment that, if changed or absent, would not prevent the organization from accomplishing its purposes. Complementary factors are environmental conditions that would have to remain unchanged for the manipulation of strategic factors to accomplish the purposes of the organization.[65] Strategic factors are the key to organizational decision making. The act of decision entails choosing an appropriate action or set of actions to manipulate the strategic factors. Once a strategic factor has been identified and some action has been chosen to deal with it, the organizational purpose is reduced to a more specific level; a search is then instituted for a new strategic factor, and a new decision process is initiated. This process continues until all strategic factors have been identified and decisions have been made to deal with them. Thus, the opportunistic element of decision making consists of constructing means-ends chains in which purpose is defined and redefined with increasing degrees of specificity and of selecting means to accomplish the organizational purposes.

The processes of decision making in the organization are, according to Barnard, necessarily specialized. Decisions made at the upper levels of the organization relate more to the ends of the organization, and those at the lower level more to the means to achieve those ends. In addition, executive communication centers that specialize in decision making are established in the organization. Consequently, the efforts of most individuals in the organization are guided by decisions that, in part, are made by organizational executives who, according to Barnard, act "impersonally"—that is, their decisions are dominated by organizational objectives.[66] As a result, although the decision processes of the organization are logical, they are not necessarily the product of the logical processes of all individuals in the organization. Many of the actions of individuals in the organization are habitual and repetitive responses to the design of the organization and to decisions made elsewhere.

Once a decision is made, it results either in an order about something to be done or not done, or in no communication for the time being. However, the decision may also be "not to decide." Of this possibility,

Barnard writes, "This is a most frequent decision, and from some points of view probably the most important." He next observes that "*the fine art of executive decision consists in not deciding questions that are not now pertinent, in not deciding prematurely, in not making decisions that cannot be made effective, and in not making decisions that others should make.*"[67]

Though Barnard emphasizes the logical character of organizational decision making, he also recognizes the necessity of what he calls "nonlogical processes," particularly in regard to executive decision making. Logical processes involve "conscious thinking" or reasoning that "could be expressed in words, or other symbols."[68] Nonlogical processes, in contrast, cannot be expressed in words or as reasoning; they are made known only by judgment, decision, or action. It is worthwhile to quote Barnard at some length on this distinction:

> Nonlogical mental processes run all the way from the unreasoning determination not to put the hand in the fire twice, to the handling of a mass of experience or a complex of abstractions in a flash. We could not do any work without this kind of mental process. Some of it is so unexplainable that we call it "intuition." A great deal of it passes under the name of "good judgment." Some of it is called "inspiration" and occasionally it is the "stroke of genius." But most of it is called "sense," "good sense" or "common sense," "judgment" or the "bright idea."[69]

Building upon Pareto's idea that nonlogical motives drive history's institutions, Barnard observes that "decision does not occur without most of its processes lying permanently below the level of consciousness, i.e., except as these processes are responsive or intuitive in character."[70]

The process employed in organizational decision making depends on three factors: the purpose of the decision, the speed required in making the decision, and the quality of the information available to the decision maker. Barnard maintains that if the purpose of the decision process is to ascertain truth, the process itself must be logical; if the purpose is to determine a course of action, too many intangibles are likely to be involved and so the process cannot be totally logical; if the purpose is persuasion, the process requires rationalization but is ultimately nonlogical in character. The second factor determining the decision process to be employed is the speed required in making the decision: if time is short, logical processes cannot be employed. Finally, the process of decision making used is a function of the quality of the information available to the decision maker. Precise information permits the use of logical processes, whereas uncertainty necessitates the use of nonlogical processes. Thus, organizational decision making, to the extent that it is involved with choosing courses of action or persuasion, must be performed in a short time frame, and if based on imprecise information, will require varying degrees of nonlogical processes.

Executive Functions

Having established the groundwork by discussing the genesis of complex formal organizations, their basic characteristics, and their dynamics, Barnard next turns to his primary topic: the functions of the executive in the organization. He identifies the fundamental executive functions as the performance of processes that deal with the relationships between the system of cooperation and its environment, and the performance of processes concerned with the creation and distribution of satisfactions to organizational participants.[71] The adjustment of cooperative systems to changes in the environment and to new purposes requires the development of an executive organization; in complex organizations, the necessities of communication require the location of executive functions in a single body. The creation and distribution of satisfactions involve altering individual behavior by the inculcation of motives and the construction of incentives to achieve organizational objectives. Executives occupy centers of communication in the organization and maintain the organization's operations in a fashion analogous, according to Barnard, to the relationship between the brain and the rest of the body.

More specifically, Barnard identifies three executive functions: providing a system of communication, securing individual effort, and formulating and defining organizational purposes.[72] In order for executive decisions to be implemented, they must be appropriately communicated. Barnard posits several requirements for effective communication in the organization.[73] First, the channel of communication should be definitely known. Second, a definite formal channel of communication to each individual is required. Third, the line of communication should be as short as possible to avoid time lags. Fourth, the complete line of communication usually should be used to avoid conflicting communication. Fifth, persons serving as communication centers must have adequate competence. Sixth, the line of communication should not be interrupted when the organization is functioning. Finally, every communication should be authenticated, and status plays an important role in this regard by appropriately identifying the issuer of the communication. The provision of communication is partially a function of formal organizational design and personnel. Of even greater importance is the establishment of an informal executive organization, which both eliminates the necessity of formal orders on routine matters and expands the available means of communication through informal contacts. Thus, the executive fosters cooperation through formal and—more importantly—informal means.[74]

Securing essential services requires both bringing people into the organization by use of the techniques of propaganda and persuasion, and then eliciting their contributions. The latter function involves the maintenance of morale, the maintenance of a system of inducements, the maintenance of a scheme of deterrents, supervision, control, inspection, education, and the provision of appropriate training.

The formulation and definition of purpose, although primarily an executive function, is a shared responsibility. Overall objectives are initially established at the executive level. But the process of formulating objectives, according to Barnard, is an iterative process in which communication passes up and down the chain of command to report difficulties and accomplishments. Accordingly, purpose may be redefined and modified throughout the organization. In this sense, organizational purpose is less a formal statement than an aggregate of actions. In Barnard's words, organizational purpose is a "residuum of decisions ... resulting in closer approximations to concrete acts."[75] Responsibility for general long-run decisions is delegated upward, while responsibility for definition and action resides at the base of the organization, within the constraints imposed by executive decisions.

To perform these functions adequately, the executive must have a sense of the total organization and of the organizational environment. This understanding, Barnard argues, is more a matter of art than of science, more aesthetic than logical. In his responsibility for the total organization, the executive must be concerned with both organizational effectiveness and efficiency. At the organizational level, effectiveness is primarily a matter of integrating technologies so that the organization achieves its objectives, while organizational efficiency is more personal than technological. The executive must coordinate four economies in the organization: the material economy; social relationships that are either external or internal to the organization, and personal economies.[76] The sum of these four economies is the organizational economy, whose entirety cannot be captured in a mere financial statement because it ignores the personal and social considerations vital to the organization. The only valid statement of the status of the organizational economy is the success or failure of the organization itself, and the maintenance of that overall economy is the responsibility of the executive because only the executive has the necessary perspective to accomplish the task.

Leadership

Because one is an executive does not necessarily mean that he or she is a leader—the former status rests on position, the latter on function. Barnard defines leadership as "the power of individuals to inspire cooperative personal decisions by creating faith,"[77] or, "the quality of behavior of individuals whereby they guide people or their activities in organized effort."[78] Since Barnard maintains that executive capacity in the form of leadership is the most important strategic factor in human cooperation, a major task of the organization is to see that those in executive positions are indeed leaders.

Barnard lists five qualities of leaders: vitality and endurance, decisiveness, persuasiveness, responsibility, and intellectual capacity. He then singles out two—responsibility and intellectual capacity—for special attention.[79] The focus on intellectual capacity is interesting because Barnard purposely relegates it to fifth place on his list of qualities. Barnard apparently has fairly low regard for intellectuals, who, he alleges, tend to be irresponsible (that is, absentminded and nonpunctual), nondecisive, and nonpersuasive (that is, a little "queer" and not interested in people).[80] In short, intellectual preparation tends to inhibit the development of the very qualities deemed indispensable to leadership. Consequently, Barnard argues that leaders are more found than trained. As for the education of leaders, it should be general in nature and aimed at teaching the individual how further to educate himself.[81] Education should also convey an understanding of human relations, an appreciation of nonlogical behavior, and an appreciation of formal organizations as evolving organic systems.[82]

Responsibility, in contrast to formal education, is vital to leadership. Barnard asserts that responsibility derives from the existence of a moral code; he defines morals as "personal forces or propensities of a general and stable character which tend to inhibit, control, or modify inconsistent, immediate, specific desires, impulses, or interests, and to intensify those which are consistent with those propensities."[83] But morality by itself does not imply responsibility. Responsibility comes when a moral code actually governs individual behavior. Thus, it is possible for a person to be moral but not responsible, although a person cannot be responsible without a moral code.[84]

Barnard argues that organizations create their own moral codes. An individual code for organizational behavior derived from the organization's moral code is one aspect of the organizational personality. A condition of organizational responsibility is present when the organization's moral code governs the individual's behavior in the organization. Barnard notes that individual and organizational moral codes sometimes conflict, and that, more frequently, there is conflict among the several moral codes of the organization itself. Furthermore, moral complexity with a high potential for internal conflict is likely under conditions of high physical and social activity.

Executive Responsibility

This line of reasoning brings us to executive responsibility. Barnard contends that executives are, necessarily, highly active. As a result, the executive, faced with a condition of moral complexity, must have a high capacity for responsibility. In addition, the executive must possess a faculty for creating moral standards and resolving conflicts among moral codes. Accordingly, Barnard defines executive responsibility as the capacity of leaders to establish ideals by which "they are compelled to bind the wills of men to the accomplishment of purposes beyond their immediate ends, beyond their times."[85]

This leadership potential depends on the ability of the executive to establish an organizational moral code that guides individuals in the pursuit of organizational objectives. The creation of moral codes for the organization and the adjudication of moral conflicts are, thus, key functions of the executive.[86] An internalized sense of organizational morality counteracts the centrifugal forces of individual interests in the organization; organizations survive in direct proportion to the extent to which individual behavior is governed by a sense of organizational morality.

Morality and a condition of responsibility are not substitutes for the other elements of the organization, but they are necessary if those other elements are to be effective. As Barnard puts it, "the quality of leadership, the persistence of its influence, the durability of its related organizations, the power of the coordination it incites, all express the height of moral aspirations, the breadth of moral foundations."[87]

Conclusion

Barnard's observations on complex formal organizations may be summarized as follows:

1. The complex formal organization constitutes a free contractual arrangement between the organization and each of its participants.

2. The system of incentives serves to satisfy individual motives and wed individual efforts to the accomplishment of organizational objectives.

3. Since the organization constitutes a free contractual relationship from which participants may withdraw if they perceive that the terms of the contract have not been fulfilled, authority resides in the relationship between a superior and a subordinate and is exercised only on consent of the subordinate.

4. Communication plays a key role in the organization both in terms of the exercise of authority and in conveying the purpose of the organization.

5. Organizational, as opposed to individual, decision processes are necessarily logical in character. Furthermore, decision making is a specialized activity in which primary responsibility is assigned to the executives who act as communication centers.

6. Executive organization is a natural outgrowth of organizational development. Executives are responsible for providing a system of communication, securing individual efforts, and defining organizational purposes.

7. Organizational leadership requires both the adoption of a personal moral code, which governs the behavior of the executive, and the creation and inculcation of an organizational moral code, which serves as a standard of behavior throughout the organization.

Barnard's impact on the study of organizations is undeniable.[88] Nonetheless, his writings have been a source of some controversy, centering on the role of management in the organization. Barnard has been accused both of suggesting the repeal of traditional managerial prerogatives and of being an apologist for management.[89] Substantial arguments can be marshaled on both sides of the dispute.

On the one hand, it is clear that Barnard's conceptualization of the organization as a system of exchange, the definition of authority he derived from that conceptualization, and the dynamics of the organizational process he described impose constraints on the arbitrary exercise of hierarchical authority. The exchange model embodies the notion of a contractual arrangement between the organization and its participants that is subject to termination by either party if its terms are not fulfilled. The value of the inducements and contributions involved in that exchange is determined by the personal and subjective assessment of each participant in the organization. In this context, authority does not reside in a hierarchical position but in a relationship between a superior and a subordinate, and it is not exercised on issuance of a directive but on its acceptance by a subordinate.

The exercise of authority is further limited by the condition that the subordinate perceive the directive to be compatible with his or her own interests and with the interests of the organization. Furthermore, the specification of organizational objectives is an iterative process involving communication traveling up and down the chain of command in which hierarchical controls and centralized planning are limited by constraints on information and analytical capabilities. As a consequence, nonhierarchical controls in the form of multilateral, spontaneous coordination are a fundamental requirement for the effectiveness of the organization, and Barnard counsels that maximum practical decentralization be exercised in the organization.

On the other hand, Barnard exalts the organization beyond any individual in it, and cooperation is to be in the service of organizational objectives. Actions are to be determined by the needs of the organization, not by individual motives, and decisions are to be dominated by organizational objectives. Organizational behavior is "depersonalized," as an organizational personality is to be substituted for an individual identity. Executives are assigned primary responsibility for formulating organizational objectives, while subordinates are expected only to believe in the existence of a common purpose, not to possess an "intellectual understanding" of that purpose. Conflict is seen as short-term and nearsighted and is to be controlled by grouping like-minded individuals. Individuals are ascribed a measure of free will, but, because individuals are seldom rational, the techniques of persuasion are to be employed to encourage participants to value the inducements the organization has to offer, and coercion can be employed for short periods of time, if necessary. Although organizational directives can be rejected, the organization is to do what it can to enlarge the subordinate's zone of indifference so that directives will be accepted without question. Informal groups, instead of being a necessary evil, can support the exercise of hierarchical authority by encouraging a belief in the "fiction of superior authority."

In sum, while Barnard argued that managers cannot manage in an authoritarian manner, he did not argue that managers cannot manage.[90] The organization may be system of exchange, but it is an asymmetrical exchange in which hierarchical superiors maintain a position of *primus inter pares*. Nevertheless, hierarchy confers only relative, not absolute, advantage in the superior-subordinate relationship, for, like Machiavelli's prince, the superior must operate within boundaries, however loosely imposed, by the necessity of securing consent. Rather than deny the existence, and desirability, of hierarchical authority, Barnard is concerned with the preconditions for its effective exercise, which requires obtaining the consent of the governed.

Though governance entails an element of consent, Barnard did not believe that this element requires the adoption of democratic procedures in the organization. In his words: "The dogmatic assertion that 'democracy' or 'democratic methods' are (or are not) in accordance with the principles here discussed is not tenable.... No doubt in many situations formal democratic processes may be an important element in the maintenance of authority, i.e., of organizational cohesion, but may in other situations be disruptive and probably never could be in themselves sufficient. On the other hand, the solidarity of some cooperative systems ... under many conditions may be unexcelled, though requiring formally autocratic processes."[91] Indeed, Barnard expressed significant reservations about democratic processes, which, he contended, are time-consuming, conflict-ridden, incapable of dealing with complex issues, and ineffective in selecting leaders on the basis of merit. To the extent that democracy is required in the organization, it is a "silent democracy" of behavior in the form of consent and cooperation that rests on an "aristocracy of leadership" to be effective.[92]

Barnard does not attempt to resolve the apparent paradoxes in the relationship between man and the organization.[93] Instead, he accepts the inevitable tensions in that relationship while seeking a balance between the needs of the individual and the needs of the organization. In Barnard's words:

Free and unfree, controlling and controlled, choosing and being chosen, inducing and unable to resist inducement, the source of authority and unable to deny it, independent and dependent, nourishing their personalities, and yet depersonalized; forming purposes and being forced to change them, searching for limitations in order to make decisions, seeking the particular, but concerned with the whole, finding leaders and denying their leadership, hoping to dominate the earth and being dominated by the unseen—this is the story of man in society told in these pages.... I believe that the expansion of cooperation and the development of the individual are mutually dependent realities, and that a due proportion or balance between them is a necessary condition of human welfare.[94]

NOTES

1. See William B. Wolf, *The Basic Barnard: An Introduction to Chester I. Barnard and His Theories of Organizational Management*, ILR Paperback no. 14 (Ithaca: New York State School of Industrial and Labor Relations, Cornell University, 1974), 3–4.
2. Material on Barnard's life is taken from Wolf, *Basic Barnard*, chap. 2. For an intellectual biography of Barnard, see William G. Scott, *Chester I. Barnard and the Guardians of the Managerial State* (Lawrence: University Press of Kansas, 1992). We still need a good biography that places Barnard's ideas in the social and intellectual environment in which he grew up. In his review of the Scott study—in *Administrative Science Quarterly* 39, no. 3 (1994): 528—Gideon Kunda argues that a more balanced or critical view of Barnard's life and work is needed. On the basis of Scott's biography, Kunda observes that Barnard's "career ... was shaped by flagrant old-boy cronyism, and his success as the CEO at New Jersey Bell is questionable. Perhaps more tantalizing for a critical biographer of the man or a student of the period are the uninterpreted hints of Barnard's distaste for Communists in the government, 'shrewd Hebrews,' and the 'disorganized and disorderly female mind' (Scott, p. 77), and his concern that the exaggerated sex drive of the American worker was the source of major social maladjustments."
3. In 1904 Barnard was admitted to Mount Hermon School, which had been founded by the evangelist Dwight Moody to provide a thorough Christian training for young men and boys. In his personal statement to his application, Barnard wrote that "... this dormant thirst for a larger education was awakened by my conversion to the Lord Jesus Christ" (quoted in Scott, *Chester I. Barnard and the Guardians of the Managerial State*, 62). But Barnard's writings would less and less be informed by Christian ethics, which, he wrote in 1946, "... had developed in agricultural ... societies

and were chiefly expressed in terms intelligible to the people of such societies" (quoted in the opening sentences of Steven P. Feldman, "The Disinheritance of Management Ethics: Rational Individualism in Barnard's *Functions of the Executive*," in *Journal of Management History* 2, no. 4 [1996]: 34).

4. Barnard was not particularly successful in this position. In fact, during his tenure, NJBT's performance declined continuously—in part, because earnings were not invested in modernization programs. Also, the New Jersey public utility commission had not raised the telephone rates to the level that NJBT had asked for. Finally, a 1947 strike exposed NJBT's weak performance. See Scott, *Chester I. Barnard and the Guardians of the Managerial State*, 71 and 86.

5. In that capacity, Barnard was immediately forced to acquaint himself with a controversy that raged through the nation as well as through the Rockefeller Foundation. It concerned Alfred Kinsey's work on male sexuality, which had been amply funded by the foundation. Scholars questioned the methodology; public intellectuals were more concerned about the moral implications. While the Rockefeller Foundation preferred to operate on the basis of consensus, the debate about whether or not to continue funding Kinsey split its officers and the board of trustees. On April 4, 1951, the board decided, by a vote of 9–7, to continue funding. Among those voting against this decision was John Foster Dulles, who was president of the board of trustees until he was called to serve as Eisenhower's secretary of state. Throughout this controversy, Barnard urged Kinsey to improve his methodology so that the foundation would not in any way be embarrassed, but he did recognize the social importance of this work, and he finally decided to adopt a policy of watchful waiting. See James H. Jones, *Alfred C. Kinsey: A Public/Private Life* (New York: Norton, 1997), 594–595, 637–639, 649–652.

6. Mayo observed that Barnard had expanded the views developed by the Human Relations group. It has been said that in his lecture Barnard omitted several crucial elements and facts, but that this omission was not a reflection on his character—for he was believed to be a man of intellectual integrity—but more a consequence of subtle pressures working upon him, including the influence of the Human Relations group. See James Hoopes, "Managing a Riot: Chester Barnard and Social Unrest," *Management Decision* 40, no. 10 (2002): 1018.

7. See William B. Wolf, "Introduction" (to a special issue on Barnard), *Journal of Management History* 1, no. 4 (1995): 4.

8. Kenneth R. Andrews, "Introduction," Chester I. Barnard, *The Functions of the Executive* (Cambridge, Mass.: Harvard University Press, 1968), ix.

9. Wolf, *Basic Barnard*, 48.

10. Ibid., 44.

11. Ibid., 23.

12. Ibid., 18.

13. Ibid., 19.

14. Quoted in Andrews, "Introduction," xii. The remark about labored, abstract, and abstruse writing comes from Barnard's article, "Comments on the Job of the Executive," *Harvard Business Review* 18 (Spring 1940): 295–308, which he had written in response to an article by Melvin T. Copeland, "The Job of an Executive," appearing in the same issue of the journal, pp. 148–160. On Barnard's writing, see also R. Ray Gehani,

"Chester Barnard's 'Executive' and the Knowledge-based Firm," *Management Decision* 40, no. 10 (2002): 989.

15. William B. Wolf, *Conversations with Chester I. Barnard,* ILR Paperback no. 12 (Ithaca: New York State School of Industrial and Labor Relations, Cornell University, 1973), 16.

16. Andrews, "Introduction," vi. In "Chester I. Barnard and the Intelligence of Learning," in *From Chester Barnard to the Present and Beyond,* ed. Oliver E. Williamson (New York: Oxford University Press, 1990), 11–37, Barbara Levitt and James G. March describe *Functions of the Executive* as "poetic and evocative rather than precise and definitive" (11). Then, in "The Relevance of Chester I. Barnard's Teachings to Contemporary Management Education: Communicating the Aesthetics of Managements," *International Journal of Organizational Theory and Behavior* 5, nos. 1–2 (2002): 159–172, Joseph T. Mahoney expands Levitt and March's observation by arguing that Barnard continues to "resonate intensely with current students" (p. 159) because he combines "the two cultures of science and art and that it is the aesthetic reading of Barnard that explains the intensity of student's responses to his work" (p. 168).

17. Barnard, *Functions of the Executive,* xxix, xxx.

18. Ibid., 96. Barnard actually writes, "Overlaying or embedded in the complex of informal organizations, which is the aggregate we call great national and local societies, is a network of formal organizations."

19. Ibid., 119; emphasis added. Compare to Steven P. Feldman, "Incorporating the Contrary: The Politics of Dichotomy in Chester Barnard's Organization Sociology," *Journal of Management History* 2, no. 2 (1996): 27, which only quotes Barnard on formal organizations as the structural material of society. In Barnard's words, it appears that formal organizations are a necessary element of both informal organizations and large collectivities.

20. The information provided in this section is taken from Scott, *Chester I. Barnard and the Guardians of the Managerial State,* 102–103, and is based on Barnard's "A Memorandum on the Nature of the Social Sciences," which he submitted in 1942 to the Board of Trustees of the Rockefeller Foundation.

21. Barnard, *Functions of the Executive,* 10.

22. Ibid., 14.

23. Ibid., 23.

24. Ibid., 38.

25. Ibid., 40.

26. To use Barnard's example, an individual's inability to move a large stone may be viewed as a result of the size of the stone (environment) or of the physical limitations of the individual (biological). See ibid., 23, 24.

27. Ibid., 84.

28. Though Barnard discusses informal organizations as one stage of organizational development, it is not clear whether he considers it a necessary stage.

29. Barnard, *Functions of the Executive,* 116.

30. Ibid., 73.

31. Ibid., 60.

32. Ibid., 104.

33. Ibid., 79.

34. Ibid., 77.

35. Ibid., 131.
36. Ibid., 137.
37. In this stance, Barnard has been both praised as being an early exponent of "management by objectives" and castigated as being pro-management in his orientation.
38. Barnard, *Functions of the Executive*, 114–115.
39. Ibid., 122.
40. Ibid., 170–171.
41. Ibid., 199.
42. Ibid., 197.
43. Ibid., chapter 14, on "The Theory of Opportunism." See also Dave McMahon and Jon C. Carr, "The Contributions of Chester Barnard to Strategic Management Theory," *Journal of Management History* 5, no. 5 (1999): 234.
44. Barnard, *Functions of the Executive*, 82.
45. Ibid., 86–89. This separation between organizational purpose and individual motives continues Barnard's theme that the purpose of the organization has no direct meaning to the individual. Barnard asserts that organizational purpose and individual motives are seldom identical. All that is required is that there be no significant divergence between the individual's perception of the organization's purpose and the actual purpose of the organization, and that the individual believe that a common purpose exists.
46. Ibid., 293.
47. Ibid., 139.
48. Ibid., 19.
49. Ibid., 43.
50. Ibid., 142–149.
51. Ibid., 149–153.
52. Chester I. Barnard, "Functions and Pathology of Status Systems," in *Organization and Management: Selected Papers* (Cambridge, Mass.: Harvard University Press, 1962 [1949]), 207–244.
53. Ibid., 208.
54. Barnard, *Functions of the Executive*, 163.
55. Ibid., 166. Barnard's view that authority is only effective when accepted is similar to Weber's definition of authority as accepted or legitimate use of power (see chapter 1, pp. 30–32).
56. Ibid., 165–166. In "Frederick Winslow Taylor and the Idea of Worker Participation: A Brief against Easy Administrative Dichotomies" (1989), in *F. W. Taylor: Critical Evaluations in Business and Management*, ed. John C. Wood and Michael C. Wood (London: Routledge, 2002), vol. I, 127, Hindy Lauer Schachter argues that this notion of "bottom-up authority" can already be found in Morris Cooke's 1917 article, "Who Is Boss in Your Shop?"
57. In his Introduction to the 30th anniversary edition of *Functions of the Executive*, Andrews observes (xiv–xv) that Follett's "Law of the Situation" influenced Barnard's understanding of authority.
58. Barnard, *Functions of the Executive*, 167. In the case of rejection, an employee can choose to vote with his feet or to blow the whistle. See A.O. Hirschman, *Exit, Voice, and Loyalty: Responses to Decline in Firms, Organizations and States* (Cambridge, Mass.: Harvard University Press, 1970). If an individual chooses not to exit but wants to voice his objections, there are

two options: to quietly discuss concerns with management or to go the route of whistle-blowing. On the latter option, see Dae-il Nam and David J. Lemak, "The Whistle-blowing Zone: Applying Barnard's Insights to a Modern Ethical Dilemma," *Journal of Management History* 13, no. 1 (2007): 33–42.

59. Barnard, *Functions of the Executive*, 167–171.

60. Ibid., 185.

61. Ibid., 187.

62. Barnard, *Functions of the Executive*, 206. In " 'Playing by Ear' … 'in an Incessant Din of Reasons': Chester Barnard and the History of Intuition in Management Thought," *Management Decision* 40, no. 10 (2002), Milorad M. Novicevic, Thomas J. Hench, and Daniel A. Wren suggest that Barnard identified seven stages in the decision process, but that they are dispersed throughout Barnard's text.

63. Barnard, *Functions of the Executive*, 186.

64. Ibid., 195.

65. Ibid., 203.

66. Ibid., 210.

67. Barnard, *Functions of the Executive*, 193–194; italics in original. The decision not to decide appears later as non-decision making. See P. S. Bachrach and M. S. Baratz, "Decisions and Non-decisions: An Analytical Framework," *American Political Science Review* 57, no. 3 (1963): 632–642. Bachrach and Baratz, though, do not reference Barnard.

68. Barnard, *Functions of the Executive*, 302.

69. Ibid., 305. As an example of intuitive knowledge, Barnard mentions judging speed and distance of a ball—a judgment that becomes more precise with practice. The same example is used by Richard R. Nelson and Sidney G. Winter, *An Evolutionary Theory of Economic Change* (Cambridge, Mass.: Belknap Press of Harvard University Press, 1982), 80.

70. Barnard, "The Organism in the Processes of the Decision," in "Decision Processes as Analyzed by Chester I. Barnard," ed. William W. Wolf, special issue, *Journal of Management History* 1, no. 4 (1995): 80. This special issue consists of notes by Barnard written for a course on the sociology of Vilfredo Pareto, in which Barnard participated between May 1938 and November 1941. In contemporary literature, "nonlogical processes," or "intuition," is more commonly referred to as "tacit knowledge"; see, e.g., Michael Polanyi, *The Tacit Dimension* (Garden City, N.Y.: Doubleday, 1966). Barnard himself also referred to it as "behavioral knowledge"; see *Functions of the Executive*, 291.

71. Barnard, *Functions of the Executive*, 60–61.

72. Ibid., 217.

73. Ibid., 175–181.

74. Some identify Barnard as the true progenitor of participative management; see Rikki Abzug and Susan Phelps, "Everything Old Is New Again: Barnard's Legacy–Lessons for Participative Leaders," *Journal of Management Development* 17, no. 3 (1998): 208.

75. Barnard, *Functions of the Executive*, 231.

76. Ibid., 241–242. Like Mary Parker Follett, Barnard is regarded as a forerunner of stakeholder theory and strategic management at the micro level. See Kenneth E. Aupperle and Steven M. Dunphy, "Managerial Lessons for a New Millennium: Contributions from Chester Barnard and

Frank Capra," *Management Decision* 39, no. 2 (2001): 158; and Milorad M. Novicevic, Walter Davis, Fred Dorn, M. Ronald Buckley, and Jo Ann Brown, "Barnard on Conflicts of Responsibility: Implications for Today's Perspectives on Transformational and Authentic Leadership," *Management Decision* 43, no. 10 (2005): 1405.

77. Barnard, *Functions of the Executive*, 259.

78. Chester I. Barnard, "The Nature of Leadership," in *Organization and Management*, 83.

79. Ibid., 93.

80. Ibid., 98.

81. Chester I. Barnard, "Education for Executives," in *Organization and Management*, 195–196.

82. Ibid., 198–199.

83. Barnard, *Functions of the Executive*, 261.

84. Ibid., 263.

85. Ibid., 283.

86. These moral codes extend beyond the organization and are nowadays referred to as "corporate social responsibility." See Aupperle and Dunphy, "Managerial Lessons for a New Millennium," 157; and Novicevic et al., "Barnard on Conflicts of Responsibility."

87. Barnard, *Functions of the Executive*, 284.

88. Barnard's work is frequently compared to that of another practicing manager, F. W. Taylor. Both were nonacademics who learned more from experience than from formal education, lectured extensively, and shared an appreciation for "workplace cooperation." Differences are that Taylor focused on the shopfloor level while Barnard considered the entire organization; Taylor looked mainly at productivity while Barnard stressed the social system as a whole; and that Taylor believed incentives followed work while Barnard held that incentives came before work. See Satyanarayana Parayitam, Margaret A. White, and Jill R. Hough, "Juxtaposition of Chester I. Barnard and Frederick W. Taylor: Forerunners of Management," *Management Decision* 40, no. 10 (2002): 1003–1012.

89. See, for instance, Charles Perrow, *Complex Organizations: A Critical Essay* (Glenview, Ill.: Scott, Foresman, 1972), 95, on the "apologist position"; and John M. Pfiffner and Robert Presthus, *Public Administration*, 5th ed. (New York: Ronald Press, 1965), 213, for the other side.

90. This point relates to the question whether or not Barnard was an elitist. See Steven M. Dunphy and James Hoopes, "Chester Barnard: Member of the 'Elite'?" *Management Decision* 40, no. 10 (2002): 1924–1028.

91. Barnard, *Functions of the Executive*, 167–168.

92. Barnard, "Dilemmas of Leadership in the Democratic Process," in *Organization and Management*, 24–50.

93. Some authors argue that Barnard did not use seeming contradictions so much as he did dichotomies, such as individual vs. organization, formal vs. informal organization, subjective vs. objective authority, and other dichotomies mentioned in the final paragraphs of his book. See Feldman, "Incorporating the Contrary," 26–40.

94. Barnard, *Functions of the Executive*, 296.

Chapter 7

Herbert A. Simon:
A Decision-Making Perspective

In examining the work of authors such as Follett, Mayo, and Barnard, we have dealt with figures probably best regarded as transitional in the shift from the Classical to the Behavioral perspective in the study of public administration in the United States. Turning now to Herbert Simon, we present an author whose works are commonly considered a watershed rather than simply a transition. Simon's writings are firmly entrenched in the Behavioral perspective, and his work, in general, represents a radical departure from the Classical approach to public administration. Yet there are a number of similarities between Simon's positions and those of the authors who preceded him. In short, Simon's work is a combination of disjunctures and continuities, impressive in the evolutionary, rather than revolutionary, character of the views he advances.

Let us consider first the similarities between Simon and his predecessors in the field. His most obvious intellectual debt is to Chester Barnard. Simon adopts, in toto, Barnard's conceptualization of the organization as a system of exchange and the definition of authority suggested by that conceptualization. He also adopts Barnard's notion that complex formal organizations evolve from, and consist of, simple formal organizations—though Barnard ascribes the development to limits on communication, while Simon attributes it to the necessity of simplifying decisions—as well as Barnard's emphasis on decision making, although that emphasis is accentuated in Simon's works.

But Simon's intellectual indebtedness is not limited to Barnard. At the most general level, Simon shares with the Classical approach the objective of developing a science of administration, an effort to describe a value-free domain for the construction of that science, a quest for general principles of administration, the acceptance of efficiency as the criterion for decision making, and an emphasis on hierarchy as well as its justifications (coordination, superior rationality, and the location of responsibility). Indeed, Simon's assignment of responsibilities to the hierarchy—the construction of decision premises and, later, system design—is reminiscent of Taylor's charge to management. Simon's assertion that the harshness of hierarchical directives can be mitigated if determined by the "logic of the situation" echoes Follett's reliance on the "law of the situation" and Gulick's admonition that hierarchy must rely on "coordination through ideas" as well as on the structure of authority.

Simon also shares with Gulick some concern about the adequacy of the politics-administration dichotomy as the basis for the construction of a science of administration. They even agree on the general definition of an appropriate scientific domain: for Gulick, it is relationships between actions and outcome (statements of "variations and interrelationships"); for Simon, it lies in the relationship between alternatives and their outcomes (the "factual" element of decisions). Finally, there is agreement between Weber and Simon that the organization—for Weber, the bureaucratic organization—provides a broader context of rationality for individual decision making. However, while Weber believes that the bureaucratic organization has the potential to become an "iron cage," to Simon it is, instead, an essential scaffolding for thought.[1]

Nevertheless, this specification of similarities should not blind us to the fact that important differences also exist between Simon's work and that of his predecessors. Although Simon agrees with Gulick on the politics-administration dichotomy, that opinion is in opposition to the dominant stance, and Simon is considerably more determined than Gulick in pressing the fact-value dichotomy as the appropriate substitute in defining the domain for the construction of a science of administration. Although Simon adopts Barnard's exchange model of the organization and his definition of authority, he substantially elaborates the former and draws an important distinction on the latter consideration.

But the truly distinctive feature of Simon's work lies in his preoccupation with decision making in the organization. Here, Simon proposes a new unit of analysis for scientific investigation (decision premises); a different methodological approach (an inductive approach based on the tenets of logical positivism); and a revised concept of the decision maker as, in Simon's hands, Economic Man is translated into the more modest dimensions of Satisficing Man, who has features of both Economic and Administrative Man.[2] All this innovative theorizing is cast in terms of routinized decision making in an organizational environment, as Simon attempts to develop a descriptive model of organizational decision making and to remake administrative theory in the process.

This chapter focuses on Simon's elaboration of decision making in an organizational environment, since this perspective is the most pertinent to the considerations raised in this book. This focus requires that we concentrate on Simon's earlier work in public administration; we, therefore, are not able to do full justice to his more recent work as a cognitive scientist in the field of individual decision making and artificial intelligence.[3]

Life

Herbert A. Simon was born in Milwaukee, Wisconsin, on June 15, 1916.[4] He earned his BA (1936) and PhD (1943) from the University of Chicago and received honorary degrees from Yale University, Case Institute of Technology, Lund University (Sweden), McGill University (Canada), and the Netherlands School of Economics. Simon began his professional career in 1936 as an assistant to Clarence E. Ridley of the International City Managers' Association (ICMA). In 1939 he became director of Administrative Measurement Studies at the Bureau of Public Administration of the University of California at Berkeley. In 1942 Simon took a position at the Illinois Institute of Technology, where he was chairman of the Department of Political and Social Sciences from 1946 to 1949. He moved to Carnegie-Mellon University in Pittsburgh in 1949 as professor of administration and psychology and remained there until his death on February 9, 2001. At Carnegie-Mellon, Simon was head of the Department of Industrial Management, associate dean of the Graduate School of Industrial Management, and Richard King Mellon Professor of Computer Science and Psychology.

Simon compiled a substantial public service record. He worked for the U.S. Bureau of the Budget, the Census Bureau, and the Economic Cooperation Administration. In addition, Simon served as a member of the President's Science Advisory Committee, chairman of the Pennsylvania Governor's Milk Inquiry Commission, chairman of the Board of Directors of the Social Science Research Council, and chairman of the Division of Behavioral Sciences of the National Research Council. Also, he served as a consultant to a variety of governmental and business organizations.

Simon's distinguished career was marked by a number of honors and awards, including the Administrator's Award of the American College of Hospital Administrators, the Distinguished Scientific Contribution Award of the American Psychological Association, and the A.M. Turing Award of the Association for Computing Machinery. In 1978 he received the Nobel Prize in Economics.

Simon's career was distinguished by the breadth of his concerns. His interest in the study of man, originating in high school, was spurred by the library of a maternal uncle (who had studied economics at the University of Wisconsin but died in his early thirties) and by the books his older brother left behind when leaving home.[5] As an undergraduate at the University of Chicago, he wrote a term paper on relations and cooperation between city government and school boards. Another paper he wrote in 1935 for a class on "Measuring Municipal Governments," prompted the professor, Clarence Ridley, to hire Simon as a research assistant in the following year. This affiliation paid off to mutual satisfaction. It led to Simon's first article and first (coauthored) book, published when he was in graduate school.[6] As a staff member (since 1938), Simon helped with the editing of the ICMA's journal, *Public Management*, and its annual *Municipal Yearbook*.[7] Simon's interest in measuring output befitted the times. In fact, in his dissertation, he observed that there were "only a handful of research studies [that] satisfy these fundamental conditions of methodology," and he explicitly mentioned F.W. Taylor's "methods of science" for measuring the cutting of metals.[8]

Simon notes that many of the ideas contained in his first single-authored book, *Administrative Behavior*, were drawn from the Institutionalist school of economics.[9] His interests expanded to include almost all the social sciences. Perhaps the breadth of his interests is best illustrated by looking at the progression of Simon's career. He began with a PhD in political science and a major in the field of public administration. He spent much of his career teaching in a school of industrial management. He was a professor of computer science and psychology. He received the Nobel Prize for his work in the field of economics.[10] His articles appeared in the professional journals of every branch of the social sciences except anthropology.[11] His official publication list includes, at last count, 942 articles and 30 books—which amounts to 15.2 publications per annum over a sixty-four-year career. And this number excludes the translations of *Administrative Behavior* into Chinese, Dutch, Finnish, French, German, Italian, Japanese, Korean, Portuguese, Spanish, and Swedish, as well as the many reprints in various anthologies and other collections.[12] Simon maintained memberships in professional associations in the fields of political science, economics, psychology, sociology, computer science, management sciences, and philosophy. In sum, he was a man of catholic interests and a "social scientist" in the truest sense of that term.

Nevertheless, there is a common theme in Simon's interests—a central focus on individual and organizational decision making.[13] This central theme is evidenced in all his major works, although the perspective changed over time. Simon describes *Administrative Behavior* as a "prolegomena to theory," devoted to the objectives of establishing decisions as a focus of analysis and constructing a common operational language for the literature of organization theory.[14] *Public Administration*, written with Donald W. Smithburg and Victor A. Thompson, is an attempt to synthesize various perspectives on public administration, but with emphasis on organizational decision making.[15] From the mid-1950s on, Simon moves more and more into cognitive science.

In 1956 he coauthors a paper on the use of computers for modeling human thought.[16] One year later, a coauthored article appears that will become the foundation of contemporary cognitive psychology.[17] In the same year (1957), *Models of Man*, a collection of his articles—including his 1955 "A Behavioral Model of Rational Choice," which (together with *Administrative Behavior*) will secure his Nobel—Simon presents a formalization of some basic elements of his decision theory.[18] Finally, in *Organizations*, co-authored with James G. March and published in 1958, he elaborates the theoretical framework presented in *Administrative Behavior* and marshals a wide array of empirical evidence pertaining to that theory and linking it to the emerging behavioral theory of choice.[19] These publications are indicative of the direction Simon takes from then on.

In *The New Science of Management Decision* Simon offers a computer-based perspective and an assessment of the computer's consequences for organizational decision making.[20] In *The Sciences of the Artificial*, he expands his scope to artificial systems in general (only one of which is an organization) and to a model of man as an information-processing system.[21] *Human Problem-Solving* and *Models of Thought*, two more compilations of articles written by Simon and his associates and edited by Simon and Allen Newell, are concerned with the processes of human cognition; these collections are embued with the ambitious aim of presenting "a unified explanation of human cognition in all of its manifestations."[22] In the 1979 *The Sciences of the Artificial*, Simon develops a design science (curriculum included) that aims to prepare the professional to be effective in a man-made, artificial world. This study targets a variety of professionals, such as engineers, architects, business managers, educators, lawyers, doctors, and (although not specifically mentioned) civil servants.[23]

One more of Simon's many books that deserves attention here is his autobiography, published in 1991.[24] Therein he observes that every scientist would have to regard the objective of science as one of "finding meaningful simplicity in the midst of orderly complexity."[25] In the eye of one reviewer, in this work Simon pushes this "concept to a limit with an interesting result—it is the story of the problem solver trying to test his own theories of decision making and problem solving on his own life."[26]

The common focus on human decision making is clear. Simon's changing perspective is marked by a progression in which the emphasis on the organizational environment as it influences decision making is replaced by an increasingly specific concentration on individual decision-making processes. Though our primary concern in this chapter is decision making in an organizational environment—that is, we largely concentrate on Simon's objective of establishing a "science of administration," his analysis of individual decision-making processes, and his understanding of organizational decision making—we should first acknowledge the manner and language with which Simon defended his ideas and scolded others. In the absence of a contextualizing biography of Simon, some brief description of his "style" may reveal his character to some degree.

It was neither his "monomaniacal" concentration on decision making nor the quality and quantity of his publications that distinguished Simon's style of argument.[27] He was also convinced that his own reasoning and ideas were sounder than those of most others. Reflecting upon his high school years, he observed that he had skipped two years because he was "smarter than his comrades."[28] Throughout his career, he could turn "with incredible intellectual ferocity on those ostensibly capable of defending themselves who were taking an intellectual position that needed a little more thought."[29] Political scientist Jonathan Bendor thought himself "fortunate to have encountered the elderly Simon; if the stories are true, the younger man would have gone at me with hammer and tongs...."[30] Indeed, Simon titled one chapter in his autobiography "On Being Argumentative."

It was the ferocity with which he defended his brain child, *Administrative Behavior*, that helped to attract attention. What started with a full-blown attack upon prewar public administration's proverbs, and an exchange with Robert Dahl,[31] would never stop. Despite the fact that Simon reported having started his career in the "academic backwater" of public administration and having left that field because "many of the books published in public administration (and management generally) are positively embarrassing," he continued to pay attention to the reception of his ideas in that field.[32] His exchanges—some of them provoked by him, some in response to challenges from others—with Waldo (1952), Banfield (1957), and Argyris (1973), and, in political science, with Lowi (1993), are illustrative.[33]

Curiously, Simon claims in his autobiography that "I have seldom replied directly to critics, preferring to make my case on my own terms, to define the issues myself rather than to deviate within the framework defined by opponents."[34] And, in fact, when he did respond to a critic, his general method was to dismiss any challenge to his ideas "simply by denying the relevance and even the existence of any arguments other than those that appear to be only the opposite of his own."[35] Simon would debate only on his own ground.[36] Although offering examples of the language Simon used would not clearly convey the tone of an entire article, we suggest that the reader review these exchanges, if only because they show that a "gloves-off" approach can be conducted in a gentlemanly manner. For instance, no matter how strong the language of disagreement had grown between Simon and Waldo, the two frequently went out to lunch together.

As time went by, Simon mellowed. In a guest editorial in the *Public Administration Review*, written upon the occasion of receiving ASPA's Waldo Award in 1995, he alluded to the "purple prose" that he and Waldo had exchanged in 1952 but conceded that the study of public administration had absorbed both their revolutions.[37] In a particular way, this is correct. Simon's scientific approach has commanded a following, especially among those scholars of public administration who identify with political science,[38] while Waldo's holistic, historical, and philosophical approach has found more of a home in the study of public administration, though only among a fairly small groups of scholars.[39] Substantively, too, Simon mellowed later in life. For instance, in an exchange of letters with Chester Barnard between 1945 and 1947, he objected to the degree to which the latter regarded intuition as important to decision making, declaring this viewpoint to be flawed.[40] Four decades later, however, Simon would write, "It is a fallacy to contrast 'analytic' and 'intuitive' styles of management.... The effective manager does not have the luxury of choosing between 'analytic' and 'intuitive' approaches to problems."[41] With regard to research, though, he remained firmly committed to the idea that science collects data.[42]

A Science of Administration

Simon, like the authors of the Classical period who preceded him, sought to construct a science of administration. But his approach differs from that of the Classical authors in several respects. Simon focuses on decisions or, more precisely, decision premises as his unit of analysis; he designates the factual component of administrative decisions as the appropriate scientific domain; and he adopts a procedure that emphasizes systematic, empirical investigation.

A Unit of Analysis: Decision Premises

Simon contends that the logic and psychology of choice is the heart of administration, and, at times, he uses the terms "decision making" and "managing" synonymously. Nevertheless, Simon considers "decisions" to be too broad to serve as a unit of analysis in a science of administration, since they are not unitary events—that is, pieces of a decision may be made at different points in time, and more than one actor may be involved—and they involve the processes of alerting, exploring, and analyzing, which precede the act of choice.

Consequently, Simon adopts decision premises rather than decisions as his unit of analysis.[43] Decision premises provide the basis for the process of decision making, while decisions themselves are conclusions drawn from these premises. Stated in the form of an analogy to the computer, premises are comparable to data input and a program of instruction, whereas a decision is the product of applying the program to the input. Simon contends that decisions are best analyzed by examining their underlying premises, discovering the sources of those premises, and tracing the channels of communication and influence by which premises are transmitted in an organizational setting.

The Domain of a Science of Administration

Simon also differs from the Classical authors in defining the area in which a science of administration can, and should, be constructed. Following Wilson, the search for a science of administration in the Classical period was founded on a proposed institutional separation between policy functions and administrative functions—the policy-administration dichotomy.[44] Policy matters or objectives were to be decided by elected officials, whereas administrative decisions were to be limited to "the systematic and detailed execution of public law" or the selection of means to achieve those objectives.[45] By limiting administrative activity to the selection of means rather than ends, Wilson believed that he was defining a value-free domain for the construction of an empirically based science of administration, whose objective was to make the conduct of government business more efficient. Fidelity to the policy intentions of elected officials was to be ensured by the establishment of appropriate hierarchical controls.[46]

Simon rejects the policy-administration dichotomy on both descriptive and normative grounds. Descriptively, he contends that policy and administrative functions, as defined by Wilson, are performed by both political and administrative officials.[47] Political officials are often involved in the selection of means, and, more important, administrators are integrally involved in the policy function both in the initiation of policy and in the exercise of discretion in the execution of policy.[48] Consequently, the policy-administration dichotomy fails to define a value-free domain for the development of a science of administration, since administrators are involved in policy functions and thus value considerations.

Simon rejects the policy-administration dichotomy on normative grounds as well. Although he concedes that the dichotomy may have been appropriate to the historical context in which Wilson wrote, Simon contends that political institutions and the normative and practical problems they pose have changed since that time.[49] Resistance to the hierarchical controls required by the policy-administration dichotomy has increased. Moreover, governmental operations have expanded, imposing severe limits on the ability of political officials to exercise adequate oversight and control over bureaucrats. Finally, the increasing role of science in government has complicated the problem of establishing controls by generalists over professionals who have specialized expertise.[50] Simon argues that it is unrealistic to attempt to establish strict, external, hierarchical controls over the bureaucracy and undesirable to separate administrators from policy functions. Instead, we must discover ways of using the technical knowledge of administrators in the policy process.[51]

In place of the policy-administration dichotomy, Simon proposes a fact-value dichotomy—which, he argues, provides a better basis for a science of administration and a more appropriate standard for administrative conduct. Simon divides decision premises into two categories: value premises and factual premises. Value premises are ethical statements about what should be done. As such, they may be good or bad, but they cannot be true or false.[52] Factual premises, in contrast, are statements about the observable world. Consequently, it can be determined whether factual premises are true or false.[53] The factual premises of decisions are the perceived relationships between alternatives and their consequences. Factual premises are true if the alternative selected leads to the predicted set of consequences; they are false if it does not.[54]

Simon maintains that propositions about administrative processes are scientific only to the extent that their truth or falsity can be assessed. Therefore, a science of administration must be based on the factual premises of administrative decisions and cannot deal with value premises. Thus, Simon substitutes a conceptual distinction—the fact-value dichotomy—for what he considers to be a descriptively invalid institutional distinction—the policy-administration dichotomy—to define a value-free domain for the development of a science of administration.

The substitution of the fact-value dichotomy for the policy-administration dichotomy also suggests a different standard for administrative behavior. The policy-administration dichotomy requires policy neutrality on the part of administrators and the establishment of hierarchical controls to ensure the responsiveness of administrators to the policy directives of their political superiors. But Simon contends that public administrators are not, and should not be, neutral concerning policy. Instead, they should be predictable in regard to the value premises entering into their decisions.[55] The value premises of the administrator are predictable, within limits, because of the processes of recruitment, socialization, and professional identification. Simon argues that predictability is superior to neutrality because a group of value-free professionals would be the most corruptible of all bodies—a "force of janissaries."[56] In addition, since the bureaucracy is controlled by controlling its decision premises, and since the premises entering into any decision are so complex that it is impossible to control more than a few, external controls by political officials cannot be the sole guarantee of administrative responsibility. Instead, internalized professional standards must guide administrative behavior.

Although inevitably limited, external controls are still required. Facts and values cannot be entirely separated, and the administrator's value premises may not be the same as those of political officials. Therefore, procedural devices should be formulated to assign value-laden decisions to elected officials and to hold administrators responsible to community values.[57] More important, automation of decision making can assist in clarifying value premises and, by making those premises more explicit, render review and evaluation both easier and more likely.[58]

The Scientific Process

Finally, Simon differs from the Classical authors with respect to the procedures to be employed in the development of a science of administration.[59] In his view, a science of administration should be based on systematic, empirical analysis rather than on casual observation and proverbs; it should be inductive, not deductive, in nature, its "principles" the result of an accumulation of empirical evidence rather than intuition; and, at least at the outset, it should be descriptive rather than prescriptive.[60]

Simon suggests that two kinds of administrative science can be established: a "pure" science and a "practical" science. A pure science seeks to describe ways in which humans behave in organizations with the objective of discovering and verifying empirical propositions.[61] A practical science attempts to develop propositions about how decision makers would behave if they sought to achieve more efficient performance.[62] A practical science of administration can assist the administrator in making decisions. Administrative decision making can be based only partly on scientific knowledge, however, since a science of administration can deal only with efficiency in the achievement of values, not with the selection of values themselves.

Simon believes that a science of administration would be applicable to both public and private organizations. He contends that public and private organizations have more similarities than differences, and that the differences that do exist are more differences in degree than in kind. Public organizations differ from private organizations in that they are characterized by more legalism, they are subject to congressional scrutiny, they have less discretion in interpreting the relationships between organizational welfare and the general welfare, and they are more likely to be seen as inefficient and corrupt than are private organizations.[63] Simon mentions one other important difference—that government organizations are needed to provide the legal framework and the infrastructure that enable private businesses and the market to function.[64] Nonetheless, he argues that there are fundamental commonalities in human behavior in public and private organizations and that the findings of a science of administration are applicable in both settings.[65] In emphasizing the similarities between public and private organizations, Simon is in agreement with the Classical authors, although he would counsel substantially different techniques of administration than those advocated by the Classical authors.

In sum, Simon's objective is to construct a science of administration focused on decision making, defining decision premises as the unit of analysis and the factual component of those premises as the scientific domain. This science is to be based on systematic empirical investigation; it is to be inductive and primarily descriptive (although Simon's design science is clearly intended as a prescription[66]); and its findings are to be generally applicable to both public and private organizations. Simon's efforts to develop a science of administration lead him to a reconceptualization of existing models of man as a decision maker and of the interaction between man and the organization in making decisions in an organizational environment. These considerations are the subject of examination in the remainder of this chapter, in which primary emphasis is placed on decision making in an organizational context.

Individual Decision Making

In discussing Simon's view of decision-making processes, it is useful to begin at the end. That is, we reverse the chronological ordering of the development of Simon's interests as outlined earlier, and work from individual decision processes to decision making in the organization.

Simon starts his analysis by proposing a new model of decision-making man. He refers to this model as "Satisficing Man"—that is, a decision maker who, because of the limits on his cognitive and analytical abilities, accepts alternatives that are merely satisfactory or sufficient in regard to his level of aspirations.[67] Simon notes that there are several alternative models of man as a decision maker. The psychological model of man as a decision maker emphasizes affective (that is, emotional) considerations in decision making,[68] while the sociological model emphasizes role playing, leaving little room for choice and, consequently, rationality.[69] Probably the best known of the models is Economic Man, which emphasizes cognitive and analytical, as opposed to affective, processes and embodies maximizing assumptions about decision-making behavior.[70]

In proposing the model of Satisficing Man, Simon seeks a middle ground among these alternatives. Thus, Satisficing Man is distinguished from Psychological Man by his emphasis on cognitive and analytical, rather than affective, elements of decision making. Satisficing Man is distinguished from Sociological Man in that his decision making is not totally determined by social roles, and from Economic Man in that he is limited in his cognitive and analytical capabilities.

Though Simon recognizes that a mature science must accommodate both affective and cognitive elements of human behavior, his central concerns are cognitive elements. He defines his task as the reconstruction of theory to provide an explanation of rational human behavior with some pretense of realism.[71] Given this emphasis on the cognitive elements of the decision-making process, Simon is primarily concerned with distinguishing Satisficing Man from Economic Man.

Economic Man

Simon argues that the field of economics has concentrated on only one aspect of man—his reason, and the application of that reason to the problem of allocation in the face of scarcity. In this context, Economic Man is viewed as a value maximizer who can deal effectively with uncertainty. The model of Economic Man is based on the following assumptions:

1. The decision maker knows all the relevant aspects of the decision environment.
2. The decision maker knows all the alternative courses of action.
3. The decision maker knows all the consequences of those alternatives with certainty, or he knows the probability distribution of the occurrence of the consequences (risk).
4. The decision maker has a known, and temporally stable, preference function for all sets of consequences. That is, he knows how he values the sets of consequences; he can rank-order the sets of consequences; and that ordering will remain stable over time.
5. The decision maker has the required computational skills.

6. The decision maker maximizes the satisfaction of his values by choosing the alternative that is followed by the most preferred set of consequences.[72]

Given this set of assumptions, Economic Man employs a relatively simple decision procedure. First, he arrays all the alternatives. Second, he determines all the consequences attached to each alternative. Third, he makes a comparative evaluation of each set of consequences. Fourth, Economic Man selects the strategy that is followed by the preferred set of consequences.

Simon does not gainsay the importance of the economics model. He considers it an appropriate normative model of decision making and one that provides a precise definition of rationality.[73] Nevertheless, Simon charges that the economic model of man is an inadequate description of actual decision-making behavior and is based on an overly restrictive view of rationality.

The basic descriptive problems of the economic model are its neglect of uncertainty in most phases of the decision-making procedure and its failure to deal effectively with uncertainty where it attempts to do so. Simon argues that uncertainty pervades the decision process.[74] Thus, the decision maker is likely to be uncertain about objectives, the range of possible alternatives, the consequences of those alternatives, and the relationships between the alternatives and their consequences. The economic model ignores uncertainty about objectives, alternatives, and consequences, dealing with uncertainty only in regard to the relationships between alternatives and their consequences; even there, it does so unsuccessfully, since it provides no generally acceptable criterion for the selection of an alternative under conditions of uncertainty.

The descriptive inadequacies of the economic model limit its predictive capabilities. Simon argues that economists who insist on maximization in their model of man become satisficers in evaluating their own theories.[75] By this, he means that economists require only that their model be good enough to render satisfactory predictions and ignore the actual processes of choice. But, although a model should be limited in its required assumptions, it should incorporate all the assumptions necessary to account for behavior. Simon contends that the economic model cannot sufficiently account for behavior and, consequently, cannot effectively predict decision-making outcomes. Furthermore, he argues, the model of Satisficing Man is a better description of decision-making behavior and therefore has better predictive power.[76]

In regard to rationality, Simon contends that almost all behavior has a rational component, though not necessarily in terms of "economic" rationality (that is, value-maximizing behavior).[77] Consequently, he argues that the definition of rationality should be expanded to incorporate a wider range of human behavior.

Satisficing Man and Bounded Rationality

Satisficing Man represents Simon's effort to provide a suitable descriptive model of human decision making in a broadened context of rationality. Simon's reformulation casts the decision maker in the modest role of one whose intent is to be rational but who satisfices because he has "not the wits to maximize."[78] In making decisions, Satisficing Man does not examine all possible alternatives, he ignores most of the complex interrelationships of the real world, and he makes decisions by applying relatively simple rules of thumb, or heuristics.[79] In short, Satisficing Man simplifies and satisfices because he operates within bounds imposed by the limits on available information and by his own computational abilities.

Simon is not the first scholar to take note of what is now generally known as "bounded rationality." This concept dates back to the seventeenth century, but its influence grew rapidly from the 1840s on.[80] A more immediate precedent for Simon's use of it can be found in Gulick's observation that "... we are confronted at the start by the inexorable limits of human nature. Just as the hand of man can span only a limited number of notes on the piano, so the mind and will of man can span but a limited number of immediate managerial contacts."[81] However, Simon was the first to study limited rationality on a systematic and empirical basis. His version of the theories of Satisficing Man and bounded rationality emphasizes that people actually manage quite well despite cognitive limitations. This detached perspective stands in sharp contrast to the literature stressing that people constantly make mistakes even with the simplest of tasks.[82]

But can such a limited decision procedure be considered rational? Simon's answer is a qualified yes, depending on how one defines *rationality*—and Simon proposes a rather broad definition. He imposes two requirements on the definition of rationality: it must accommodate the extent to which appropriate courses of action are actually chosen (outcomes), and it should address the effectiveness and limitations of the procedures used to make decisions (process). Accordingly, Simon defines rationality as "the selection of preferred behavioral alternatives in terms of some system of values whereby the consequences of behavior can be evaluated."[83]

Furthermore, he distinguishes among six types of rationality that, taken together, serve to expand substantially the compass of the term.[84] "Objective rationality" is, in fact, the correct behavior for maximizing given values in a given situation. "Subjective rationality" is maximizing value attainment relative to the actual knowledge of the decision maker.

"Conscious rationality" is a conscious adjustment of means to ends, but this process may also be subconscious in nature.[85] "Deliberate rationality" is a process by which the adjustment of means to ends is deliberate, although it may also be nondeliberate in character. "Organizational rationality" is oriented toward the organization's objectives, whereas "individual or personal rationality" is focused on individual goals.

In short, Simon would have rationality range across a continuum bounded on one end by subconscious and nondeliberate adaptations of means to ends, based on incomplete knowledge, and on the other by conscious and deliberate adaptations, based on complete knowledge. Most decision-making behavior, of course, would fall somewhere between these extremes. In addition, the system of values by which alternatives are chosen may be either organizational or individual. We return to this point in examining organizational decision-making processes.

This enlarged definition of rationality is consistent with Simon's claim that all human behavior has a rational component and with his insistence that we look beyond the rather narrow bounds of economic rationality in analyzing and assessing human behavior. Simon would extend the reach of rationality even to psychoanalytic theory, which explains behavior in terms of the functions performed for the individual; he notes that "even madness has its methods."[86]

Individual Decision Processes

Much of Simon's later work was concerned with elaborating the ways in which Satisficing Man goes about making decisions. At the broadest level of generalization, the decision maker can be conceptualized as an artificial system—that is, a system that adapts through goals and purposes to the environment in which it exists.[87] More specifically, Simon conceives of the decision maker as an information-processing system and maintains that there are broad commonalities among humans as information-processing systems engaging in the task of making decisions.

As an information-processing system, the decision maker is limited in his capacities and deals with alternatives sequentially. That is, the decision maker can process only a few symbols at a time, and those symbols are held in memory structures of limited access, capacity, or both.[88] As a result, the decision maker is forced to deal with one or a few alternatives at a time rather than confronting all alternatives simultaneously. Problem-solving activities involve interaction between the decision maker and the decision environment; the behavior of the decision maker is determined by his internal state, by stimuli from the decision environment, and by the interaction between the two. The internal state of the decision maker is a function of his previous history, from which information is stored in a memory. Nonetheless, any specific decision-making activity can involve only a small part of the information contained in the memory. Thus, decision making is a mutual product of a process for evoking some portion of the information contained in the memory and the limited information evoked. Therefore, decision-making behavior is influenced either by changing the active determiners of current behavior (evocation) or by altering the information contained in the memory (learning).[89] In sum, the decision maker as an information-processing system is a problem solver who can do only a few things at a time and can attend to only a small portion of the information contained in his memory and presented by the task environment at any given point in time.

Stimuli. The first basic element in individual decisions is a stimulus from the decision environment. Simon distinguishes between two kinds of stimuli: repetitive and novel.[90] Repetitive stimuli evoke routinized or habitual responses. Novel stimuli evoke problem-solving responses and prompt search activity that may be either routinized or creative. Creative search activity, if necessary, proceeds until a solution is discovered or until some routinized response becomes applicable.[91]

Given his limited capacities, the decision maker is not likely to be aware of, nor will he be able to respond to, all the stimuli emanating from the decision environment. Instead, there is likely to be selective attention to stimuli that is reinforced by the existence of a mutual interaction between environmental stimuli and the information evoked from the memory. That is, not only do environmental stimuli influence what information will be drawn from the memory, but also, the information drawn from the memory will influence what environmental stimuli will be perceived.[92]

Memory. The second basic element in individual decisions is the memory. Information stored in the memory consists of criteria that are applied to determine preferred courses of action (values or goals); the alternative possible courses of action; and beliefs, perceptions, and expectations regarding the relationships between alternative courses of action and their outcomes.[93] The memory consists of two components: short-term and long-term. The short-term, or working, memory is characterized by a limited capacity and relatively quick access. It is upon short-term memory that people decide whether information that comes in from the world around them is relevant or irrelevant. If relevant, information becomes a stimulus for response and is then prioritized in relation to other stimuli. One drawback of short-term memory is that it is very small, but its role is vital. It has been called the "bottleneck" of information processing, since anything reaching the long-term memory has to go through the short-term memory. The long-term memory has no known limits, but a relatively long period of time is required to transfer information from the short-term memory to the long-term memory, and vice versa. The long-term memory encodes direct and secondary experiences into "rules that specify action to be taken in response to categories of stimuli."[94] Someone who has stored 50,000 chunks (that is, familiar units) of relevant information can be regarded as an expert who draws upon this indexed information in the same manner as a grand master of chess can play fifty simultaneous games by taking only seconds per move.[95]

Simon notes that the most serious limits on the decision maker's ability to employ appropriate decision-making strategies are the limited capacity of the short-term memory and the amount of time required to store information in the long-term memory.[96] Given the difficulties of attention and access, only a small part of the information stored in the long-term memory plays an active role in problem solving at any given time. Nevertheless, one element of the long-term memory may activate other elements based on prior learning and may increase the amount of information brought to bear on the decision problem. In the case of habitual response, the connecting links between stimulus and response and among elements of the memory may be suppressed from the decision maker's consciousness.[97]

Problem-Solving Process. The problem-solving process begins with what Simon refers to as a "problem space," which is the decision maker's subjective and simplified representation of the decision environment.[98] The problem space determines the possible programs or strategies that will be used for problem solving, as the individual extracts information from the decision environment and uses that information to make a selective search for a solution to the problem as defined. The effectiveness of problem-solving activity is thus a function of how well the critical features of the decision environment are reflected in the problem space.

Having defined the problem space, the decision maker proceeds to scan that space for viable alternative solutions. Search activity is simplified in a number of ways. First, search takes place only in the area defined by the problem space. Second, search is patterned, rather than random; the pattern is determined by simplified rules of thumb (heuristics) suggesting which path should be followed. Selectivity in search is made possible by trial-and-error experimentation and, more importantly, by learning from previous experience.[99] Third, search is sequential rather than simultaneous in nature, which means that alternatives are not considered all at once but are scanned one at a time, evaluated, and accepted or rejected. Only when a given alternative is rejected does the decision maker move on to another alternative. Fourth, the decision maker will attempt to reduce the problem to one already solved, by limiting creative search to bridging the gap between the new problem and the old solution. Finally, search will be limited, and consequently simplified, by feasibility considerations—the activity cannot extend beyond the boundaries imposed by the amount of resources available to conduct the search.

The decision maker may employ any of several strategies in searching the problem space. When there is a standardized response (routine), search is minimal or nonexistent, and the decision maker simply applies the routine. If a routine is not applicable, search may be standardized and based on a pattern or rule stored in the memory to calculate successive moves—Simon calls this "pattern-driven" search. If neither a routine nor a patterned search procedure is applicable, search will take one of two forms: stimulus-driven search, which uses visual cues to determine successive moves; or goal-driven search, which employs a goal or subgoal structure to determine successive moves.[100] Heuristic search in its pattern-driven, stimulus-driven, and goal-driven forms proceeds by defining the difference between current and desired states, finding an operator relevant to each difference, and applying that operator to reduce the difference.[101]

The final step in the individual's decision process is choice. The decision maker will choose the first alternative that satisfices in terms of an aspired level of performance along each relevant dimension. In evaluating alternatives, the decision maker operates with what Simon calls "simple payoff functions" that are "partially ordered."[102] By this he means that the decision maker will examine the consequences of a given alternative in terms of the presence or absence of a particular attribute (a simple payoff function) and will compare alternatives on the basis of at least minimal satisfaction of aspirations in regard to each relevant attribute (a partial ordering of the payoffs). In this way, the decision maker both simplifies the problem of choice and deals with the potential noncomparability of outcomes.

The discovery of a satisficing alternative will normally terminate search and result in a choice. An exception to this rule occurs when a satisficing alternative is discovered too easily. In this case, the level of aspiration will be raised, and search will continue. If a satisficing alternative is not discovered and the cost of additional search is considered to be excessive (that is, greater than the potential benefits), the decision maker will lower his level of aspiration to accommodate alternatives already discovered.[103]

Decision Making in an Organizational Environment

Having outlined the individual's decision process, we can now consider that decision process in an organizational environment and, more particularly, the impact of organizations on individual decisions. Simon states that formal organizations are those in which roles are highly elaborated, relatively stable, and well-defined; transactions among organizational participants are preplanned and precoordinated; and the processes of influence are specific. As an environment for decision making, Simon says the organization can be considered a complex network of decision processes that are oriented toward influencing individual behavior.[104] The organization creates stimuli that determine the focus of attention for specific decisions, provides premises for those decisions, and maintains stable expectations about the actions and reactions of other participants in the organization. The organization also creates personal qualities and habits in the individual (an organizational personality) and provides those in positions of responsibility with the means for exerting authority and influence. In short, Simon states, the organization takes from the individual some of his or her decision autonomy and substitutes for it an organizational decision process.[105]

The behavior of the individual acquires a "broader context of rationality," however, through the environment of choice provided by the organization. In this perception, Simon agrees with Weber, who contended that the organization can overcome the computational limits of man by such devices as specialization and the division of labor, which bring expert knowledge to bear on organizational decisions and limit the required focus of attention. In Simon's words, "The rational individual is, and must be, an organized and institutionalized individual."[106] The behavior of the individual acquires a broader context of rationality as the organization places the individual in a psychological environment that adapts individual decisions to organizational objectives and provides the individual with information to make decisions correctly.

Although Simon is in basic accord with the Classical authors in this formulation, he differs in respect to his assessment of the degree of control that the organization can exercise over individual decisions. Simon argues that the Classical model is not sufficiently attentive to the character of the human organism. It ignores the wide range of roles that participants perform simultaneously and does not treat the coordination of those roles effectively. As a result, the Classical model fails to recognize that only some influences on individual decision making in the organization are under the control of the organization and that individual behavior is manipulable only within limits imposed by potential or actual individual and/or group resistance.[107]

Accordingly, Simon takes as his objective the construction of a model of the organization that more fully accounts for human nature and the relationship of the individual to the organization. In so doing, he addresses what he believes to be the two central concerns of any theory of organizations: (1) why people join, remain in, or leave organizations (the decision to participate), and (2) behavior while people are in the organization (the decision to produce).

The Decision to Participate

In addressing the question why people decide to participate in the organization, Simon adopts Barnard's basic framework, in which the organization is viewed as a system of exchange involving inducements for participation offered by the organization and contributions required by the organization of each participant—or, more precisely, the utilities attached to those inducements and contributions. Each participant will agree to participate, and will continue to participate, in the organization only as long as that individual perceives that he or she is receiving a net positive balance of inducements over required contributions. The organization is in equilibrium when all participants perceive that they are receiving such a balance, and it is solvent as long as the inducements offered by the organization are sufficient to elicit required contributions from the participants.

Simon refers to the perceived utility of inducements and contributions as the Inducement-Contribution Utility Scale.[108] Positions on this scale are a function of two considerations: the perceived desirability of moving from the organization and the perceived ease of such movement. The perceived desirability of moving from the organization depends on the individual's satisfaction with his or her participation. Satisfaction, in turn, is conditioned by a broad range of personal, social, and economic considerations. The perceived ease of movement is a function of the availability of alternatives to participation in the organization and the participant's awareness of those alternatives.

The nature of the "contractual" relationship between the participant and the organization varies among classes of participants. For most participants, the contract is in the form of a "sales contract" in which specific considerations (inducements and contributions) are exchanged. For one class of participants—employees of the organization—the contract is in the form of what Simon calls an "employment contract," in which the employee makes a general agreement to accept organizational authority rather than to exchange specific considerations with the organization.[109] Simon argues that the employer is willing to enter into an employment contract, and to pay additional compensation, because he is likely to be uncertain about the specific task requirements of a position; the employee is willing to enter into an employment contract because he is "substantially indifferent" about the specific tasks to be performed. The result of this contractual arrangement, according to Simon, is that the employee signs, in effect, a "blank check" giving the employer authority over the employee's behavior in the organization.

The nature of the employment contract has important consequences for both the organization and the employee. From the organization's viewpoint, the employee's willingness to sell his services and, consequently, to become a neutral instrument in the performance of those services means that the importance of personal motives is reduced or eliminated and that the employee will accept criteria unrelated to personal values as the basis for his organizational decision making. From the viewpoint of the employee, acceptance of the terms of the employment contract reduces the cognitive demands on his decision-making capacity by restricting his attention to organizational decision-making criteria. These criteria then determine both the alternatives scanned and the alternative selected in a decision situation. In short, the decision environment is simplified.

There are also significant consequences for Simon's theory of the organization. By positing an employment contract, Simon can ignore personal values and the affective components of an employee's behavior in the organization and focus narrowly on the cognitive aspects of individual behavior. It should be noted that Simon does not deny the importance of personal values and motives. Instead, he relegates these considerations to "boundary decisions"—that is, decisions influencing the decision to participate in the organization—not to decisions made once the individual has agreed to participate. Simon admits that this is an oversimplified view, but it is an analytical simplification that plays an important role in the elaboration of his theory.[110]

Consonant with his notion of the employment contract, Simon distinguishes between motives and goals and between individual goals and organizational goals.[111] Motives are forces that lead individuals to select some goals rather than others as decision premises. Personal motives, as implied by the employment contract, pertain only to the decision to participate in the organization. Goals are the result of motives, and they serve as value premises for decisions. Individual goals in the organization are selected by reference to organizational roles, not personal motives. Since individual goals act as constraints on the behavior of others in a mutually interdependent organizational setting, Simon defines organizational goals as "widely shared constraint sets," or—not necessarily equivalent—the constraint sets and criteria of search that define the roles of persons in the upper levels of the organization.[112] Thus, personal motives determine the decision to participate in the organization, but organizational roles determine the selection of organizational goals and the selection courses of action to achieve those goals.

The Decision to Produce

According to Simon, once the individual has decided to participate in the organization, he or she takes on an organizational personality. In so doing, the individual adopts a generalized deference to organizational authority and is "substantially indifferent" regarding the specific tasks to be performed. It then becomes the strategic task of the organization to translate that generalized deference to authority into specific deference to organizational directives. This task raises two central, and related, concerns: employee motivation and compliance.

Whereas the decision to participate in the organization is a function of the Inducement-Contribution Utility Scale, Simon argues that the motivation to produce in the organization is a function of the Satisfaction Scale.[113] The two scales are related, since a higher perceived net positive balance of inducements over required contributions is associated with higher levels of satisfaction. The scales are different in that the Inducement-Contribution Utility Scale, as noted earlier, is a function of both the desire to move and the perceived ease of movement, whereas the Satisfaction Scale is a function of the desire to move only. In other words, the Inducement-Contribution Utility Scale includes opportunity-cost calculations, and the Satisfaction Scale does not. This means that, though functionally related, the scales differ in the location of their zero points.[114] If it is perceived that alternative employment is available and that the employment possibility is superior to the individual's current position, a satisfied employee may leave the organization. In contrast, if alternative employment opportunities do not seem to be available, an employee who is not satisfied may remain in the organization.

Although arguing that one's position on the Satisfaction Scale is related to the decision to produce, Simon rejects the suggestion that there is a simple and direct causal relationship between satisfaction and productivity. Indeed, he would reverse that causal ordering. Simon argues that the motivation to produce stems from a present or anticipated state of discontent and a perception that there is a direct connection between individual productivity and a new state of satisfaction.[115] Thus, the employee produces more to achieve a state of greater satisfaction; he is not more productive simply because he is more satisfied. Nevertheless, the organization must arrange incentives so that the employee perceives a linkage between work effort and rewards.

On compliance, Simon starts with Barnard's concept of authority. He agrees with Barnard that authority resides in a relationship between a superior and a subordinate, not in a position, and that the critical act in the authority relationship is the acceptance of a directive, not its issuance. But Simon proposes an important revision of Barnard's concept of authority. Barnard's position is that authority is exercised when the subordinate either accepts a directive without examining its merits or accepts a directive after examining its merits and being convinced that it is appropriate. In the first case, the directive falls within the subordinate's "zone of indifference"; in the latter case, it falls outside the zone of indifference but within the "zone of acceptance." Simon defines authority as the power to make decisions in the form of a directive or a command that guides the actions of another and, in contrast to Barnard, he contends that authority is exercised *only* when the subordinate holds his critical faculties in abeyance.[116] Thus Simon argues that authority is exercised only in the zone of indifference and in those instances wherein the subordinate examines the merits of a directive and accepts the directive *despite* the fact that he is not convinced of its merits or thinks the directive is wrong. Instances in which the subordinate is convinced of the merits of a directive and accepts the directive fall within the domain of influence or persuasion rather than that of authority.

The questions of motivation and compliance are joined in Simon's consideration of why subordinates defer to organizational authority. Broadly speaking, employee deference to organizational authority is a function of the perceived balance between inducements and contributions required. The larger the perceived net positive balance of inducements over required contributions, the more likely it is that an employee will accept an organizational directive. More specifically, Simon identifies four bases of organizational authority that both derive from, and reinforce, the operation of the organizational incentive system: "authority of confidence" is based on functional status and/or the charismatic qualities of the person issuing the directive; "authority of identification" is the product of the acceptance of a directive by a group with which the individual identifies; "authority of sanctions" is derived from the anticipation that a sanction will be applied; and "authority of legitimacy" springs from the beliefs, mores, and values of a society establishing the right of the superior to command and the duty of the subordinate to obey.[117]

Decision Premises

When the individual has decided to participate and produce, the organizational problem is reduced to one of providing the appropriate premises for individual decision making in the organization. For Simon, the primary responsibility for the provision of decision premises lies with the hierarchy. In this view, he echoes Taylor's injunction that management first make itself efficient before expecting efficiency from its subordinates. The executive's responsibility is both to make decisions and to see that other individuals in the organization make decisions effectively.[118]

Simon offers a number of justifications for his emphasis on hierarchical control in organizational decision making. In a traditional vein, hierarchy is seen as a means for securing coordination, specialization, and accountability.[119] Coordination is achieved as hierarchy synchronizes the disparate elements produced in the process of horizontal specialization in complex organizations.[120] In addition, hierarchy is a method of *vertical* specialization that affords those with greater expertise greater authority in the organization and, consequently, assures that technical experts will play a commanding role in organizational decision making. Finally, by making relatively precise assignments of authority and jurisdiction, hierarchy is a means for assigning responsibilities in the organization and thus locating accountability.

In addition to these traditional arguments, Simon argues that hierarchy simplifies the decision-making task. Indeed, he contends that hierarchy is *the* adaptive form for finite intelligence to take in the face of complexity.[121] Simon maintains that complex hierarchical organizations evolve from relatively stable subsystems that are largely independent units of the overall organization. In this "room-within-rooms" structure, complexity is independent of size, since interdependencies are minimized. The result is that a complex hierarchical organization requires less information transmission, and, consequently, the decision-making process is simplified.[122]

Simon assigns a wide range of critical functions to superiors in the organizational structure. Management sets goals, allocates work by establishing the overall structure of the organization and assigning tasks to its subunits, takes responsibility for innovation and long-range planning, settles disputes, and—most important, from the perspective of decision making—establishes decision premises for the organization. Broad premises (policy) are framed at the upper reaches of the hierarchy; more specific premises are developed as one descends the hierarchy and standard operating procedures are constructed for organizational decision making.

The criterion of efficiency serves as a standard for decision making throughout the organization and, indirectly, as means for hierarchical control. Simon defines efficiency as the maximization of the ratio of net positive results (that is, positive results minus negative results) to opportunity costs.[123] In other words, efficiency is getting the greatest possible results with the lowest possible opportunity costs. Simon argues that the criterion of efficiency should become an internalized standard of performance for each organizational employee. Though each individual seeks efficiency in terms of his or her own values, those values should be the product of an organizational role and, to the extent that management has been successful in establishing organizational objectives, efficiency will be measured in reference to the goals of the management group.[124]

The organizational hierarchy has a variety of means at its disposal for performing its functions. The most important is transmitting the right decision premise to the right person at the right time. The exercise of authority is a central means of establishing decision premises by formal directive. Communication in forms other than formal directives also serves to establish decision premises by influencing which decision stimuli will be encountered and how forcefully particular courses of action will be brought to the attention of the decision maker. Selection processes allow management to choose employees whose values and skills are consistent with the needs of the organizations. Once the individual is in the organization, training can assist in translating general values and skills into specific organizational values and skills as the employee develops a sense of loyalty to the organization.

Organizational Decision Making

To this point, we have examined Simon's ideas on the role of decision premises in organizational behavior and on mechanisms for establishing decision premises. The next concern is the actual processes of decision making in the organization. Simon deals with two basic kinds of decision procedures: programmed and nonprogrammed. Before discussing these decision procedures, we can elaborate on some characteristics that are common to both.

First, both programmed and nonprogrammed decision making start with what Simon calls a "definition of the situation"—a simplified model of reality that is constructed to reduce the complexities of the actual decision environment. The definition of the situation includes the decision maker's perception of the likelihood of future events, the range of alternatives seen as possible, expectations regarding the consequences of those alternatives, and rules for ordering the consequences according to the preferences of the decision maker.[125]

A second characteristic common to the two decision procedures is that some form of means-ends analysis is conducted to link specific actions with the ultimate objectives of the organization. The means-ends chain has both factual and value elements. The factual element is the relationship between alternatives and their consequences. Since lower-level objectives in the means-ends chain are both the ends of lower-level means and the means to achieve higher-level objectives, a factual element exists at all levels except the highest of the means-ends chain. The value element of the means-ends chains is the selection of the ultimate objective or objectives of the organization. Since the ultimate objective of the organization is, by definition, not a means to a higher end, there is no factual element involved in its selection.[126]

The means-ends chain is characterized by increasing uncertainty about the relationship between alternatives and their consequences as one ascends the chain. This factor has two important implications. First, uncertainty introduces a level of indeterminateness in the decision process and forces the use of judgment regarding relationships between alternatives and consequences that though knowable, are not known.[127] Second, uncertainty means that the decision maker will likely use "value indicators" rather than ultimate objectives to choose among alternatives. The value indicator is the highest-level objective in the means-ends chain that can be stated operationally—that is, in such a way that the steps required to meet the objective can be elaborated and that the objective can be measured to determine whether it has, in fact, been achieved.[128]

A third characteristic common to both programmed and nonprogrammed decision making is that decisions (problems) are factored or divided into nearly independent parts and assigned to organizational subunits.[129] The upper levels of the hierarchy make broad determinations and delegate more specific considerations to subordinate units. It is likely that this process will result in what Simon calls a "loosely coupled" system, in which the objectives of the organization and its subunits are only imperfectly reconciled. But since organizations typically operate under conditions of organizational "slack"—that is, resources in excess of the amount required for survival—the organization can tolerate some inconsistency among its objectives.[130]

A fourth common characteristic is that "satisficing" rather than "optimizing" criteria are used in choosing among alternatives. Simon distinguishes between these two standards on the following basis: For optimization, one posits a set of criteria that permits all alternatives to be compared; the optimizing decision maker selects the alternative preferred, by these criteria, to all other alternatives. For satisficing, one posits a set of criteria that describe minimally satisfactory alternatives; the satisficing decision maker simply selects an alternative that meets or exceeds all these criteria.[131]

A fifth common characteristic is that the decision-making process is likely to involve uncertainty absorption. Uncertainty absorption entails drawing conclusions from data that themselves take on an aura of unwarranted certainty. The conclusions become decision premises for the rest of the organization, and points of uncertainty absorption are thus critical locations of power in the organization.[132]

A final common characteristic is that decision making in the organization is routinized. The degree of routinization ranges from specified responses in programmed decision making to routinized search procedures in nonprogrammed decision making.

Simon identifies four phases of the decision-making process that will be used to compare programmed and nonprogrammed decision making in the organization:

1. Finding occasions to make decisions
2. Finding alternative possible courses of action
3. Choosing among alternatives
4. Evaluating past choices[133]

Programmed Decision Making. Programmed decision making occurs when a decision stimulus is repetitive, and the organization has developed a definite procedure for handling the situation. The procedure is embodied in what Simon calls a "performance program," which determines the sequence of responses to a task.[134] Performance programs vary in regard to their degree of specificity. The most specific of the performance programs are organizational routines, in which decisions are made by reference to approved practices rather than by consideration of alternatives on their merits. Thus, choice is fixed, and no search activity is involved. Simon compares organizational routines to individual habit and, perhaps more aptly, to computer programs. In performance strategies, as opposed to routines, the responses are not fixed, although search is restricted to the contingencies and alternatives specified by the strategy. In either case, the performance program deals with a restricted range of situations and consequences, and each program is executed in relative independence from other programs.

Performance programs can be constructed at various levels of the organization. In general, higher levels are more concerned with coordinating programs developed elsewhere than with the development of new programs. Once the organization has established a repertory of standard responses, it develops a classification of program-evoking situations and a set of rules to guide the individual decision maker in determining the appropriate response for each class of situations.

Simon identifies a number of techniques for making and/or influencing programmed decision making in the organization.[135] The traditional methods have been habit, clerical routines, and organizational structure. Habit, the most pervasive technique, is established by such mechanisms as educational and training systems maintained by society and the selection and training processes within the organization. Clerical routines—or standard operating procedures—are explicit statements used to formalize habitual patterns. The organizational structure influences programmed decision making by dividing decisions, providing a common set of presuppositions and expectations regarding role behavior, establishing a structure of goals and subgoals, and instituting a well-defined communication system. More modern techniques include operations research and simulation.[136] Operations research relies on mathematical analysis and model construction to establish programs for organizational decisions. Simulation replicates, in simplified fashion, system operations under a variety of conditions and stipulates appropriate decision rules for those situations.

In terms of the phases of the decision process cited earlier, programmed decision making is a truncated process in which search activity is either severely restricted or nonexistent. Repetitive stimuli serve as a means for identifying occasions for making decisions. Performance programs, in the limiting case of organizational routines, determine the alternative of choice. In performance strategies, the range of alternatives scanned is restricted, and the criterion of choice is defined. Evaluation is relevant only to the extent that, over time, the performance program produces noticeably unsatisfactory outcomes.

Nonprogrammed Decision Making. Nonprogrammed decisions are made in response to novel stimuli for which no structured response exists. Consequently, nonprogrammed decision making requires some search activity, which will follow predictable and prescribed patterns.

Search activity is prompted by the perception of a "performance gap," or a deficiency in the actual as opposed to the desired level of performance. The performance gap may be the product of unsatisfactory performance in regard to previous levels of aspiration, of heightened aspirations resulting from factors such as encounters with new opportunities, or a combination of those factors.[137] The size of the performance gap generally determines the intensity of the search effort—that is, the larger the gap, the more intense will be the search. If the gap is too small, however, it may produce apathy; if too large, it may produce frustration. In those cases, a performance gap will not stimulate search activity. Simon refers to points between these extremes as "optimum stress"; performance gaps in that range lead to the initiation of an action program to eliminate the gap.[138] The goals of the search procedure are determined by desired levels of performance in the organization that are stated in satisficing rather than optimizing terms. The levels of aspiration, in turn, are determined by factors such as the past performance of other similar organizations, changes in the organizational environment, and/or accidental encounters with opportunities.

The search activity of the organization is both sequential and routinized in character. Search is sequential in that one alternative at a time is examined rather than a range of alternatives being scanned simultaneously.[139] Search is routinized in that it follows predictable and prescribed patterns. Variables under the direct control of the organization are examined first. If a satisfactory alternative is not generated, search proceeds to variables not under the direct control of the organization. If the search procedure still has not produced a satisfactory alternative, the level of aspiration is lowered, and the search procedure returns to its initial phase. Search activity continues until an alternative is found that closes the performance gap, in terms of either the original or the revised level of aspiration.[140]

As with programmed decision making, Simon identifies a number of procedures that have been employed in nonprogrammed decision making. Traditionally, organizations have relied on judgment, rules of thumb, and the selection and training of executives to cope with nonprogrammed decision situations.[141] Simon indicates that these techniques can be improved somewhat by training in orderly thinking, the assignment of primary responsibility for nonprogrammed decision making to top executives, and the designation of a specific unit in the organization to deal with nonprogrammed decisions. More recently, Simon believes that major advances have been made in developing techniques for dealing with nonprogrammed decision making.[142] These techniques fall under the general rubric of heuristic problem solving, which involves looking for simplifying clues or hints for right directions to follow in addressing problems. Modern techniques of heuristic problem solving are based on computer simulations of actual decision makers as they engage in problem-solving tasks. This simulation is intended to expose, evaluate, systematize, and routinize the traditional techniques of judgment, intuition, and creativity.

In reference, once again, to the phases of the decision process, in nonprogrammed decision making the occasion of choice is identified by the perception of a performance gap. The alternatives scanned are limited by previous organizational practices, the range of alternatives being incrementally expanded only in the absence of the discovery of a satisfactory alternative. Choice is determined by an encounter with the first satisfactory alternative. Evaluation takes place at each stage of a sequential search process. The major difference between programmed and nonprogrammed decision making is that in the former process, the organization determines the alternative of choice in the form of either an organizational routine or a performance strategy, whereas in the latter, the organization merely provides the parameters for the search procedure and the criterion of choice embodied in an organizationally determined level of aspirations.

Rationality and Organizational Decision Making. We can raise the same question here that was raised in regard to Simon's model of individual decision making: Can the organizational decision procedures just described be considered rational even within the expanded boundaries of Simon's definition of rationality? To the extent that subordinates accept organizational decision premises in the form of routines, such behavior would fall toward the unconscious and nondeliberate end of Simon's rationality continuum but could nonetheless be rational for organizational objectives in terms of the outcomes of the decisions. The employment of performance strategies and nonprogrammed decision procedures represent conscious and deliberate processes in the pursuit of organizational objectives, but they are processes that are likely to fall in the realm of subjective rationality—that is, bounded by the limits on the informational resources and analytical capabilities of the decision maker. In short, although they are not likely optimal, Simon would not summarily dismiss the organizational decision-making procedures described as nonrational.

Nevertheless, although Simon would expand the compass of the term "rationality," he would not contend that all organizational decisions are necessarily rational, even in that expanded context. Available information and analytical capabilities may not be used to the fullest extent. The definition of the situation used in problem solving may not be a sufficiently accurate representation of the decision environment, and, consequently, the problem itself may not be formulated correctly. The process of uncertainty absorption may also lead to nonrational outcomes if the inferences drawn from the raw data are not appropriate to the information received and thus provide faulty premises for subsequent decision making in the organization. Indeed, the very nature of routinized decision making may result in nonrational outcomes if the routines employed are not appropriate to the accomplishment of organizational objectives. This is a particular problem when, as is likely, the application of the routine falls within the individual's zone of indifference and, consequently, is applied without evaluation.

A major concern for Simon regarding the rationality of organizational decisions is the phenomenon of displacement of goals, a process in which instrumental values or goals either are substituted for the ultimate objectives of the organization or become valued because they have desirable consequences that were not originally anticipated.[143] Simon notes two major sources of possible goal displacement: loyalty to organizational subgoals and the use of value indicators in constructing means-ends chains.

Loyalty to organizational subgoals may develop as problems are factored and assigned to subunits in the organization. The result is that members of the subunits may concentrate on the goals of their subunit and lose sight of broader organizational objectives. Loyalty to subunit objectives is, in turn, generally the product of cognitive limits on rationality.

That is, given the inability to think of everything at once, members of the subunit concentrate on considerations limited to the goals of the subunit rather than on broader organizational goals. Thus, selective perception may lead to concentration only on information that is relevant to subgoals. Communication within the subgroup may shape the focus of information and exclude information seen as unrelated to subgoals. The formal division of labor in the organization may limit the information received by the subunit to that considered appropriate to the subgoals of the unit. Finally, professional identification may restrict the focus of attention as professionals emphasize information that is consistent with their calling.[144]

Displacement of goals may also result from the use of value indicators in the decision process. It will be recalled that value indicators are the highest-level operational objectives in the means-ends chain. Value indicators are employed because of uncertainty at the upper levels of the means-ends chain and the consequent inability of organizational decision makers to fully elaborate the chain. If pursuit of the objectives represented by the value indicators leads to the accomplishment of the ultimate objectives of the organization, no displacement of goals occurs. If it does not, a displacement of goals does occur, as instrumental values (the value indicators) replace the terminal values (ultimate objectives) of the organization.[145] Moreover, the displacement of goals is likely to go unnoticed, since, of necessity, the ultimate objectives of the organization cannot be stated operationally, and the organization will have no way of determining whether its ultimate objectives have been achieved.

In summary, the decision-making processes described by Simon are likely to be rational only in a subjective and bounded sense, and they may not be rational even in that sense.

Conclusion

Simon's work and impact are, perhaps, best understood in the characterization by Hunter Crowther-Heyck, who labels research that assumes the freedom of choice of the individual—such as game theory, neoclassical utility theory, and statistical decision theory—as "sciences of choice." The Economic Man is the example of such a decision maker. Behaviorist experimental psychology, sociology, social psychology, anthropology, and political science, instead, assume that individuals are shaped and molded by their social environment, and are, hence, "sciences of control." This decision maker is an Administrative Man. By placing the concept of bounded rationality at the core of his approach, Simon attempted nothing less than the integration of decision theory (choice) and organization theory (control) into an interdisciplinary theory. The exemplar decision maker of this approach is Satisficing Man (or, in Crowther-Heyck's words, Adaptive Man).[146]

As befits the format of this book, so far we have allowed Simon to speak, but given the influence of the bounded rationality concept in various fields of study, we find it necessary to elaborate upon its impact. Let us first consider the study of economics. For decades, economists largely ignored bounded rationality, perhaps because it is so difficult to model.[147] In the 1980s, Kenneth Arrow asked, "Why ... has the work of Herbert Simon, which meant so much to all of us, ... had so little direct consequence?"[148] It seems, though, that economists in the past decade or so have been attempting to model bounded rationality.[149] The concept has also had some influence in political science.[150] But what about its influence in public administration? In the early 1990s, two authors observed that Simon's influence must have been limited because few proverbs had been laid to rest, administrative argument had not at all improved, and positivism was less respected than at the time that Simon wrote "in" public administration.[151] Each of these arguments can easily be countered: Simon merely said that proverbs had no place in a *science* of administration; he never expressed a desire to change the practice of administrative argument; and positivism's alleged loss of respect is irrelevant. Actually, we suggest that logical positivism is still highly respected, even if it is no longer seen as the only approach either to developing a science of public administration or to understanding government. Indeed, this circumstance explains why Simon is less successful in influencing public administration, for here his approach shares the stage with, for example, Gulick's "usable knowledge," Waldo's practical wisdom, and various postmodern approaches.[152]

Perhaps Simon's impact is largest in the field of cognitive psychology. As Simon developed the concept of bounded rationality, he focused predominantly on individual limitations in storing and processing information. While he acknowledged that the social and cultural environment was relevant, he never really sought to model it.[153] Of bounded rationality's four principles—intended rationality, adaptation, uncertainty, and trade-offs[154]—the most exciting recent research concerns the last. First, it has been claimed that bounded rationality is actually closer to maximizing behavior than is often realized, but that the term itself is confusing in its suggestion that maximizing behavior is rejected.[155] Second, and closely related to the first, is that the domain (that is, the relevant environment) of bounded rationality varies with the complexity of the issue at hand. In the case, for instance, of a medical diagnosis, if symptoms clearly point to one diagnosis or a few overlapping diagnoses, it can be said that bounded rationality and maximization are very close; but if symptoms point to thousands of potential illnesses, the gap between them is much larger.[156] Another way of recognizing how close the two concepts can get is to say that bounded rationality must be close to maximization when regret for having taken the wrong decision is low. In public administration and policy, this means that one can expect bounded rationality and maximization to be very close in the case of completely technical and/or politically noncontentious issues and policies, such as highway repair, or in decision domains that are cleanly demarcated from others.[157] However, in the case of so-called wicked problems,[158]—wherein multiple actors clash because of multiple interpretations of a problem— the gap between bounded rationality and maximization is huge.

In reviewing Simon's work, we have raised three primary considerations: Simon's objective of constructing a science of public administration, processes of individual decision making, and decision making in an organizational environment. Simon's proposed foundation for the construction of a science of public administration is the fact-value dichotomy, by which he sought to describe a value-free domain in which scientific investigation could be conducted. That domain consists of the factual premises of administrative decisions, defined as the relationship between alternatives and their consequences. Since that relationship is empirically observable, it is amenable to systematic (that is, scientific) investigation. Simon proposes that two kinds of science be developed: a practical science focused on the objective of developing more efficient administrative procedures, and a pure science, which is to examine the basic processes of human behavior as they relate to decision making.

There are problems with Simon's proposed fact-value dichotomy as a basis for either a practical or a pure science of administration. Acceptance of the standard of efficiency, which is the selection criterion of a practical science of administration, is in itself a value judgment.[159] Thus, a practical science cannot be totally "scientific." Moreover, the fact-value dichotomy defines a rather narrowly circumscribed area for the construction of a practical science of administration. Values are involved in the selection of the ultimate objectives of the organization and, accordingly, fall outside the province of a practical science of administration. But values may also be present at other points in the means-ends chain. The selection of means is not valuationally neutral. That is, whether a means will accomplish a given objective is a factual (empirically observable) consideration, but the selection of the means is not necessarily value-free— one does not rob a bank to obtain funds for a charity even if that alternative leads to a desired consequence. Even an assessment of the relationship between an alternative and its consequences may be contaminated by values if uncertainty exists about the relationship, if judgment therefore must be exercised, and if that judgment is conditioned by the values of the observer. In sum, values may be present throughout the means-ends chain, which limits the area of applicability of a practical science of administration.

The fact-value dichotomy also fails to describe fully the scientific domain for a pure science of administration. Decisions do not constitute the entirety of administrative behavior, and more is empirically observable than the relationship between alternatives and their consequences. Group relationships, styles of supervision, levels of satisfaction, and even whether particular values are held are only a few examples of empirically observable phenomena falling beyond the purview of a science based on facts as defined by Simon.

The second major component of Simon's work is his description of individual decision processes. Here, Simon substitutes the concept of Satisficing Man for the omniscient and lightning-quick calculator of utilities envisioned in economic theory. Simon's view of the decision maker prompts him to expand the definition of rationality, so that rational decisions can be seen to range from conscious and deliberate adaptations of means to ends based on complete information to subconscious and nondeliberate adaptations based on incomplete information.

The concept of Satisficing Man and the associated concept of rationality raise troublesome questions. Simon would seem to stretch the definition of rationality to the breaking point by including within it all forms of functional adaptation, particularly functional adaptation to psychotic disturbances. This inclusiveness raises the question whether rationality as defined by Simon provides any basis for distinguishing between rational and nonrational behavior. Simon contends that all human behavior has a rational component, but the logical implication of that contention is that human behavior also has a nonrational component, and Simon's definition of rationality provides little basis for distinguishing between the two.

In addition, the model of Satisficing Man has limited predictive value. As is acknowledged by Simon, the model does not provide unique solutions or, therefore, precise predictions. In particular, the level of aspirations is an elusive concept that Simon is unable to fully explain. Without a prior definition, the theory has a tendency to degenerate into ex post facto explanations rather than be a predictive construct. Moreover, the model requires a great deal of information in order to generate any predictions—that is, it is not parsimonious. The question here is how much precision we require of prediction. Simon may be right that the model of Satisficing Man yields different behavioral predictions than does the model of Economic Man, but he gives us no criteria to assess whether the difference is worth the cost of acquiring the required information.

The third major component of Simon's work is the description of organizational decision making, which raises two concerns. The first is

Simon's emphasis on cognitive, as opposed to affective, elements of organizational behavior. The second is the intent of Simon's analysis—is it descriptive, prescriptive, both, or neither?

Throughout his analysis, Simon stresses the cognitive aspects of organizational behavior while admitting that a mature science must ultimately deal with both the cognitive and the affective dimensions. Several key elements of Simon's theory illustrate his relative emphasis on cognitive, as opposed to affective, dimensions of organizational behavior. Most basic, of course, is the employment contract, under which, according to Simon, the employee agrees to be a neutral instrument, holding affective considerations in abeyance in regard to behavior in the organization. Simon's assertion that the criterion of efficiency should be the standard for organizational performance is also based on the assumption that the employee is affectively neutral about the means selected to achieve organizational objectives. The exercise of authority itself is characterized as "an abdication of choice," in which the employee either is indifferent about an organizational directive or sets aside his disagreement with the directive. In regard to informal groups, the focus of many discussions of affective considerations, Simon simply advises that the formal organization should set limits on informal relationships and encourage the development of informal groups in ways that are compatible with the accomplishment of organizational objectives. The displacement of goals is interpreted in terms of cognitive limits on rationality rather than its affective dimensions.[160]

Even conflict within the organization is reduced to its cognitive dimensions. Simon does not deny that differences exist between organizational and individual interests; on the contrary, he explicitly rejects the assumption that there is some preordained harmony of interests in the organization.[161] Nevertheless, Simon contends that when the individual decides to participate in the organization, an organizational role is assumed and organizational loyalties are adopted. Thus, potential conflict between individual and organizational interests is resolved. What remains is potential conflict stemming from cognitive limits on rationality.[162] One such source of conflict is the nature of organizational goals themselves. Simon argues that conflict regarding organizational goals is likely to be the product of a cognitive inability to find courses of action satisfactory to the multiple constraints embodied in goals that are only loosely coupled and probably imperfectly reconciled. Another source of potential conflict is parochial loyalties, which Simon attributes to the cognitive inability to fully elaborate means-ends chains for organizational decision making. Finally, potential conflict may derive from such cognitive factors as lack of an acceptable alternative, incomparability of the consequences of alternatives examined, differing perceptions of reality used in constructing the definition of the situation, and/or uncertainty about the relationship between alternatives and their consequences.

Where Simon does deal with affective considerations, he simply argues that affective needs will be well served in the organizations he describes. Simon contends that individuals are uncomfortable in unstructured situations. Accordingly, organizations are most humane—that is, they best serve affective needs—when they strike a balance between freedom and constraint.[163] For lower-level employees, service of affective needs does not mean an absence of hierarchical constraints. It simply means that those constraints should be reasonable and understandable. Furthermore, if a person is motivated to work for organizational objectives, appropriate behavior can be determined by the "logic of the situation" rather than by personal impositions of hierarchical authority.[164]

For middle management, the primary benefits stem from increased centralization, made possible, in part, by the application of computer technology. Centralization allows middle management to concentrate on overall objectives, since subgoal formation is discouraged; it reduces the amount of nonprogrammed decision making that middle management must contend with as hierarchically prescribed performance programs are developed; and it substitutes machine-paced for man-paced operations—which, Simon argues, is less grating on the individual.[165] There are also benefits for top management. The development of programmed decision-making procedures relieves top managers of the tedium of dealing with routine matters and frees them to deal with critical functions such as system design and innovation.[166]

Simon's emphasis on cognitive, as opposed to affective, considerations is clear. Whether such an emphasis is justified is a more difficult matter, for there is a considerable body of literature indicating that affective considerations do influence organizational behavior. The *relative* importance of cognition and affect in the organization, although an empirical question, is one that, despite Simon's insistence on systematic empirical analysis, he fails to address. Simon admits that his formulation of the employment contract, for instance, is at least suspect on descriptive grounds. Nevertheless, he disregards evidence indicating that affective considerations are not abandoned once the employee crosses the threshold of the organization. Thus, the employment contract and all that it implies for organizational behavior stands more as an analytical simplification than as an empirical finding.

This problematic emphasis suggests a broader question about Simon's intent: is his work meant to be descriptive, prescriptive, both, or neither? The apparently anomalous, but nonetheless appropriate, response is probably "all of the above." Simon's original intent was clearly descriptive in nature. In *Administration Science*, he faults the Classical authors for con-

centrating on prescriptions for the allocation of functions and the establishment of an appropriate formal structure of authority. Simon argues
that "the first task of administrative theory is to develop a set of concepts
that will permit the description, in terms of a relevant theory of administration, of administrative situations."[167] Simon's discussions of individual
decision processes and at least some aspects of organizational behavior
would appear to be primarily descriptive.

But Simon also argues that description alone is not sufficient. Instead,
description should provide the foundation for prescription. In Simon's
words, "Until administrative description reaches a higher level of sophis-
tication, there is little reason to hope that rapid progress will be made
toward the identification and verification of valid administrative principles."[168] In other words, the derivation of principles and prescriptions
based on those principles should be the result of an accumulation of descriptive, empirical findings. Simon goes even further in the direction of
prescription in *The Sciences of the Artificial*, where he argues that the fundamental problem of an organization as an artificial system is one of design
to ensure appropriate adaptation to the external environment. Design, in
turn, is concerned with what ought to be (prescription) in devising artificial systems to attain goals.[169] Simon seems to adopt a prescriptive stance
in discussing design elements such as the establishment of hierarchical
control structures, the assignment of design and innovation responsibilities to top executives, the establishment of hierarchically prescribed decision premises, and the development of communication processes.

Finally, in the case of the employment contract, Simon's treatment appears to be neither descriptive nor prescriptive in nature. The concept itself is more a simplifying assumption than a description of, or a
prescription for, organizational behavior. As Simon himself points out,
his notion of the employment contract is "highly abstract and oversimplified, and leaves out of account numerous important aspects of the real
situation."[170]

The problem is not so much that Simon is sometimes descriptive, sometimes prescriptive, and sometimes neither. The problem is determining
when he is which. In the absence of clearer guidelines regarding his intent, the reader is hard-pressed to distinguish one intent from the others.

These qualifying assessments are not meant to detract from the significance of Simon's contributions to the fields of public administration and
organization theory. If there are shortcomings in Simon's analysis, they
should be adjudged as such only by comparison to his ambitions—the
construction of a science of administration and a unified explanation of
human cognition in all its manifestations. Simon proved to be a remarkably insightful and innovative theorist, and his esteemed position in the
social sciences is both assured and well-deserved.

NOTES

1. Cf. chapter 1 on Weber, note 98; and Hunter Crowther-Heyck, *Herbert A. Simon: The Bounds of Reason in Modern America* (Baltimore: Johns Hopkins University Press, 2005), 117.

2. In *Administrative Behavior: A Study of Decision-Making Processes in Administrative Organization*, 2nd ed. (New York: Free Press 1957 [1947]), 39. There is some confusion about when, exactly, the first edition was published. In his second edition, Simon lists 1945 as the first edition, although that version was not issued formally by a publisher; instead, it consisted of 200 mimeographs, produced on the departmental copy machine, and distributed, via a direct-mail campaign, to those he thought might be interested (see Crowther-Heyck, *Herbert A. Simon*, 131). In his early years, Simon regarded that early mimeographed version as his first edition, but official bibliographies list 1947 as the first.

   Simon mentions "administrative man" but does not define the term. We consider Administrative and Satisficing Man as distinct concepts, but they can be regarded as separate—as, for instance, when "administrative man" describes the situation wherein an organization's values displace individual values while "satisficing man" emphasizes the effort at bounded utility maximization. Such a distinction is suggested by Peter L. Cruise in a section title, but he does not discuss the distinction. See Cruise, "Are Proverbs Really So Bad? Herbert Simon and the Logical Positivist Perspective in American Public Administration," *Journal of Management History* 3, no. 4 (1997): 353. For clarification of the nature of Administrative Man as someone who leaves personal considerations and emotions aside in favor of organizational objectives and directives, see Crowther-Heyck, *Herbert A. Simon*, 166–167.

3. While Simon's work is generally described in terms of the fields and disciplines he influenced, the designation "cognitive scientist" best fits the last forty years of his scholarship; see Jonathan Bendor, "Herbert A. Simon: Political Scientist," *American Review of Political Science* 6, no. 2 (2003): 433. There is another reason that we cannot do full justice to Simon: his output was so voluminous that few, if any, scholars can claim to have digested it completely. For instance, his colleague at Carnegie Mellon, Patrick Larkey, observes that "even direct beneficiaries of his work . . . failed to understand and appreciate the breadth and depth of Simon's contributions"; see Patrick D. Larkey, "Ask a Simple Question: A Retrospective on Herbert Alexander Simon," *Policy Sciences* 35, no. 2 (2002): 239–268, 243. Hal Rainey wrote that a committee should write the review of Simon's 1991 autobiography ". . . because most of us do not have the range to assess his work in all the different areas where he contributed"; see Hal G. Rainey, "A Reflection on Herbert Simon: A Satisficing Search for Significance," *Administration & Society* 33, no. 5 (2001): 491–507, 491.

4. Basic data on Simon's life is taken from *Who's Who in America*, vol. 2 (Chicago: Marquis Who's Who, 1976, 1977), 2889. An excellent intellectual biography was published in 2005: Crowther-Heyck's *Herbert A. Simon*. However, in his review of the Crowther-Heyck study (in *Journal of American History* 93, no. 3 [December 2006]), James H. Capshew observes that very little attention is paid there to Simon's non-research life. In other words,

we still need a good overall biography. For a start, we can look at Katherine Simon Frank, "He's Just My Dad!" in *Models of a Man: Essays in Memory of Herbert A. Simon*, ed. Mie Augier and James G. March (Cambridge, Mass.: MIT Press, 2004), 33–43.

5. Herbert Simon, "Rationality as Process and as Product of Thought," *American Economic Review* 68, no. 2 (May 1978): 1. See also Reva Brown, "Consideration of the Origin of Herbert Simon's Theory of 'Satisficing' (1933–1947)," *Management Decision* 42, no. 10 (2004): 1248.

6. Herbert A. Simon, "Comparative Statistics and the Measurement of Efficiency," *National Municipal Review* 26 (1937): 524–525; and a monograph with Clarence Ridley, *Measuring Municipal Activities* (Chicago: International City Managers' Association, 1938).

7. See Brown, "Consideration of the Origin of Herbert Simon's Theory of 'Satisficing,'" 1250.

8. Simon, *Administrative Behavior*, 43. This output measurement orientation has a history dating back to the late 18th century; see, e.g., James C. Scott, *Seeing Like a State: How Certain Schemes to Improve the Human Condition Have Failed* (New Haven, Conn.: Yale University Press, 1998). To be sure, the collection of population statistics became common throughout the Western world between 1790 and 1850. Until the 1980s the aggregation of output measures seems to have been embraced mostly in the United States. One of the earliest activities of the New York Bureau of Municipal Research was to count potholes in New York and thus disprove the mayor's claim that the state of the city's streets was fine. See Camila Stivers, *Bureau Men, Settlement Women: Constructing Public Administration in the Progressive Era* (Lawrence: University Press of Kansas, 2000), chap. 1. From the 1970s on, output measurement conquers the Western world (and beyond) through New Public Management; see Mie Augier and James G. March, "Remembering Herbert A. Simon (1916–2001)," *Public Administration Review* 61, no. 2 (2001): 397.

9. Apparently, Simon also developed an early interest in decision making, since, as a high school student, he worked out a decision-tree analysis to prove that, if played properly, a game of Tic-Tac-Toe would always end in a draw. See Herbert Simon, *Administrative Behavior: A Study of Decision-Making Processes in Administrative Organization*, 2nd ed. (New York: Free Press, 1945), xxviii.

10. Interestingly, given his research concerns, Simon's formal training in mathematics stopped short of calculus. He later taught himself calculus by reading through a textbook and working the problems. See Herbert Simon, *Models of Man: Social and Rational* (New York: Wiley, 1957), ix.

11. Ibid., vii.

12. See Augier and March, "Remembering Herbert A. Simon," 396; and Frank P. Sherwood, "The Half-Century's 'Great Books' in Public Administration," *Public Administration Review* 50, no. 2 (1990): 252. For a complete listing of Simon's bibliography, organized by decade, see www.psy.cmu.edu/psy/faculty/hsimon/hsimon.

13. Simon often said that during his life he really tackled only one huge research problem: understanding decision making in individuals and organizations. See Mie Augier and Edward Feigenbaum, "Herbert A. Simon: Biographical Memoirs," *Proceedings of the American Philosophical Society* 147, no. 2 (2003): 194.

14. Simon, *Administrative Behavior*.

15. Herbert Simon, Donald W. Smithburg, and Victor A. Thompson, *Public Administration* (New York: Knopf, 1950).

16. Allen Newell and Herbert A. Simon, "The Logic Theory Machine," *IRE Transactions on Information Theory* 2, no. 3 (1956): 61–79.

17. Allen Newell, J. C. Shaw, and Herbert Simon, "Elements of a Theory of Human Problem Solving," *Psychological Review* 65, no. 3 (1958): 151–166.

18. Simon, *Models of Man*.

19. James G. March and Herbert A. Simon, *Organizations* (New York: Wiley, 1958). Bryan D. Jones called 1957–1958 Simon's critical year; see Jones , "Bounded Rationality and Public Policy: Herbert A. Simon and the Decisional Foundation of Collective Choice," *Policy Sciences* 35, no. 2 (2002): 270.

20. Herbert Simon, *The New Science of Management Decision*, rev. ed. (Englewood Cliffs, N.J.: Prentice-Hall, 1977).

21. Herbert A. Simon, *The Sciences of the Artificial* (Cambridge, Mass.: MIT Press, 1969).

22. Herbert A. Simon, *Models of Thought* (New Haven: Yale University Press, 1979), xi.

23. Simon, *Sciences of the Artificial*, 129; the curriculum example is on p. 190 et seq.

24. Herbert A. Simon, *Models of My Life* (New York: Basic Books, 1991).

25. Ibid., 275.

26. See Robert Faggan, review of *Models of My Life*, in *Modern Language Studies* 22, no. 4 (1992): 107. The most peculiar example of the effort to apply his theory to his personal life is found in chapter 15, entitled "Personal Threads in the Warp," wherein he analyzes his response to falling in love with another woman; see pp. 244–246.

27. Simon allegedly described himself as a "monomaniac about decision making." See Armand Hatchuel, "Toward Design Theory and Expandable Rationality: The Unfinished Program of Herbert Simon," *Journal of Management and Governance* 5, no. 1 (2001): 260; and Mie Augier and Edward Feigenbaum, "Herbert A. Simon," *Proceedings of the American Philosophical Society* 147, no. 2 (2003): 194.

28. Quoted in Brown, "Consideration of the Origin of Herbert Simon's Theory of 'Satisficing,'" 1248, and taken from an autobiographical chapter that Simon published in 1980.

29. Quoted in Larkey, "Ask a Simple Question," 241.

30. Bendor, "Herbert A. Simon: Political Scientist," 466.

31. Herbert A. Simon, "The Proverbs of Administration" (1946), in *Readings on Modern Organizations*, ed. Amitai Etzioni (Englewood Cliffs, N.J.: Prentice-Hall, 1969), 32–49; Robert A. Dahl, "The Science of Public Administration: Three Problems," *Public Administration Review* 7, no. 1 (1947): 1–11; Simon, "A Comment on 'The Science of Administration,'" comment on article by Robert Dahl (1947), in *Administrative Questions and Political Answers*, ed. Claude E. Hawley and Ruth G. Weintraub (New York: Van Nostrand, 1966), 34–37.

32. Simon, *Models of My Life*, 114.

33. In order of appearance: Dwight Waldo, "Development of Theory of Democratic Administration," *American Political Science Review* 46, no. 1 (1952): 81–103; Herbert A. Simon, "Development of Theory of Demo-

cratic Administration: Replies and Comments," *American Political Science Review* 46, no. 2 (1952): 494–496; Waldo, "Development of Theory of Democratic Administration: Replies and Comments," *American Political Science Review* 46, no. 2 (1952): 500–503; Edward C. Banfield, "A Criticism of the Decision Making Schema," *Public Administration Review* 17, no. 3 (1957): 278–285; Simon, "'The Decision-Making Schema': A Reply," *Public Administration Review* 18, no. 1 (1958): 60–63; Simon, "Applying Organization Technology to Organization Design," *Public Administration Review* 33, no. 3 (1973): 268–278; Chris Argyris, "Some Limits of Rational Man Organizational Theory," *Public Administration Review* 33, no. 3 (1973): 253–267; Simon, "Organizational Man: Rational or Self-Actualizing?" *Public Administration Review* 33, no. 4 (1973): 346–353; Lowi v. Simon in *PS: Political Science and Politics* 1, no. 1 (1993): 49–53, and in *Journal of Public Administration Research and Theory* 2, no. 1 (1992): 110–112.

34. Simon, *Models of My Life*, 277.
35. See Linda F. Dennard, "Neo-Darwinism and Simon's Bureaucratic Antihero," *Administration & Society* 26, no. 4 (1995): 475–476.
36. Inviting Waldo and others to do the same, in his response to Waldo's challenge in *APSR*, Simon wrote: "I suggest that as the first step they acquire a sufficient technical skill in modern logical analysis to attack the positivists on their own ground." See Simon, "Development of Theory of Democratic Administration: Replies and Comments," 501.
37. Herbert A. Simon, Guest Editorial, *Public Administration Review* 55, no. 5 (1995): 404–405.
38. See John W. Ellwood, "Political Science," in *The State of Public Management*, ed. Donald F. Kettl and H. Brinton Milward (Baltimore: Johns Hopkins University Press, 1996), 56. There are, however, public administration scholars working in the tradition of Simon who believe that public administration no longer fits in political science. See, e.g., Kenneth J. Meier, "The Public Administration of Politics, or What Political Science Could Learn from Public Administration," *PS: Political Science & Politics* 40, no. 1 (2007): 3.
39. These scholars include, i.a., those involved in the Minnowbrook I and II conferences, such as H. George Frederickson and Frank Marini, and those involved with the Blacksburg Manifesto, including Gary L. Wamsley. See chapter 10 for more on this.
40. In a letter dated April 27, 1945, Simon asked Barnard to read a draft of *Administrative Behavior*. Barnard wrote a lengthy reply on May 11, in which he observed, i.a., "It seems to me you have to bring to the front that the ascertainment of fact even in physics … is in a fundamental sense a process of valuation." Simon did hold on to a strict fact-value separation. On September 23, 1946, he writes to ask if Barnard would be willing to write an introduction to the book, and Barnard agrees. A year later, Barnard informs Simon that he is "… frankly amazed at the simplicity and clarity of the book because the first attempt was so much the reverse." The letters are published in William B. Wolf, "The Simon-Barnard Connection," *Journal of Management History* 1, no. 4 (1995): 88–99. The quotations in this note can be found on pp. 91 and 96, respectively.
41. Quoted in Milorad M. Nivocevic, Thomas J. Hench, and Daniel A. Wren, "'Playing by Ear' … 'in an Incessant Din of Reasons'": "Chester Barnard

and the History of Intuition in Management Thought," *Management Decision* 40, no. 10 (2002): 999.

42. See "Herbert A. Simon, Testimony on the Social Sciences: Senate Committee on Commerce, Science, and Technology, September 29, 1989," *PS: Political Science and Politics* 23, no. 1 (1990): 33–34.

43. Simon, *Administrative Behavior*, xii.

44. Woodrow Wilson, "The Study of Administration," in *Classics of Public Administration*, ed. Jay M. Shafritz and Albert C. Hyde (Oak Park, Ill.: Moore Publishing, 1978), 10.

45. Ibid., 11.

46. Ibid., 12.

47. See Simon, *Administrative Behavior*, 58; and Herbert A. Simon, "The Changing Theory and Practice of Public Administration," in *Contemporary Political Science*, ed. Ithiel de Sola Pool (New York: McGraw-Hill, 1961), 87–88.

48. Simon, *Administrative Behavior*, 58–59.

49. Simon, "Changing Theory," 88.

50. Ibid., 89–91.

51. Ibid., 106.

52. Simon, *Administrative Behavior*, 47.

53. Ibid., 45–46.

54. Ibid., 5, 46, 48.

55. Simon, "Changing Theory," 99.

56. Ibid.

57. Simon, *Administrative Behavior*, 58.

58. Simon, "Changing Theory," 113.

59. Care should be taken to distinguish among Classical authors in drawing this difference. Simon approved of the techniques, if not the organizational *gestalt*, of the Scientific Management movement, which had emphasized systematic, empirical investigation. However, he had little use for the "principles" of the Departmentalists, arguing that those principles amount to little more than rules of thumb for organizational analysis and, like proverbs, tend to occur in contradictory pairs. See Simon, *Administrative Behavior*, 20–41.

60. Simon does not deny the utility of prescriptive analysis. Instead, he believes that description should precede prescription and that prescription should be based on a better understanding of how organizations actually operate. See Simon, *Administrative Behavior*, 37. For a recent reassessment of the usefulness of proverbs, see Cruise, "Are Proverbs Really So Bad?" 342–359.

61. Simon, "A Comment on 'The Science of Administration,'" 34.

62. Simon, *Administrative Behavior*, 253.

63. Simon, Smithburg, and Thompson, *Public Administration*, 10–12.

64. See, i.a., Herbert A. Simon, "Why Public Administration?" *Journal of Public Administration Research and Theory* 8, no. 1 (1998): 7; Herbert Simon, "Public Administration in Today's World of Organizations and Markets," *PS: Political Science and Politics* 33, no. 4 (December 2000): 754. Of course, he was not the first to say this. Back in the nineteenth century, Robert Owen observed that complete self-regulation of the market would create great and permanent evils; mentioned in Karl Polanyi, *The Great Transformation* (New York: Rinehart, 1944), 130.

65. Simon, Smithburg, and Thompson, *Public Administration*, 8.

66. See Hatchuel, "Toward Design Theory and Expandable Rationality."

67. Simon, *Administrative Behavior,* xxiv.
68. Ibid., xxiii.
69. Ibid., xxx, xxxi.
70. Ibid., xxiii.
71. Simon, *Models of Man,* 200.
72. Ibid., 241; March and Simon, *Organizations,* 138; and Herbert Simon, "Rational Decision Making in Business Organizations," *American Economic Review* 69, no. 4 (September 1979): 500.
73. March and Simon, *Organizations,* 138; and Herbert Simon, "The Behavioral and Social Sciences," *Science* 209, no. 4 (July 1980): 75.
74. March and Simon, *Organizations,* 138.
75. Simon, "Rational Decision Making in Business Organizations," 495.
76. Ibid., 497.
77. Simon, "Rationality as Process and as Product of Thought," 2. Prolific scholars such as Simon are frequently misunderstood or taken out of context. See, for instance, John W. Murphy, "Reason, Bounded Rationality, and the *Lebenswelt*: Socially Sensitive Decision Making," *American Journal of Economics and Sociology* 51, no. 3 (1992): 293–304.
78. Simon, *Administrative Behavior,* xxiv.
79. Ibid., xxvi. David Dequech argues that Simon overemphasizes conscious rule-following and neglects the influence of habits and of nonorganizational institutions. See Dequech, "Bounded Rationality, Institutions, and Uncertainty," *Journal of Economic Issues* 35, no. 4 (2001): 912, 921.
80. See Matthias Klaes and Esther-Mirjam Sent, "A Conceptual History of the Emergence of Bounded Rationality," *History of Political Economy* 37, no. 1 (2005): 27–59.
81. As quoted in Thomas J. Hammond, "In Defence of Luther Gulick's 'Notes on the Theory of Organization,'" *Public Administration* (UK) 68, no. 1 (1990): 167.
82. On this contrast in the literature regarding how bounded rationality is approached, see Bendor, "Herbert A. Simon: Political Scientist," 438–439.
83. Simon, *Administrative Behavior,* 75.
84. Ibid., 76–77.
85. Simon cites some steps in mathematical invention as evidence of subconscious rationality. Ibid., 76.
86. Simon, "Behavioral and Social Sciences," 75.
87. Simon, *Sciences of the Artificial,* ix.
88. Ibid., 53.
89. March and Simon, *Organizations,* 10.
90. Ibid., 140.
91. It has been argued that bounded rationality applies only to some specific situations, that it does not apply to situations of fundamental uncertainty, and that it does not allow for novelty and creativity. Bounded rationality "... either neglects the connection between genuine innovation and rationality or implies that innovating is not rational. It does so by overemphasizing rule following and overlooking rule breaking." See Dequech, "Bounded Rationality, Institutions, and Uncertainty," 922–923.
92. March and Simon, *Organizations,* 10.
93. Ibid., 11.
94. On short- and long-term memory, see also Bendor, "Herbert A. Simon: Political Scientist," 437; and Jones, "Bounded Rationality and Public Policy," 275.

95. In psychology, a "chunk" is defined as "a technical unit of measurement of mental storage." See Herbert A. Simon, "Decision Making: Rational, Nonrational, Irrational," *Educational Administration Quarterly* 29, no. 3 (1993): 402–403; and Herbert A. Simon, "Bounded Rationality and Organizational Learning," *Organization Science* 2, no. 1 (1991): 129.

96. Simon, *Sciences of the Artificial*, 53.

97. March and Simon, *Organizations*, 11.

98. Herbert Simon, "Information-Processing Theory of Human Problem Solving," in *Handbook of Learning and Cognitive Processes*, vol. 5, ed. W.K. Estes (Hillsdale, N.J.: Lawrence Erlbaum Associates, 1978), 272–273.

99. Indeed, Simon maintains that the distinguishing characteristic of humans is their ability to anticipate the consequences of alternative courses of action based on previously observed regularities. This is what Simon refers to as "docility," or the ability of individuals to observe the consequences of previous behavior and to adjust their behavior on the basis of those observations to achieve desired purposes. See Simon, *Administrative Behavior*, 85–86.

100. Simon, "Information-Processing Theory of Human Problem Solving," 283.

101. Ibid., 278.

102. Simon, *Models of Man*, 246–248, 250–252.

103. Simon acknowledges that, in contrast to the optimizing criterion of Economic Man, the satisficing criterion of choice does not provide a unique solution to the problem of choice and thus reduces the utility of his model in regard to predicting decision-making behavior. However, he contends that if we learn enough about the dynamics of setting levels of aspiration, a near-unique solution is possible. That enterprise has not yet been successfully completed. See ibid., 253.

104. Simon, *Administrative Behavior*, 220.

105. Ibid., 8.

106. Ibid., 102.

107. March and Simon, *Organizations*, 81–82.

108. Ibid., 85.

109. Simon, *Models of Man*, 183–195.

110. Ibid., 167.

111. Herbert Simon, "On the Concept of Organizational Goals," in *A Sociological Reader on Complex Organizations*, 2nd ed., ed. Amitai Etzioni (New York: Holt, Rinehart, and Winston, 1969), 158–174.

112. Ibid., 174.

113. Ibid., 51.

114. Ibid., 85–86.

115. Ibid., 51.

116. Simon, *Administrative Behavior*, 126.

117. Simon, Smithburg, and Thompson, *Public Administration*, 188–201.

118. Herbert Simon, "Decision Making and Organizational Design," in *Organization Theory*, ed. D.S. Pugh (Baltimore: Penguin, 1971), 193.

119. Simon, *Administrative Behavior*, 9.

120. But Simon does not feel that unity of command is required to secure coordination. Decision premises may originate from a number of sources. It is only necessary that these premises be satisfactorily synchronized. In this stance, Simon agrees with Taylor and departs from a fundamental "principle" of the Departmentalists. Ibid., 22–26, 140–147.

121. Simon, "Decision Making and Organizational Design," 204.
122. The degree of decentralization possible within the hierarchical structure varies with the decision-making needs of the organization. The question for Simon is not *whether* to decentralize—he says this is a laudable, and necessary, objective—but how far to decentralize. The permissible degree of decentralization in the organization is dependent on the level of interaction required for organizational decision making. An organizational division of labor that minimizes interdependencies permits the maximum amount of decentralization, since organizational subunits can then select their own decision premises with minimal impact on other parts of the organization. March and Simon, *Organizations*, 208.
123. Simon, Smithburg, and Thompson, *Public Administration*, 493. Opportunity costs are simply opportunities foregone by selection of a particular project as opposed to other possible projects.
124. Simon, *Administrative Behavior*, 172. The criterion of efficiency assumes that employees are neutral regarding the means employed to achieve organizational objectives. This assumption is consistent with the terms of the employment contract, in which the employee becomes a neutral instrument of the organization. As such, the employee values not the act of production but the right to consumption, which that production entails. Simon does caution that employees will be neutral only to the extent that minimal standards have been reached in terms of the satisfaction of the employee. See Simon, Smithburg, and Thompson, *Public Administration*, 493–497.
125. March and Simon, *Organizations*, 150–151.
126. Simon, *Administrative Behavior*, 50.
127. Ibid., 50–51.
128. March and Simon, *Organizations*, 155–156.
129. Ibid., 192–193.
130. Ibid., 126.
131. Ibid., 140.
132. Ibid., 165.
133. Simon, *New Science of Management Decision*, 40–41.
134. March and Simon, *Organizations*, 141–142.
135. Simon, *New Science of Management Decision*, 50–51.
136. Ibid., 54–62.
137. March and Simon, *Organizations*, 182–183.
138. Ibid., 184.
139. Ibid., 180.
140. Ibid., 179–180.
141. Simon, *New Science of Management Decision*, 51–54.
142. Ibid., 62–77.
143. March and Simon, *Organizations*, 38–39.
144. Ibid., 152–153.
145. Simon, *Administrative Behavior*, 176.
146. See Crowther-Heyck, *Herbert A. Simon*, 5–6, 166–167.
147. As, for instance, Rajiv Sarin notes when writing about "... our very limited ability to describe and model bounded rationality"; see Sarin, review of Jennifer J. Halpern and Robert N. Stern, *Debating Rationality: Nonrational Aspects of Organizational Decision Making* (Ithaca, N.Y.: Cornell University Press, 1998), *Journal of Economic Literature* 37, no. 3 (1999): 1182–1183. In his lecture upon accepting the Nobel Prize for Economics, Simon ob-

serves this difficulty in terms of two specific challenges. First, a multitude of facts on organizational decision making are available that fit the behavioral model he proposes, but it is not yet known how to test this model in a formal way, nor "... do we quite know what to do with the observation that the specific decision-making procedures used by organizations differ from one organization to another." Second, while the basic mechanisms of rational human behavior are "relatively simple," human behavior cannot "be accounted for by a handful of invariants." For it "... operates in interaction with extremely complex boundary conditions imposed by the environment and by the very facts of human long-term memory and of the capacity of human beings, individually and collectively, to learn." See Herbert A. Simon, "Rational Decision-making in Business Organizations," Nobel Memorial Lecture, Economic Sciences, December 8, 1978, 363, 367.

148. As quoted in Oliver E. Williamson, "Chester Barnard and the Incipient Science of Organization," in *Organization Theory: From Chester Barnard to the Present and Beyond*, ed. Oliver E. Williamson (New York: Oxford University Press, 1990), 182.

149. Sarin, review of Halpern and Stern, *Debating Rationality*, 1183–1184. See also Herbert A. Simon, "Bounded Rationality in Social Science: Today and Tomorrow," *Mind & Society* 1, no. 1 (2000): 25–39, in which he observes that bounded rationality is rapidly replacing maximization assumption in economics.

150. See the chapters on Herbert Simon by Robert E. Goodin and Bryan D. Jones in *Competition & Cooperation: Conversations with Nobelists about Economics and Political Science*, ed. James E. Alt, Margaret Levi, and Elinor Ostrom (New York: Russell Sage Foundation, 1999). In his response to both pieces, Simon writes (112) that "... my tribal allegiance is to political science." But see Bendor, "Herbert A. Simon: Political Scientist," 443, on how limited Simon's impact on political science has been.

151. See Christopher Hood and Michael Jackson, *Administrative Argument* (Aldershot, Hants, England: Dartmouth, 1991), 20–21.

152. Public administration scholars find it difficult to outline why Simon's *Administrative Behavior* was so influential. See, e.g., Frank P. Sherwood, "The Half-Century's 'Great Books' in Public Administration" and Rainey, "A Reflection on Herbert Simon," 495. On these four main approaches in public administration (i.e., scientific knowledge, practical experience, practical wisdom, and relativist perspectives), see Jos C.N. Raadschelders, "Understanding Government: Four Intellectual Traditions in the Study of Public Administration," *Public Administration* (UK) 86 (2008 forthcoming).

153. Early on, Simon pointed to the need for understanding the environment—see, e.g., *Administrative Behavior*, 240. He is credited with preparing the ground for the contingency theory of organizations, but he never went beyond basic levels of analyzing decision processes. See Hal G. Rainey, "Products of Simon's Progress: Similarities and Contrasts in Three Major Contributions," *Public Administration Quarterly* 12, no. 4 (1989): 398 and 408. Later in his career, Simon said about the mind-environment interface, "Human rational behavior ... is shaped by scissors whose two blades are the structure of the task environment and the computational capabilities of the actor." Quoted in Joseph Porac and Zur

Shapira, "On Mind, Environment, and Simon's Scissors of Rational Behavior," *Journal of Management and Governance* 5, nos. 3–4 (2001): 206–207.

154. These four principles are discussed in Jones, "Bounded Rationality and Public Policy," 272–275. See also Bryan D. Jones, "Bounded Rationality and Political Science: Lessons from Public Administration and Public Policy," *Journal of Public Administration Research and Theory* 13, no. 4 (2003): 397–399.

155. Ibid., 274.

156. Based on author's discussions with Dr. Rick Thomas, a cognitive psychologist at the University of Oklahoma, and William Hanson, ABD, University of Oklahoma, who works on a study of decision making. For the example of varying bounded rationality domains in determining medical diagnoses, see Thomas's coauthored work in progress: Rick Thomas, Michael R. Dougherty, Amber Sprenger, and J. Isaiah Harbison, "Diagnostic Hypothesis Generation and Human Judgment," referenced with permission from Thomas.

157. We must keep in mind that Simon was quite optimistic about the possibility that fairly high levels of rationality could be achieved in carefully designed organizational units. See Rupert F. Chisholm, "The Storing Critique Revisited: Simon as Seen in the Science of Politics," *Public Administration Quarterly* 12, no. 4 (1989): 434. See also note 82 above for Bendor's contrast between the "glass is half full" and the "glass is half empty." Simon is actually close to Max Weber in believing that bureaucracy is the best available type of organization for advancing rationality and efficiency; on this point, see Charles R. Davis, "The Administrative Rational Model and Public Organization Theory," *Administration & Society* 28, no. 1 (1996): 39–60.

158. The term "wicked problems" was coined by H. Rittel and M. Webber, in "Dilemmas in a General Theory of Planning," *Policy Sciences* 4, no. 1 (1973). "As distinguished from problems in the natural sciences, which are definable and separable and have many solutions that are findable, the problems of governmental planning—and especially those of social or policy planning—are ill-defined: and they rely upon elusive political judgment for resolution . . ." (160), and, "In a setting in which a plurality of publics is politically pursuing a diversity of goals, how is the large society to deal with its wicked problems in a planful way? How are goals to be set, when the valuative bases are so diverse . . ." (168).

159. Simon, Smithburg, and Thompson, *Public Administration*, 491.

160. For an interpretation of displacement of goals based on affective considerations, see Robert K. Merton, "Bureaucratic Structure and Personality," in *Reader in Bureaucracy*, ed. Robert K. Merton et al. (New York: Free Press, 1952), 361–371.

161. Simon, Smithburg, and Thompson, *Public Administration*, 502.

162. March and Simon, *Organizations*, 112–135.

163. Simon, *New Science of Management Decision*, 98.

164. Ibid., 121.

165. Ibid., 119.

166. Ibid., 33.

167. Simon, *Administrative Behavior*, 37.

168. Ibid., 38.

169. Simon, *Sciences of the Artificial*, 59.

170. Simon, *Models of Man*, 192.

Chapter 8

Charles E. Lindblom:
Probing the Policy Process

As with some other authors discussed in this volume, inclusion of the works of Charles Lindblom in a book on public administration appears, at first blush, somewhat odd.[1] Lindblom's formal training was in economics, and, though he ventured into political science—which some consider the disciplinary home of public administration—he never identified himself as a political scientist, let alone as a theorist in the study of public administration. The majority of his writings did not appear in the usual public administration publication outlets; only the *Public Administration Review* published three of his pieces (in 1959, 1964, and 1979). Thus, including Lindblom here is yet another affirmation of the eclectic nature of the field of public administration, and of its determination to incorporate helpful ideas and knowledge regardless of their disciplinary origins.

Lindblom's thinking has had a profound impact on the field of public administration in a number of ways. His work on decision making—encompassing, as we shall see, an alternate view of rationality—differs substantially both from the rational-choice, or synoptic, model and from Simon's offering of simplified search and bounded rationality. It is in this realm of organizational decision making that the connections between Lindblom and public administration are most obvious. Lindblom may not have been centrally interested in decision making within the organization (as Simon was), but, early on, he was aware of the relevance of his thoughts to the study of public administration.[2] If the compass of public administration is extended to matters of public policy, as many have argued it should be, then the processes Lindblom describes are directly relevant to public administration. Clearly, partisan mutual adjustment and incrementalism are integral to the administrator's involvement in the policy process, regardless of one's evaluation of those concepts. And, if the province of public administration is extended into the political realm, as Dwight Waldo also thought necessary, then Lindblom's treatment of broader social and political matters is a vital approach to understanding the environment in which the public administrator must operate. Indeed, in the second half of his career, Lindblom turned his attention again (as he had in his 1949 study) to the broad social and political processes that transcend the traditional boundaries of public administration.

Even if one is interested only in organizational decision making, Lindblom's approach can best be understood in the context of his wider range of interests. Consequently, this chapter starts with a consideration of those broader interests and then narrows to issues more directly and palpably related to the enterprise of public administration. We will offer a critique of Lindblom's conceptual endeavors (that is, incrementalism and mutual adjustment) and assess his worldview (that is, domination of elites, impairment of thought) in a separate, penultimate section.

Life

Charles Edward Lindblom was born in California on March 21, 1917, and attended Stanford University, where he earned a BA in economics and political science in 1937.[3] He received a PhD in economics at the University of Chicago in 1945; his dissertation was published as a book, *Unions and Capitalism*, in 1949. Lindblom served on the Economics faculty at the University of Minnesota from 1939 to 1946, then moved to Yale University, where he retired in 1991. He is currently Sterling Professor Emeritus of Economics and Political Science at Yale. Lindblom gained experience as a practitioner when working temporarily at the RAND Corporation in the late 1950s and at the State Department between 1963 and 1965, as economic adviser to the head of the U.S. Agency for International Development mission to India, among other positions.[4] He has served as president of both the American Political Science Association (1981–1982) and the Association of Comparative Economics Studies.

However, that simple picture masks an underlying complexity in both Lindblom's professional career and his writings, leaving him in a somewhat ambivalent position between disciplines and a somewhat ambiguous role as social critic. The disciplinary ambivalence was evidenced early on. As an undergraduate, Lindblom vacillated in his choice of a major—first choosing economics, then abandoning it for political science. He complained that economics was overly "narrow, complacent, and formalistic," but, apparently, he overcame those objections somewhere along the line, for he later entered the University of Chicago to study for his doctorate in economics, "because the mushiness of political science, indeed its frequent emptiness ... were no easier to bear."[5] While at Chicago, Lindblom encountered Frank Knight, whom he described as an extraordinary economist, philosopher, and teacher. Lindblom attributed to Knight his fascination with "the hidden intricacies, but especially the hidden rationalities, of complex social institutions,"[6] as well as his interest in incrementalism and in processes of mutual adjustment. All of these concepts were to be integral to Lindblom's subsequent academic pursuits.

His commitment to economics lasted through his graduate studies and into his subsequent faculty appointment at the University of Minnesota. However, disenchantment soon returned. Though Lindblom found economics attractive because of its strong theoretical core, he was dismayed by its reluctance to venture beyond inquiries permitted by its restricted, albeit formidable, analytical techniques. Lindblom's ambivalence was deepened by his perception that the Economics faculty at Minnesota failed to appreciate the kind of work he wanted to do. By his own account, he had barely started teaching there when the department chair criticized him for giving a talk about market socialism before undergraduate students. In his words: "Eventually I was 'let go' rather than promoted," and he decided that "... more caution was called for with respect to the kinds of scholarly interest I pursued."[7]

His lack of acceptance by the Economics faculty at Minnesota, coupled with his reservations about the field itself, led Lindblom to seek both a more supportive environment and a new disciplinary home. His quest took him to Yale and, eventually, to its Political Science Department, but even there, happiness and resolution proved elusive.

Though originally appointed to Economics, Lindblom's involvement with the department waned over time. A graduate seminar jointly taught with political scientist Robert Dahl was a turning point in Lindblom's academic identification and in the direction of his research. The seminar led to a collaboration on a book entitled *Politics, Economics, and Welfare* (1953), which addressed the big issues that Lindblom felt were proscribed by the analytical myopia of the field of economics. Described by Lindblom as an "amateurish project selection"[8] and borne of the legacy of the social disorganization of the Great Depression,[9] the book investigated the structures and processes of social control, thereby setting the stage for the subsequent work of both its distinguished authors. In Lindblom's case, it led to two more books and several articles.[10] In *A Strategy of Decision*, written with David Braybrooke (1963), he expanded upon the concept of disjointed incrementalism, which he had begun to develop in his study with Dahl. In *The Intelligence of Democracy* (1965), the subtitle—*Decision Making through Mutual Adjustment*—captures what aspect of the earlier book with Dahl he would elaborate upon. Lindblom summarized his ideas on mutual adjustment and partisan analysis in *The Policy-Making Process*, a small textbook that enjoyed three editions (1968, 1980, 1992).

Despite the immediate, and lasting, impact of *Politics, Economics, and Welfare*, the book was not well-received by Lindblom's colleagues in the Economics Department at Yale. In fact, the department chair asked him to resign (even though Lindblom was a tenured associate professor) and warned that he would never be promoted to the rank of full professor. When he finally became a full professor nonetheless, the department chair "... explained that it was warranted by [his] reputation 'elsewhere.'"[11] Ever the contrarian, Lindblom only intensified his interest in political science and the role of social critic. Still, the ambivalence remained.

Lindblom has maintained his involvement in both economics and political science, though he remains a critic of both, and though, it seems, he doesn't feel fully appreciated by either.[12] Nor has he fully embraced his adopted role of social critic. Lindblom maintains that, early in his career, he found it safer to focus on the "hidden rationalities" of the social order than on its defects: "It is true that the earlier work emphasizes what works (though badly) in politics, the more recent work what does not work (though it persists)."[13] Thus, in the early years of his career, he yielded to institutional criticism and disciplinary expectations. With the attitude of a distant observer, Lindblom later describes his career as being "no chronicle of a conspicuous dissenter bravely fighting the constraints of bigots. It is an ordinary story of a conventional career, some prudent adaptations to its milieu, a confining set of disciplinary traditions, and a willingness to disregard them growing only slowly with age and security."[14]

Lindblom does avow a continuing and underlying concern with "ugly" social processes and the defects of social organization that becomes more apparent in his later writings. This concern started with *Politics and Markets* (1977), which won the Woodrow Wilson Award of the American Political Science Association[15]; continued in *Usable Knowledge* (1979, coauthored with David Cohen); and culminated in the radical social critique, *Inquiry and Change* (another winner of the APSA's Woodrow Wilson award), in which he focused on "the dark side of the human accomplishment that we call culture, and the dark side as well of the socialization of children into law-abiding adults, both of which create impairments of people's capacities to think."[16]

A self-proclaimed liberal, radical, or radical-liberal,[17] Lindblom lists his interests as reducing inequalities, ameliorating the misery of the Third World, and conserving the planet.[18] But even here, the victory is not complete. Late in his career, Lindblom confesses to finding himself "both critical of all existing societies ... and yet fascinated by such feats of social organization as are achieved by unplanned and superficially untidy, even ugly, mutually adjustive social interaction.... It is understandable ... that as a result I seem to be a radical critic but a cautious rather than radical reformer."[19] His fascination with mutual adjustment led to his latest book, *The Market System* (2001), in which he continues to criticize individual and organizational actors.

While admitting to the influence of contemporary liberal and social democratic thought, he finds it impossible to fully escape the "prison" of classical nineteenth-century liberalism.[20] He observes his inclination to lean more and more toward the left, as illustrated by his increasing opposition to unfair, unequal, unjust, and irrational political and economic arrangements. He is, though, leery of radical change because he is even more concerned about the incompetence of impaired people and their leaders. Considering whether Americans should do something about the shortcomings of their Constitution, he recoils: "Would I welcome a constitutional convention to write a new Constitution? My God. When I think who would participate in this convention and the values they would write in a new Constitution ... it would be a catastrophe."[21]

Lindblom's work has attracted significant support in various disciplines and fields of study, including public administration, political science, accounting, budgeting and finance, organization theory, and foreign policy. A variety of authors have suggested that Lindblom's views and attitudes changed over time from a scholarly (that is, distant) focus on policy and decision making as an incremental process of mutual adjustment to the protestations of an engaged social critic against the complacent understanding of pluralism that does not take into account the disproportionate influence of business and the fundamental impairment of people.[22] But Lindblom himself believes and suggests that both positions can be found in his work from early on.[23]

When analyzing social and organizational structures and processes, Lindblom has focused throughout his career on the difference between centrally controlled groups or societies, whether large or small, and mutually adjusted groups and societies, large or small.[24] He organizes his thoughts consistently around one key issue: (the extent of) central planning versus (the extent of) mutual adjustment.[25] Central planning—

which is evidenced at the societal level in totalitarianism, and at the organizational level in hierarchy and bureaucracy—is an extreme, which he does not discuss much. Spontaneous order, or mutual adjustment, is discernible at societal and organizational levels in the economic (market) and political systems, wherein mutual adjustment—that is, polyarchy, the price system, and bargaining—is the coordinating mechanism.[26] The analytical instrument fitting central planning and policymaking is the synoptic or rational-comprehensive model, while incrementalism best serves as the analytical instrument for mutual adjustment.

We will first address Lindblom's ideas about social and organizational structure by distinguishing between unilateral (totalitarianism, hierarchy, bureaucracy) and multilateral controls (market, polyarchy). Against that background, we can discuss his ideas about policymaking, distinguishing between the analytic (rational, incremental, scientific approaches) and the interactive approach (partisan mutual adjustment).

Social and Organizational Control Structures

Any interactive activity, large or small, requires the coordination, through unilateral and/or multilateral social control structures, of a potentially unlimited number of individuals who may not know each other on a personal basis. Lindblom claims that the study of unilateral controls—totalitarianism and hierarchy/bureaucracy—is extensive, while the study of multilateral controls—market and polyarchies[27]—is limited, consisting either of rather general description or of detailed studies of specific elements. In discussing both methods of social and organizational control, he attempts to redress this imbalance.

Unilateral Controls

The bulk of Lindblom's work focuses on multilateral controls in Western systems (especially in the United States). His attention to unilateral controls is rather limited initially but expands somewhat in his later work.[28] The totalitarian regime is the political system that basically uses unilateral controls, which Lindblom believes to be a limiting case, seldom if ever realized in actual social situations. At the organizational level, unilateral control is exercised through hierarchy and bureaucracy.

Totalitarian Regimes. At the societal level, unilateral controls are expressed in totalitarian regimes, in which there is a concentration of political authority in the hands of a single person or a ruling committee. This pattern contrasts with the diffusion and fragmentation of power that is characteristic of mutually adjusting societies, including polyarchies, but the distinction is one of degree. The exercise of authority is not absolute in totalitarian regimes; it is simply less constrained by rules or constitutionalism than in a polyarchy. Nonetheless, though a polyarchical façade may be maintained, a totalitarian regime generally rules in an authoritarian manner guided by a political ideology that is taken as "truth."

In both totalitarian and polyarchical regimes, government operates through persuasion. German and Italian fascism represents the primary example of an effort at "massive, centrally managed, and saturating political indoctrination," making extensive use of the media (radio, film, and advertising).[29] Communist systems are different, because they do not exalt unilateral authority and they promise a democratic future. Lindblom calls them "preceptoral systems" because they seek to teach, persuade, and transform an entire population. A preceptoral system is ideologically hostile to bureaucracy. Indeed, in communist bureaucracies, coordination is rather loose, and technical competence is considered less important than correct attitudes.[30]

Hierarchy and Bureaucracy. At the organizational level, unilateral controls are exercised in hierarchical structures. As is the case with totalitarian regimes, hierarchy is not a pure case, but simply a form of organization in which leaders exercise a very high degree of unilateral control over nonleaders.[31] Leaders in hierarchical organizations maintain control primarily through the exercise of authority. However, echoing Weber, Lindblom argues that the key to the hierarchical exercise of authority is not command but legitimation—that is, the ability to create the perception that the leader has the right to command and the subordinate the duty to obey. Consequently, command always mixes with other forms of control (such as persuasion and exchange) and, in itself, is not sufficient to achieve central control.[32]

Lindblom contends that hierarchy runs counter to the ideology and ethos of democracy.[33] First, hierarchy violates the democratic commitment to equality, for even if there is "equal opportunity," those who get to the top are more powerful than those below. More importantly, hierarchy—particularly industrial hierarchy—is difficult to control, even by means of competing hierarchies such as government and labor unions, because they are incapable of unified, coordinated, cohesive action.

Hierarchical organizations are the means by which totalitarian regimes perpetuate themselves. In this sense, Lindblom sees communist regimes as cousins of fascist regimes. Both need a larger, multi-skilled supporting organization to carry the ideological campaign against democracy to those who are learning to demand it. Top leadership employs and controls a privileged mobilizing organization that is ideologically trained and loyal to the regime. In totalitarian regimes, this formal organizational control supersedes other forms of social coordination, including ethnic solidarity, religious belief, market, family, and moral code.

Like Weber, Lindblom sees bureaucracy as a special case of hierarchy. According to Lindblom, bureaucracy is an organizational form that is hierarchical in structure, but it also embodies a bundle of characteristics, including hierarchical organization, conscious adaptation of means to ends, prescribed and limited discretion, specialization of skill and function, and separation of ownership from management. The basic advantage of bureaucracy is that it is an effective means by which a relatively small number of people can coordinate the activities of a relatively large number of people.[34]

However, that advantage may involve familiar costs that are both minor and major in scope.[35] The minor costs are internal "red tape," a reluctance to make decisions, rigidity and inflexibility, impersonality, and overcentralization. With regard to red tape, Lindblom—echoing Robert Michels[36]—asserts that communist parties tend to lose their innovative zeal as they come to rely on the formal organization and authority of bureaucracy.

There are several well-known major costs. First, there is the possibility that members of a bureaucracy will obtain disproportionate benefits, and that the bureaucracies themselves may become more interested in acquiring political power and in feathering their own nests than in fostering political equality. Communist systems may be more egalitarian than market systems, but they engender inequality nonetheless because the bureaucratic elite resists any change that disrupts its privileged position. A second major cost is the limited opportunity for outsiders to influence the hierarchy. Bureaucrats serve as the principal immediate source of analysis and advice for ostensible policymakers.[37] The problem with this role is that the bureaucracy is difficult to control and may usurp the rightful function of the legislative branch.

There are two ways in which bureaucratic identifications may frustrate efforts at control. First, bureaucrats may see themselves as part of a professional, educated corps of managers with knowledge and experience outweighing that of their elected superiors. Second, bureaucrats are also a part of a particular organization with which they are likely to strongly identify, and they may be willing to sacrifice the greater good to the interests of their own organization. Thus, operating under a shroud of secrecy and cloaked with the aura of expertise, the bureaucracy may be able to manipulate the flow of information in order to frustrate the policy intentions of its nominal superiors. This thwarting of control is possible in both public and private organizations,[38] for market coordination stops at the door of the enterprise, where authoritative command and hierarchy await. Indeed, the enterprise is, in Lindblom's words, an "island of authority in a market sea."[39]

Multilateral Controls

Lindblom argues that human beings find it easier to conceive of an identifiable coordinator than a "hidden" process that coordinates. He holds that multilateral controls are far more efficient than has been realized, yet are very little understood. In fact, central coordinators can make a mess of things.[40] Lindblom distinguishes several types of multilateral controls: the market for the economy, the polyarchy for the political system, and the development of languages and moral codes among people. The market system and polyarchy are systems of control that differ in the following respects:

1. Within market organizations, islands of central decision making exist, while, within policymaking agencies, fragmented decision making is inescapable (though not to the exclusion of central decision making).[41]

2. The market is controlled predominantly through a system of inducements, while the political system is generally one of commands.[42]

3. In the market, some control over output is possible (that is, voting with money), while, in the political system, some control over process is possible (that is, voting with ballots).[43]

How are the two multilateral control systems related? In Lindblom's words, "If the market system is a dance, the state provides the dance floor and the orchestra."[44] Conversely, polyarchy and democracy have not existed without a market system.[45] Both systems are directed by the same mechanism—mutual adjustment among competing interests—and are governed by structures wherein centrality and command are dispersed rather than concentrated.[46] However, as we shall see, Lindblom is also cynical about the connection between the two systems—which is not just a matter of mechanics and structure, but also of the fact that business and government elites both largely endorse or accept the market system. In that sense, the historical connection between the two rests upon a state of mind.[47]

The Market. Given his training as an economist, it is not surprising that Lindblom turned to the market as his first (and last—in his 2001 book) and perhaps strongest example of multilateral controls and their hidden rationalities. The market is a decentralized mode of decision making that is designed to achieve results not necessarily intended by any participant within the organization in which the entrepreneur plays the central role.[48] The market system "is a method of social coordination by mutual adjustment among participants rather than by a central coordinator."[49]

The market offers multilateral controls in an environment characterized by consumer sovereignty and free choice—by which individuals, driven by self-interest, seek mutually beneficial exchanges. Exchange is the method by which behavior is controlled and social cooperation is organized. In the market, one can assert a personal claim only by offering a benefit sufficient to induce someone else to grant that claim.[50]

This system of exchange is moderated by the operation of the price system, which Lindblom describes as "a highly differentiated sociopolitical process for controlling the relations between leaders and non-leaders in the economizing process."[51] In a price system, an enormous number of different values are represented by prices, which thus serve as a common denominator of values. The price system dispenses with the necessity of a central authority and delegates decisions to a large number of individuals whose decisions are coordinated without the aid of even a supervisory agency. Moreover, the price system always facilitates rational calculation. It does so, first, by providing the information necessary for the individual consumer to make rational choices about the value of exchanges offered. Second, the price system facilitates social rationality more broadly, as each individual's pursuit of his own interest, through the process of mutually beneficial exchanges, leads to the realization of the general interest—here defined as the greatest happiness of the greatest number.

Lindblom maintains that, as a method of social coordination or organization, the market is unmatched in scope, detail, and precision of control. However, he recognizes that, like all controls, those of the price system function imperfectly—there are "market failures." That is, even when the market system operates perfectly, it may fail to produce optimal results for the following reasons: the market is subject to cyclical fluctuations that, in the extreme case, can end in depression; the motivation of primitive self-interest is often not congenial to those who are driven by other concerns in their noneconomic roles; the outcomes of market transactions can be inequitable and inhumane; and imperfect competition can allow the businessman to ignore the "marginal principle" that is so vital to the proper operation of the price system.[52]

Given these imperfections—or, some would say, to correct these imperfections—the exercise of governmental authority is required. As Lindblom observes, all societies are mixtures of governments and markets. Indeed, he asserts that the greatest distinction between one government and another is the degree to which market replaces government or government replaces market.[53] Lindblom lists three forms of governmental control over the market: direct authoritative control, indirect manipulation of the markets, and, as a special form of indirect control, planner sovereignty.

Direct authoritative control is the limiting case, as was true of totalitarianism and hierarchy. Just as Lindblom argues that markets do not function effectively without governments, so, too, does he claim that governments do not function effectively without markets. Though some socialists may have hoped that hierarchy could replace the price system, it has proven to be difficult and inefficient to eliminate discretionary entrepreneurial power.

Indirect manipulation of the market can range from governmental intervention to correct for imperfections in the market system, to what is known as "market socialism." In market socialism, the intent is to employ the market mechanism within a completely socialized economy. In this case, the market is not eliminated, but a mandatory price mechanism is substituted for a spontaneous market price system, and government officials replace private managers at the top of the organization. In this system, the objective is still to serve the preferences of individual consumers, but hierarchy replaces bargaining as the primary control mechanism.[54]

In the case of *planner sovereignty*, the objective of serving consumer preference is abandoned in favor of satisfying a planner's preference function. That is, the judgment of the planner is substituted for that of the consumer in determining what is to be produced, and for allocating resources to the chosen lines of production. Planner sovereignty is based on the assumption that planners, motivated by their concept of the general interest, will arrive at more rational decisions—in regard to social needs—than will consumers acting on the impulse of self-interest. Planner sovereignty may employ a price mechanism, as long as the final assortment of outputs is determined by the planners. Lindblom notes that all market-oriented systems are, in part, planner sovereignty systems simply because government is a buyer of many final outputs.[55]

Democracy, Polyarchy, Multiplism, and Pluralism. Multilateral controls are also exercised in the political process. Lindblom asserts that the First Problem of Politics is how to keep our rulers from becoming tyrants.[56] It is typically assumed that democracy is the multilateral response to that problem, but Lindblom argues that this cannot be. Like a perfectly competitive price system, democracy is a limiting case, never fully realized—nor even attempted—in practice.[57] Indeed, Lindblom suggests that, even if true democracy could be achieved, it would not be an appropriate method for dealing with the First Problem of Politics since democracy provides no effective means of preventing our leaders from becoming tyrants.

The rules of democracy, Lindblom argues, endow the citizen with important powers and liberties but confer only a loose control over policy.[58] Democratic rules create large policymaking systems that are difficult to understand, unpredictable, and, consequently, difficult to participate in effectively. Democracy assumes that preferences are expressed and that they are binding in the policy process; neither assumption is true, according to Lindblom. Preferences are not expressed in the policy process—they are discovered. What is needed is a process that leads to the construction of integrated rather than compromised solutions.[59] Such a process requires more than simply a vote or majority rule, which are the foundations of simple democracy. In short, democracy promises neither a significant degree of popular control over top authority nor a concern for the populace among those in authority.[60]

It is not democracy that offers a solution to the First Problem of Politics, but polyarchy, which is a rough approximation of liberal democracy.[61] Polyarchy is a process in which nonleaders exercise a relatively high degree of control over leaders. It is a special combination of unilateral and multilateral controls in which the tendency to reciprocity counteracts the tendency to unilateral decision making. The majority seldom rules. Instead, secondary majorities decide most issues, while a grand majority coalesces only on issues of massive and long-standing agreement. Polyarchy is distinguished from hierarchy by the high degree of control exerted by nonleaders, and from democracy in that control is not shared equally.[62]

More specifically, Lindblom lists the following characteristics of polyarchy: most adults have the opportunity to vote; the vote of each member has about the same weight; nonelected officials are subordinate to elected leaders; elected leaders, in turn, are subordinate to nonleaders (i.e., the population); alternative sources of information exist; and parties offer rival policies and candidates without severe penalties for their doing so.[63] Polyarchy does not exist in a vacuum; nor will it succeed without the following preconditions: social indoctrination in the process of polyarchy and belief in the desirability of democracy, agreement, at least among the politically active, on basic processes and policies; a considerable degree of social pluralism—that is, a diversity of social organizations with a large measure of autonomy to prevent an accumulation of power and the arbitrary exercise thereof; a relatively high degree of political activity by all citizens and the opportunity for nonleaders to become leaders (and vice versa); and, finally, a considerable degree of psychological security, limited disparity of wealth and income, and widespread education.[64] These are not inconsiderable requirements, and, to the extent that they are not met, polyarchical control will suffer in its ability to deal with the First Problem of Politics. (We will have more to say about this problem later.)

As noted previously, all societies consist of mixtures of market and governmental controls. Lindblom is concerned both with comparison of these types of control and with their interaction. Though markets and polyarchy are both systems of popular control, the systems may differ in the type of control exercised. In *Politics, Economics, and Welfare*, Dahl and Lindblom specify four types of social control: *spontaneous field controls* (signals about rewards and deprivations that are produced as the unintended consequence of one's behavior); *manipulated field controls* (signals about rewards and deprivations that are intended to evoke a definite response); *command* (control over another by virtue of a penalty prescribed for noncompliance with a directive); and *reciprocity* (two or more people controlling one another).[65] Note that the choice is not between control and noncontrol, but among the types of control that will inevitably exist in any society.

The forms of control differ in their impact on the controllee's subjective sense of equality. Spontaneous field controls are usually not damaging in this way since they are not intended, although they may be the most tyrannical because they are so difficult to escape. Manipulated field controls may not be damaging to the subjective sense of equality if the manipulation is not discovered.[66] Command is inherently damaging to the subjective sense of equality; moreover, it is costly, cumbersome, difficult to legitimize, and inherently frustrating, and, therefore, is used only sparingly. The forms of control also differ in the degree to which they can be exercised reciprocally. Command is least compatible with reciprocity, while some degree of reciprocity—although not complete reciprocity, which is a separate category—is possible in both spontaneous and manipulated field controls.

The market can be compared to a political system: in both, claims adjustment is delegated to elites that are authorized to make decisions. To the extent that a perfectly competitive market exists, the market is more likely to rely on spontaneous field controls than on government. If the assumption of perfectly competitive markets is relaxed, the market is more likely to employ manipulated field controls or—in the case of monopoly— even command, as a form of control. Government is more likely to rely on manipulated field controls or—in the case of totalitarian regimes—command. Indeed, Lindblom argues that imperfections of popular control in a price system are analogous to the imperfections of popular control in government.[67] As more imperfections are introduced into the system, more discretion is delegated to elites, and the effectiveness of popular controls is reduced. In the case of the market, businessmen can exercise substantial discretionary controls over the timing and fullness of their responses to consumer demands.[68] In the case of government, control is also ceded to an elite that is subject to only loose controls by the public.

However, although both polyarchal and market controls give the populace direct control over no more than a small proportion of necessary decisions, they differ greatly on how large that proportion is. It is smaller in government because polyarchal governments are designed not simply to achieve popular control but to curb the power of top authorities through devices such as separation of powers and constitutional limitations on the exercise of power. No such formal devices exist to curb the power of corporate executives. And yet, while Lindblom argues that the corporation is increasingly recognizable as a challenge to democracy,[69] such informal devices as market competition, the "invisible hand," and reciprocity do limit the power of corporate executives.

As stated previously, Lindblom asserts that there is no necessary connection between the market and polyarchy. But there is a historical association: it is only in market-oriented systems that political democracy arises. One possible explanation, he argues, is that both polyarchy and the market are manifestations of constitutional liberalism and its emphasis on equality and liberty, dispersion of power, and mutual adjustment of interests. Another interpretation that becomes more prominent in his later writings is that governmental controls such as central planning threaten the "prerogatives, privileges, and rights" of the business and property-owning groups. This suggestion raises the paradoxical possibility that polyarchy is tied to the market system not because the market is democratic but because it is not.[70] The influence of business can result in the removal from the government agenda of items that would otherwise be governmental; it adversely affects the equal distribution of income and wealth; and it can lead to a privileged role for business in government. In the process, public discourse degenerates as advertising and public relations "drown us in unilateral communication," carrying with it "an enormous freight of misinformation and obfuscation."[71]

The limitations of polyarchy can be overcome through a combination of pluralism, multiplism, and mutual adjustment in a *self-directing* or *self-guiding* or *self-seeking society*.[72] Pluralism, the widest possible representation of various interests, has already been mentioned, and mutual adjustment will be discussed later in the chapter. Multiplism is the situation wherein vast numbers of people probe social problems. Very few people choose not to or fail to probe, and inequality in terms of education or in terms of availability of information and time does not reduce the quality of probing or the number of participants.[73]

One feature of the self-guiding society that provides a bridge to our next topic is best voiced in Lindblom's own words: "The model of the self-seeking society, multiplistic, pluralistic, takes account, as the Enlightenment failed to do well, of the irrational, non-rational, often tormented side of the human personality that is hostile to inquiry, though incapable of stopping it."[74]

Policymaking as Analytical and Interactive Process

Rational problem solving was the Enlightenment's answer to the increasingly complex social problems and interactions created by slowly emerging demands for political emancipation and by the combined effects of industrialization, urbanization, and population growth. At the center of the social problem-solving process would be the intellectual, or expert. This pattern had its roots in Plato's idea about philosopher-kings and guardians, and it gathered support from Hegel in the nineteenth and Lasswell in the twentieth century. It is what Lindblom calls Model I of the intellectually guided society, based on an optimistic view of people's intellectual capacities. This model assumes that the guiding elite knows and understands the needs of the people at large. In contrast to this pattern stands Model II of the conflict-ridden society, which is grounded in the thought of Aristotle, Hobbes, and Kant. In this model, interaction leads not to mere compromise but to new integration. Polyarchy approximates Model II, but ambitions for the scientific problem-solving characteristics of Model I have not been discarded.[75]

In a later work, Lindblom introduces another contrast. In Vision I, the role of the state is to establish a legal foundation for the market system and provide a framework of regulations, while in Vision II, the state goes much further—managing money and credit, providing subsidies and tax concessions, engaging in research and development, redistributing income and wealth, and acting as the largest buyer and seller in the market system. Lindblom prefers Vision II, which he finds more realistic.[76] In the Model II and Vision II society, Lindblom attempts to balance the benefits of state interventionism (Vision II) with the advantages of integrative interaction (Model II). He clearly does not favor unilateral central planning based on rational analysis conducted by a small group of intellectuals.[77]

Throughout his work, Lindblom explored the limits of the classical version of rational analysis and elaborated an alternative that was still rational but took account of human beings' limited intellectual capacities. In this section, we explore policymaking as analytical activity and discuss the two main approaches contrasted by Lindblom—the synoptic model and the bargaining/incremental model. Included in our survey are Lindblom's views about the nature of knowledge and about the necessary elements of any analysis: the use of partisan and nonpartisan (that is, expert) knowledge, the use of lay and professional (expert) knowledge, and the use of ordinary and scientific knowledge.

The Synoptic/Rational-Choice Model

The theme of unilateral versus multilateral controls is continued, and extended, in Lindblom's discussion of decision- and policymaking processes. Here, the contrast is between the rational-comprehensive, or synoptic, model of decision making and bargaining (partisan mutual adjustment)/incrementalism. The former model is associated with unilateral control mechanisms, and the latter with multilateral controls.

The synoptic model assumes that decision makers possess full information and can choose the best alternative to accomplish known objectives. The decision process is one that is based on nonpartisan and scientific analysis that is not "contaminated by ethical issues." Indeed, it was in the spirit of Harold Lasswell, whose career had been devoted to developing a scientific policy analysis, that expertise was considered superior to what Lindblom calls "lay knowledge." This perspective is nicely illustrated in the following remark by President John Kennedy:

> The fact of the matter is that most of the problems ... that we now face are technical problems, are administrative problems. They are very sophisticated judgments, which do not lend themselves to the great sort of passionate movements which have stirred this country so often in the past. [They] *deal with questions which are now beyond the comprehension of most men.*[78]

Elevated to the policy level, the decision process is seen as linear and staged, proceeding from problem definition to identification of alternatives, to choice of an alternative, to planning, to implementation, and, finally, to evaluation. All of this rational analysis is to occur in a unified system, be it organizational or political.

For Lindblom, this process is simply too tidy. It fails to describe the messy business that constitutes real-life decision- and policymaking. Specifically, the synoptic ideal suffers from seven problems, caused by its lack of adaptation to (a) people's limited problem-solving capacities; (b) the inadequacy of information; (c) the costliness of analysis; (d) failure in constructing a satisfying method of evaluation; (e) bridging fact and value; (f) the analyst's need for strategic sequences of analytical moves; and (g) the various forms in which policy problems actually occur.[79]

More broadly, there are two fundamental problems confronting the synoptic model—uncertainty and multiple decision makers. Uncertainty, which may be expressed as limited information, is the product of a complex decision environment. Moreover, it probably pervades the decision process. That is, the decision maker may be uncertain about objectives, about the alternative means of accomplishing objectives, about the relationship between alternatives and their consequences, and about the consequences of those alternatives. The rational-choice model attempts to deal with uncertainty only in the relationship between alternatives and their consequences—and there with only middling success—while largely ignoring uncertainty about objectives, alternatives, and consequences.

The second problem with the synoptic model is the involvement of multiple decision makers, or a collective decision environment. Actually, the problem of multiple decision makers must be further specified, for the mere presence of multiple decision makers poses no threat to the rational-choice model. If there are no conflicting interests, the model can rely on consensus. If power is not shared, the decision can be hierarchically imposed. It is the presence of conflicting interests and shared power that causes the problem, and it is precisely that situation, Lindblom argues, that is likely to be encountered in polyarchal systems such as the American political process. The synoptic model yields little practical guidance for dealing with this type of collective decision environment. It suggests the formation of public preference functions, but it fails to provide a measure that permits the interpersonal comparison of utilities necessary to construct such a preference function. An alternative is substituting a planner sovereignty system, but that solution simply avoids the problem by replacing public preferences with planner preferences.

Simon attempted to deal with the problem of uncertainty (limited information and limited capabilities) by offering his concept of Satisficing Man—that is, one who satisfices because he has not the wits to maximize. However, he avoided the problem of a collective decision environment by resorting, by default, to a hierarchical solution. In other words, individual decision making in the organization would be guided by organizational objectives that have been framed by hierarchical superiors, encouraged by the proper structuring of incentives in the organization, and assured by the construction of performance programs that capitalize on member docility.

Lindblom, in contrast, attempts to deal with these problems of the synoptic model by means of his concepts of incrementalism and bargaining, both of which quickly evolve into more complex forms. Uncertainty is countered by simplifications introduced in both the bargaining and incremental elements of Lindblom's approach. A collective decision environment in which individuals share power and have conflicting interests is addressed in the bargaining (mutual adjustment) portion of his approach. Moreover, while Simon was content to offer a descriptive decision model, Lindblom undertakes the heroic task of constructing a paradigm that aspires to be both descriptive and normative—that is, addressing not only the way decisions are made, but also the way they should be made.

Incrementalism

Incrementalism offers the most radical simplification in Lindblom's decision-making approach. What Dahl and Lindblom called "incrementalism"—a process that they believed had much in common with Popper's "piecemeal social engineering"[80]—is a concept that took twenty-six years to define. Initially, they described it as "a method of social action that takes existing reality as one alternative and compares the probable gains and losses of closely related alternatives by making relatively small adjustments in existing reality, or making larger adjustments about whose consequences approximately as much is known as about the consequences of existing reality, or both."[81] A few years later, Lindblom contrasted this comprehensive method with four features of the "second method" of incrementalism: relatively less reliance upon theory, a fragmented view of important variables, intertwinement of facts and values, and no use of policy presumptions.

Incrementalism as a policymaking process unfolded as a sequence of approximations, or, in Lindblom's terms, as a method of successive limited comparisons that would allow the decision maker to easily revisit earlier decisions and rectify them if necessary. Hence, this type of policy process was serial and remedial.[82] In a 1958 article, he spoke for the first time of "muddling through"[83]—a label that featured prominently in the title of his most well-known article, published a year later in the *Public Administration Review*.[84] Over the following years, Lindblom expressed surprise at its apparent success, observing time and again that he had merely pointed out what he considered to be common sense. To underscore the fragmented nature of actual decision making, he added the qualification "disjointed" to the incrementalism concept in 1963.[85]

Some degree of discrepancy emerges in the 1963 analysis. While in 1953 Dahl and Lindblom observed that opportunities for rational calculation increase with the repetitiveness of events, Braybrooke and Lindblom note ten years later that the more repetitive a change is, the more incremental it is.[86] More important, however, is the line of reasoning in both coauthored studies, where a distinction is made between repetitive and nonrepetitive, and small versus large change, that implicitly foreshadows Etzioni's mixed scanning as a combination of "bit-by-bit decisions" and "contextuating decisions."[87]

In 1965 Lindblom argued that disjointed incrementalism is intended as an instrument not for solving social problems but merely for helping to deal with social problems.[88] Nevertheless, confusion about the nature of incrementalism remained, as illustrated by the strong comments from a slew of reviewers (summarized in a later section). Partially in response to their comments, Lindblom further refined the concept of incrementalism in a 1979 *PAR* article and apologized for the confusion he had created by not distinguishing incremental politics from incremental analysis. As politics, the process represented change by small steps; as analysis, he now distinguished three types of incrementalism that were hierarchically related. *Simple incrementalism*—defined as the situation wherein analysis is limited to considering only alternative policies that differ incrementally from the status quo and thus simplify decision making—he regarded as one element of *disjointed incrementalism* (DI), wherein the consequences of alternative policies are, either intentionally or accidentally, simply ignored. Simple incrementalism allows the decision maker to consider and profit from feedback from previous experiences and decisions.

Disjointed incrementalism, in turn, was one element of *strategic analysis*—what Lindblom had called Model II in 1977—which focuses on a limited but calculated and thoughtfully chosen set of stratagems to simplify complex policy problems,[89] thus avoiding large, irreversible errors. In the third edition (1992) of *The Policy-Making Process*, he and his new coauthor, Edward J. Woodhouse, distinguished between incrementalism as an analytic strategy, as a political process intended to support a strategy of disjointed incrementalism, and as a policy outcome that consists of small steps.[90]

Whatever its particular incarnation, incrementalism serves to simplify the decision process by limiting the conceptual space in which the decision maker operates. It simplifies the decision process in the following ways:

1. limiting the number of alternatives that are considered, since only those that are marginally different from previous practices are included;

2. allowing the decision maker to rely on feedback from previous experience in rendering a decision; and

3. managing risk by making the process serial and remedial and thereby avoiding the possibility of large, irreversible errors.

Note that the incrementalism portion of Lindblom's approach does not address the normative aspects of the decision process. Instead, the concept is presented merely as a necessary concession to the difficulty of decision making—that is, it is inevitable, not necessarily desirable. The normative implications of the process are derived from the concept of bargaining/mutual adjustment, by which Lindblom also addresses the problem most vexing to the rational-choice model of decision making: a decision environment wherein there are multiple decision makers who share power and whose interests conflict.

Partisan Mutual Adjustment

While Lindblom is probably best known for his writings about incrementalism, the real core of his thought—though generally undervalued—is the notion of mutual adjustment, which he designated early on as the "hidden hand in government."[91] He believes that mutual adjustment is not only more common than, but also generally superior to, centralized decision making.[92] He distinguishes between two main types of adjustment: adaptive adjustments, whereby people simply modify their behavior to suit that of others around them, and manipulated adjustments, whereby actors actively pursue responses from others.

Lindblom went into some detail to define these concepts. For instance, in 1965, he noted that negotiation was one type of manipulated adjustment that included partisan discussion, bargaining, and reciprocity.[93] The price system, figuring prominently in a 1955 article written while he was at the RAND Corporation, was a limited case of bargaining, and we will not discuss this example of mutual adjustment at length.[94] Polyarchy, discussed earlier in this chapter, represented another case of mutual adjustment. But here, rather than outlining in detail his various definitions and examples of mutual adjustment, we will focus on three basic aspects: the nature, the process, and the objective of mutual adjustment, with some special attention to the role of bargaining.

The Nature of Mutual Adjustment. In the RAND Corporation article, Lindblom defines bargaining as "the methods, stratagems, and tricks ... (including) throwing one's weight around, forming alliances and coalitions, taking a partisan position, scheming for advantage, as well as horsetrading, backscratching, log-rolling, jockeying, threatening, deceiving, lying, bluffing, but not to exclude persuasion and courteous negotiation."[95] Lindblom thus provided a provocative starting point for his discussion of a process that would eventually evolve into his concept of partisan mutual adjustment.

Lindblom's notion of mutual adjustment was not novel. As we observed earlier, it had its origins in Adam Smith's notion that higgling in the market is guided by the "invisible hand" of the price system. Indeed, the parallel with the operation of the market system is compelling for Lindblom, particularly in his earlier works. Much as actors in the market system seek out mutually beneficial exchanges, actors in government seek out areas of agreement as the basis for constructing winning coalitions. One is reminded of Follett's circular response, evocation, and integrative solutions. The motivating force in both instances is self-interest. An important difference is that the operation of the market is monitored by a price mechanism that signals the value of the exchanges to the various participants in the process, whereas there is no such mechanism in government, and so the relative value of the items of exchange is more problematic. As a result, the operation of the system of adjustment in government is less elegant and more loosely bound than that in the market.

The Process of Mutual Adjustment. How does this mutual adjustment happen? Clearly, if it is unconscious, it cannot be unilaterally pursued through hierarchy. Traditional policy- and decision-making theory assumes that a system of hierarchical relations is in place that coordinates policymaking. But in a government of thousands of organizations and millions of public servants, is it realistic to assume that every decision maker is directly adjusting to every other decision maker? Is it not rather the case that no single decision maker has the supervisory authority over others that is assumed under the notion of central coordination?[96]

Lindblom was the first to point out that policymaking and decision making do not proceed hierarchically and unilaterally, but depend highly upon the supportive organization. Although hierarchy confers relative advantage on superiors and thus conditions the process of mutual adjustment, it does not necessarily determine the outcome of that process. Indeed, subordinates have power over supervisors through the information and analysis they provide. The notion that subordinates not only feed but have substantial influence upon policymaking and decision making at surprisingly junior levels in public organizations has recently been empirically confirmed.

Thus it is that all decisions on policy are reached through a combination of "brains and brawn"—that is, the rationality of the expert and the power of the higher-ranked official. How brains and brawn are linked varies from situation to situation, but in whatever mix they emerge, mutual adjustment makes enormous demands on all participants.[97]

The Objective of Mutual Adjustment. In the process of mutual adjustment, the choice ultimately made is based not on compromise, whereby all parties "lose some and win some," but on true integration of different ideas. (This point is where Lindblom comes very close to Follett's notion of reciprocity.[98]) But, whereas, in the synoptic model, the substance and outcome of the ultimate decision are what is to be assessed, in the system of mutual adjustment, it is the process that counts. In Lindblom's words, mutual adjustment "… cannot show directly that its outcomes are superior to other outcomes. As with most social processes, we argue the superiority of the outcome from the process, not the process from the outcome."[99] The closest we can get to the general interest is recognition of the areas of agreement emerging from partisan mutual adjustment. The rationality of synoptic decision making is thus in the substance, while that of mutual adjustment is in the procedure.

This process of mutual adjustment is open-ended, while hierarchical decision making seeks closure. Mutual adjustment is fed by ideas from all participants, while hierarchies develop small channels of input. Mutual adjustment thrives on diversity of thought, has its sleeves rolled up. Whereas hierarchies dignify decisions by declaring them to be correct and final, mutual adjustment expects that decisions remain open to challenge.[100] Whatever choice is made, it is ultimately and only authoritative when it is the product of an accepted process.

Simplifications from Mutual Adjustment. As did incrementalism, bargaining addresses the problem of complexity in the decision process. Bargaining offers a number of simplifications that reduce decision making in the public sector to manageable proportions. Bargaining limits the number of interests that need be considered to those with sufficiently intense preferences to seek representation in the process. And it limits the type of interest calculation required of each participant—in the bargaining process, all participants need be concerned only with their self-interest.

The general interest emerges from the bargaining process as areas of agreement are discovered. Indeed, Lindblom argues, these areas of agreement are the best feasible definition of the general interest. Lindblom refers to this process as the translation of private vices (the pursuit of self-interest) into a public virtue (the realization of the general interest). The criterion of a "good policy" is simply agreement. Finally, the bargaining process requires agreement only on the policy itself, not on objectives. This limited focus simplifies the process because it allows different parties to agree on the same policy for different reasons.

Bargaining is a method of decision making that is appropriate to— and, Lindblom would argue, inevitable in—a decision environment marked by multiple decision makers who share power and whose interests conflict. One such arena is the American political system, which Richard Neustadt has aptly characterized as one of separated institutions sharing power.[101] Like its successors, "partisan mutual adjustment" and "multiplism," bargaining treats values as central to the process rather than excluding them, as Simon had done, and it takes us into a palpably political setting. It also facilitates the transition from decision making to policymaking in the public sector, as, during the bargaining, individuals make decisions and create organizations to frame public policy. Bargaining is also the basis on which Lindblom claims normative superiority for this decision process.

Even if the analogy with the market is imprecise, Lindblom argues that there are identifiable benefits from the use of bargaining in the public decision process that parallel those of the market system. Bargaining is good because it leads to the pursuit of widely shared values in the form of the areas of agreement that emerge from the bargaining process (the equivalent of mutually beneficial exchanges in the marketplace). Bargaining is good because it assists rational calculation. This benefit refers, in part, to the simplifications itemized earlier, but, beyond that rationalizing effect, Lindblom argues that bargaining encourages the representation of all important interests. Here he is contrasting bargaining with hierarchical approaches that are designed to preclude, rather than encourage, participation.

Lindblom is not entirely sanguine about the problem of representation, even at this stage of his career. However, there is at least the implication that, if there is a problem with representation, the solution is to improve representation, not to abandon bargaining. Next, bargaining is good because it leads to the realization of the general interest, which is defined—tautologically, perhaps—as the areas of agreement that emerge from the bargaining process. This benefit is the automaticity produced by the operation of the "hidden hand" in government that Lindblom claimed was at least the rough equivalent of Adam Smith's invisible hand in the market.

There are two other benefits that are not drawn from the market analogy. First, Lindblom asserts that bargaining is good because it is ubiquitous and inevitable. Of course, this statement (which was also Simon's view) smacks of a naturalistic fallacy—namely, that one cannot deduce what ought to be from what is. Actually, though, Lindblom's point is a little more subtle. His argument is that even though bargaining and incrementalism may not constitute the best of all conceivable worlds, they may represent the best of all *possible* worlds in a polyarchal political system. And if we value the political system, we should seek good in the decision processes it inevitably embraces. The second non-market-like benefit, which is related to the first, is that bargaining contributes to the health of democracy. It does so because the act of participation encouraged by the bargaining process creates a greater sense of citizenship and empowerment in the polity.

Most of these ideas were expressed early, primarily in the RAND Corporation essay (1955) and in Lindblom's 1959 article in the *Public Administration Review*. However, the basic elements outlined here remain essentially the same throughout Lindblom's writings. He does develop an increasingly intricate taxonomy of bargaining as the characterization of the process is transformed into partisan mutual adjustment and multiplism. He also expands the concept of incrementalism from simple incrementalism into disjointed incrementalism and strategic analysis. However, Lindblom's assessment of all of these processes undergoes a dramatic change. In particular, he expresses increasing reservations about the normative attributes of mutual adjustment, culminating in an abrupt reversal at the publication of *Politics and Markets* in 1977. The problem is representation—which he comes to view as being intractable. (We shall have more to say later about this concern.)

Mutual Adjustment and the Nature of Social Science Knowledge. It has been said that democracy is a form of government for people who aren't sure that they are right. The same may be said of Lindblom's model of decision making. A self-identified liberal with classical liberal sympathies, Lindblom becomes a populist in the realm of information and analysis. The decision/policy process he defends would not be limited to experts nor would it be based solely—or even primarily—on scientific information. To the contrary, the policy process would assign a central role to ordinary citizens employing ordinary knowledge. Practitioners of Professional Social Inquiry (PSI) may be "nonpartisan" experts, but the most important of their activities is to provide information and analysis suited to the interactive roles of participants in interaction. PSI helps to diagnose, to evaluate, and to improve the process of interaction. Practitioners of PSI should not strive for independent authoritativeness, since problem complexity can only make them fail.[102] The idea that PSI facilitates mutual adjustment is nowadays known as "process management in networks," and a new occupation has emerged in the world of public policymaking: that of process facilitator, process manager, or game manager.

From the onset of his career, Lindblom observed that research by trained experts had become the main policymaking tool in the twentieth century.[103] In response to this trend, he warned against the exclusion of the recipients and beneficiaries of policy, and deplored the possibility that policy substance would be determined by so-called experts only (and then in cahoots with corporate elites). His call for a more engaged citizenry intensified in the second part of his career, starting with *Usable Knowledge* in 1979. Also, from early on, he insisted that scientific analysis must be considered only supplementary to other knowledge sources— that is, as an additional aid to rational calculation, but nothing more.[104]

Lindblom's attacks on scientific policy analysis became relentless. With Cohen, he argued that although practitioners of Professional Social Inquiry may use scientific analysis, most of their activities are accomplished through practical judgment—a form of "ordinary knowledge." Two years later, he observed that "a scientific theory of decision making can make a significant contribution only by not attempting to wholly displace the ordinary knowledge."[105] Policymaking as problem-solving process can only be successful, in his view, when both ordinary and scientific knowledge are used.

He expanded upon these ideas in his 1990 *Inquiry and Change*, in which he further denounces the pretensions of the social sciences. He argues that the natural and the social sciences cannot be judged by the same standard, and that the scientific method should not be identified with a narrow concept of science (such as logical empiricism or positivism). Dryly (or sarcastically?), he observes that, despite all efforts to develop social science methods, none measures up to those of the natural sciences. Furthermore, he cannot "identify a single social science finding or idea that is undeniably indispensable to any social task or effort." Finally, he charges that social scientists practicing PSI make far too little use of partisan and lay knowledge, which is especially problematic because, in his view, most ideas generally appear first as lay ideas.[106]

Lindblom reinforced his critique of positivism in a piece about the state of political science in the 1940s–1950s, observing, "Largely what we find are refinements of already familiar hypotheses or beliefs." In fact, he says, none of the so-called political science accomplishments seem to be clearly connected to any of society's achievements; he cannot think of any human accomplishment that unambiguously and undeniably could not have been achieved without social science.[107] As for himself, he notes that none of the 110 ideas that have been attributed to him can claim any origin in social science. Even his writing on incrementalism, for instance, only became significant because academics had been so enamored of rational decision making that they had forgotten how policymaking unfolded in reality.[108] With deadpan certainty, he dealt with the fact-value split: "I do not see how a social scientist can achieve a very profound intelligence about the social world unless his studies are guided by values."[109]

So, how did Lindblom propose to approach social problem solving? In his view, analysis of facts by means of the scientific method is only one way—and not a very effective one. As important, if not more so, is interactive problem solving, wherein expert and allegedly nonpartisan professionals hammer out policy in constant cooperation with lay and partisan citizens. After all, he argues, policy is made not by policymakers but by interaction among a plurality of citizens.[110] Indeed, the notion of a nonpartisan pursuit of the public interest, the central claim of social science research, is, to him, nothing but a betrayal of pluralism. Who can deny that citizens' version of the public interest—and thus of their preferences—varies, or that it can be anything but partisan?[111] In other words, the social scientist follows common sense, and that is reason enough to take the notion of mutual adjustment seriously.

Lindblom's Worldview

Lindblom's discussion of the role of ordinary knowledge in the policy process and of the importance of the participation of the ordinary citizen starts his transformation from proponent (albeit sometimes a reluctant one) to radical critic of the American political process. Whereas, previously, he seemed to think that the system could be rectified by improving representation, he becomes increasingly pessimistic about that prospect. The problem is impairment, and the culprit is business—which, Lindblom contends, occupies a privileged position in the American political process.

From the start of his career, Lindblom identified himself as a liberal, standing to the left of the political spectrum. His ideas about policy- and decision making as an incremental process of mutual adjustment in the public and the private sectors have been greatly influenced by a worldview that can be summarized in one word: *impairment.* This condition has biological, psychological, and political origins. As so many had recognized already—Simon and Lindblom among them—the cognitive limitations of the human brain are partially imprinted by our genetic and biological makeup. Simon's research explored the link between biological and psychological limitations, while Lindblom focused on the connection between psychological and political limitations, or rather manipulation. While psychological and political limitations are intertwined, we will address them separately for analytical reasons.

Impairment as Consequence of Psychological Manipulation

To Lindblom, impairment of thought is the consequence of systematic and continuous indoctrination and manipulation. He firmly believes that the forces that profit from impairing the masses gained in strength over the course of the twentieth century through the use of mass media and widespread, overwhelming advertising campaigns. He especially targets advertisements that convey non- and misinformation, that are designed to move consumers by appealing to emotions, that thwart rational thought, and that obfuscate. He writes: "Pepsi is an 'up thing' according to an ad, something to be identified with good spirits and perhaps the phallus."[112] More than ever before, in his view, humankind is crippled in its capacity to think critically and independently about social problems. Impairment of thought is not random, but patterned: by parents who control rather than edify their children; by clerics who control rather than illuminate an errant mass; by a political and economic elite who are more interested in holding onto and expanding their power than in advancing equality. Finally, " ... we are all impaired, crippled by learned incompetences."[113]

To be sure, impairment is an affliction of all times, as Lindblom points out by citing a number of philosophers contemplating the same or quite related phenomena: Plato's "shadows in caves," Francis Bacon's "idols," Immanuel Kant's "tutelage," John Locke's "insinuations," Rousseau's reference to "capturing volitions," Karl Marx's "false consciousness," the "manufactured will" noted by Joseph Schumpeter, the "distorted communication" of Jürgen Habermas, Elmer Schattschneider's wry perception that "the heavenly chorus sings with a strong upperclass accent."[114] Lindblom argues that in antiquity, when agrarian societies emerged, elites developed a hostility to "probing"—the activity through which people arrive at an understanding of social problems. The secular and religious elites, especially, trumpeted the merits of hierarchy and authority, thus securing their domination over the (uneducated) masses.

Lindblom is particularly scathing in his attitude toward religious, political, and business elites. About the first, he observes that in Christian societies a hostile attitude toward probing was turned into a moral virtue, peddling submission to faith rather than reasoned skepticism. He writes: "If for many people of religious faith their impairment is enormous, I shall not press the point. Aside from the futility of doing so, it is considered discourteous, bad form, even unethical to engage in reason on this subject (a fact that is in itself a monument to impairment)."[115] His secular perspective on organized religion is truly rooted in the Enlightenment's enthrallment with reason.[116] By way of example, Lindblom mentions the evolution of the word *heresy*: the Greek word *heiretikos* (or, *hairesis*) signifies "choice," but that meaning has been distorted, so that its derivative now refers to adherence to a religious opinion contrary to established dogma.[117] Of all Western countries, he considers the United States to be one of the most impaired societies, while the Scandinavian countries are the least impaired.[118]

Several sources contribute to the overall impairment of thought. Children are taught to profess allegiance to flag and country rather than to be politically active when mature or to develop such virtues as compassion and sympathy for others. Workers are indoctrinated to believe that equality harms the economy, even though two centuries of increased legal, social, and economic equality has improved the economy. Americans are raised to believe that their system is No. 1, the moral guardian of polities. We are taught to believe that the good citizen is one who does not criticize government, who does not question the fundamental institutions of the country. We are taught that democracy is best identified in the secret ballot, even though we all know that money talks—and that, finally, speech is not free, but, in fact, very expensive.[119]

There is hope, though, since impairment can be reduced by support for the competition of ideas and the expansion of free speech, and by decreasing inequalities in the distribution of control, influence, and power.[120] This process of reversal will not be easy, however, for at least four conditions must be met if impairment is to be reduced. First, messages must challenge each other. Second, loud voices must not silence others. Third, contesting messages must contain some empirical content. And, fourth, contestants must not depart too far from respect for truth.[121]

We are all impaired; no one can escape this human condition. Perpetuating this condition, however, cannot be attributed entirely to the nature of humankind, but is the role of a rather select group of elite individuals and interests. It seems that these elites have more impairing abilities than others, and that some associations—church, state, business elites—are more impairing than are other interest groups or associations. Lindblom, thus, appears to agree with George Orwell, who observed in

Animal Farm that "some animals are more equal than others." Of those considered to be part of this "more equal" group, Lindblom targets the political and corporate business elites especially.

Impairment as Consequence of Manipulation by Business and Political Elites

As early as his first book, Lindblom showed suspicion of business elites when observing that employers often take advantage of their close relations with politicians to corrupt the democratic process.[122] His irritation and impatience with business and political elites then increased over the years and burst to the surface in *Politics and Markets*. In this study, he conveys strong criticism of corporate executives who escape popular control, who can actually disregard consumer demand for a while, who exercise enormous discretionary authority, and who seek to escape unfavorable regulation.[123] The powerful and privileged position of business is due to its extraordinary financial resources, to its organizational capacity, and to its special access to government. This position of privilege obstructs polyarchy and is the major institutional barrier to a fuller democracy. On what seems to be a more personal note, Lindblom writes: "Elites have always feathered their nests...."[124]

How can it be that business elites enjoy this powerful and privileged position? Lindblom is quite clear about his answer: their privileged position could not be acquired and sustained without the help of substantive government policies that support business (such as tax breaks for business activity, bailouts from pending bankruptcy, relaxation of environmental regulations, and so forth) and the political arrangements that allow business leaders to participate directly, if not always visibly, in policymaking. No other category of citizens is granted similar influence and participation in policymaking. Why? Because business executives will accept the responsibility to pursue high profits and economic growth—which assure, to some degree, employment—only when awarded a privileged position in the power play of policymaking.[125] These corporate executives have a stake in maintaining the status quo, since they wish to hold on to their decision-making authority in their own businesses and to their right of recruiting from among themselves. They support policies that do not upset the existing distribution of income and wealth as well as policies that curtail the labor movement.[126]

Corporate executives could not enjoy this kind of influence were it not for the political elites, and Lindblom is equally critical of them. Of political parties, he observed in his APSA presidential address (1981), that they basically obstruct the translation of mass preferences into public policy. (As for the audience of political scientists that he was addressing, he charged them with having become complacent about the liberal

democratic political process.)[127] Of the political executive, and specifically the presidency, he noted, "... in the Reagan administration we now
hear remarkably candid acknowledgements that we must learn to be
happy in our prison," and he declared that "we are governed by presidents of dubious qualifications, often working with teams of cronies
rather than experienced political leaders, and deferred to by congress-
men and senators many of whom pursue interests more pressing to them
than problem solving for the nation."[128]

The corporate and political elites may challenge one another, but they
agree on some fundamental beliefs and values: hierarchy, inequality,
their own competence (see, by way of comparison, Plato's philosopher-
king), the danger of political agitation, and the importance of loyalty,
obedience, and deference from the masses.[129] In fact, in all political systems—not just market systems—both groups of elites largely escape mass
control. They will deny being hostile to the masses, and they may not always recognize that they are.[130]

The Lindblom Critique

It is not surprising that an author as prolific and outspoken as Lindblom
has attracted quite a bit of critical attention. The most general thread in
the critique of Lindblom's work is that he presents sweeping generalizations but does not support them sufficiently with empirical evidence.
Commenting on *Unions and Capitalism*, John T. Dunlop observed that
Lindblom and others should "put up or shut up" about the influence of
unionism on the structure of wage rates, for example, since ample data
were available testifying that unions had very little independent influence.[131] It was not the last time that Lindblom would be charged with
vagueness and lack of specificity about theory and method. For instance,
in his review of *The Intelligence of Democracy*, John C. Harsanyi wrote that
Lindblom made "... little use of precisely defined theoretical concepts or
of clearly specified analytical models."[132]

Jonathan Bendor implicitly charged Lindblom with relying exclusively
on informal reasoning and not using formal models.[133] In a review of *Usable Knowledge*, William H. Panning complained, "Even sympathetic readers will soon become impatient with the prevalence of sweeping
conclusions that are imprecisely stated and supported by only the most
casual argument and evidence."[134] Charles W. Anderson declared that
"much of what Lindblom has to say is provocative and original and much
of it is familiar. Large portions of conventional wisdom are simply embedded in the argument without much reflection or criticism," and that
his review of market failures did not exceed the level of an introduction
to economics.[135]

The bulk of the criticism has targeted Lindblom's exposition of the rational-choice model, his claims about incrementalism, and his views on elite manipulation. We will address each in turn.

Lindblom's views on the synoptic model attracted attention from several top scholars. Agreeing with Braybrooke and Lindblom's assertion, in *A Strategy of Decision*, that the intellectual abilities of people are limited, Kenneth J. Arrow observed that the authors had not considered the possibility that in some cases small steps might be pointless, and that the synoptic model as ideal at least forced decision makers to consider as many relevant factors as possible.[136] Reviewing the same book, Jan Tinbergen felt that the authors had created a rather imaginary controversy; he argued that the synoptic model was fitting for the macro-level of policymaking, while incrementalism was useful at the micro-level.[137] C. West Churchman went further, saying that "the authors are afraid of comprehensive and calculating people like Tinbergen, Arrow, or E.A. Singer." And he could not "appreciate their wish to keep assumption about the whole system unconscious, because whether one likes it or not, any recommendation to change or not to change entails a commitment about the whole system. How can we possibly justify the position that these whole-system commitments should be suppressed?"[138]

Reviewing *The Intelligence of Democracy*, Amitai Etzioni felt that limiting the choice between rationalism and disjointed incrementalism was a major mistake; regarding the latter as an overreaction to the limitations of rationalism, he advised that Lindblom should have paid attention to the more common mixes between the two models.[139] Finally, reviewing both that book and *The Policy-Making Process*, Eric C.B. Schoettle argued that Lindblom had judged the synoptic and the incremental models by different standards, overlooking the limitations and disadvantages of incrementalism.[140]

With regard to incrementalism, one might conclude that its meaning was not made clear initially, given the gestation period of the concept (1953–1979). Several reviewers suggested as much, and one even argued that contrasting the synoptic model with incrementalism was not appropriate since the latter still was inspired by a desire for rationality.[141]

In addition to the charge of confusing meaning, there have been three basic critiques. First, several authors opined that incrementalism lacked goal orientation. Kenneth E. Boulding commented, "Just because we cannot see the whole way before us ... does not mean that we should never invest in a better lamp." Morton A. Kaplan wrote that incremental adjustment would lead to blind policy choices. Gordon Tullock feared that incrementalism disregards long-term outcomes, while Etzioni noted that nothing in incrementalism would guide the small steps' accumulation toward a large step. And Paul R. Schulman warned that incrementalism would not help to understand nonincremental policy.[142]

A second critique—namely, that incrementalism was inherently biased in favor of elites—was particularly ironic in light of Lindblom's later explicit radicalism in opposition to elite domination.[143] Related to this charge was the feeling that incrementalism was only appropriate in stable, noncrisis situations. Arrow remarked that incrementalism represented "a complacent acceptance of imperfections; in Dror's words, it reinforced the pro-inertia and anti-innovation forces in society"; this point was also made by Etzioni.[144]

A third, and much later, criticism of incrementalism was that threshold or sleeper effects undermined its usefulness. That is, when a series of small steps lead to a big change, the last incremental step no longer represents a small change. Furthermore, when a threshold is crossed, it becomes impossible to pursue the kinds of serial adjustment that made incrementalism an attractive approach in Lindblom's eyes. The sleeper effect would occur when a decision maker is deprived of prompt feedback.[145]

Lindblom's response to the critique of incrementalism over the years is best summarized by his own reconsideration in 1988: incrementalism was weak, inefficacious, inadequate to problems at hand, often controlled by the wrong people, and yet ... usually the best possible course of action.[146] The reason for this ultimate acceptance was to be found not so much in the outcome as in the process of policymaking that he called partisan mutual adjustment. We will return to that point shortly.

The strongest critique of Lindblom's views was that reserved for his attack on the influence of business elites. Several authors pulled together in a single volume their reviews of Lindblom's *Politics and Markets*. In line with earlier critiques, Eugene Bardach observed therein that Lindblom provides very little evidence to support the claim that business dominates government, and, furthermore, he said, business leaders are not the only ones who seek access to government. (Aaron Wildavsky, writing elsewhere, concurred in these assessments.[147]) In the same consolidated review volume, Ithiel de Sola Pool charged that Lindblom focuses too much on Fortune 500 executives at the expense of the larger group of small-business owners.[148]

James Q. Wilson judged Lindblom's outline of market and planning to be brilliant, and thought his analysis of how totalitarian systems had been looking for an alternative to the market system illuminating, but he found Lindblom's claim that the large corporation is a threat to democracy positively embarrassing. As Wilson put it, "... one cannot assume that disproportionate possession of certain resources leads to disproportionate exercise of power."[149] Wilson also pointed out that Lindblom does not support his observations with empirical evidence.

In another venue, Tom Mayer observed that Lindblom's critique of business power made it hard to believe that democracy could exist at all in market societies.[150] Finally, Richard Adelstein asserted that Lindblom exaggerates business influence and underrates the fact that the people themselves have chosen wealth over liberty and, by implication, self-inflicted impairment over active, critical participation.[151]

So, where does Lindblom stand as a scholar? As noted, he has attracted serious criticism for the lack of empirical evidence cited in support of his generalizations and for the ideological slant in his later work. Still, he has surely made his mark. Incrementalism is a concept that will be forever tied to his name because it is so familiar. His notions about mutual adjustment are rather less widely recognized, but they are likely to be(come) more important as other scholars explore their implications in the future.

Conclusion

In his concluding remarks to the Redner volume, Lindblom declares that he has merely served as a conduit for existing common sense, and this excess of modesty may have influenced the overall judgment of his work. For instance, in 1999 William C. Mitchell wrote that Dahl and Lindblom broke new ground but never attained the status that might be expected from a pioneering attempt to connect economics and political science. Indeed, he said, these authors "... failed because they made an effort to integrate existing scholarship rather than present strikingly innovative theorems as did Arrow, Black, Downs, and Buchanan and Tullock, who largely ignored the past and set forth totally new perspectives."[152] What we need to keep in mind, though, is that Mitchell's assessment of how Lindblom stacks up against the Arrows—and one could add Simon to his list—is based on a rather narrow view of scholarship, namely, that science should result in innovative theorems. But whatever happened to the notion that connecting existing scholarship can be just as scholarly as conjuring innovative theorems and models?

Also, why is it considered less scholarly to raise difficult questions without providing a solution? Lindblom has often been charged—implicitly, for the most part—with providing no guidance as to how he would propose to solve the conundrums he describes. The level of uncertainty (and contradiction) that one experiences when reading his work is uncomfortable to the rationalist, positivist mindset; it appears to fit better with alternative approaches such as postmodernism. Nonetheless, the difficult questions must be raised, and Lindblom has done so. Furthermore, is Lindblom's thought really less innovative than that of the other authors discussed in this volume? As we have seen, all the authors considered so far were successful because they advanced existing (lay! and often commonsensical) knowledge with a dogged conviction. In that sense, Lindblom certainly belongs among them.

Lindblom's work shows substantial continuity over time in regard to his basic concepts about the dynamics of decision making and political processes. However, his interpretation of those phenomena changed substantially during the 1970s, when he moved from a basically apologetic posture to a nearly apoplectic one over a relatively short period of time. The motivating force for that transformation was his focus on impairment and elite influence. Like Marx's "false consciousness" and Galbraith's "created demand" before him,[153] Lindblom's view of impairment denies a primitive assumption of classical economics—namely, that individuals are the best judges of their own interests. Unfortunately, Lindblom adduces little evidence in support of his position, and, in the absence of empirical support, we are left with only assertions based on his own observations about the political process, which themselves changed considerably over time.

When it comes to solutions, both Marx and Galbraith would seem to be a step ahead of Lindblom. Marx's answer was that the "vanguard of the proletariat" was to rule in the interests of the people until the people were capable of ruling in their own interests. This popular takeover would occur with the emergence of "full communism"—an elusive, if not illusory, goal. Galbraith's solution was a truncated version of pluralism in the form of "counterveiling powers," as the competition among big business, big government, and big labor was to keep them all relatively honest. Lindblom's solution is not so clear, for the equivocation demonstrated early in his career continues into its denouement. He is attracted like a moth to flame by the hidden rationalities of complex social systems, but he recoils in horror from some of the implications of that position.

Lindblom's ideas take us neither into a world enjoying a perfect government of socialist welfare economics, nor into a world featuring a perfect market of laissez-faire economics. Instead, we are forced to deal with an imperfect government and an imperfect market. The lingering dilemma, in Lindblom's world of imperfections, is how we are to choose between these imperfect institutions. Is there some appropriate mix of government and market? Are we simply to choose the lesser of the two evils? Lindblom has no clear answers. At one point, it seemed that he would counsel improving the process of mutual adjustment, not abandoning it. However, that solution became less clear with his increasingly acerbic attacks on that very process. If Lindblom believes the process can be improved, how can that be done? If he believes it must be abandoned, what is the alternative?

Despite the lack of finality in Lindblom's work—or perhaps because of it—there has been ample attention to his ideas and scholarship. In fact, the large number of reviews his books have attracted indicates that he was taken seriously. Possibly his most lasting contribution consists of incrementalism in policymaking and mutual adjustment as mechanisms of social coordination. He believes in the rationality of the invisible hand but has never formalized his observations in the mathematical formulae so characteristic of those who wish to advance social science beyond descriptive statement. Indeed, in his interpretative and hermeneutic social science, Lindblom is the heir to Dewey, who championed scholarship as inquiry into meaning.[154] And he is an heir to the Enlightenment, in the sense that his social critique sprang from a secular perspective that places reason above belief or faith. But he is a heretical heir to the Enlightenment, both in the sense that he has fought the domination of a narrow view of science, and in the sense that he passionately believes in a people who choose to be active, critical citizens, rather than impaired, passive cattle.

Perhaps Lindblom's views about the causes of impairment and his advocacy of a self-guiding society place him among the utopians. He is most certainly an American, for the notion of a self-guiding society can easily be placed within the context of Jefferson's belief in the self-reliant citizen. Of the authors introduced in this volume, Lindblom generated the most controversy, for he did not eschew—indeed, he actively embraced—provocative discourse that pierced, or at least tried to pierce, longstanding and sacred beliefs. His relevance to the study of public administration will endure, for no one can ignore incrementalism as both an important perspective on and a basic element of policy- and decision-making theory. As to mutual adjustment, his contribution in that regard may not yet be discernible in a large body of references in literature on, for instance, networks or chaos theory, but it certainly looms in the background, and it may well become a more significant legacy than his concept of incrementalism.

Lindblom's most important legacy, though, is his unabashed conviction that public policymaking is not an analytical, problem-solving activity—as the large majority of policy scholars believed between the 1940s and the 1980s—but a fundamentally political process that is driven by a distinct collective rationality.[155]

NOTES

1. We appreciate the factual, stylistic, and substantive comments on an earlier version of this chapter that Professor Lindblom provided by e-mail correspondence, December 1, 2007.
2. Cf. Robert A. Dahl and Charles E. Lindblom, *Politics, Economics, and Welfare: Planning and Politico-Economic Systems Resolved into Basic Social Processes* (New York: Harper & Row, 1953), 349: "... among students of public administration one finds often a tendency to idealize the rationality and responsiveness of government bureaucracies...." Twelve years later, in *The*

Intelligence of Democracy: Decision Making through Mutual Adjustment (New York: Free Press, 1965), 303, Lindblom observed that mutual adjustment was hardly recognized in public administration as a systematic alternative to central coordination.

3. Of the nine authors profiled in this volume, the biographical information available on Charles Lindblom is the most limited. The discussion in this section is drawn from comments made by Lindblom in several publications; from a brief intellectual biography of his work as viewed from a public administration angle—Rob Hoppe, "Feilbaarheid, rationaliteit en politiek. Het werk van Charles E. Lindblom," in *Bestuurskunde: Hoofdfiguren en Kernthema's*, ed. A.F.A. Korsten and Th.A.J. Toonen (Leiden/Antwerpen: H.E. Stenfert Kroesxe bv., 1988), 323–342; and from a brief intellectual biography of his work as viewed from the economist's perspective—Richard P. Adelstein, "Charles E. Lindblom," in *New Horizons in Economic Thought: Appraisals of Leading Economists*, ed. Warren J. Samuels (Aldershot, England: Edward Elgar, 1992), 202–226.

4. That he temporarily worked at the State Department is clear from the institutional affiliation listed in Charles E. Lindblom, "Contexts for Change and Strategy: A Reply," *Public Administration Review* 24, no. 3 (1964): 157. His work as adviser during a mission to India is mentioned in Amitai Etzioni, review of *The Intelligence of Democracy*, in *Science* 152, no. 3723 (1966): 746. The exact years of his time in India, which he used to study both theory and action on Indian economic development, are mentioned in a brief Lindblom bio at the Web site of the International Leadership Forum, ILF Post home, to which Lindblom is a frequent participant; a recent entry by him appeared August 6, 2007.

5. Charles E. Lindblom, "Political Science in the 1940s and 1950s," *Dædalus* 126, no. 1 (1997): 229.

6. Charles E. Lindblom, introduction to *Democracy and the Market System* (Oslo: Norwegian University Press, 1988), 15.

7. Ibid., 17.

8. Lindblom, "Political Science in the 1940s and 1950s," 245. In his view, this mode is the most common basis for choosing a research project in the social sciences, whose practice is not even close to "the path of accomplishment in physics [that] pointed most emphatically at any time toward *necessary next research projects*" (emphasis added).

9. Ibid., 250.

10. Two articles deserve to be mentioned specifically. In "Policy Analysis," *American Economic Review* 68, no. 3 (1958): 298–312, Lindblom systematically contrasts the comprehensive method of policy analysis with the method of successive comparisons. Also in that article, he first mentions "muddling through" (311); that concept takes center stage in his most famous article, published as "The Science of 'Muddling Through,'" *Public Administration Review* 19, no. 2 (1959): 79–88.

11. Lindblom, introduction to *Democracy and the Market System*, 18 and 19.

12. In his review of *Politics and Markets*, Charles W. Anderson observed that Lindblom's ideas appear to be more cited than seriously argued, *American Political Science Review* 72, no. 3 (1979): 1012.

13. Charles E. Lindblom, "Still Muddling, Not Yet Through," in *Public Administration Review* 39, no. 6 (1979): 525.

14. Lindblom, introduction to *Democracy and the Market System*, 19.

15. The Mobil Corporation denounced this book in an op-ed piece published in the *New York Times* on February 9, 1978. In spite of—or perhaps because of—this attack, Lindblom's book was listed as an Editor's Choice in the *Times* on February 26, 1978.

16. Charles E. Lindblom, *Inquiry and Change: The Troubled Attempt to Understand and Shape Society* (New Haven, Conn.: Yale University Press, 1990), viii. Interestingly, Lindblom later recalled that the National Science Foundation was unwilling to support either this single-authored work or the volume he coauthored with David K. Cohen—*Usable Knowledge: Social Science and Social Problem Solving* (New Haven: Yale University Press, 1979)—unless he could specify in advance which specific research methods he intended to use; see Lindblom, "Political Science in the 1940s and 1950s," 246.

17. He describes himself thus already in his first book, *Unions and Capitalism* (New Haven, Conn.: Yale University Press, 1949), vi, but he is as critical of liberals as of conservatives—charging ideologues on both sides of ordering their beliefs to follow those of their ancestors, and observing that liberals were quick to recognize the union's potential for social reform while not acknowledging its power to disrupt the economy (vii).

18. See Lindblom's introduction to *Inquiry and Change*, vi–vii.

19. Lindblom, "Political Science in the 1940s and 1950s," 251.

20. Lindblom, *Inquiry and Change*, x.

21. Lindblom made this remark in an interview conducted upon the publication of *The Market System*: Hans Blokland, "Charles Lindblom heroverweegt de markt" ("Charles Lindblom Reconsiders the Market"), in *Sociaal-Wetenschappelijk Magazine* 9, no. 2 (2001): 16.

22. Several reviewers and authors suggested that Lindblom had turned to the left in *Politics and Markets*. Among them was Rick Tilman, "Social Value Theory, Corporate Power, and Political Elites: Appraisals of Lindblom's *Politics and Markets*," *Journal of Economic Issues* 17, no. 1 (1983): 115–131. In his own contribution to his edited volume on Lindblom, Harry Redner observes that *Politics and Markets* represents a break with Lindblom's earlier work on pluralism and a new focus on the privileged role of business entrepreneurs; see "From Pluralism to Multiplism: The Theory of Representative Democracy from Hamilton to Lindblom," in *An Heretical Heir of the Enlightenment: Politics, Policy, and Science in the Work of Charles E. Lindblom*, ed. Harry Redner (Boulder, Colo.: Westview Press, 1993), 63–96.

23. Lindblom, introduction to *Democracy and the Market System*, 10.

24. Dahl and Lindblom, *Politics, Economics, and Welfare*, 520.

25. Adelstein, "Charles E. Lindblom," 203; see also idem, "Review of *The Market System* by Charles E. Lindblom," *Constitutional Political Economy* 13, no. 2 (2002): 287, in which Adelstein observes that Lindblom never used the term "spontaneous order" but had written about it throughout his career.

26. In *Politics, Economics, and Welfare*, Dahl and Lindblom analyze four central sociopolitical processes: hierarchy, price system, bargaining, and polyarchy. In *Politics and Markets*, x, Lindblom for the first time groups together price system, bargaining, and polyarchy as forms of mutual adjustment.

27. Charles E. Lindblom, "Success through Inattention in School Administration and Elsewhere," *Educational Administration Quarterly* 30, no. 2 (1994): 199–200.

28. One reviewer of the Dahl and Lindblom volume observed that although the authors mentioned planned economy, there was "... a surprising paucity of reference to this major example of planned economy [i.e., the USSR] in their book"; see Francis X. Sutton, "Review of Robert A. Dahl; Charles E. Lindblom (1953), *Politics, Economics, and Welfare*," in *Review of Economics and Statistics* 36, no. 1 (1954): 116.

29. Lindblom, *Politics and Markets*, 53.

30. Ibid., 54–60.

31. Dahl and Lindblom, *Politics, Economics, and Welfare*, 227.

32. Lindblom mentions exchange and persuasion as other types of control; see *Politics and Markets*, 4. He also observes (18) that he and Dahl identified authority with command backed by penalties (*Politics, Economics, and Welfare*, 106) but did not recognize how authority always mixes with other forms of control. On authority, persuasion, and exchange, see also Lindblom, *The Policy-Making Process* (Englewood Cliffs, N.J.: Prentice-Hall, 1980), 50, 68.

33. Dahl and Lindblom, *Politics, Economics, and Welfare*, 230.

34. Ibid., 237.

35. On minor and major costs of bureaucracy, see ibid., 247, 255–261, 372.

36. See, for instance, Robert Michels, *Political Parties: A Sociological Study of Oligarchical Tendencies of Modern Democracy* (1915; New York: Free Press, 1962), 188–202. Michels consistently speaks of socialist parties.

37. Lindblom observes that this arrangement has resulted in something of an anomaly in American political science, where the study of policy analysis is associated with public administration rather than with the study of the legislature. See *Policy-Making Process*, 70.

38. Lindblom, *Politics and Markets*, 11.

39. Lindblom, *The Market System* (New Haven, Conn.: Yale University Press, 2001), 184.

40. E.g., "Legend has it that the greatest coordinator of them all flooded the earth to erase some creative mistakes" (ibid., 24).

41. Charles E. Lindblom, "Tinbergen on Policy-Making," *Journal of Political Economy* 66 (1958): 536–537.

42. Charles E. Lindblom, "The Market as Prison," *Journal of Politics* 44, no. 2 (1982): 327.

43. Lindblom, *Market System*, 71.

44. Ibid., 42. Richard Adelstein observes that "corporations call the tune"; see Adelstein, "Review of *The Market System* by Charles E. Lindblom," 287–292.

45. Lindblom, *Politics and Markets*, 162; *Market System*, 12, 226.

46. Lindblom, *Market System*, 5. He does not precisely date the emergence of the market system, but we can infer from his writing that he considers the eighteenth century to be the period in which the modern market system developed, since before that time wider coordination was accomplished mainly, if not solely, through central direction (6–9). We have to keep in mind, though, that extensive interregional trade and production for sale go back to antiquity, so, in that sense, the market system is of earlier origin but was indeed highly dominated by the state (whether city-state or empire).

47. Ibid., 230.

48. In various places, Lindblom indicates that entrepreneurs are the most influential parties in the market system. But he also says that the state is the

dominant partner in the market system as the rule- and price-maker; see *Market System*, 86. In other words, Lindblom is not always clear.

49. Ibid., 23.
50. Lindblom, *Politics and Markets*, 12; *Market System*, 54–55.
51. Dahl and Lindblom, *Politics, Economics, and Welfare*, 177.
52. In imperfect competitive environments, the supplier can affect prices and need not set marginal revenue equal to marginal cost. This means that prices are higher than they would be in perfectly competitive markets, and the notion of Pareto Optimality is threatened.
53. Lindblom, preface to *Politics and Markets*, ix.
54. Ibid., 95–97.
55. Ibid., 98–103.
56. Dahl and Lindblom, *Politics, Economics, and Welfare*, 273.
57. Ibid., 41–49; *Policy-Making Process* 22–24, 122. He also observed that genuine democracy does not depend upon the market system. In a market society, democracy cannot develop because the market imprisons policymaking. Polyarchies exist because of undemocratic control by government and business elites. See Lindblom, *Politics and Markets*, 77, 169; and "Market as Prison," 327.
58. Lindblom, *Policy-Making Process*, 58–59.
59. Lindblom, *Politics and Markets*, 137; note that he is very close to Follett in this respect.
60. On the various problems with the concept of "sovereignty of the people," see Thomas J. Catlaw, *Fabricating the People: Politics and Administration in the Biopolitical State* (Tuscaloosa: University of Alabama Press, 2007), especially chaps. 3 and 4.
61. Lindblom, *Politics and Markets*, 233.
62. Dahl and Lindblom, *Politics, Economics, and Welfare*, 279, 284.
63. Ibid., 277–278.
64. Ibid., 287–318.
65. Ibid., 99–109.
66. Dahl and Lindblom observe that the Human Relations movement distinguished itself by manipulation of employees, thus strengthening the manager's control in the organization; see ibid., 104, 119–120. Lindblom observes the same effect again in "Democracy and Economic Structure" (1962), reprinted in Lindblom, *Democracy and the Market System*, 45.
67. Lindblom, *Democracy and the Market System*, 35.
68. Lindblom, *Politics and Markets*, 152–157. The extent to which business entrepreneurs enjoy discretion became clear in the corruption scandals in corporate America in 2001–2003.
69. Ibid., 348; *Market System*, 240. Lindblom's idea that the corporation potentially threatens democracy seems to contrast with his earlier opinion that unionism undermined managerial authority and, thus, the market; see *Unions and Capitalism*, 19, 156, 214, 226.
70. Lindblom, *Politics and Markets*, 168–169.
71. See Charles E. Lindblom, "Modes of Inquiry," *Journal of Public Administration Research and Theory* 4, no. 3 (1994): 330, 331; *Market System*, 217.
72. For the concept of self-directing, self-guiding, or self-seeking society, see Lindblom, *Inquiry and Change*, 7, 213, 301. The notion of self-guiding society is rooted in the thought of, i.a., Polybius, Hume, Rousseau, and Dewey, and it stands in contrast to the scientifically guided society advocated by,

i.a., Plato, Bacon, Condorcet, Bentham, and Sidney and Beatrice Webb. See ibid., 214–216.

73. Ibid., 231–233.

74. Ibid., 301.

75. Lindblom, *Politics and Markets*, 248–260.

76. Lindblom, *Market System*, 256–258.

77. As was suggested by Royall Brandis, "An Alarmist View of Corporate Influence," in *Does Big Business Rule America? Critical Commentaries on Charles E. Lindblom's "Politics and Markets,"* ed. Robert Hessen (Washington, D.C.: Ethics and Public Policy Center, 1982), 21.

78. President Kennedy at a press conference in May 1962, as quoted in Christopher Lasch, *The Culture of Narcissism: American Life in an Age of Diminishing Expectations* (New York: Norton, 1978), 77; emphasis added.

79. Braybrooke and Lindblom, *A Strategy of Decision*, 48–54; on points (e) and (g), see also Lindblom, *Intelligence of Democracy*, 141, 143.

80. See Dahl and Lindblom, *Politics, Economics, and Welfare*, 82n; also see *A Strategy of Decision* (New York: Free Press, 1963), in which David Braybrooke and Charles Lindblom mention Popper (45) and Simon (46).

81. Dahl and Lindblom, *Politics, Economics, and Welfare*, 82.

82. Lindblom, "Policy Analysis," *American Economic Review* 48, no. 3 (1958): 301–302; and Albert O. Hirschman and Charles E. Lindblom, "Economic Development, Research and Development, Policy Making: Some Converging Views," *Behavioral Science* 7, no. 2 (1962): 211–222; and Braybrooke and Lindblom, *Strategy of Decision*, 125. What Lindblom called "successive limited comparisons" resembles Michael Polanyi's notion of problem-solving through "successive approximations"; see Polanyi, *The Logic of Liberty: Reflections and Rejoinders* (Chicago: University of Chicago Press, 1951), 141.

83. Lindblom, "Policy Analysis," 299, 311.

84. The title of that article was suggested by William B. Shore, who was then managing editor of the journal. See Lindblom, "Still Muddling, Not Yet Through," 525n2; and Lindblom, "This Week's Citation Classic," in *Current Contents*, no. 45 (November 7, 1983), 22. Lindblom's article, "The Science of Muddling Through," *Public Administration Review* 19, no. 2 (1959): 79–88, has recently been voted a "top three policy piece" by the readers of *Policy Currents*, the newsletter of ASPA's public policy section; see Matthias Klaes and Esther-Mirjam Sent, "A Conceptual History of the Emergence of Bounded Rationality," *A History of Political Economy* 37, no. 1 (2005): 36.

85. Braybrooke and Lindblom, *Strategy of Decision*, 61.

86. Dahl and Lindblom, *Politics, Economics, and Welfare*, 63; Braybrooke and Lindblom, *Strategy of Decision*, 64, 67.

87. Braybrooke and Lindblom, *Strategy of Decision*, 67; Etzioni, review of *Intelligence of Democracy*, in *Science* 152, no. 3727 (1966): 747.

88. Lindblom, *Intelligence of Democracy*, 148.

89. Lindblom, "Still Muddling, Not Yet Through," 517–518. Already in 1962, he had, in an article coauthored with his colleague A.O. Hirschman, considered intentional and accidental neglect of consequences; see "Economic Development, Research and Development, Policy Making." With regard to disjointed incrementalism, Robert Gregory argues that at the micro-level it can be deliberately chosen, but at the macro-level it is inevitable because of societal complexity and because the coordination of control of

political complicatedness is impossible; see Gregory, "Political Rationality or 'Incrementalism'? Charles E. Lindblom's Enduring Contribution to Public Policy Making Theory," *Policy and Politics* 17, no. 2 (1989): 145.

90. See also Edward J. Woodhouse and David Collingridge, "Incrementalism, Intelligent Trial-and-Error, and the Future of Political Decision Theory," in Redner, *Heretical Heir of the Enlightenment*, 137.

91. Charles E. Lindblom, "Bargaining: The Hidden Hand of Government" (1955), in *Democracy and the Market System* (1988), 139–170; see also Adelstein, "Charles E. Lindblom," 210.

92. E-mail correspondence from Charles Lindblom to authors, December 1, 2007.

93. On adaptive adjustments, see Lindblom, *Intelligence of Democracy*, 35–52; on manipulated adjustments, see ibid., 53–84; on negotiation, see ibid., 66.

94. Lindblom, "Bargaining," 143.

95. Ibid., 140.

96. Lindblom, *Intelligence of Democracy*, 26–27.

97. E-mail correspondence from Lindblom.

98. As observed by, for instance, Michael Harmon, *Public Administration's Final Exam: A Pragmatist Restructuring of the Profession and the Discipline* (Tuscaloosa: University of Alabama Press, 2006), 94; see also O.C. Mc-Swite, *Legitimacy in Public Administration: A Discourse Analysis* (Thousand Oaks, Calif.: Sage, 1997), 164–166.

99. Charles E. Lindblom, "Decision Making in Taxation and Expenditures," in National Bureau of Economic Research, *Public Finance: Needs, Sources, and Utilization* (Princeton, N.J.: Princeton University Press, 1961), 323. See also Gregory, "Political Rationality or 'Incrementalism'?" 146.

100. Lindblom, "Success through Inattention in School Administration and Elsewhere."

101. See Richard E. Neustadt, *Presidential Power: The Politics of Leadership from FDR to Carter* (New York: Wiley, 1980).

102. Cohen and Lindblom, *American Behavioral Scientist* 22, no. 5 (1979): 60, 75–76; see also idem, *Usable Knowledge* (New Haven, Conn.: Yale University Press, 1979), 45, 51.

103. Dahl and Lindblom, *Politics, Economics, and Welfare*, 79.

104. Ibid., 82.

105. Cohen and Lindblom, *Usable Knowledge*, 90; and Charles E. Lindblom (1981), "Comments on Decisions in Organizations," in Andrew T. Van der Ven and William F. Joyce, *Perspectives on Organization Design and Behavior* (1981; Minneapolis: University of Minnesota Press, 2004), 247.

106. Lindblom, *Inquiry and Change*, 137.

107. Lindblom, introduction to *Democracy and the Market System*, 21. In *Public Administration's Final Exam*, 54, Harmon proceeds along these lines of thought when observing that the failure of social scientists to produce a single predictive law-like generalization (i.e., not a probabilistic observation) has not dampened the enthusiasm of believers in positivism. Indeed, "That empiricists themselves have achieved very limited predictive success simply shows, from that standpoint, that tighter theories, more rigorous methods, additional data, and harder work are needed in the future" (47).

108. Lindblom, *Inquiry and Change*, 63, 136, and 276; and "Political Science in the 1940s and the 1950s," 235, 240–241. In his "Concluding Comment:

A Case Study of the Practice of Social Science," in Redner, *Heretical Heir of the Enlightenment*, 343–372, Lindblom wrote for the first time that his work merely elaborated upon preexisting ordinary knowledge.

109. Lindblom, "Political Science in the 1940s and 1950s," 248.
110. Cohen and Lindblom, *Usable Knowledge*, 64.
111. Charles E. Lindblom, "Who Needs What Research for Policy Making?" *Knowledge* 7 (June 1986): 345–366.
112. Lindblom, *Market System*, 217.
113. Lindblom, "Political Science in the 1940s and 1950s," 249.
114. Lindblom, *Inquiry and Change*, 62; *Market System*, 222.
115. Lindblom, *Inquiry and Change*, 115.
116. For instance, the French priest Meslier died in 1729, convinced that religion was a device of the rich to oppress the poor. See Karen Armstrong, *A History of God: From Abraham to the Present: The 4000-Year Quest for God* (London: Mandarin Books, 1993), 392. Thomas Paine wrote that Christianity was too repugnant to reason; see Thomas Paine, *Age of Reason, being an Investigation of True and Fabulous Theology* (1794; New York: Willey, n.d.), 248.
117. Lindblom, *Inquiry and Change*, 86. We could add another example: the word *anarchy* is not much associated with society without government—its original meaning—but with lawlessness.
118. Ibid., 100.
119. Lindblom, "Modes of Inquiry," 333–338. On inequalities in voting power, see Charles E. Lindblom, "Democracy and Economic Structure," in *Democracy in the Mid-Twentieth Century: Problems and Prospects*, ed. William N. Chambers and Robert H. Salisbury (St. Louis: Washington University Press, 1960), 65.
120. Lindblom, *Inquiry and Change*, 299.
121. Lindblom, *Market System*, 222.
122. Lindblom, *Unions and Capitalism*, 13. See also his later remark that corporate policy has consequences for politics through the conscious manipulation of employees, in Lindblom, "Democracy and Economic Structure," 44.
123. Lindblom, *Politics and Markets*, 152–157. On unfavorable regulation, see Charles E. Lindblom, "The Accountability of Private Enterprise: Private—No. Enterprise—Yes," in *Social Accounting for Corporations: Private Enterprise versus the Public Interest*, ed. Tony Tinker (New York: Markus Wiener, 1984), 33.
124. Lindblom, *Politics and Markets*, 194–198, 201, 356; the comment about elites is at 273. In *Capitalism, Socialism, and Democracy* (New York: Harper, 1942), Joseph Schumpeter arrived at a position opposite of Lindblom's, arguing that capitalism will fail because businessmen are ineffective in the art of persuasion and overmatched in the political arena.
125. Lindblom, *Policy-Making Process*, 73–77.
126. Lindblom, "Market as Prison," 330.
127. Lindblom, "Another State of Mind," presidential address, annual meeting of the American Political Science Association, 1981, in *American Political Science Review* 76, no. 1 (1982): 9. Reprinted in *Discipline and History: Political Science in the United States*, ed. James Farr and Raymond Seidelman (Ann Arbor: University of Michigan Press, 1993), 327–343.
128. The quote on Reagan is from "Market as Prison," 330; the quote about presidents comes from "American Politics since 1970" (1982), in *Democracy and the Market System*, 112.

129. Lindblom, *Market System*, 222–224.
130. Ibid., 66, 68.
131. John T. Dunlop, review of *Unions and Capitalism* by Charles E. Lindblom, *American Economic Review* 40, no. 3 (1950): 465. Lack of attention to empirical evidence, in this case substantiating that the knowledge utilization literature had gone wrong, is also observed by Rohii Deshpandé, "The Use, Nonuse, and Abuse of Social Science Knowledge," in *Knowledge: Creation, Diffusion, Utilization* 1, no. 1 (1979): 170, 174.
132. John C. Harsanyi, review of *The Intelligence of Democracy* by Charles E. Lindblom, *American Economic Review* 55, no. 5, part 1 (1965): 1191. In his review of Dahl and Lindblom, Francis X. Sutton also observed a fuzziness in the methods and theories used; see Sutton, "Review of Robert A. Dahl; Charles E. Lindblom (1953), *Politics, Economics, and Welfare*," 116.
133. Jonathan Bendor, "A Model of Muddling Through,"*American Political Science Review* 89, no. 4 (1995): 819.
134. William H. Panning, review of *Usable Knowledge: Social Science and Social Problem Solving* by Charles E. Lindblom and David K. Cohen, *Ethics* 91, no. 1 (1981): 162–163.
135. Charles W. Anderson, "Review: The Political Economy of Charles E. Lindblom,"*American Political Science Review* 72, no. 3 (1978): 1014.
136. Kenneth J. Arrow, review of *Strategy of Decision* by Braybrooke and Lindblom, *Political Science Quarterly* 79, no. 4 (1964): 587, 588.
137. Jan Tinbergen, review of *Strategy of Decision* by Braybrooke and Lindblom, *American Economic Review* 54, no. 6 (1964): 1094.
138. C. West Churchman, review of *Strategy of Decision* by Braybrooke and Lindblom, *Operations Research* 13, no. 1 (1965): 160.
139. Etzioni, review of *Intelligence of Democracy*, 747.
140. Eric C. B. Schoettle, review of *Intelligence of Democracy* and *Policy-Making Process*, in *American Political Science Review* 64, no. 4 (1970): 1270.
141. See Morton A. Kaplan, review of *Strategy of Decision* by Braybrooke and Lindblom, in *Annals of the American Academy of Political and Social Science* 352 (1964): 189–190; Kaplan feels that the authors should have clarified whether incrementalism is a description or a prescription. See also Robert D. Calkins, review of *Strategy of Decision* by Braybrooke and Lindblom, in *Administrative Science Quarterly* 10, no. 4 (1966): 553; Calkins notes that incrementalism is less a method than a strategy. Camila Cates made the observation about incrementalism being basically a rational model; see Cates, "Beyond Muddling: Creativity,"*Public Administration Review* 39, no. 6 (1979): 528. More recently, Andrew B. Whitford regarded bounded rationality and incremental decision making as corresponding ideas, hence belonging to a group of rational theories; see Whitford, "Adapting Agencies: Competition, Imitation, and Punishment in the Design of Bureaucratic Performance," in *Politics, Policy, and Organizations: Frontiers in the Scientific Study of Bureaucracy*, ed. George A. Krause and Kenneth J. Meier (Ann Arbor: University of Michigan Press, 2003), 161. Jonathan Bendor also observes that Simon and Lindblom had been thinking along similar lines, speculating that the traditional model of rationality was inaccurate, but where Simon focused on one heuristic (bounded rationality), Lindblom looked at several, of which incrementalism is the best known; see Bendor, "Herbert Simon: Political Scientist," *Annual Review of Political Science* 6, no. 4 (2003): 446. Indeed, in response

to Dror's review of the 1963 volume, Lindblom insisted that one model of decision making would be insufficient; see Lindblom, "Contexts for Change and Strategy: A Reply," *Public Administration Review* 24, no. 2 (1964): 157–158. Intriguingly, Simon regarded dealing with uncertainty (including learning about the reactions of other actors) as an element of a systematic theory of bounded rationality, and this thinking appears to be quite comparable with Lindblom's partisan analysis; see Herbert A. Simon, "Bounded Rationality in Social Science: Today and Tomorrow," *Mind & Society* 1, no. 1 (2000): 35.

142. Kenneth E. Boulding, review of *Strategy of Decision*, in *American Sociological Review* 29, no. 6 (1964): 931; Kaplan, review of *Strategy of Decision*, 190; Gordon Tullock, review of *Strategy of Decision* in *Ethics* 75, no. 1 (1964): 68; Amitai Etzioni, "Mixed Scanning: A 'Third' Approach to Decision Making," *Public Administration Review* 27, no. 5 (1967): 387; Paul R. Schulman, "Nonincremental Policy Making: Notes toward an Alternative Paradigm," *American Political Science Review* 69, no. 4 (1975): 1355. While much of this literature suggests that fundamental changes require institutional reform, it has more recently been argued that fundamental changes are possible without punctuating the institutional equilibrium; see Benjamin Cashore and Michael Howlett, "Punctuating Which Equilibrium? Understanding Thermostatic Policy Dynamics in Pacific Northwest Forestry," *American Journal of Political Science* 51, no. 2 (2007): 533.

143. Harry Cain, "Lindblom: A Partisan Analyst of the Policy Process," review of *The Policy-Making Process*, in *Policy Sciences* 2, no. 1 (1971): 198; and Aaron Wildavsky, "Impairments Come from Cultures: The Anti-Gramsci, or the Confessions of a Culturally Biased Social Scientist," in Redner, *Heretical Heir of the Enlightenment*, 51–62.

144. Arrow, review of *Strategy of Decision*, 588; Yehezkel Dror, "Muddling Through: 'Science' or Inertia?" *Public Administration Review* 24, no. 3 (1964): 155; Etzioni, "Mixed Scanning," 387. See also David Braybrooke, "Review: Scale, Combination, Opposition—A Rethinking of Incrementalism," review of *The New American Dilemma: Liberal Democracy and School Desegregation* by Jennifer L. Hochschild, *Ethics* 95, no. 4 (1985): 920–933, in which Braybrooke counters several of the criticisms.

145. Woodhouse and Collingridge, "Incrementalism, Intelligent Trial-and-Error, and the Future of Political Decision Theory," 136.

146. Lindblom, introduction to *Democracy and the Market System*, 11.

147. Eugene Bardach, "Pluralism Reconsidered," in Hessen, *Does Big Business Rule America?* 14. Wildavsky's remark was made in a review of *Politics & Markets* in the *Yale Law Journal* and is referenced in Tilman, "Social Value Theory, Corporate Power, and Political Elites"; on this point, see also Wildavsky, "Impairments Come from Cultures."

148. Ithiel de Sola Pool, "How Powerful Is Business?" in Hessen, *Does Big Business Rule America?* 23, 30.

149. James Q. Wilson, "Democracy and the Corporation," in Hessen, *Does Big Business Rule America?* 37.

150. Tom Mayer, "Markets and Democracy: A Critique of Charles E. Lindblom," *New Political Science*, Summer–Fall 1982, 71–92.

151. Adelstein, "Charles E. Lindblom," 220; and Adelstein, "Review of *Market System*, 289.

152. William C. Mitchell, "Political Science and Public Choice: 1950–1970," *Public Choice* 98 (1999): 241.
153. Cf. "Production only fills a void that it has itself created," in John Kenneth Galbraith, *The Affluent Society* (New York: Mentor Books, 1958), 125; see also Galbraith's *The New Industrial State* (Boston: Houghton Mifflin, 1967).
154. As noted by James Farr, in "John Dewey and American Political Science," *American Journal of Political Science* 43, no. 2 (1999): 527. Lindblom's ideas about causes of impairment are reminiscent of John Dewey's criticism of the existing education system as being too much focused on the imposition of adult standards, subject matters, and methods from above and from outside, while he favored a participative pedagogical process; see Dewey, *Experience & Education* (New York: Touchstone Books, 1938), 18–19. Perhaps it is not a stretch to recognize cooperative partisan mutual adjustment in the following comment from the same book: "... the general conclusion I would draw is that control of individual actions is effected by the whole situation in which individuals are involved, in which they share and of which they are co-operative or interactive parts" (53). Also consider John Dewey, *Reconstruction in Philosophy* (1920; Boston: Beacon Press, 1957), 192–203, outlining how activities and decision making in organizations are usually based on voluntary cooperation and guided by blind rule rather than scientific method.
155. Gregory, "Political Rationality or 'Incrementalism'?" 147, 151.

Chapter 9

Dwight Waldo:
An Eclectic View of Public Administration

The reasons for discussing the works of Dwight Waldo in this collection differ from those for considering the works of the other authors chosen. Waldo is included because of his observations on the contributions of others, because of his own astute criticism and knowledgeable chronicling of the history of the study of public administration, and because of his insistence that public administration "has distinct political theoretical elements, aspects and implications," and may even *be* political theory.[1] He is also representative of an approach to public administration—the Administration-as-Politics approach—that, combined with the Behavioral approach, constituted a devastating critique of the Classical paradigm of public administration. Waldo is thus included both because of his views on the development and current state of the field of public administration and as a representative of a particular perspective on the field.

As a commentator on, and critic of, public administration, Waldo came to his task with reservations, always approaching his subject with a certain wariness. When he was a student, his intellectual interests centered on political philosophy, not public administration. His dissertation dealt with public administration, but it was intended as an exposé of the political theory that he believed to be implicit in the Classical approach to public administration. Waldo argued that by concentrating on the technical aspects of public administration, the Classical approach embodied a philosophy and constituted an ideology that effectively supported the existing political order. The publication of the book based on his dissertation earned for Waldo, by his own estimation, the status of a pariah in the field. Waldo's views softened over time, but there remained an element of the skeptic in him. He denied the possibility of constructing a science of public administration, doubted the existence of "principles" of administration, questioned the plausibility of a unified theory of organizations, mistrusted those who would indiscriminately intermingle politics and administration, and even despaired of reaching common agreement on a definition of the field of public administration. Nonetheless, he believed that the fate of civilization may well rest on our ability to master the functions of administration.

Waldo was also representative of a perspective on public administration—the Administration-as-Politics approach—that emerged in the 1940s. His position was initially based on his response to the Classical approach, but his later writings extend elements of that critique to the Behavioral approach. Waldo denies that politics and policy considerations can be excluded from administration. Moreover, facts cannot be separated from values. Consequently, administration is inevitably both art and science, and perhaps more art than science. Also, since administration cannot be separated from politics, Waldo argues that public administration is different from private administration, being distinguished by the political environment in which the public administrator must operate. Our objective, Waldo argues, should not be to keep administrators out of policy and political matters but to encourage cooperation between the political and administrative domains and to discover ways in which we can benefit from the creative potential and substantive contributions of administrative officials.

Waldo's works serve as a fitting conclusion to the author-focused chapters in this volume. He presents an overview of the field, offers a series of penetrating original insights and criticisms, comments on some more recent developments, and speculates about the future of the enterprise of public administration. Perhaps more important, he reveals the implicit assumptions, the hidden premises that underlie the various approaches to public administration. Although Waldo may not provide definitive answers, he certainly leads us to the right questions and provides some insights that better equip us to make more informed choices among difficult alternatives.

Life

Clifford Dwight Waldo was born in Dewitt, Nebraska, on September 28, 1913.[2] His father, Cliff Ford Waldo, owned a livery stable and raised hogs, while his mother, Grace Gertrude (Lindley), managed the household. In commenting on his youth, Waldo says only that it was largely misspent for his future purposes—he cites his victory in a hog-calling contest as a major achievement—and that his ultimate career developed largely by accident.

Upon graduation from high school, Waldo entered Nebraska State Teachers College in Peru, Nebraska. Earning his BA in 1935, he then looked for a job as an English teacher, but, in the depths of the Great Depression, he was unable to locate a position. In what he describes as an act more of desperation than of choice, Waldo accepted a job reading papers at the University of Nebraska and enrolled in the master's program in political science. In 1937 he received his MA, married Gwen Payne (with whom he would eventually have three daughters), and accepted the offer of a Cowles Fellowship at Yale University. There Waldo studied political science, with a specialization in the history of political thought. He served as an instructor in the Political Science Department from 1941 to 1942 and received his PhD in the spring of 1942.

Waldo's dissertation at Yale, initially entitled "Theories of Expertise in the Democratic Tradition," was originally intended to address the question of how much democracy should be yielded to expertise.[3] But, as is often the case, both the intent and the scope of the project changed over time. Waldo's central concern remained political theory, but the final dissertation dealt with only one chapter of his original design, focusing on public administration.[4] This change of focus was prompted largely by his discovery that public administration had an underlying matrix of theory, and his intent became that of "exposing" the theory of public administration.

Waldo came to his newly defined task with a self-described "animus toward, even contempt for" his chosen subject matter.[5] He viewed public administration as a "lower" field of endeavor, preoccupied with such relatively mundane matters as counting manhole covers.[6] Although he thought public administration and political theory to be at opposite ends of the applied-theoretical continuum, Waldo's objective was to treat public administration as yet another chapter in political theory and thereby prove the usefulness and relevance of political theory itself.

Waldo's attitude and intent resulted in a dissertation—later to be published as *The Administrative State*—which he admits was "presumptuous, smart alec, and hostile."[7] In Waldo's words, "I savored over much the paradox and the irony. Occasionally the warranted critique tended toward the unwarranted exposé."[8] Although the book was toned down at the behest of his publisher, who advised that making unnecessary enemies would not help his career, Waldo observes that it took him nearly a decade after the publication of *The Administrative State* to achieve a measure of respectability in the field.[9] First, his critical appraisal of the prewar search for principles of administration did not exactly endear him to the majority of public administration scholars of the then-orthodox persuasion. Second, his book issued at least an oblique challenge to the newly emergent Behavioral approach to public administration and political science. In what was to become a continuing, and not always pleasant, exchange with Waldo, Herbert Simon observed that Waldo doubted the possibility of any science of administration, but that his argument was "stated in a far too brief, superficial, and confused fashion to cast much light on the issues."[10] Looking back on the "sometimes bitter encounters" between Behavioralists and others in political science and public administration, Waldo observed that by 1965 these clashes had become "too complex, too subtle, [with] opinions too tempered, [and with] emotions too exhausted."[11]

In the eight years intervening between conception and publication of *The Administrative State,* Waldo's ideas and attitudes about public administration changed substantially. In the spring of 1942, he was offered a university teaching position in political theory. He declined the offer, perhaps because it was not suitable, and, through the help of Harvey Mansfield, found a job in Washington, D.C., where he spent the next four years. Between 1942 and 1944, Waldo worked as a price analyst for the Office of Price Administration and, from 1944 through 1946, as an administrative analyst in the Bureau of the Budget. Though Waldo considered himself a failure as a bureaucrat, his administrative experience started a process of resocialization that resulted in an identification with public administration rather than political theory. He reports that he emerged from governmental service with respect for the difficulties of administration, empathy for administrators, and a conviction that no one should be allowed to teach political science without experience in public affairs.[12]

After the war, Waldo was hired to teach political theory at the University of California at Berkeley. He proceeded to teach courses in everything but political theory; and he found himself increasingly interested in, and identified with, public administration. He participated in a movement to establish a Graduate School of Public Affairs, he was involved in changing the University Bureau of Public Administration to the Institute of Governmental Studies, and he served as director of the institute from 1958 to 1967. Waldo's interests in public administration were also widening. An encounter with Weber's writings stimulated an interest in comparative administration, and, in the early 1950s, Waldo offered a course in Comparative National Administration. Later, he went to Italy on a project to improve Italian administration—an experience that, he reports, made him acutely aware of the limitations of "principles" of administration.[13] In the early 1960s, Waldo became actively involved in the Comparative Administration Group of the American Society for Public Administration.

Having endured his decade of "intellectual exile" following publication of *The Administrative State*, Waldo now also became centrally involved in the administration of his professions. Between 1957 and 1960, he served on the Council and then on the Executive Committee of the American Political Science Association, becoming vice president of that organization in 1961. He also served on the editorial board of the *American Political Science Review* from 1959 to 1963. In public administration, Waldo served on the Council of the American Society for Public Administration (1963–1966) and on the editorial board of the *Public Administration Review* (1958–1966). In 1966 he became editor-in-chief of *PAR.* To date, he remains its longest-serving editor, having stepped down in the summer of 1977. Between 1963 and 1983, Waldo was also a member of the editorial board of the *International Review of Administrative Sciences.*

Waldo's stay at Berkeley was thus characterized by an increasing and expanding interest in public administration, accompanied by a similarly increasing disaffection from political science, either as a disciplinary "home" for public administration or as a supportive environment for those who wish to study it.[14] By 1967, Waldo stated that his interests were running to sociology, business administration, and organization theory and that he found those subjects more germane to the agenda of public administration than political science.[15] Moreover, he felt that the political science environment was inhospitable to his interests.[16] As a result, Waldo moved to Syracuse University to become professor of political science and Albert Schweitzer Professor of Humanities in the Maxwell School of Citizenship and Public Affairs. Reflecting later on his career, Waldo describes Syracuse and the Maxwell School as one of the few places where public administration is valued and viewed with respect.[17] While at Syracuse, he served as vice president (1976–1977) and president (1977–1978) of the National Association of Schools of Public Affairs and Administration. In 1979 Waldo retired from Syracuse as professor emeritus, and he then spent the next two years at the Woodrow Wilson International Center for Scholars of the Smithsonian Institute. Thereafter, like the other authors considered in this volume, Waldo remained active in his retirement years—studying, writing, lecturing, and mentoring young scholars.

Over the course of his distinguished career, Waldo received a number of awards, including the Silver Medallion of the University of Bologna; an honorary PhD from the University of Nebraska; an honorary life membership in the International City Managers Association; the William E. Mosher and Laverne Burchfield awards of the American Society for Public Administration; and the Berkeley Citation of the University of California at Berkeley. He was a member of the National Academy of Public Administration, the American Society for Public Administration, the American Political Science Association, the American Society for the Advancement of Science, the International Institute of Administrative Sciences, and the International Political Science Association.

From June 27–29, 1996, a symposium was held in his honor at the Maxwell School.[18] At the opening dinner of this gathering of about 100 former colleagues, students, and other relations, each participant related in what manner Dwight Waldo had helped him or her to get started in a career. As Gary Wamsley recalls, "nearly all had personal vignettes to tell … vignettes about Dwight's impact on them and their lives—lessons learned from Dwight Waldo, the scholar as mensch."[19] In his brief editorial introduction as the new editor-in-chief of *PAR*, Louis C. Gawthrop observed that "Dwight Waldo is a gentleman in the finest sense of the word. Moreover, he is a gentle man"—words he reiterated in at a toast during the dinner.[20] Waldo was more critical of himself, noting that he identified with political theory in the humanist-liberal tradition, but that, sometimes, his "other side [displayed] archness and arrogance, pretentiousness and preciousness. I now judge that in some cases my words reflected those qualities." He passed away on October 27, 2000.

Waldo on the Classical Approach to Public Administration

Since so much of Waldo's writing dealt with the history of public administration, we start with a review of his conception of, and commentary on, that history before proceeding to his own view of public administration.

Waldo emphasizes that public administration did not begin in the twentieth century. Instead, a stream of administrative technology was developed over the centuries to which, until recent times, the public sector made the more important contributions. Indeed, he says, "in the sweep of history overall, public administration has been leader, not follower, in the development of administrative technology."[21] Waldo does credit the late nineteenth and early twentieth centuries with the development of the self-conscious study of public administration on a scale new in human history, and he identifies the United States as a major focal point of administrative studies. Although a number of forces were important in shaping the overall contours of the field, Waldo asserts that the proximate determinants of the specific content of public administration in the United States were the reform movement and the Progressive era, which emphasized executive leadership, civil service reform, and education for citizenship and sought to expose inefficiency through scientific investigations.[22] All these characteristics, to one degree or another, were incorporated in what has become known as the Classical approach to public administration.[23]

General Characteristics of the Classical Approach

Waldo identifies five basic characteristics of the Classical approach to public administration, which dominated the field until roughly 1940. These characteristics were acceptance of the politics-administration dichotomy,[24] a generic management orientation, the search for principles of administration through scientific analysis, an emphasis on centralization of executive authority, and a commitment to democracy.

A fundamental premise of the Classical approach was that politics should be separated from administration. Despite some differences, Waldo argues that, on the whole, the authors of the Classical period accepted the distinction between politics and administration, asserted that administration is in the realm of expertise from which politics should be excluded, and argued for a strengthened chief executive to curb the centrifugal forces of the administrative branch.[25]

A second basic characteristic of the Classical approach was a generic management orientation, which assumed that the techniques of private management were applicable in the public sector. Waldo argues that public administration accepted both business procedures and a business ideology, as the business model was used to deprecate the balance of powers and aggrandize the role of the chief executive, as well as to justify hierarchical control mechanisms, merit appointment, and the adoption of businesslike budgetary procedures.[26]

A third characteristic of the Classical approach was the search for a science of administration. The Classical approach had a practical rather than an idealistic orientation, for it was believed that the scientific study of administration could lead to the discovery of general "principles" of administration on which efficient government could be based.[27]

Next, the Classical approach emphasized the centralization of executive activities. The general prescription was centralization, simplification, and unification. The objectives of this emphasis were to centralize responsibility, to build the power of the chief executive by establishing stronger hierarchical controls within the executive branch, and to abolish superfluous offices in the name of efficiency.[28]

Finally, the Classical approach maintained a basic commitment to "democracy." Democracy was defined substantively rather than procedurally, however—it was to be achieved by establishing a strong, responsive, and responsible government designed to serve efficiently the needs of the people in an emergent "Great Society." [29]

Ideological and Philosophical Aspects of the Classical Approach

Although the authors of the period purportedly avoided value commitments, ideology, and philosophy, Waldo contends that strong elements of each were contained in the Classical approach to public administration. The value orientation of the Classical approach, according to Waldo, was embodied in a tacit commitment to individualism, materialism, and equality; a preference for harmony over conflict; a belief in the superiority of urban life; and a dedication to science as a primary instrument of progress.[30] By adopting these values and by concentrating on means and methodology, Waldo contends, the early authors on public administration effectively accepted and supported the existing political order.

Waldo also maintains that the Classical approach had an implicit ideological framework. This ideology embraced the idea of a democratic "mission of America," a belief in fundamental law, adherence to the doctrine of progress and progressivism, adoption of the "Gospel of Efficiency," and a faith in expertise on which a "democratic ruling class" could be founded. The so-called mission of America was seen as "witnessing Democracy before mankind, bearing democracy's ideals of freedom and equality, and its material blessings to the nations of the world."[31] It was held that this mission could not be accomplished in competition with ethically inferior ideals unless greater efficiency in governmental operations could be achieved. The belief in fundamental law was expressed in the search for "principles" of administration that were to reflect a "higher law and a fundamental moral order." Waldo attributes a pervasive "aura of evangelical protestantism" in the reform movement to this belief in fundamental law.[32] Progress was to be achieved through a planned and administered society. The "Gospel of Efficiency" represented an attempt to reconcile traditional democratic institutions with the requirements of new administrative technology. More efficient organization and administration were seen as means of creating responsive and responsible government that would better serve the needs of the people. This purpose required both the assembling of scientific knowledge and the placement of experts in government, as the Classical authors sought to establish a governing class of expert administrators who would exercise governmental power to preserve democracy.[33] In sum, Waldo concludes that the early students of public administration were "part of a well-known company of political theorists, not removed from political theory," despite their protestations to the contrary.[34]

Finally, Waldo argues that the Classical approach to public administration had a recognizable philosophical component consisting of pragmatism, utilitarianism, and positivism.[35] Pragmatism was reflected in the concentration on the efficiency of means. Utilitarianism was reflected in the objective of achieving the "greatest happiness of the greatest number," presuming a practical equality of persons. Positivism was reflected in the opposition to intangible criteria and the attempt, in Waldo's terms, "to substitute measurement for metaphysics."[36]

Weber on Bureaucracy

Before we leave Waldo's description of the Classical period, it is probably appropriate to discuss his views on Max Weber. One must say "probably" because Waldo, like many others, has some difficulty in defining a suitable niche for Weber in the development of administrative thought. As he puts it, Weber has been seen as a traditional systems builder, a seminal Behavioralist, and even a disguised metaphysician.[37] Although he acknowledges some validity in each of these views, Waldo is primarily concerned with Weber's concept of bureaucracy, which he regards as the single most important statement on formal organization.

Waldo considers Weber's genius to lie in his ability to relate the concept of bureaucracy to history, economic life, technological development, political philosophy, and social structure and social processes. In short, Weber saw the development of bureaucracy as related to the development of civilization itself—a view that, as we shall see, Waldo shares. Waldo assesses Weber's formulation of bureaucracy as having a "plausible fit" for his time, but he has some reservations about the desirability of bureaucratic organizations, a point to which we will return.[38]

Waldo's Critique and Comments on the Classical Approach

So much for Waldo's recounting of the Classical approach to public administration. What is his reaction to that approach? Characteristically, Waldo gives it a mixed review—as has perhaps been implied in the preceding discussion.

On the politics-administration dichotomy, Waldo contends that the separation is inadequate, either as a description of reality or as a prescription for administrative behavior.[39] This dichotomy, according to Waldo, was intended to resolve the conflict between bureaucracy and democracy by making elected officials responsible for framing policy while restricting administrators to the execution of that policy. Democracy itself was then defined in terms of an efficient response to public needs that could best be accomplished by a cadre of experts. But Waldo argues that public administration in the Classical period was, in actuality, false to the ideal of democracy. Democracy was seen as desirable but peripheral to the concerns of administration and hostile to the central principle of efficiency.[40] The Classical movement indicted "centrifugal democracy" and sought to implement its own version of "centripetal democracy" by proposing a separation between politics and administration and relying on what Waldo calls the "dogmas of centralization" and the "canons of integration" as a solution to the problem of efficiency.[41]

The politics-administration dichotomy was also intended to solve the value problem. Here it was asserted that the political system would establish values and set goals for administration. Waldo regards this solution as disingenuous, since it ignores the desire to extend the compass of the science of administration to an ever-larger complex of phenomena. As a result, public administration threatened to "overrun the realm of policy—as the British conquered India—not by intent and plan, but by a continuous process of tidying up the border."[42] Waldo contends that the real question raised by the Classical authors is not whether politics and policy should be separated from administration but how far the administrative function should extend in determining values and policies—a question for which they failed to provide a suitable answer. Waldo's own view is that we should move toward a philosophy that encourages cooperation among powers, be they administrative or political, not competition among separated powers.[43]

Waldo is similarly critical of the organizational paradigm of the Classical approach. He criticizes both the emphasis on supposed principles or commonalities among organizations and the rationalist bias of Classical organization theory. In regard to the search for commonalities, Waldo contends that Classical organization theory ignored the specificity that is the "stuff of administration." Organizations, Waldo maintains, should be defined and structured to meet purposes, not general principles, and the organizational form and process actually adopted should be suited to the specific situation confronting the organization.[44] He asserts that Classical organization theory prescribed general organizational forms and processes that were not readily adaptable to specific situations or changing circumstances.[45]

Waldo also argues that the Classical "principles" were based on an idea of law—he calls it Cosmic Constitutionalism—that mixes a scientific, descriptive concept of the "natural order of things" (what is) with the notion of moral necessity (what ought to be). Waldo observes that even if the Classical principles were based on empirical observation and could tell us what exists, that does not necessarily constitute a prescription for the way things should be.[46] Finally, he claims that the Classical approach ignores the irrational and informal aspects of organizations. A case in point is Weber's concept of bureaucracy. Waldo argues that Weber placed undue emphasis on the functional side of bureaucracy, ignored the informal and socioemotional aspects of organizations, and elevated position over knowledge as the basis for hierarchical authority.[47]

Waldo also chides the Classical authors for their "scientific" pretensions. In his view, the Classical "science" of public administration relied primarily on a "heaping up of facts," and its principles were little more than an extension of common sense.[48] Waldo is even more critical of the intent of the Classical authors than he is of the execution of that intent. In a theme that recurs throughout his writings, Waldo expresses reservations about the possibility of developing a science of administration. He contends that public administration must deal with thinking and valuing human beings and that the techniques of science are inappropriate to such subjects. Values cannot be treated scientifically, and human free will means that the principles of mechanical cause and effect are inapplicable.[49] This does not mean that Waldo thinks that science is unnecessary. Even if an administrative science is not possible, he believes that a scientific mentality might at least make common sense more sensible, and that some parts of administration may well be amenable to scientific investigation. Nevertheless, he warns that we should not try to force on a subject matter a method that is not suitable to it.

Finally, Waldo challenges the Classical emphasis on efficiency, which was originally intended to replace a moralistic approach to public administration. Waldo maintains that the idea of efficiency itself became imbued with a moral significance, however, as the pursuit of "technical efficiency" was transformed into the pursuit of "social efficiency."[50] Moreover, he asserts that, although efficiency is not a value in itself, it is a useful concept only within a framework of consciously held values. In other words, one must consider the object of efficiency, since it is not reasonable to assume that it is desirable to accomplish *any* end efficiently.[51]

Although, as is evidenced by the preceding comments, Waldo was initially highly critical of the Classical approach to public administration, time and exposure to proposed alternatives served to temper his views. He continued to consider the Classical approach to be an ideology, but, as he put it, that "is not to imply that it is a myth that a sensible man must summarily reject."[52] In Waldo's judgment, the Classical approach contains much truth and represents an intelligent response to a historical situation. In particular, he suggests that the politics-administration dichotomy served—and still serves—a useful purpose in stimulating political reform and improvement in administration.[53] Moreover, the Classical approach is still deeply engrained in our culture, and no consensus on an alternative has yet emerged to replace the Classical paradigm of public administration.[54]

Contemporary Public Administration

A series of challenges to the Classical approach to public administration arose in the 1940s, as, in Waldo's words, "heterodoxy replaced orthodoxy."[55] The Classical claim to having discovered a science of public administration was branded as, at best, premature. The Classical principles of administration were relegated to the status of proverbs. The Classical emphasis on economy and efficiency was denigrated as having been too narrowly conceived. The politics-administration dichotomy was questioned. The generic management approach was seen as overly simplistic.

Waldo contends that the field of public administration is now characterized by a diversity of perspectives in which the Classical approach has not been so much repudiated as absorbed, amended, extended, and joined by new perspectives. In the process, some of the ideological and philosophical underpinnings of the Classical approach have been rejected, and others have simply gone underground. The influence of the business mentality has diminished, the idea of "fundamental law" as a higher moral order has been largely abandoned, and there is increasing skepticism about the notion of "progress." Though pragmatism has declined as a "fashionable" philosophy, Waldo maintains that it continues to be the unarticulated working philosophy of public administration and that it is manifested in the effort to construct a new science of administration in a manner consistent with the tenets of Behavioralism.[56]

Concurrent with the Behavioral emphasis has been the assertion that administration is both art and science, and perhaps more art than science. This new perspective has been the result of the rejection of the politics-administration dichotomy and the consequent inclusion of both politics and policy within the legitimate purview of public administration. The concern with policy, Waldo notes, has raised normative questions that were previously excluded from the domain of public administration. Thus, contemporary public administration has witnessed both a continuing interest on the factual side in the form of the Behavioral approach and an awakening of interest on the value side in the form of renewed concern with the role of the administrator in political and policy processes.[57]

Waldo identifies four basic, though not entirely separate, currents of thought in contemporary public administration: organization theory, comparative public administration, a public policy orientation, and the "new public administration."

Organization Theory

Waldo divides the development of organization theory into three stages.[58] The first stage was the Classical period, epitomized by the works of authors such as Taylor, Gulick, Fayol, and Mooney. The Classical stage of organization theory was based on the "machine model" of the organization and emphasized the rational aspects of human behavior. This stage reached it zenith in the 1930s and culminated in the publication of the *Papers on the Science of Administration.*[59] Waldo labels the second stage in the development of organization theory the "neoclassical" approach.

This stage began with the Hawthorne experiments in the 1920s and retained major importance through mid-century. In contrast to the Classical stage, the neoclassical approach emphasized the emotive and sociopsychological dimensions of human behavior in organizations.

The final stage in the development of organization theory is modern organization theory, which, according to Waldo, began with the publication of James March and Herbert Simon's *Organizations* in 1958.[60] Modern organization theory is based on an "organic" or "natural system" model of the organization and stresses organizational growth and survival. The modern approach endorses organizations that have less reliance on hierarchical controls, more recognized sources of authority, greater opportunity for personal mobility, and greater receptivity to organizational change. Modern organization theory is decidedly Behavioral in orientation, adopting the methods of the physical and biological sciences and seeking a value-free "general theory" of organizations that is true for all times and places.

Neoclassical Organization Theory

In Waldo's scheme of things, the neoclassical stage of organization theory was dominated by the Hawthorne studies and its intellectual progeny, the Human Relations movement. Placing its emphasis on the affective and social aspects of organizational behavior, the Human Relations movement focused on considerations such as morale, perceptions and attitudes, group relationships, informal groups, leadership, and the bases for cooperation in organizational behavior. Waldo considers the Human Relations movement to be simultaneously a repudiation and a continuation of the Classical approach.[61] In its concentration on social and psychological factors in organizational behavior, the Human Relations movement demonstrated the limitations of perspectives such as Scientific Management. According to Waldo, however, the Human Relations movement was originally seen as merely an extension of, and a corrective to, Scientific Management, laying a continuing stress on the values of science, managerialism, and efficiency. The objective was to bring the newly discovered "nonrational" under the control of the "rational." Thus, Waldo contends, Human Relations represented more a refinement of means than a radical departure from the Classical approach in terms of either goals or methodology.

Modern Organization Theory

Waldo finds modern organization theory to be a more elusive subject matter. It is, he says, diverse and heterogeneous and highly subject to changing fashions.[62] Modern organization theory has drawn its ideas from such varied sources as management science (which Waldo considers to be the principal legatee of the Scientific Management movement), sociology, social psychology, economics, and anthropology. Modern organization theory is founded on a belief in the "universals" of organizational behavior and, as a result, has shown little concern for public organizations as a potentially separable subject of analysis. Finally, Waldo contends that modern organization theory continues to be grounded in the values of twentieth-century Western culture—namely, science, rationality, effectiveness, efficiency, and productivity. This cultural orientation has eventuated in a perceptible shift from description to prescription, from theoretical to applied science. Waldo cites Simon's focus on organizational design, the productivity movement, and the pursuit of "softer" values such as humanism, job enrichment, and self-actualization as illustrative of this trend.[63]

Reflecting the diversity of the period, Waldo includes several perspectives under the rubric of modern organization theory. Simon's work on decision making is but one aspect of modern organization theory—albeit, in Waldo's opinion, a crucial aspect. Waldo considers Simon's work to be, in some respects, a radical departure from Classical organization theory but, in other respects, a conservative approach that is only partial in perspective.[64] Simon's approach to organization theory constitutes a radical departure in its insistence on more rigorous scientific standards and its focus on administrative decision making. Waldo also sees Simon as a conservative in that he seeks to establish a science of administration, retains efficiency as the criterion of organizational decisions, attempts to salvage the Classical principles (if only as diagnostic criteria), and maintains a twofold structuring of the universe by substituting the fact-value dichotomy for the old politics-administration dichotomy. This conservatism, Waldo contends, is the reason that Simon's formulation has not been accepted as the solution to the identity crisis in public administration.

The second perspective of modern organization theory in Waldo's schema is organizational humanism, represented by works of authors such as Chris Argyris, Warren Bennis, and Rensis Likert. Waldo observes that organizational humanism focuses on much the same kinds of concerns as the Human Relations movement. From the humanist perspective, according to Waldo, the objective is to achieve organizational effectiveness and self-fulfillment simultaneously, under the assumption that the interests of the individual and the organization are compatible.[65] Thus, although organizational humanism has been proposed as a means for escaping the impersonality of bureaucracy, it is also a pragmatic attempt to develop more flexible, knowledge-based organizations that can achieve rationality and efficiency in changing circumstances.

The third major strand of modern organization theory is what Waldo terms the systems-based, "scientific and managerial" literature. He includes contingency theory in this literature, arguing that it is a natural outgrowth of the system perspective in that it addresses the problem of specifying appropriate managerial strategies in a changing and uncertain environment. Other components of the scientific and managerial literature include elements of decision theory, organizational development, computer technology, and organizational futurism.[66] In assessing the scientific and managerial literature, Waldo notes that, like organizational humanism, this literature does not so much repudiate the old values of rationality and efficiency as it seeks to realize those values under more difficult circumstances.[67]

Waldo's attitudes toward neoclassical and modern organization theory are mixed and, in his words, range from "unqualified admiration, through curiosity and hope, to indifference and annoyance stopping short of hostility."[68] Waldo's first concern is that the techniques of modern organization theory may be used by managers "only to more skillfully manipulate their 'human material.'"[69] In a colorful comment on Elton Mayo and the Human Relations movement, Waldo says: "I have a persistent vision of a modern dairy farm, managed to perfection, each cow in its gleaming stanchion, contentedly munching vitaminized food, milking machines barely audible through the piped-in Vienna waltzes."[70] Waldo also charges that much of modern organization theory is "anti-individual" and "dwarfs and de-humanizes man."[71] This tendency is most vividly reflected, Waldo asserts, in Simon's concentration on the rational and logical aspects of the organization. Simon, Waldo contends, does not just demystify rationality, he dehumanizes it.

Second, Waldo notes that the authors dealing with organization theory are not very specific in defining their object of analysis. Using the fable of the blind man and the elephant as an analogy, Waldo remarks, "It is not clear that the [authors] are talking about the same elephant, or even members of the same species ... if they all concern the same elephant, it is a very large elephant with a generalized elephantiasis."[72] The absence of definitional delimitation is consistent with the objective of developing a universal and unified "theory of organization," but the assertion that such universals exist and that, therefore, a unified theory is possible, is, according to Waldo, more hope than certainty. Waldo charges that modern organization theory, despite its pretensions, presents no unified "theory of organization." By becoming everything, systems theory runs the danger of becoming nothing in particular.[73] Contingency theory's central point that "it all depends" is plausible enough, but little indication has been given of what to do beyond that point.[74] Waldo also notes that modern organization theory has given little attention to public organizations and that it is "ironical that an enterprise that aspires for universality in its fruits should be so parochial in its roots."[75]

Finally, Waldo contends that, like the Classical approach, the newer theory of organizations is value-laden. He asserts that the shift from "administration" to "organization" was, at least in part, intended to counter the value problem. The concept *organization* suggests that there is something out there that can be dealt with on a descriptive basis.[76] But Waldo claims that organizations, like administration, inevitably mirror the values of the societies in which they reside. In twentieth-century America this means, among other things, an attachment to the values of rationality and efficiency. Waldo maintains that there is no way to study organizations apart from the values they embody and the aims toward which they are directed. Consequently, in his opinion, a value-free theory of organizations is unattainable.[77]

Comparative Public Administration

The second major focus of the contemporary period has been comparative public administration. According to Waldo, comparative public administration both resembles and differs from modern organization theory. It shares with modern organization theory a concern for methodological problems; a reliance on models such as the systems framework and structural functionalism; an interdisciplinary orientation; a search for universal concepts, formulas, and theories; and an emphasis on empirical description. Comparative public administration differs from modern organization theory, however, in its explicit comparative perspective, its focus on cultural diversity, and its fascination with Weberian bureaucracies.

Though it was at one time widely believed that comparative public administration was the "area of greatest promise" in contemporary public administration, Waldo feels that promise has yet to be fulfilled. Comparative public administration, according to Waldo, taught us much about the relationship between administration and social ends, the critical dependence of civilization on effective governmental administration, and the difficulties in transferring the Western model of administration to other cultures. But the basic problem of the comparative administration movement was the distance between the theoretical models employed and the evidence of field research.[78] And despite its strong theoretical bent, Waldo asserts, the movement failed to produce anything in the way of rigorous theory.[79]

The pressure for practical results led to a switch from comparative to "developmental" administration, a switch that Waldo at one time endorsed.[80] The results, however, have not been much more encouraging: we have simply learned much about what will not work, and no general "science of development" has yet emerged. Waldo charges that the developmental perspective has assumed that to be "developed" is to be Western. The result, he asserts, is that developmental administration has become a "powerful and subtle ideology" with the characteristics of a "world-girdling religion," and the effort to achieve development has amounted to little more than an effort to reproduce the Weberian model of bureaucracy.[81]

Public Policy

The third major focus of contemporary public administration has been public policy, which initially took the form of the case-study approach. Essentially a teaching method, the case-study approach was designed to offer the student a vicarious experience in administration by giving an account of actual administrative happenings as recounted by an interested but impartial observer. The case studies focused on decision making in a holistic manner and attempted to raise basic questions about both policy and ethics. The motives of the approach were "scientific" in that the cases were to be based on careful observation and were to result in the accumulation of empirical data on the administrative process. But the approach also constituted a rejoinder both to logical positivism and to Simon's fact-value dichotomy that was viewed as an overly simplistic cleavage, all too reminiscent of the old politics-administration dichotomy. Waldo judges the case-study approach to be potentially useful but not sufficient as a means to study and teach public administration.[82]

Other than the case-study approach, Waldo says, little has been done with public policy within the field of public administration. Authors such as Paul Appleby, Norton Long, and Emmette Redford have addressed questions of policy and politics. Until recently, however, policy as a focus has been largely ceded to other disciplines, especially economics, and those disciplines have been attending to matters that Waldo feels ought to have been addressed by public administration.[83]

The New Public Administration

A development with which Waldo's own name is connected is the New Public Administration movement. The Schweitzer chair enabled him to finance a meeting of young scholars (those under the age of thirty-five) that was convened in 1968 at the Minnowbrook conference center in the northern Adirondacks. This movement, spawned by the social and political ferment of the late 1960s and early 1970s, was, according to Waldo, part of the rebellion of youth and the counterculture of the non-Marxian left.[84] The New Public Administration criticized the "old" public administration for its lack of an explicit ideological-philosophical framework and supported an activist role for the administrator in the pursuit of social equity. Waldo referred to the movement as a "New Romanticism," because it shared with that philosophical movement the assumption that man is inherently good but is corrupted by bad institutions, and because it reacted to rationalism by emphasizing the role of feeling over reason, senses over the mind, and spontaneity, creativity, and self-fulfillment over convention and rules.[85]

The basic themes of the New Public Administration were participation, decentralization, and representative bureaucracy. Participation was supported both as a political process and as an organizational process. Political participation was seen as a means of dispersing power and increasing citizen involvement in government. The movement rejected both simple majoritarianism and pluralism in favor of alternatives described by Waldo as ranging from "organic communitarianism" to moral and political elitism.[86] Support for organizational participation was part of what Waldo sees as the movement's "massive hostility" to any factor perceived as "bureaucratic." Organizational participation was to be a means for promoting change and dispersing power within the organization. Decentralization, like participation, was intended to disperse power and increase citizen involvement in governmental and organizational processes. Representative bureaucracy was meant to produce client-centered administration and representation of clientele interests by administrators.

Waldo confesses a "sympathetic interest" in the ideas of the New Public Administration movement, but he also expresses some substantial misgivings. On participation and representative bureaucracy, he asserts that the arguments are often "*ad hoc* and inconsistent, if not indeed dishonest."[87] Supporters of participation, Waldo argues, seem to assume that some "invisible hand" will resolve the problems of coordination, order, and survival in the new system of highly dispersed power. Moreover, he finds the movement to be inconsistent in its desire to have democracy while rejecting majoritarianism and pluralism and, in effect, supporting rule by the minority.[88] On decentralization, Waldo points out that a cogent case can also be made for centralization, and that neither case is universally right or wrong.[89]

Waldo finds some validity in the antiorganizational stance of the New Public Administration, but he considers much of its indictment to be "unfair, spurious, and above all unrealistic."[90] Although our administrative ethos has been oriented toward the rational end of the spectrum, in his view, this orientation does not constitute a blind dedication to rigid organizational procedures and bureaucracy. Moreover, those very bureaucratic organizations have often proven to be a force for change. Waldo notes that most innovative techniques and technologies have been created in—or at least at the behest of—bureaucratic organizations, and that the era of bureaucracy has been an era of rapid change. Furthermore, even if bureaucracy serves the status quo, the status quo itself is not a monolithic interest but a diversity of interests, all of which must be served. Finally, in addressing the question of efficiency, Waldo charges that the

critics attack a narrow conception of efficiency that has long been discarded. Even the critics do not support inefficiency, but Waldo says that
he hopes that he will never have to "fly with an airplane, have surgery in a
hospital, or even stay in a hotel run in the new 'ideal style.' "[91]

To the extent that the New Public Administration movement simply
reflects a conflict of youth versus age, Waldo observes that "children's
crusades and youth movements have not on the whole written happy, brilliant pages in the history of civilization."[92] Even more acidly, he asserts
that the young represent a "continuing barbarian invasion" that must be
socialized and civilized if a return to barbarism is to be prevented.[93]

In regard to contemporary public administration as a whole, Waldo
describes it as "like Poland, open to invasion from every side," as no new
synthesis has emerged to replace the old Classical formulation.[94] The
field is marked by an increasing perimeter, but no agreed-upon intellectual core or "public philosophy." Waldo maintains that the problem now
is to find the boundaries of public administration.[95]

Waldo's World of Public Administration

To this point we have examined Waldo's "map" of the field of public administration and his reactions thereto. Waldo himself was more a commentator and critic than a creative theorist, or even a synthesizer.
Scattered throughout his voluminous writings, however, are a series of
observations that, while not constituting the elusive unified theory of
public administration, at least provide some insight into Waldo's own perspectives on public administration.

History and Public Administration

If there is a single dominant theme in Waldo's work, it is probably the importance he attaches to history, or, as he puts it, a strong sense that "what
is past is prologue."[96] Although he "confess[es] [to] have written more
about it than *in* it,"[97] Waldo believes that there is much to be learned
from history, and he deplores the fact that much of the public administration literature has been antihistorical in nature. He asserts that history
does indeed repeat itself, though "in different keys and with endless variations of its themes," and that ignoring the past denies an important
source of "insights, hypotheses, and scientific conclusions."[98]

An important lesson of history, Waldo argues, is that the techniques of
administration are at the center of the political-governmental evolution.
Indeed, he maintains that government and administration are substantially equivalent. In Waldo's phrase, administration "frames civilization"
by giving it a foundation or stage and by providing a base for growth.[99] In

short, government qua administration and civilization are always intimately joined.

Accordingly, Waldo considers government and its administration to be more than merely an artificially created intruder in a state of nature that would otherwise be serene and prosperous.[100] Government, Waldo argues, is no more a "creation" than are markets or private enterprise; and the "sustaining, nurturing, and creative" role of government has been largely ignored. Waldo acknowledges that "government is always marginally oppressive and sometimes massively so" and that "there are things that government cannot do or can do only clumsily."[101] He argues, however, that government and its administrative apparatus have performed their functions with at least moderate success despite increases in the scale and complexity of their activities.

Waldo's focus is mainly on the development of government in the Western world. His initial forays into this topic focused on the influence of Rome (passed on through the Catholic Church) and the early modern state's emerging nationalism supported by a " ... military force, in itself in many ways increasingly 'bureaucratic.'"[102] Later, he observes that the modern state's politics and administration is firmly rooted in two very different traditions: "One is a civic culture tradition that arises in the thought and experience of classical Greece and draws from the Roman Republic and some of the medieval and early modern city-states. The other is an imperial tradition arising in the ancient empires of the Middle East and the Mediterranean basin.... The United States reflects both traditions. Our politics are Greek, but our administration is Roman."[103] The features of both these traditions came to the United States "as a function of the English antecedents to the American experiment in government."[104]

Public Administration and the State

What was the nature of this "American experiment in government"? The title and content of his dissertation hold the answer to this question. From the late nineteenth century on, scholars had observed that administrators qua civil servants became more and more important to government functioning. According to Frank Goodnow, "The execution of the law, the expressed will of the state, depends in large degree upon the active initiative of the administrative authorities."[105] More than four decades later, W.A.R. Leys wrote, "Legislators admit that they can do little more with such subjects as factory sanitation, international relations, and public education than to lay down a general public policy within which administrators will make detailed rules and plans of action."[106] What had started out as a political experiment and "a revolt against the old administrative order planted the seeds of a new administrative order."[107] Indeed, one of the ironies Michael Nelson suggested is that the spoils system helped to "hasten the reorganization of federal administrative agencies along bureaucratic lines."[108]

In his dissertation, Waldo analyzed the characteristics of the American administrative state, some of whose features were shared with Western government at large, which had become dominated by administrators rather than political officeholders.[109] This study, in fact, is why Waldo must be regarded as a political philosopher as well, and it is why he cannot simply be labeled a commentator on public administration. Waldo's work on the state and its bureaucracy in relation to politics and citizenry is nothing less than original. He articulated the concept of "the administrative state," even though notions of it had existed earlier. As bounded rationality became the dominant concept to describe human decision making, the administrative state became the dominant concept to describe modern government. Waldo astutely recognized the political force that administrators had become, and he would continue to point out that much of what could be found in public administration had been stated before in the language of political theory.[110] This observation, too, is original, because much of the research in the sixty to seventy years before publication of his study had been focused on developing a practically oriented public administration that was divorced from the influence of politics. So divorced, in fact, that few realized how much public administration could be regarded as political theory in action.

Bureaucracy and Democracy

As government and administration have been intimately joined, so too, Waldo says, has administration been joined with bureaucracy. And it is the potential conflict between bureaucracy and democracy that Waldo identifies as the central issue of our time.

In applying the word *bureaucracy*, Waldo takes care to distinguish his usage both from the common pejorative connotation and from Weber's ideal type, which identified bureaucracy with rationality. Instead, Waldo employs the term in a descriptive-analytical sense, connoting simply large-scale, formal, complex, task-specialized, and goal-oriented organizations. He asserts that bureaucratic organizations, so defined, have proven to be crucially important and that they perform unrecognized, or at least unappreciated, functions relating to order and stability by virtue of the very rigidity and permanence for which they are commonly condemned.

Democracy, according to Waldo, is a "striving toward equality and freedom."[111] By this definition, democracy is characterized by an ethic or a set of values rather than by its procedural trappings. Moreover, "democracy" is a term that is equally applicable to both political affairs and administrative-bureaucratic matters. Waldo notes that bureaucratic organization is not totally incompatible with the concept of democracy, for bureaucracies provide important support for democratic values, such as universalistic criteria and opportunity based on ability and expertise. There are also conflicting characteristics, such as the bureaucratic emphasis on the rule of hierarchy versus the democratic value of equality, and the bureaucratic reliance on discipline and supervision versus the democratic principle of liberty.

Waldo sees the conflict between bureaucracy and democracy as a dilemma. On the one hand, power is viewed as a dangerous commodity that should be fragmented and dispersed. On the other hand, it is recognized that power, if properly channeled, can serve good purposes. In administrative terms, this dual potential means that bureaucratic power is seen as a possible force for immorality and that decentralization should be encouraged. At the same time, it is held that democracy is possible only if power is concentrated so that it can both act and be held accountable. The dilemma deepens as the activities and services that democracy increasingly seeks from government are rendered more difficult to deliver within democratic restraints and expectations.

In Waldo's opinion, the clash between bureaucracy and democracy has elicited no little hypocrisy. Conservative authors brand public organizations as inferior while failing to acknowledge that bureaucracy is also the organizational mode of capitalism. Liberals want participatory administration, but not when the client is a defense contractor. The artist or the novelist "eagerly accepts with one hand the material goods of an organizational society he vigorously flogs with the other."[112] Waldo expresses his disdain for such hypocrisy in declaring that "the reaction to [bureaucracy] (right, left, and center) is essentially Ludditist, high in emotion and low in social knowledge and skill, ignorant and confused, dishonest and misleading in suggesting that in some simple fashion we can have our cake and eat it, that we can return to the simple life, but retain the high standard of living which is the product of present scientific, technological-administrative skills."[113]

The solution to the problem, according to Waldo, is to seek an optimal mix of democracy and bureaucracy, recognizing that while democracy is desirable, bureaucracy is necessary. He argues that we should accept the fact that we have an administrative culture and that we should use that culture to get as much as possible of the goods of life. We must also be concerned with the values of human equality and participation. Even though a considerable amount of authority, hierarchy, and even coercion is necessary and inevitable, the bureaucratic game should be played with everyone knowing the basic rules and being allowed to play to the extent that skill and inclination dictate.[114] Moreover, we should plan carefully to preserve areas of freedom and spontaneity. In short, Waldo would have us reform the world—not attempt to escape from it or abolish it—and seek a reasonable balance between accommodation to authority and rebellion.

Public Administration and Politics

Related to the question of bureaucracy and democracy is the role of administration in politics. Here, Waldo seeks some new formulation to replace the politics-administration dichotomy. Politics and administration, he asserts, are not separable realms but related realms, and perhaps even a single realm.[115] Waldo does not pretend to have the solution to the problem of relating administration to politics, but he does suggest that moving toward a professional perspective may be helpful.[116] That professional perspective should recognize that public administration is characterized by an interlocking set of values, not by a rigid paradigm or doctrine, and thus should be receptive to ideas and techniques from many sources. The professional perspective should have a moral component drawn from the values of democracy. Finally, the professional perspective should incorporate the concepts of political and social rationality, as well as economic rationality, and the idea of the "public interest" should play an important role lest public administration lose its ethical aura and thereby degenerate into mere "governmental administration."[117]

Morality and Public Administration

Waldo recognizes that rejecting the idea that the function of the administrator is simply to efficiently execute the will of the state raises a bewildering array of value problems. In its early decades, he charges, public administration simply avoided questions of values and morality by focusing on technical and scientific matters in the pursuit of efficiency. This focus, Waldo claims, is both unrealistic and insufficient. Instead of being divorced from questions of values and morality, he asserts, public administration is inevitably both a morality and an ideology. Consequently, administrative theory must embrace ethical theory, which, in turn, requires that values be treated as more than merely data. Waldo maintains that values should be studied consciously and should be used to give direction to empirical research. He does not envisage a "set of hornbooks to give 'Easy Ethical Answers'" to complex ethical problems. But he does believe that the conscious study of values can assist in reducing confusion and stress, and that it may lead to the development of a "moral creativeness" or "moral architecture" in administration matters.[118]

Waldo himself offers some tentative first steps in his proposed study of values and morality. History, he tells us, presents two traditions concerning morality in public affairs—one public and one private.[119] In the Greek tradition, as reflected in the writings of Plato and Aristotle, the polity itself is seen as the source of morality. Accordingly, the good man and the good citizen are one and the same.[120] The Stoics, in contrast, maintained that above the political community there exists a community of mankind that should be governed by a "natural law." Thus, considerations of right and wrong rest on interests beyond those of the polity.[121] With the rise of the Christian church came the claim that the church has a right to govern spiritual concerns independent of the political regime. The emergence of the modern theory of the state signaled a return to the Classical position that there is a unity of public and private morality. It was maintained that the state has the authority to determine right and wrong, but based on a higher law, and that public morality transcends matters of private morality. This formulation reached its extreme in the doctrine called Reason of State, which justifies actions serving the objectives of creating, preserving, or enhancing governmental power, even though those actions would be considered immoral in the private sphere.[122]

The political theory of liberal democracy, Waldo says, attempts to encompass both of these historical traditions. Consequently, "fortune, honor and life" may depend not only on a choice between morality and immorality but also on the choice among differing versions of morality.[123] Waldo asserts that "all decision and action in the public interest is inevitably morally complex," and, like a Greek tragedy, is apt to be not so much a conflict between good and evil as a conflict among competing goods.[124] That is, the individual is likely to have to weigh the moral claims of the state against the competing claims both of other collectivities (such as family, organization, or profession) and of higher law or conscience.

Waldo maintains that all governments are conceived in sin and survive by at least occasional and moderate sinning. As he puts it, "Those in government who decide and act on behalf of the public will from time to time, of necessity ... be lying, stealing, cheating, and killing."[125] Furthermore, Waldo contends that some cost in immorality is the price of any substantial act of public morality and that governmental actions are inevitably a mixture of morality and immorality. He does not attempt to resolve the dilemmas posed by moral complexity in public affairs—indeed, he feels that they are insoluble. Instead, he would call attention to the problems, suggest that they deserve serious study, and warn against facile moral judgments. Self-righteousness, Waldo notes, is equally distributed, and, under its influence, "thinking about public morality is likely to be partial and circumstantial no matter what universals are enunciated as the basis of judgment."[126]

Logical Positivism and Public Administration

His commitment to the study of public administration combined with a political theory perspective emerged full-blown in an article that was published in the first issue of the *American Political Science Review* in 1952; it was written on the occasion of the retirement of Francis W. Coker, Waldo's dissertation adviser at Yale.[127] In this piece, he outlined why a theory of democracy should "embrace administration," and he raked prewar scholars and thinkers over the coals.[128] He criticized Taylor for regarding "his laborers essentially as draft animals."[129] He observed that business or private administration had mellowed in the regard of thinkers "whose motivation has been primarily religious or ethical," such as Ordway Tead and Mary Parker Follett—he called Follett "as much theologian as social philosopher."[130] Mayo's Hawthorne experiments, he charged, had resulted in "a much more subtle and sophisticated (and therefore potentially more vicious) paternalism."[131] About Max Weber's viewpoint that bureaucracy was technically superior, he wondered " ... was not Weber perhaps a victim of the common foible of imagining one's own time and place the terminus of the creative process, in his picture of western civilization moving slowly and haltingly toward the type of organization typical of his own day?"[132]

Waldo perceived the central problem of public administration studies to be that of reconciling the desire for democracy with the demands of authority (or bureaucracy).[133] This would be a lifelong theme. Most memorably, he remarked, "To maintain that efficiency is value-neutral and to propose at the same time that it be used as the central concept in a 'science' of administration is to commit one's self to nihilism, so long as the prescription is actually followed." He elaborates: "In this contention, the present 'weight of authority' is against. But I believe that there is no realm of 'factual decisions' from which values are excluded. To decide is to choose between alternatives; to choose between alternatives is to introduce values. Herbert Simon has patently made outstanding contributions to administrative study. These contributions have been made, however, when he has worked free of the methodology he has asserted."[134] This brash pronouncement clearly threw down the gauntlet, and Simon was not slow in picking it up, thereby beginning a famous repartee between these two noted authors.

In the next issue of *APSR*, Simon criticized Waldo's portrayal of the fact-value question and his apparent bias against positivism and empiricism. And, since Waldo had introduced an element of heightened rhetoric in his initial sally, Simon felt justified in indulging in a bit of his own: "The standard of unrigor that is tolerated in political theory would not receive a passing grade in the elementary course in logic, Aristotelian or symbolic."[135] Waldo, in his rejoinder, observed that "... Professor Simon seems to me that rare individual in our secular age, a man of deep faith. His convictions are monolithic and massive. His toleration of heresy and sin is nil. The Road to Salvation is straight, narrow, one-way, and privately owned. We must humbly confess our sins, accept the

Word, be washed pure in the Blood of Carnap and Ayer. Then, he says, we will no longer be 'enemies.'"[136] Simon was not the only one who could be acerbic.

Waldo's insistence on the inclusion of values in the study and practice of public administration leads him to question the utility of logical positivism as an analytical perspective. Waldo considers logical positivism to be an important and respectable viewpoint, but one that dismisses "ought" questions "with a wave of the hand."[137] He argues that logical positivism takes a distinction in logic—that is, the distinction between facts and values—and employs it as a distinction in life. In reality, Waldo contends, facts and values are joined organically and cannot be separated, even in a "pure" science, as long as that science is social. He admits that facts and values *can* be logically separated and that values *can* be treated merely as data, but he maintains that logical positivism goes beyond that separation in dismissing the consideration of values qua values as a useless pursuit. That dismissal he considers to be a "dogmatic and intolerant evasion of value problems."[138]

A larger, but related, problem of the logical-positivist perspective is that logical positivism leads to a premature technological orientation, in which public administration is seen as simply a tool for the achievement of externally determined goals. Thus, wide areas of human experience—namely the aesthetic, moral, and metaphysical—are abandoned, and the "rational" is put at the service of the "irrational," or, at least, of matters judged to be beyond rational inquiry.[139] Waldo concludes that we need to be self-aware and self-critical of values; he warns that we should not seek rigor at the price of relevance; and he expresses the hope that we may be reaching a modus vivendi between the "scientific" and the normative.

Science and Public Administration

Waldo's views of science did not come out of the blue, and they were neither solely nor primarily a response to Simon. In fact, in the year that he defended his dissertation, he had also published an article in which he asserted, "There is no indication that our social sciences have contributed anything to the current scene except confusion—*opposing sets of dogmas*—each claiming to be 'scientific,' and all equally useless to anyone who, honestly trying to face all facts, has a decision to make concerning human lives, values, and the future. A social science that is of no value in the judgment process is at best a secondary tool and at worst a fraud and delusion."[140] In that article, Waldo approvingly discussed Graham Wallas's 1915 study, writing:

His [Wallas's] argument was not, then, that social science could not or should not become "scientific." His quarrel was rather with those devotees of the social studies whose conception of scientific method is adherence to popularizations of the scientific theory of the previous decade—or century—in this case nineteenth century physics and biology. His notion was that the nature of the subject matter and the nature of the task must define the method, and that the imposition of modes of thought appropriate to another subject matter in another era could not be regarded, in any proper sense, as scientific.[141]

Waldo's insistence upon the fact that public administration is a fundamentally normative study that transcends empirical fact was acknowledged by at least one reviewer of *The Administrative State*.[142]

Waldo also raises the question whether a science of public administration has been achieved, is being achieved, or can be achieved. His response to that question is equivocal. In part, Waldo asserts, the response depends on how one defines "science." In its broadest sense, science is simply knowledge that leads to the control of "concrete transformations."[143] Waldo adjudges the social sciences, including public administration, to be scientific by this definition. He observes that social science has achieved a high degree of control over human behavior and is capable of making many accurate predictions. Indeed, he argues that, since the progress of social science technology and physical science technology are so intimately related, all science is, in an important sense, social science.[144]

However, Waldo concedes that this reasoning rests on a rather generous definition of science. If science is defined in the stricter sense of "highly abstract and systematized concepts which 'order' empirical reality" with hypotheses and laws, and knowledge obtained and legitimated according to the canons of a specified methodology, Waldo doubts the existence, or even the possibility, of a science of public administration.[145] He asserts that although there may be universal "principles" of administration, we do not know whether this is true or what they might be. Moreover, he questions whether "management science" is anything more than a covert, class-based ideology seeking control in the interests of the managers.[146] Waldo's view—based on what he describes as a "mild commitment" to the proposition that, through study, administration can become more scientific, if not "a science"—is that there are lawful regularities in organizational phenomena about which we can learn more through science.[147] But, to Waldo, the scientific approach is one among and equal to other approaches, as is testified by the frequently quoted concluding remark of his thesis: " … administrative thought must establish a working relationship with every major province in the realm of human learning."[148]

Although Waldo did not say so explicitly, he advanced throughout his career the idea that public administration ought to develop a "scientific" approach of its own. He admitted in the early 1980s that "my rearing and education disposed me to the soft side: to a humanist approach to social science and to a suspicion of all philosophies and methods that offered

Truth." Indeed, "even a crude and unsophisticated science is bett
none," and he claimed to have learned much "from the 'hard sci
behaviorally oriented literature" of which Simon was the prime repr
tative in public administration.[149]

Public Administration: Discipline, Profession, Enterprise

If public administration is not a "pure" science, what is it? Waldo asserts that public administration can, at best, be considered an applied science, and is probably better thought of as an art, a profession, or something else. He has wrestled with several alternatives in trying to arrive at an acceptable characterization of public administration.

Whether or not, for instance, public administration should be considered a *discipline* depends on how that term is defined, and, in any case, Waldo considers it preferable to think of public administration as being composed of the many disciplines required in preparation for a career in the public service.[150] Waldo is emphatic in rejecting the idea that public administration is merely a subdiscipline—particularly a subdiscipline of political science. Political science, he maintains, has been too much influenced by logical positivism, so that it now focuses on "what is interesting, but inconsequential, what is quantifiable, but trivial."[151] Waldo views the traditional relationship between public administration and political science as part convention and part inertia, and he predicts for it a problematic future, since political science has failed to provide an understanding and nurturing environment for public administration. Nor, he asserts, should public administration be subsumed in business schools or "generic" schools of management. Waldo argues that neither the values nor the techniques of administration can be universalized, and that public administration requires both a differentiated technology and a distinctive philosophy. Moreover, as with political science, Waldo warns that public administration programs in business or generic schools are likely to face "slow death from lack of nutrition or atrophy from a lack of attention and affection."[152]

Waldo is more sympathetic to a "professional" orientation in public administration. He acknowledges that public administration is not a profession in a strict sense, is not about to become one, and perhaps should not even be one. Nevertheless, he considers professionalism to be a good attitude or strategy and asserts that public administration should move from a disciplinary to a professional perspective, occupying a separate professional school status in the university.[153] Waldo's favorite analogy in this regard is medicine, which, he says, is both science and art, both theory and practice, has a multidisciplinary focus rather than a single theory, and is given direction by a broad social purpose. Thinking of public administration as a profession, Waldo maintains, frees it from its second-class status in colleges of liberal arts, relieves it of a sense of guilt about not having a distinctive paradigm, and gives it license to seek whatever is needed, wherever it is located. Thus, he suggests that public administration might act as a profession without being one, or even hoping to become one.

Waldo's ultimate judgment is that public administration is not a single entity but a focus of interest best characterized as an "enterprise." That enterprise contains many facets, perspectives, interests, and methodologies, and it is eclectic, experimental, and open-ended in addressing the problems of an untidy, swiftly changing world. The enterprise of public administration should have "a solid center as well as an active circumference" and an emphasis on expanding its range of professional concerns.[154]

A Pedagogy for Public Administration

Waldo was known not only for his criticism of prewar administration and his characterization of trends in the field after the war. He also was concerned about how to teach in a field of study consisting of so many different theories, concepts, and approaches. In 1955 he devotes a section in a small volume to teaching, discussing the "textbook method" that aims to provide an overview of the study as a whole, the "case method" that seeks to illustrate and illuminate theoretical concepts, and the practice of "in-service training" (both as internship and as on-the-job training).[155] He believes that the case method is applicable to public administration, although in a manner different than its use in the study of law, where established categories or cases are illuminated by authoritative statements.[156] Still, the case study method is useful for pedagogical reasons; it has no scientific value.[157]

One favored "technique of analysis and ... form of pedagogy"[158] was that of using antinomies or "paired alternatives." The first example that comes to mind is the leitmotiv for Waldo's scholarship—democracy and bureaucracy—but he also discussed, both in class and in writing, various others, such as politics and administration, fact and value, centralization and decentralization, efficiency and inefficiency, stability and change, and so on. Note that we write "and" instead of the more common usage, "versus," when mentioning these paradoxes. Although, as far as we know, Waldo never explored his use of antinomies, he was certainly ahead of his time.[159]

Public Administration and the Future

Where do we go from here? Waldo, a self-described "amateur futurist," sees the future as a world of turbulence and change. A major force for change is the current transition from an industrial to a postindustrial society. Although Waldo notes that many of the prophesies for the 1970s failed to come to pass, there is still validity in the notion that the postindustrial society will see the emergence of knowledge as a crucial factor in productivity, the creation of new technologies for processing information, the decline of the factory, the establishment of new power elites and power centers based on scientific-technological knowledge, and a shift in emphasis from production to distribution and service occupations.[160] All this transitional energy will result in an accelerated pace of economic-social-political change that will generate institutional and psychological-social crises.

These forces raise an array of problems that must, at least in part, be addressed by public administration. A particular problem for public administration, Waldo observes, will be dealing with new forms of organization and management and with calls for the assumption of new responsibilities. Waldo predicts that organizations of the future will be less bureaucratic; increasingly of a mixed public-private nature; more "chains, complexes, or systems of organizations" than unitary organizations; and more international or multinational in their operations.[161] These new organizational styles raise questions about how to develop less bureaucratic organizations without encouraging chaos—that is, with "adaptive" organizations, what happens to such matters as stability, predictability, and responsibility?—how to deal with increasing ethical complexity, and how to cope with the increasing likelihood of conflict and crisis. Moreover, public administration is apt to be called on to perform even more functions, which raises the danger of overload in a system that, according to Waldo, already has responsibility beyond the authority it can command or the virtue it can summon.[162]

The implications of this supercharged future for public administration are manifold. Public administration, Waldo contends, is government's primary mechanism for dealing with the forces noted, and so it will be centrally involved in change and transformation. The decisions of public administrators will necessarily be a combination of policy judgments, instrumental judgments, legal judgments, and moral judgments. The enterprise of public administration will be marked by philosophical, disciplinary, and methodological pluralism as we attempt to survive, adapt, and control change.

In looking to the future, Waldo observes that there are two major scenarios: the totalitarian and the anarchist.[163] The totalitarian scenario reconciles public and private morality by definition, as government totally integrates and controls. The anarchist scenario, which Waldo sees as preferable, or at least less undesirable, envisions the future as characterized by a multiplicity of diffuse and complex economic-social-political institutions, accompanied by considerable ambiguity in the concept of public morality. In reaction to the anarchist scenario, Waldo asserts that he feels as if he is watching a film run backward, as the sovereign state is dissolved and its clear vertical structure of authority is replaced by complicated, contractual, and informal horizontal relationships. This does not mean that he thinks history will repeat itself. Waldo believes that the future must be created—it cannot be copied—and he expresses the hope that "reciprocal learning, mutual adjustment, and institutional intervention may now be speeded; that a world unified, but not unitary, harmonious, but not homogenized, may develop."[164]

Conclusion

As stated previously, Waldo was a frequent critic and commentator on the field of public administration, as well as a creator early in his career. He thus played a different role than that of the other authors considered in this book. Yet, his approach to the study earned the epithet "Waldonian thought," which James D. Carroll described as, in its method, antinomic, pluralistic and multidimensional, historical, reflective, and comparative, and, in its content, concerned with the relation between civilization and administration, with the core and other functions of government and its relation to bureaucracy and change, with the relation between democratic and bureaucratic processes and values, and, finally, with formalistic (that is, legal) answers to perceived public discontent.[165]

Waldonian thought is to be regarded as opposite to Simonian thought: whereas Waldo emphasized that very little in (P)public (A)administration[166] was clear-cut and so most of its phenomena could be subject to various interpretations, Simon firmly continued to point out that complex problems could be simplified into measurable facts.[167] Waldonian and Simonian thought have one thing in common: their insistence upon multidisciplinarity. To Waldo, though, this inclusive approach served to elucidate and resolve social problems; to Simon, of course, it served the effort to build a discipline around the concept of bounded rationality. Like Simon, Waldo had soaked up a particular literature. In Waldo's case, it was the body of work connected to political theory. His own ideas, thus, may not have been completely new, but, then, neither were those of Simon. In the minds of both of these scholar-critics, streams of thought came together, although in different ways.

Waldo helped to understand the increasing uneasiness with a technocratic public administration that was already visible in prewar literature by linking administration to political theory.[168] Up to that point, that linkage had not been made—not by the Greek philosophers; by Machiavelli, Hobbes, or Locke; by the French Enlightenment philosophers; by the American founding fathers; nor by the public administration scholars of the seventeenth through the nineteenth centuries. There had been no need; administration had for the longest time been a rather small element of government. But the administration of the twentieth century had assumed unprecedented proportions in the state, and that sudden expansion required its own political theory. Waldo provided it.

Waldo shared with Weber a rather pessimistic outlook on the balance between bureaucracy and democracy. While he never went as far as Weber—who claimed to expect a continuous march forward of bureaucratization—Waldo did recognize the political power of the new expert administrator. He could have compared Weber's concern with the more optimistic assessment of G.W.F. Hegel, who regarded the civil service as the new guardians (in clear reference to Plato) of democracy and as the indispensable backbone to the advance and preservation of democracy.[169] Clearly, Waldo shared with Weber a concern for machine bureaucracy within democracy, while most practitioners and academics only saw the good side of efficient management.

It is possible to quibble with the particulars of Waldo's approach to the history of public administration, but the larger problem with Waldo's work is his essential ambivalence. He insists that public administration is necessarily involved in politics, but he sees some continuing value in the politics-administration dichotomy. He states that public administration is both art and science, but he fails to specify an area in which each might be applicable. He argues that public administration is both different from and the same as private administration—but without specifying in any detail the similarities and differences, or their consequences. He thinks we should have both democracy and bureaucracy, but he does not tell us either how the conflicts between those forces can be resolved or what is the optimal balance between them. He says that public administration is not, and perhaps should not be, a profession, but he urges that it act like one. Perhaps Waldo best expresses his own ambivalence in stating, "I am skeptical of all faiths and philosophies. This includes, emphatically, skepticism."[170]

This pattern of ambivalence does not mean that Waldo was necessarily wrong. He admitted to the problem but found his position defensible. In addressing the applicability of physical science methods to the social sciences, he remarks, "I must confess (on the evidence I could not do otherwise) to a certain indecisiveness and ambivalence.... But I don't find this posture, this attempt to find a middle ground, as 'error.'"[171] Perhaps so, but that posture does lead to a problem. Waldo's curious mixture of intellectual promiscuity and skepticism, in which he sees all perspectives as flawed (when presented as superior to other perspectives) but regards each as having something to contribute, makes him subject to his own criticism of systems analysis—that is, by attempting to include everything, public administration, in his hands, can potentially become nothing in particular. Nor can the problem simply be passed off with such felicitous phrases as this one: "As the island of knowledge has expanded, the shore-line of mystery has lengthened."[172] It may be fair to say that public administration should have an active periphery, but Waldo ignores his own pronouncement that it should also have a recognizable core. At least, he does not define such a core.

Having defined the subject matter as broadly as he does, Waldo seems to be overwhelmed by the enormity of the task facing the study and practice of public administration. If that task is overwhelming, it is one of Waldo's own construction. Despite his call for the recognition of the limits of administration and the circumscription of administrative responsibilities, Waldo seems to see almost all problems as problems of administration.[173] This tendency is, in large part, a product of his view that administration and civilization are intimately linked and that administration is government's central mechanism for dealing with change. Once again, his ambivalence appears, as Waldo seems torn between his desire to confine public administration to some appropriate sphere that he feels has already been overreached and his belief that public administration will inevitably be involved in addressing most of the major problems of the present and the future.

Wallace Sayre once chided Waldo about his "youthful pessimism" regarding a perceived "identity crisis" in contemporary public administration.[174] Waldo never so much resolves the problem as he apparently learns to live with it. Waldo poses heroic demands on public administration, even if he does not necessarily see a heroic future for the enterprise. In this conception of public administration and in his call to action, Waldo has already provided what he claims is needed in public administration—namely, an "inspirational literature." In characteristic fashion, however, Waldo's "inspiration" is liberally sprinkled with pessimism and doubt.

NOTES

1. In "Leaders in the Field: Dwight Waldo," *Public Administration Review* 53, no. 5 (1993): 411–412, Frank Marini took issue with Fry's comment (in the first edition of this book, 243) that "... Waldo has been more of a critic and commentator on the field of public administration than a creator." Marini notes that this impression is, in part, Waldo's own doing. For instance, Waldo later wrote that "having no talent for creativity, [I] had specialized in 'perspectives'"; see Dwight Waldo, "Epilogue," in *Public Management in an Interconnected World*, ed. Mary Timney Bailey and Richard T. Mayer (New York: Greenwood, 1992), 177; as quoted in Marini, "Leaders in the Field," 417n6. The distinction between public administration as political theory and public administration as inundated with political theory elements, aspects, and implications is found in ibid., 414–415.

2. Information on Waldo's early life is taken from material provided by Professor Waldo and from *Who's Who in America*, 42nd ed., vol. 2 (Chicago: Marquis Who's Who, 1982), 3451. More about Waldo's life can be found in various obituaries, e.g., James D. Carroll and H. George Frederickson, "Dwight Waldo, 1913–2000," in *Public Administration Review* 61, no. 1 (2001): 2–8; George Lowery, "Dwight Waldo: Putting the Purpose in P.A.," *Maxwell Perspective: The Magazine of the Maxwell School of Syracuse University*, Spring 2001, available at www.maxwell.syr.edu/perspective/spr01_Waldo_main (accessed March 31, 2007); Richard J. Stillman, "A Tribute to Dwight Waldo," *Public Affairs Report* 42, no. 1 (Spring 2001), Institute of Governmental Studies, Berkeley, Calif.; Gary L. Wamsley, "Reflections on the Passing of Dwight Waldo," *Administration & Society* 33, no. 3 (2001): 247–250. Neither an intellectual nor a general biography has been pursued, but either would surely be worthwhile, especially in light of Waldo's enormous impact on the careers of a wide range of scholars; see Wamsley, "Reflections on the Passing of Dwight Waldo," 250. But see also Marini, "Leaders in the Field," 409–418.

3. Dwight Waldo, introduction to *The Administrative State: A Study of the Political Theory of American Public Administration*, 2nd ed. (New York: Holmes & Meier, 1984). The first edition of this work was published in 1948 by Ronald Press. The second edition (cited here) contained a new 55-page introduction by Waldo, titled "Retrospect and Prospect" (pp. ix–lxiv). In 2006 a third edition was published by Transaction, with a new introduction by Hugh T. Miller.

4. The final dissertation was entitled *Theoretical Aspects of the American Literature in Public Administration*.

5. Dwight Waldo, "The Administrative State Revisited," *Public Administration Review* 25, no. 1 (March 1965): 6.

6. Waldo, "Introduction," 3.

7. Waldo, "Administrative State Revisited," 7. See also footnote 5 in the introduction to the 2nd edition of *Administrative State*, lix.

8. Waldo, "Introduction," 3.

9. Waldo, "Administrative State Revisited," 7. Clearly, Waldo's study has grown in reputation since.

10. See Herbert A. Simon, review of Waldo's *Administrative State*, in *Journal of Politics* 10, no. 6 (1948): 844. Simon clearly distinguishes Behavioralism in political science from behaviorism in psychology; see Herbert A. Simon, "Human Nature in Politics: The Dialogue of Psychology with Political Science," *American Political Science Review* 79, no. 2 (1985): 295.

11. Dwight Waldo, "Political Science: Tradition, Discipline, Profession, Science, Enterprise," in *Political Science: Scope and Theory*, vol. 1 of *Handbook of Political Science*, ed. Fred I. Greenstein and Nelson W. Polsby (Reading, Mass.: Addison Wesley, 1975), 61–62.

12. Waldo, "Administrative State Revisited," 6–7.

13. Dwight Waldo, *The Enterprise of Public Administration* (Novato, Calif.: Chandler and Sharp, 1980), 119.

14. It appears that this separation of public administration and political science has only become stronger. For the past several years, the annual APSA editorial reports no longer mention public administration as a subfield, even though the APSR publishes a steady stream of articles on bureaucracy. We will return to this point in the concluding chapter.

15. Waldo, *Enterprise of Public Administration*, 6.

16. In his "Tribute to Dwight Waldo," Stillman writes: "Eventually, the Free Speech movement, student protests, and the election of Ronald Reagan as governor in the mid-1960s brought a different climate to the University of California, forcing Dwight to make the difficult decision to leave."

17. Waldo, *Enterprise of Public Administration*, xii.

18. Papers presented at this gathering were published in the *Public Administration Review* 57, nos. 3–4 (1997), and in the *Journal of Public Administration Research and Theory* 7, no. 3 (1997).

19. Wamsley, "Reflections on the Passing of Dwight Waldo," 250. While not a colleague or student, the second author of this volume was invited to the symposium as a relation of Waldo who had taken the time to review his *Handbook of Administrative History*, recommending changes, and, finally, writing Transaction Publishers a letter most supportive of publication.

20. In *Public Administration Review* 37, no. 5 (1997): 441; see quotation from Gawthrop in Carroll and Frederickson, "Dwight Waldo, 1913–2000," 7–8.

21. Waldo, preface to 2nd edition of *Administrative State*, xxxii.

22. Dwight Waldo, "Public Administration," *Journal of Politics* 30, no. 2 (May 1968): 447–448.

23. The term "Classical approach" was coined by James G. March and Herbert A. Simon in *Organizations* (New York: Wiley, 1958). See Dwight Waldo, "Organization Theory: An Elephantine Problem," *Public Administration Review* 21, no. 4 (1961): 219.

24. In "Leaders in the Field," 412, Marini claims that Waldo was the first to use that term.

25. Waldo, *Administrative State*, 114–115.

26. Ibid., 44.

27. Dwight Waldo, *The Study of Public Administration* (New York: Random House, 1955), 41; and idem, "Public Administration," in *International Encyclopedia of the Social Sciences*, ed. David Sills (New York: Macmillan and Free Press, 1968), 148.

28. Waldo, *Administrative State*, 133–134.

29. Dwight Waldo, "Public Administration," in *The Dimensions of Public Administration: Introductory Readings*, ed. Joseph A. Uveges Jr. (Boston: Holbrook Press, 1971), 26.

30. Ibid., 71–73, 74.

31. Ibid., 12.

32. Ibid., 15.

33. Waldo, *Administrative State*, 19–20, 91.

34. Ibid., 21.

35. Ibid., 77–85.

36. Ibid., 80.

37. Waldo, "Public Administration," 456.

38. Dwight Waldo, "The Future of Management," *Bureaucrat* 6, no. 3 (Fall 1977): 109–110.

39. Dwight Waldo, *Democracy, Bureaucracy, and Hypocrisy* (Berkeley, Calif.: Institute of Governmental Studies, 1977), 9.

40. Dwight Waldo, "Development of the Theory of Democratic Administration," *American Political Science Review* 46, no. 1 (March 1952): 87.

41. Waldo, *Administrative State*, 133.

42. Ibid., 57.

43. Ibid., 128.

44. Ibid., 175.
45. Waldo, "Future of Management," 105.
46. Waldo, *Administrative State*, 159–161.
47. Dwight Waldo, *The Novelist on Organization and Administration: An Inquiry into the Relationship between Two Worlds* (Berkeley, Calif.: Institute of Government Studies, 1968), 40.
48. Waldo, *Administrative State*, 181, 177.
49. Ibid., 181–182.
50. Ibid., 193–197.
51. Ibid., 202. Waldo suggests that a hierarchy-of-purpose approach may be useful in assessing the utility of the concept of efficiency, and that efficiency is an appropriate framework at the lower levels of the hierarchy where purpose can be taken as a given. See ibid., 204–205.
52. Waldo, "Public Administration," in Uveges, *Dimensions of Public Administration*, 27.
53. Waldo, *Enterprise of Public Administration*, 69.
54. Ibid.
55. Waldo, "Public Administration," in Sills, *Encyclopedia of the Social Sciences*, 148.
56. Dwight Waldo, "Administrative State Revisited," 11. Waldo describes Behavioralism as a "mood" or "persuasion" that adopts most of the elements of logical positivism, particularly the view that values are unverifiable and thus removed from the realm of scientific investigation. In general, Behavioralism involves a movement from the philosophical to the positive (i.e., a focus on observable behavior), the separation of facts and values, the use of "proper" scientific methodology, and the search for a more unified empirical theory of human behavior. See Dwight Waldo, *Comparative Public Administration: Prologue, Problems, and Promise*, Papers in Comparative Administration, Special Series no. 5 (Washington, D.C.: Comparative Public Administration Group, American Society for Public Administration, 1964), 7.
57. Waldo, *Study of Public Administration*, 47.
58. Dwight Waldo, "Organization Theory: Revisiting the Elephant," *Public Administration Review* 38, no. 6 (November–December 1978): 589–590. See also his "Organization Theory: An Elephantine Problem," 210–225. Comparing the state of organization theory between 1961 and 1978, he concludes that, while we know much more, the elephantine problem has only increased.
59. Luther Gulick and L. Urwick, eds., *Papers on the Science of Administration* (New York: Institute of Public Administration, 1937).
60. March and Simon, *Organizations*.
61. Waldo, "Public Administration," in Sills, *Encyclopedia of the Social Sciences*, 150; and Dwight Waldo, "Theory of Organization: Status and Problems," in *The Study of Organizational Behavior: Status, Problems, and Trends*, Papers in Comparative Administration, Special Series no. 8 (Washington, D.C.: Comparative Administration Group, American Society for Public Administration, 1966), 6.
62. Waldo, "Organization Theory," 590.
63. Ibid., 592.
64. Waldo, "Public Administration," in Sills, *Encyclopedia of the Social Sciences*, 149; idem, "Public Administration," in Uveges, *Dimensions of Public Admin-*

istration, 28–29; and Dwight Waldo, "Scope of the Theory of Public Administration," in *Theory and Practice of Public Administration: Scope, Objectives, and Methods*, ed. James C. Charlesworth (Philadelphia: American Academy of Political and Social Science, 1968), 6.

65. Waldo, "Future of Management," 111.
66. Ibid.
67. Waldo, *Enterprise of Public Administration*, 146.
68. Waldo, "Theory of Organization," 1.
69. Dwight Waldo, "Administrative Theory in the United States: A Survey and Prospect," *Political Studies* 2 (1954): 72.
70. Waldo, "Development of the Theory of Democratic Administration," 89. Also see notes 135 and 136 below, for a rather acid exchange between Waldo and Simon.
71. Waldo, *Novelist on Organization and Administration*, 43–44.
72. Waldo, "Organization Theory: An Elephantine Problem," 216.
73. Waldo, "Organization Theory: Revisiting the Elephant," 592.
74. Ibid.
75. Waldo, "Organization Theory: An Elephantine Problem," 211.
76. Ibid., 217.
77. Waldo, "Theory of Organization," 16.
78. Waldo, *Comparative Public Administration*, 27.
79. Waldo, *Enterprise of Public Administration*, 127.
80. Waldo, *Comparative Public Administration*, 29.
81. Dwight Waldo, "Reflections on Public Administration and National Development," *International Social Science Journal* 21, no. 2 (1969): 298, 304.
82. Waldo, "Public Administration," *Journal of Politics*, 466–469.
83. Waldo, *Enterprise of Public Administration*, 73.
84. Dwight Waldo, "Developments in Public Administration," in *Current Issues in Public Administration*, ed. Frederick S. Lane (New York: St. Martin's Press, 1978), 554.
85. Dwight Waldo, *Some Issues in Preparing Science Administration Leadership for Tomorrow*, Program of Policy Studies in Science and Technology, Occasional Paper no. 6 (Washington, D.C.: George Washington University, 1969), 6–7. The NPA suggestion that human beings are born good but corrupted through civilization dates back to Jean-Jacques Rousseau.
86. Dwight Waldo, "Some Thoughts on Alternatives, Dilemmas, and Paradoxes in a Time of Turbulence," in *Public Administration in a Time of Turbulence*, ed. Dwight Waldo (Scranton, Pa.: Chandler, 1971), 271.
87. Ibid., 263. The Minnowbrook conference resulted in a volume edited by Frank Marini, who served as Waldo's managing editor at *PAR*; see *Toward a New Public Administration: The Minnowbrook Perspective* (Scranton, Pa.: Chandler, 1971). Waldo was appreciative but critical, and he responded with his own collection (see previous note). For a critical review and explanation as to why the Minnowbrook perspective failed to impact the study, see Richard J. Stillman, *Preface to Public Administration: A Search for Themes and Direction* (Burke, Va.: Chatelaine Press, 1999), 2–3, and especially footnote 9 on p. 17.
88. Waldo, "Some Thoughts on Alternatives, Dilemmas, and Paradoxes in a Time of Turbulence," 267.
89. Ibid., 259–260.
90. Ibid., 273.
91. Ibid., 280–281.

92. Ibid., 268.
93. Ibid., 281.
94. Waldo, "Public Administration," *Journal of Politics*, 454.
95. Ibid.; and Dwight Waldo, "Education for Public Administration in the Seventies," in *American Public Administration: Past, Present, and Future*, ed. Frederick C. Mosher (University: University of Alabama Press, 1975), 107.
96. Waldo, *Enterprise of Public Administration*, 34.
97. Letter from Dwight Waldo to Irving Horowitz, Transaction Publishers, April 13, 1995 (in possession of second author).
98. Dwight Waldo, "Toward World 'Development,'" *African Administrative Studies* 16 (1976): 100; and idem, "Organization Theory: An Elephantine Problem," 225.
99. Waldo, *Enterprise of Public Administration*, 18.
100. Ibid., 19.
101. Ibid., 29.
102. Waldo, "Some Thoughts on Alternatives, Dilemmas, and Paradoxes in a Time of Turbulence," 282. For the influence of the ancient world and the (Catholic) Church upon government structures and processes, see also Jos C. N. Raadschelders, "An Administrative-History Perspective on Church-State Relations: On the Varied Impacts of Judeo-Christian Heritage and Organized Religion," in *Church and State in Western Europe in an Administrative-History Perspective*, ed. Jos C. N. Raadschelders (Baden-Baden: Nomos Verlagsgesellschaft, 2002), 1–20.
103. Dwight Waldo, "Politics and Administration: On Thinking about a Complex Relationship," in *A Centennial History of the American Administrative State*, ed. Ralph Clark Chandler (New York: Free Press, 1987), 90.
104. Ibid.
105. Frank Goodnow, *Politics and Administration: A Study in Government* (New York: Macmillan, 1900), 44.
106. W. A. R. Leys, "Ethics and Administrative Discretion," *Public Administration Review* 3, no. 1 (1943): 10.
107. Cf. Michael Nelson, "A Short, Ironic History of American National Bureaucracy," *Journal of Politics* 44, no. 3 (1982): 751.
108. Ibid., 760. While this reorganization mostly happened after the 1880s, the first steps were actually made during the Civil War. See Jos C. N. Raadschelders, "Abraham Lincoln's Presidency as the Foundation of the Modern Administrative State?" *Public Administration Review* 67, no. 3 (2007): 943–946.
109. Nowadays, between 0.5% and 2% of the total public workforce holds elected office. More than 400 years ago, and in four Dutch municipalities, political officeholders accounted for almost 24% of the workforce; their numbers steadily declined. See Jos C. N. Raadschelders, "Understanding the Development of Local Government: Theory and Evidence from the Dutch Case," *Administration & Society* 25, no. 4 (1994): 417. Obviously, one cannot generalize on the basis of this limited case, but, to our knowledge, no other reliable figures are available.
110. For a discussion of how much organization theory at the time reminded Waldo of interests shared by Plato, Aristotle, and Machiavelli, see Waldo, "Organization Theory: An Elephantine Problem," 225. For a persuasive argument about Waldo's originality, see Hugh Miller's introduction to the 3rd edition of *Administrative State*.

111. Waldo, *Enterprise of Public Administration*, 86.
112. Waldo, *Novelist on Organization and Administration*, 66.
113. Dwight Waldo, "Public Administration and Culture," in *Public Administration and Democracy*, ed. Roscoe C. Martin (Syracuse: Syracuse University Press, 1965), 61.
114. Ibid., 45.
115. Waldo, *Enterprise of Public Administration*, 80.
116. Ibid., 78.
117. Ibid.
118. Waldo, "Administrative Theory in the United States," 85.
119. Dwight Waldo, "Reflections on Public Morality," *Administration and Society* 6, no. 3 (November 1974): 273.
120. Waldo, *Enterprise of Public Administration*, 101.
121. Ibid., 102.
122. Waldo, "Reflections on Public Morality," 272.
123. Ibid., 273.
124. Ibid., 271.
125. Waldo, *Enterprise of Public Administration*, 100–101. This is reminiscent of the "dirty hands problem" as discussed in ethics literature. For an early discussion of "dirty hands," and an expansion upon Machiavelli's insights, see Michael Walzer, "Political Action: The Problem of Dirty Hands," *Philosophy and Public Affairs* 2, no. 2 (1973): 160–180.
126. Waldo, "Reflections on Public Morality," 269.
127. Carroll and Frederickson, "Dwight Waldo, 1913–2000," 4.
128. Dwight Waldo, "Development of Theory of Democratic Administration," 81.
129. Ibid., 83.
130. Ibid., 84–85. He discusses Follett at greater length on pp. 94–96. See also his introduction to the 2nd edition of *Administrative State*, in which he writes (p. xxviii): ". . . for the formative period of public administration, Follett's theories seemed largely irrelevant if not perverse."
131. Waldo, "Development of Theory of Democratic Administration," 89.
132. Ibid., 100.
133. Ibid., 102.
134. Ibid., 97.
135. Herbert Simon, " 'Development of Theory of Democratic Administration': Replies and Comments," *American Political Science Review* 46, no. 2 (1952): 494–496.
136. Dwight Waldo, in ibid., 501.
137. Waldo, "Administrative State Revisited," 13, 23.
138. Waldo, "Administrative Theory in the United States," 86.
139. Waldo, *Study of Public Administration*, 62–65.
140. Dwight Waldo, "Graham Wallas: Reason and Emotion in Social Change," *Journal of Social Philosophy & Jurisprudence* 7, no. 1 (1942): 145; as quoted in Marini, "Leaders in the Field," 417, footnote 9. We have added emphasis to the phrase "opposing sets of dogmas" since it is reminiscent of what Simon four years later calls "proverbs."
141. Waldo, "Graham Wallas," 152; as quoted in Marini, "Leaders in the Field," 413. The study Waldo discussed was Graham Wallas, *The Great Society: A Psychological Analysis* (New York: Macmillan, 1915).

142. Arthur W. Macmahon, "Reviews of Books and Documents: The Administrative State," *Public Administration Review* 8, no. 3 (1948): 203–211, esp. 207.

143. Waldo, *Enterprise of Public Administration*, 21.

144. Ibid., 24.

145. Waldo, "Administrative Theory in the United States," 81; and Dwight Waldo, "Political Science: Tradition, Discipline, Profession, Science, Enterprise," 1–2.

146. Waldo, "Future of Management," 104.

147. Waldo, "Reflections on Public Administration and National Development," 306.

148. Waldo, *Administrative State*, 203.

149. Quoted matter from the preface to the 2nd edition of *Administrative State*, xlix and l. In the same passage, Waldo observes again that using physical science methods in relation to human affairs has its limitations. In footnote 43, he writes: "What is said about economics (pp.173–174 [in 1st edition]) is especially relevant in view of the present disarray in that discipline. In the 1960s I thought it just possible that I had been wrong, that the economists could walk on water. But now I judge that they, like the rest of the social scientists, are lucky if they can swim reasonably well" (lxiii).

150. Waldo, "Education for Public Administration in the Seventies," 223.

151. Waldo, *Enterprise of Public Administration*, 6.

152. Waldo, "Administrative State Revisited," 29.

153. Ibid., 28.

154. Dwight Waldo, *Perspectives on Administration* (University: University of Alabama Press, 1956), 137.

155. Waldo, *Study of Public Administration*, 24–37. (A second edition of this title was published in 1955 by Doubleday, and a third edition in 1967 by Random House.)

156. Ibid., 36.

157. Waldo, "Organization Theory: An Elephantine Problem," 224.

158. Carroll and Frederickson, "Dwight Waldo, 1913–2000," 5.

159. In *Responsibility as Paradox: A Critique of Rational Discourse on Government* (Thousand Oaks, Calif.: Sage, 1995), 7, Michael Harmon argues that the study of public administration works too much with dichotomies—which he calls "schismogenic paradoxes," because they involve two principles regarded as opposites to each other. Simon's scholarship is a good example of this tendency. However, Harmon advises that two principles that appear to be opposing—in terms of language, e.g., centralization-decentralization; in terms of function, e.g., politics-administration; in terms of process, e.g., mechanistic-organic organizations—ought to be regarded as antinomial paradoxes, or two principles that coexist in creative tension with one another. Harmon thus continues in Waldo's footsteps, and he extends his argument in *Public Administration's Final Exam: A Pragmatist Restructuring of the Profession and the Discipline* (Tuscaloosa: University of Alabama Press, 2006).

160. Waldo, *Enterprise of Public Administration*, 158–160.

161. Waldo, "Developments in Public Administration," 538–542: idem, *Enterprise of Public Administration*, 167–168.

162. Ibid., 187.

163. Waldo, "Reflections on Public Morality," 277.
164. Waldo, *Enterprise of Public Administration*, 134.
165. See this listing, and more discussion, in James D. Carroll, "The Warfare On and Over American Government in Waldonian Perspective," *Public Administration Review* 57, no. 3 (1997): 202.
166. Waldo sometimes uses capital letters to refer to the study and lowercase letters to refer to government.
167. Simon's success and fame was already established by the mid-1950s. Reviewing in 1961 a series of organization theory books, Waldo observes that what is striking in all of them is "... pre-eminence of the name of the unique and all but ubiquitous Herbert Simon, and on the manifest evidence of a Simon Admiration Society of respectable size...." Waldo, "Organization Theory: An Elephantine Problem," 212. Waldo, however, gathered his own following in the decades to come.
168. By way of illustration, consider that the following two comments could very well have come from Waldo. First: "... in the last fifty years, American citizens have developed an attitude toward the term 'efficiency' which is nothing short of worshipful.... In this country the connotation of efficiency definitely conveys the mechanical, utilitarian meaning. Efficiency becomes tantamount to economy, penny-pinching, and profit-making." And, second: "The mechanical view of efficiency cramps the style even of those who are responsible for management. Machine-like efficiency is to the responsible executive of an enterprise as chilly aloofness is to an orator. Successful administration is warm and vibrant. It is human. Mechanical efficiency is coldly calculating and inhuman. Hence it cannot be expected to produce morale and enthusiastic co-operation. It relies upon the instincts of fear and survival rather than upon 'associatedness' and creativeness." These remarks can be found in Marshall E. Dimock, "The Criteria and Objectives of Public Administration," in *The Frontiers of Public Administration*, ed. John M. Gaus, Leonard D. White, and Marshall E. Dimock (Chicago: University of Chicago Press, 1936), 116–117, and 120.
169. See G.W.F. Hegel, *Elements of the Philosophy of Right* (Cambridge: Cambridge University Press, 1991); also, Carl K.Y. Shaw, "Hegel's Theory of Modern Bureaucracy," *American Political Science Review* 86 (1992): 381–389; and Jos C.N. Raadschelders, Theo A.J. Toonen, and Frits M. Van der Meer, "Civil Servants in the Enabling Framework State of the 21st Century," in *The Civil Service in the 21st Century: Comparative Perspectives*, ed. Jos C.N. Raadschelders, Theo A.J. Toonen, and Frits M. Van der Meer (Houndsmills, England: Palgrave, 2007), 299–315.
170. Waldo, introduction to 2nd edition of *Administrative State*, note 39.
171. Ibid., 48.
172. Ibid., 45.
173. Waldo, *Enterprise of Public Administration*, 47.
174. Wallace S. Sayre, "Comment on Waldo's Paper," in Waldo, *Theory and Practice of Public Administration*, 27.

Chapter 10

The Study of Public Administration: Origins, Development, Nature

The study of public administration has clearly come of age. The sheer growth of the enterprise is indicated by the wide range of generic and specialized journals that have come into existence in the United States and abroad, the increasing number of public administration programs,[1] and the burgeoning number of undergraduate and graduate students, scholars, and public-sector consultants in the field. Not only has the enterprise grown, but it has established its organizational independence from other disciplines. The top twenty-five programs in American public administration are all independent programs, and, of the top fifty, only two are situated in political science departments.[2] What a century ago was a specialization in the study of law (in Europe) or in political science (especially in the United States) has become a study that has branched out and expanded in scope far beyond the early-twentieth-century interest in (local) government management and reform policies. In the process, the study of public administration has sought, and largely gained, recognition; in the United States and in a variety of European countries, this recognition reflects the attainment of organizational independence, while, only in Europe, public administration sometimes retains the status of an organizationally independent specialization within political science or law.

In a field that is diverse, eclectic, and pragmatic, it is only fitting that the influential authors treated here come from a variety of backgrounds. Weber's (law and history), Simon's (social science), Lindblom's (economics and political science), and Waldo's (philosophy and political science) work transcend, and defy, disciplinary boundaries. Follett's interests, if not her education, were in social work. Mayo's degrees were in philosophy and psychology. Barnard relied on his experience in business organizations. What connects the writings of this wide-ranging

343

group is the determined pursuit of ideas, and a willingness (particularly on the part of Weber and Simon) to use whatever appeared relevant. Some worked primarily as scholars (Weber, Mayo, Simon, Waldo, Lindblom), others primarily as practitioners (Taylor, Barnard) and/or as social commentators (Follett). Gulick managed to keep one leg in the university and the other in practice.

These authors also had a variety of personal experiences that shaped their theories, concepts, and judgments—and even their writing styles.[3] By way of example, consider the influence of:

- early exposure to Hegel and growing up in rule-bound German society upon Max Weber's theories about bureaucracy;
- working in a factory environment upon Frederick Taylor's formulation of Scientific Management;
- fairly early involvement in the reform movement upon Luther Gulick's ideas about organization and management;
- working in Boston's community centers upon Follett's ideas about cooperation, integration, and institutional dynamics;
- witnessing labor union strikes and fierce conflicts with management in Australia upon Mayo's ideas about hierarchical management;
- running a big company or addressing a crowd of discontented workers upon Barnard's ideas about balancing management and employee needs;
- noticing how a public works administrator and a recreation administrator in Milwaukee budgeted according to very different rationales for a playground—as a physical facility that needs maintenance, or as a social facility that needs supervision—upon Simon's conceptualization of bounded rationality;
- Frank Knight's fascination with the hidden rationalities of complex social institutions and Michael Polanyi's theories about mutual adjustment upon Lindblom's analysis of bargaining, incrementalism, and the great social institutions of our time;
- Francis W. Coker's doubt that principles of administration could be scientifically established or that efficiency was the central concept of the study[4] upon Waldo's thoughts about the connection between facts and values and the nature of the study of public administration.

Only the authors themselves can distinguish between what was of primary influence upon their thinking and what was not, but, clearly, each of them was affected by early experiences in life and work, by mentors, and by ideas.

Though each of these authors can, thus, be considered a product of his or her times, their ideas remain timely, and the contemporary study of

public administration is obviously deeply indebted to them
tion, they set the agenda for most of the issues still being a(
study. Their diversity of opinion also anticipated the tens¹
in attempts to address those issues. Their legacy is the power ᴏ₁ .
ideas, which still resonate in the study and practice of public administration. We shall examine that agenda and legacy, and then conclude with
some thoughts on the state of the field of public administration.

Setting the Agenda

There can be little dispute that the nine authors presented and discussed
in this volume addressed big issues. Weber and Waldo were intrigued by,
and concerned about, the survival of democracy in the face of a burgeoning bureaucracy. Taylor and Gulick sought to discover general principles of management. Mayo and Barnard sought to balance managerial
prerogatives with employee needs. Weber, Simon, and Lindblom attempted to make sense of rationality, by exploring its limits. Follett and
Barnard delved into the nature of authority in cooperative social systems.
And that is only a beginning.

Attesting to the cumulative nature of knowledge, the ideas, theories,
and concepts presented by these authors are not quite new. Lindblom, for
instance, writes that there are no original concepts in his work but that he
may sometimes have given a vague or incomplete concept fuller formulation.[5] All of these authors present ideas that are more carefully elaborated, more systematically pursued—and sometimes employed in
different settings—than in their previous appearances. Weber built upon
Hegel, though he treated the bureaucrat as a less heroic figure than did
Hegel. Taylor built upon engineering principles as applied to the relationship between man and machine. Gulick built upon early work done
in the New York Bureau of Municipal Research, acting upon a general
sense that the discovery of principles of administration was tantamount to
science. Mayo built upon previous studies of fatigue, extending them into
the psychological realm with surprising, and often unanticipated, results.

Follett built upon a Rousseauesque egalitarian idea of cooperation
and horizontal relations, but applied these concepts to intra-organiza-
tional relationships. Barnard built upon the notion of intuitive knowledge and upon management ideas prevalent in his time, while
challenging, though not fully rejecting, traditional concepts of authority
and leadership. Simon built upon an eighteenth-century sense of limited
rationality and borrowed directly from the Institutionalist perspective in
economics to develop his model of organizational decision making. Lindblom built upon ideas about the relation between polity and market in
developing his theory about governmental decision making and policy

processes and in his critique of institutions of social control. Waldo, like Weber, built upon theories about balancing democracy and bureaucracy. Enamored of originality, contemporary scholarship is seldom as ready to acknowledge precursors as was Lindblom, who recognized that good work often follows from initial steps and that the full meaning of initial findings may not become clear until much later.[6]

With regard to agenda setting, let us consider the positions of our nine authors in relation to two issues chosen because of their continuing salience in the field and the controversy surrounding them. These issues—the relationship between public and private administration, and the question whether a science of public administration is attainable or desirable—have attracted the attention of all nine authors, if intermittently and to varying degrees.

Public Administration and Business Administration

On the first issue—the relationship between public and business administration—opinions among our authors are divided, as they are in the study as a whole. A typical formulation is that administration is essentially the same in both the public and private sectors, and, since the private sector is more efficient than the public sector, we should borrow techniques from the private sector to improve efficiency in the public sector. Dating back to late-nineteenth-century America, this is a canard that has remarkable resilience. Among the authors considered here, Frederick Taylor perhaps comes closest to this position.

More typical is the assumption that organizations are organizations, and the same management techniques are applicable in both the public and private sectors—note the absence of the invidious comparison between them. This indifference would seem to be the position, if only implicitly, of Gulick, Barnard, Mayo, Follett, and Simon. For Weber, bureaucracy is a product of the process of rationalization and is associated with the rise of capitalism; thus, bureaucracies are characteristic of both the public and private sectors, which share the virtues and vices of that organizational form. Lindblom argues that forms of social control are generic, though power is likely to be more equally shared in the public sector because of the institutional arrangements of democratic government. While he does not directly address the relative efficiency of the two sectors, it is unlikely that Lindblom would favor the private sector, given his general attitude toward business corporations and their executives. More likely, he would simply contend that both sectors are "political." Waldo falls at the other end of the spectrum, arguing that public administration is different from private administration and that, even if private organizations are more efficient, quality is not the primary criterion by which public organizations should be judged. Criteria such as representativeness, responsiveness, due process, fairness, and equity would be more important for Waldo.

These differences among our authors pretty much mirror differences in the study as a whole. Perhaps it is most accurate to say that prewar American public administration built upon studies of business (Taylor, Mayo, Barnard), of government (Gulick), and of society at large (Follett). Postwar public administration appears to be no different. Driven by the quest for "The Theory of Organizations," organizational and decision-making theories were thought applicable to both the public and the private sectors. Contingency theory promised to be different, but it never used "public" versus "private" as a contingency. Organizational humanism returned to the universalistic theme, but posed satisfaction of human needs rather than productivity as the objective of organizational endeavors.

The New Public Administration emphasized the difference between public and private administration, and, accordingly, stressed the values of representativeness and equity over efficiency. However, between the 1970s and the 1990s, many public administration scholars withdrew into studies of specific programs and agencies, with a renewed interest in productivity.[7] They were drawn especially to expanding and improving techniques of measuring the outputs and, to a lesser extent, the outcomes of organizational activities. One detects more than a touch of Taylorism in this New Public Management literature. Generally, it seems that the study of public administration is—once again?—very much enamored of concepts (such as efficiency) and approaches (such as performance management and measurement) that seem to fit better in a private context.

We note that some of this debate about the relationship between public and business administration seems to have been miscast, being based on the idea that the study of public administration has borrowed from business management to improve productivity. A number of factors belie that claim. First, there was a study of public administration at least two centuries before there was a study of business administration.[8] Second, and in the same vein, the conceptual distinction between public and private sectors was not made until the late eighteenth century. Whatever can be considered private organization in early modern Europe, back to the ancient world, was heavily intertwined with government—if not in terms of laws and directives, then certainly in terms of personal unions. Higher-level government officials usually combined their work with lucrative positions in, for instance, trade and church organizations.[9]

Third, early-twentieth-century American scholars were impressed by the management successes of late-nineteenth-century private corporations, especially in the United States, not recognizing the extent to which expanding market freedoms actually fueled corruption in the private sector.[10] This lapse is ironic, since public-sector reform was inspired, in part, by the desire to battle corruption. Fourth, quite a few concepts and theories-in-use in public administration and organization theory actually originated in public administration and not in business administration.[11] Indeed, in the light of history, business administration and management have only briefly offered an example to public management—certainly not "through the ages," as the National Performance Review claimed.[12] Finally, however plausible theoretically, there is no convincing evidence beyond the anecdotal that private organizations are more efficient than public organizations.

A Science of Public Administration

The second issue we have chosen for use in comparing our nine authors concerns the development of a science of public administration. Any discussion of whether or not public administration is a science must consider which definition of science to use: one that emphasizes a natural-science orientation, or one that describes science as a branch of knowledge.[13] In the modern, positivist sense, science is based on empirical observation of facts for which the explanation is ideally expressed in terms of a universal law (which is more possible in the natural sciences) or, at least, in terms of law-like generalizations (which are more common in the social sciences). The methodology associated with this concept of science typically involves systematic empirical investigation relying on sophisticated quantitative analysis. This concept of science is also identified with "objectivity" in the sense that it is assumed that research results can be generated independently from the observer.

While the bulk of the preceding chapters has been devoted to our authors' substantive ideas about organization, management, decision making and policymaking, most of them also had specific ideas about the science of public administration and its appropriate methods.[14] They are almost evenly divided on the prospect of developing a science of administration: Weber, Taylor, Gulick, Mayo, and Simon are all proponents of a science of administration, though each offers a variation on that theme; Follett, Barnard, Waldo, and Lindblom are at least skeptics, if not outright opponents.

Simon is most emphatically committed to a positivist, empirical science of administration that studies facts and leaves value-judgment to practitioners and politicians. His focus is on strengthening the internal validity of findings (that is, establishing causal relations between alternatives and their consequences). Taylor was, of course, a strong supporter of the effort to develop a science of management, but he was largely atheoretical and rather narrow in his focus—Simon would view Taylor's work as a "practical" science. Taylor's approach was inductive (a heaping up of facts), in contrast to the hypothetical-deductive method typically preferred by the positivists.

Gulick was an equally firm supporter of empirical study, but less positivist. In his view, management science—that is, systematic and frequent observation of organizational behavior—was the method through which public administration should define itself; this opinion was no doubt influenced by the prevalence of Taylor's Scientific Management movement in the 1920s and 1930s. Gulick believed that administrative science should focus on studying the relation between action and outcome, a topic that has received renewed attention among those who study performance measurement and advocate New Public Management. In contrast to Taylor's reasoning, Gulick's was largely theoretical, since in his search for principles he mustered precious little empirical support for those putative principles. Weber is more equivocal. While he engaged in large-survey research and in the development of quantitative methods, he is best known for his qualitative method of using the ideal type to arrive at a better understanding of reality. Mayo was, as usual, an enigma. He clearly had scientific aspirations, but he relied on highly subjective participant-observer techniques and generally paid scant attention to the niceties of research design.

Let us consider now the forces of the opposition. Barnard—as one would expect from a practicing executive—was not centrally concerned with developing a science of administration. He was more pragmatic in his thinking, as likely to rely on "nonlogical" processes as on science in executive decision making. Intriguingly, Follett, even though a member of the Taylor Society, regarded linear logical positivism and nonlinear social dynamics as an antinomial paradox. Instead of choosing a side, she advocated a method of circular response, advising students to make an effort at understanding the relation between quantitative and qualitative approaches. In her view, those whom she called "subjective idealists" had focused too much on the subject, while the "realists" were too much concerned with the object. It is striking to see how close Follett comes to Weber's position of embracing both positivism and hermeneutics as methods of study. To Weber and Follett both, the choice of method is subordinate to the objective of rational explanation—which, to Weber, is synonymous with understanding (that is, *Verstehen*).

Also comparable to Weber are Lindblom and Waldo, given their habit of engaging in wide-ranging and theoretical perspectives upon major social trends. Lindblom was not entirely unsympathetic to the idea of a science, but he considered scientific methodology and its results as, at best, complementary to lay knowledge and probing. Indeed, he argued that social science generally could not claim findings that had not been preceded by lay thought. Waldo is probably the most vociferous in his opposition to the scientific method as described earlier. His problem is with the treatment of values. He argues that, whereas the Classical approach disguised its values under the mantle of scientific analysis, the positivists simply dismiss them. It is not that the scientific method is inappropriate; it is simply incomplete.

So where does this leave us when attempting to assess the state and nature of public administration as a science? The answer is: divided, as always. Scientific (that is, objectivist) aspirations persist, but performance lags. When we look at the articles and books published in the United States, it appears that empirical research is overwhelmingly favored over questions of political theory, history, law, and so on. This empirical research is presented in two ways, but quantitative-statistical methods are clearly favored over qualitative and narrative methods. Quantitative research is facilitated by ever-more sophisticated statistical techniques and by an increasing use of formal, mathematical modeling. This tendency is especially prevalent in the United States, but it is also found, to a significantly lesser extent, in other Western countries. Quantitative research is motivated by a desire to develop an administrative science that is unique in its own methods[15] and can compete, in terms of rigor, with such social sciences as cognitive psychology and economics.

Yet, reviews of publications in major journals suggest that most articles are conceptual in nature and that, even where statistics are employed, little attention is paid to research design, there are few multivariate or longitudinal analyses, and the statistical methods employed are often inappropriate to the question addressed. An obvious rejoinder to the positivist approach is that it defines science too narrowly. Knowledge based on intersubjectively observed phenomena and subjective experiences can be considered scientific if a broader and more classic definition of science is applied. We specifically have the German concept of *Wissenschaft* in mind, wherein *Wissen* is knowledge and *schaft* is branch. According to that perspective, public administration, like political science, is a branch of knowledge, belonging to the larger branch of the social sciences.

Moreover, there are those (Lindblom and Waldo among them) who would deny the desirability of "scientific analysis" narrowly construed. A postpositivist critique has arisen that challenges the positivist methodology, arguing that there are ways of knowing beyond systematic empirical analysis. Various alternative approaches have been suggested, but the postpositivists "share a distrust of systematic analysis, a belief in qualitative analysis, and a taste for methodological diversity."[16] Qualitative methods are equally on the rise in the United States and other Western countries even as their rigor is challenged.

Supporters of a narrowly conceived science of administration assess the rigor of research in terms of the theory and methods employed in the analysis, regardless of the potential range of knowledge relevant to the topic. What they desire is a disciplinary status for public administration in terms of theory, and even more, so it seems, of method. When they speak of public administration's lack of rigor, they generally refer to the limited use of quantitative-statistical techniques and lament the continued use of single-case-study and narrative methods. In this sense, the study of public administration clearly fails the litmus test of "science." In other words, the question about the state of the art and nature of public administration can be addressed only when we move away, first, from a narrow definition of science, and, second, from the unproductive—now almost classical, and certainly stereotypical—dichotomy between science, on the one hand, and practice/profession, on the other.

In the prewar decades, American public administration was riding high on a wave of optimism about the possibility of developing a science of administration. While doubts were expressed as early as the 1920s,[17] it was not until the late 1940s that this optimism was shattered by Simon's proverbs article and by both Simon's and Waldo's dissertations. In the two decades following, it appeared that the positivists had won the day, while those embracing a more holistic approach to public administration were, it seemed, on the defensive. The latter could not make the claim stick that public administration was a science, but one of a different nature than, say, economics or psychology. This failure prompted Waldo to regard public administration increasingly as a professional study such as medicine,[18] while at the same time noticing that the study was suffering from an identity crisis.[19]

In the 1980s and 1990s, various articles and books were published that advocated either a public administration that was scientifically rigorous[20] or a public administration that was more holistic in its concerns.[21] To date, this debate is not resolved—and, we suggest, it may never be resolved, for at least two reasons. The first reason is that the wide range of theories and concepts used and of interests pursued in the study of public administration defies unity of knowledge on an epistemological and methodological basis. That is, public administration scholars are divided among themselves. The second reason is that public administration scholars do not "own" their subject matter. The wit of Frank Knight is particularly applicable to this point, and we take the liberty of quoting him at length:

In the field of natural science the masses can and will gladly take and use and construct appliances in regard to whose scientific basis they are as ignorant as they are indifferent. It is usually possible to demonstrate such things on a moderate scale,

and literally knock men down with "results." In the field of social science, however, fortunately or unfortunately, these things are not true. Our whole established tradition tends to the view that "Tom, Dick, and Harry" know as much
about it as any "highbrow"; the ignorant will not in general defer to the opinion of
the informed, and in the absence of voluntary deference it is usually impossible to
give an objective demonstration.[22]

Indeed, public administration is one of those studies that cannot own
its subject matter because of the following circumstances:

1. Knowledge sources of and for public administration are dispersed across a variety of academic disciplines, but also across a huge
variety of organizations.
2. Its search for knowledge is driven not only by pure academic
interests (that is, knowledge for the sake of knowledge—see, for
instance, Simon), but also by the desire to help solve, or at least better
understand, social problems (that is, usable knowledge—see, for
instance, Taylor, Gulick, Mayo, and Lindblom).
3. The organized complexity of government in modern society cannot be captured in any simplification of reality (see Weber, Follett, and
Waldo).
4. And, finally, government and its study not only deal with solving
simple problems but are especially challenged by and judged on how
they deal with solving "wicked problems"—those that are ill-defined,
rely upon political judgment, and attract a plurality of publics (that is,
interests—see, for instance, Lindblom).[23]

With all this in mind, one cannot but conclude that public administration has matured as a study, although not in the sense that Thomas Kuhn
had in mind when he distinguished between pre-paradigmatic and para-
digmatic phases. If the concept of paradigm is at all relevant to the study
of public administration—and we do not think it is[24]—we conclude that
there are several paradigms-in-use. This means that we cannot judge the
study by the standards of "science" (in its limited, objectivist sense) only,
and that the study is and ought to be the home to any approach, theory,
concept, or construct that helps to advance the understanding of the role
and position of government in society in relation to the understanding of
the internal structures and functioning of public organizations. In that
sense, each of the authors discussed in this volume contributed one piece
or a few pieces to a better overall understanding of government and its
study; Weber, Follett, Lindblom, and Waldo focused primarily on government in society, while Taylor, Gulick, Mayo, Barnard, and Simon were
more concerned with the dynamics internal to an organization.

Legacy

The authors included in this volume not only set an agenda for the investigation of fundamental issues still under consideration but also had more specific impact on how we study and manage public organizations and policies. Determining an author's direct influence is, however, a perilous undertaking. Influence is difficult to assess because there is no hard-and-fast measure on which all would agree. Should we measure influence in terms of what has been attributed to the author? Or, should we measure it in terms of salience, in terms of honors received (Simon would probably win that one), in terms of citations, or scope, or empirical quality, or originality? Moreover, even if scholars could agree upon a measure, establishing a direct linkage to current research or present-day authors is often difficult.

Accordingly, we shall settle for an explication of the relationship between ideas rather than attempting to establish direct linkages between the authors discussed in this volume and their influence, direct and/or indirect, on contemporary scholarship. Since we do not want to repeat what has been said in the preceding chapters, we simply offer a few examples:

- Weber's primary legacies, as far as public administration is concerned, include the ideal-typical conceptualizations of bureaucracy and authority, and his understanding that the civilizing process is one of rationalization. The ideal-type-of-bureaucracy concept, especially, has been used as a foil—if often inappropriately—in many studies of bureaucracy (or, how to avoid it).
- The spirit of Frederick Taylor and Scientific Management lives in industrial management departments everywhere. Taylor's perspective has been extended beyond his focus on man-machine relationships to decision-making and planning processes, now known as the "management sciences." Some have even claimed that he is the father of modern personnel administration because of his emphasis on scientific recruitment, selection, and training processes.
- Gulick identified the core processes of personnel and finance, which remained a major focus for many years in public administration. In addition, his concern with organizational structure has continued in the form of the organizational design movement.
- Follett's ideas have extraordinary currency, even if it is not always acknowledged, or even recognized. A direct, and acknowledged, descendant is the Harvard Negotiations Project and its proposed processes of conflict resolution.[25] However, that direct influence only begins to describe her legacy. Pieces of Follett's approach to interpersonal relationships in the organization can be found in

popular initiatives such as W. Edward Deming's Total Quality Management and Peter Senge's Learning Organization. Also, her emphasis on integration rather than compromise is repeatedly echoed in Lindblom's work.

- Mayo may fairly be considered the progenitor of the Human Relations movement, and, by indirection, of the Contingency Theory and Organizational Humanism approaches that developed in response to it.

- Barnard's conceptualization of the nature of authority in the organization, and the notion of leadership conditioned thereby, are widely, if not universally, accepted in organizational analyses.

- Simon, a somewhat ungrateful follower of Barnard, was enormously influential in his development of descriptive decision theory, in providing an "institutional" perspective on organizational decision making, and, ultimately, in his work in the area of artificial intelligence.

- Lindblom embedded traditional public policy concerns in the political and social (pluralist) environment within which the public administrator must operate.

- Waldo coined the concept of "the administrative state," thus stressing the extent to which democracy has come to rely upon—while still being potentially threatened by—bureaucracy (reflecting Weber). He will, perhaps, be best remembered as a chronicler of, and often a skeptic about, modern developments in the field of public administration. Because of his constant reminders of its shortcomings, we might consider Waldo to be the "conscience" of public administration.

Additional examples are presented in Figure 10-1.

No matter how different their interests and approaches, our nine authors have some things in common. They all believed in their ideas, pursued the exploration of their initial interests, and continued along the same paths despite frequent confrontations and disagreements with colleagues and critics. Some of them really hammered away on the same anvil over and over again. This tenacity is especially evident in the works of Taylor (driven by belief in Scientific Management), Simon (driven by belief in bounded rationality), and Lindblom (driven by belief in incrementalism and, later, in partisan mutual adjustment). Of them all, Weber was probably the most diversified in his substantive interests and methodological approaches.

Generally speaking, the influence of these nine authors transcends American borders, though we should note that the impact has been reciprocal. Some of them were foreign-born, which likely had some influence on their thinking. Weber, of course, was German, and that intellectual tradition had a decided impact on his writings. Mayo was born, received his formal education, and spent his early career in Australia; his experiences there with unions and victims of shell-shock clearly affected his thinking. Gulick was born in Japan, but the effect of that circumstance on his writings is not clear.

However, the cross-border influence goes beyond place of origin. Throughout the development of the field, there has been a close relationship between its adherents in the United States and Europe. The first generation of American scholars identified with public administration—including some of our authors—either received part of their education in Europe[26] or traveled in Europe to learn about its governing traditions and, especially, about specific methods and techniques used in such areas as mail service, garbage collection, financial management, police organization, municipal organization, and so forth.[27] Typically, European administrative customs and techniques were adapted by these authors to befit the specific features of a more pragmatically oriented American government.

More to our point, American authors have had a considerable influence on the study and practice of public administration elsewhere. Pre–World War II American authors—especially Taylor, Follett, Gulick, and Mayo—not only learned from European scholarship but also contributed to the further development of the study at home and abroad. After the war, the study of public administration everywhere was touched by the vigor of American scholarship. American ideas regarding both methodology (including sophisticated quantitative-statistical techniques) and substance (defining the relevant questions and their answers) have found their way across the globe in translations of textbooks and other seminal works of American authors.

What about the influence of non-American scholars upon American public administration? We can assume that the exchange between public administration scholars from the United Kingdom and its Commonwealth partners and their U.S. colleagues has been extensive, especially since the 1960s, simply because there is no language barrier. And, given that English has become the lingua franca of international scholarship, the transmission of knowledge between English-speaking scholars and those whose native language is not English has also increased substantially. But this interchange of ideas does not yet amount to "influence." We suggest that the influence of one public administration tradition upon another can be assessed by gauging the frequency of translations of seminal works and of textbooks.

With regard to the translation of seminal works from another language into English, the prime examples are two studies by Max Weber

FIGURE 10-1
Public Administration: Achievements of the Major Theorists

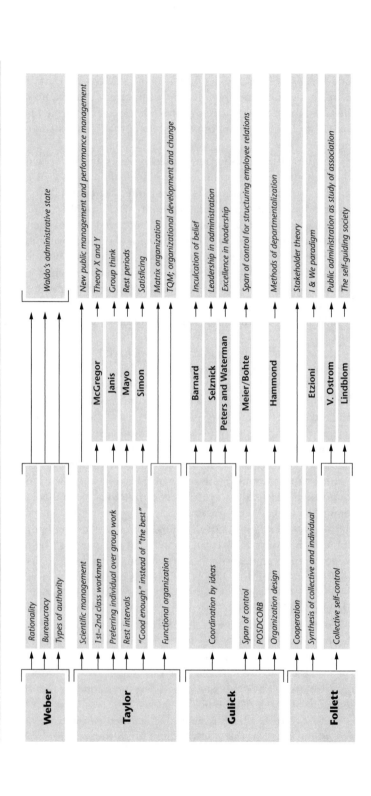

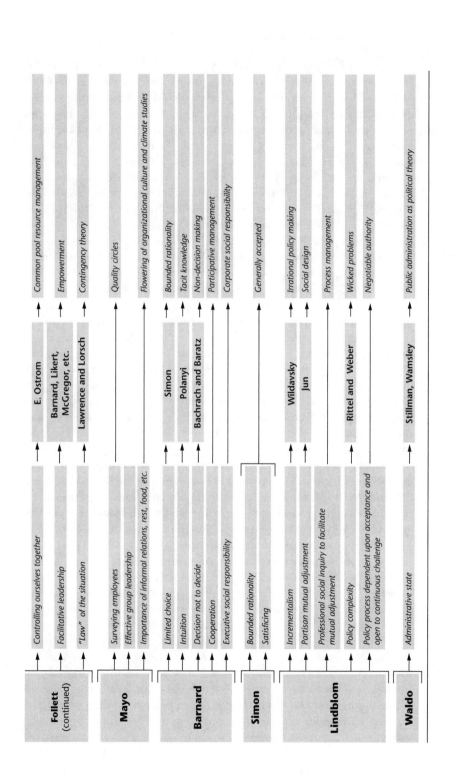

Follett (continued)		**E. Ostrom**	
Controlling ourselves together	→	Common pool resource management	
Facilitative leadership	→	Empowerment	**Barnard, Likert, McGregor, etc.**
"Law" of the situation	→	Contingency theory	**Lawrence and Lorsch**

Mayo			
Surveying employees	→	Quality circles	
Effective group leadership			
Importance of informal relations, rest, food, etc.	→	Flowering of organizational culture and climate studies	

Barnard		**Simon**	
Limited choice	→	Bounded rationality	
Intuition	→	Tacit knowledge	**Polanyi**
Decision not to decide	→	Non-decision making	**Bachrach and Baratz**
Cooperation	→	Participative management	
Executive social responsibility	→	Corporate social responsibility	

Simon			
Bounded rationality	→	Generally accepted	
Satisficing			

Lindblom		**Wildavsky**	
Incrementalism	→	Irrational policy making	
Partisan mutual adjustment	→	Social design	**Jun**
Professional social inquiry to facilitate mutual adjustment	→	Process management	
Policy complexity	→	Wicked problems	**Rittel and Weber**
Policy process dependent upon acceptance and open to continuous challenge	→	Negotiable authority	

Waldo		**Stillman, Wamsley**	
Administrative state	→	Public administration as political theory	

(*Economy and Society* and *Methodology of the Social Sciences*) and two by Michel Crozier (*The Bureaucratic Phenomenon* and *The World of the Office Worker*)—though, obviously, several others could be mentioned. With regard to the translation of textbooks, the influence of non-American works is pretty much nonexistent. That is, American textbooks are translated into French, German, Korean, and Chinese (among other languages), but textbooks from France, Germany, Italy, or the Netherlands—each of which boasts at least a two-centuries-long tradition of studying public administration—are much less often translated into English, if at all. This neglect probably reflects the fact that the study of public administration addresses not only generic administrative problems (such as policymaking, bureaucracy, and political-administrative relations) but also country-specific challenges, and hence is rooted in disparate national traditions of government and governance. Why would a French or German textbook be useful to an American audience?

Of course, that perspective also raises the question why American textbooks are translated in other languages even though some of their content is of limited significance in a different culture? Perhaps the answer is simply that American public administration appears attractive to other countries. After all, the United States is the earliest large-scale democracy in the world, and certainly the first in the modern age to emphasize efficiency rather than equality. It is possible that practitioners and scholars in other countries therefore think that they may benefit from U.S. scholarship in public administration. Also, American scholars have been very active since the Second World War as consultants to developing nations in Africa, Asia, and—since the early 1990s—in the new independent states in Eastern Europe and Asia. But these are tentative answers to the question why American public administration textbooks are often translated into other languages, while those from non-English-speaking countries are seldom translated into English. Clearly, more research is needed to explain this indicator of one-way influence.

Next to influencing one another, Western scholars of public administration have left their imprint in the study and practice of government elsewhere. Especially during the postwar period, national and international consultancy intensified. Among the authors in this volume, Taylor, Mayo, and Barnard, especially, were active consultants in the domestic scene. Gulick was very active for a while in international consultancy, as was Lindblom (at least once). Nowadays, American, Australian, and European scholars are regularly involved in national and international consultancy. On the domestic front—that is, advising local, regional, and national government—this activity is, we suspect, most often conducted through universities and through consulting bureaus, either on an individual basis (university professors working part-time as consultants) or through the many institutes within university departments. International consultancy is more often channeled through international organizations such as the International Monetary Fund, the Organization for Economic Cooperation and Development, the United Nations, and the World Bank. Most scholars of public administration will know at least a handful of colleagues who are actively engaged in advising governments in Central and Eastern Europe, or in Africa, Asia, or Latin America. These consultants bring a mixture of usable knowledge drawn from their national traditions and scholarly knowledge of theories and concepts in Western public administration. Indeed, science and praxis blend when faced with the challenge of social and/or institutional problem solving.

The State of the Enterprise

Controversies still rage about the definition and nature of public administration. Is it simply a branch of political science? Is it merely an extension of private management techniques? Should it be concerned with matters of public policy? Should the public administrator be involved in political processes? Should public administration be considered a science? These are all quandaries that resist—perhaps defy—resolution. One is reminded of Waldo's assertion that public administration, like Poland, lies open to invasion from all sides, while at the same time it is a study that has branched into the realms of other studies and disciplines.

The process of selecting the authors to be included in this volume is a case in point. That selection did not start with a priori definition of the field. Indeed, had a fixed definition been a requirement, it is likely that this book would never have been written. Instead, authors were selected who have made significant contributions to what is commonly thought of as public administration. Most of those selected would not think of themselves as students of public administration; only Gulick and Waldo identified with the field. Simon did so originally, but he later seceded, increasingly identifying himself in a more generic sense as a "social scientist." All of the others maintained closer ties with other disciplines.

Perhaps, like Charles Schultz's comic character Charlie Brown, we may better identify the general contours of the study by looking at the characteristics of our authors rather than by pursuing an abstract, and elusive, definition. If so, then it can be said that public administration is international, interdisciplinary, eclectic in its methodology, ambiguous in its boundaries, and beset by internal tensions. All of that description seems fair enough. And it is not all bad. From this perspective, public administration can be thought of as in a continuing process of becoming as it responds to previous excesses and strives to adapt to continuous changes in its environment. The tie that binds is not techniques and methods of analysis but the focus of analysis—and, even here, there is disagreement. It may be that, as students, scholars, and public administrators, we are condemned always to live in interesting times.

Our preference is for an inclusive rather than an exclusive interpretation. Under this "big tent" approach, the study of public administration is and ought to be home to positivism and interpretation, to empirical research and philosophical reflections, to quantitative and qualitative methods, to public choice and postmodern approaches, and to any substance or theory/method developed in the future. Its identity is interdisciplinary in the fullest sense of that concept: borrowing from any discipline, building knowledge around specific questions, and thus serving as the umbrella for knowledge about government. While its subject matter is not unique to the study, at present it is the only study that focuses both on developing the understanding of the internal structure and process of government as well as the relations between society and government.

Any effort to define the nature of public administration along the lines of science in a strict sense (Simon), of usable knowledge (Taylor, Gulick, Mayo, Lindblom), of professional skills (Barnard, Waldo), or of political theory and social philosophy (Follett, Waldo) will attract individual scholars. Even Simon, while adhering to a rather narrow vision of science—defining a science of administration as the domain of scientists only—acknowledged that "the proper training of 'administrators' lies not in the narrow field of administrative theory, but in the *broader field of the social sciences generally.*"[28] A year later, in the last paragraph of *The Administrative State,* Waldo wrote that "administrative thought must establish a working relationship with *every major province in the realm of human learning.*"[29] This view was not unique to the late 1940s. Already in the early 1930s, Charles Merriam, one of the University of Chicago's champions of positivism, had observed, "It is to be presumed and desired that students of government will play a larger role in the future than in the past in shaping of the types of civic education; but this will not be possible unless a *broader view is taken of the relation of government to the other social sciences, and the function of the political in the social setting.*"[30]

But we have to regard the work of individual scholars in relation to that of others. We can understand what the individual scholars discussed in this volume have done, but we have not probed how they contributed to a more holistic understanding of government. Scholars today are in the position of connecting the ideas and theories developed by authors who came before them. Also, any debate about the nature of public administration should transcend concern with method, and celebrate its interdisciplinary, pragmatic, and eclectic nature, by welcoming any effort at understanding that meets scholarly standards. This openness means that no theoretical or methodological approach is off-limits. While we keep in mind that what is considered scholarly in public administration is time-bound in terms of theory and method, it is not so in terms of careful, intellectual, and—dare we say it—rational exposition of facts in relation to how they are valued. In that sense, Weber and Waldo serve as the perfect bookends to this volume: between them, anything is possible in terms of theory and method, and anything is welcome in terms of substance.

Public Administration and Political Science

The comment from Merriam quoted earlier leads us to our last topic of discussion: the often troublesome relationship between public administration and political science. The search for public administration's identity has, since the 1940s—and especially in the United States—been pursued in the context of efforts to define the study in relation to political science. In a process of maturation, a study comes into its own, seeking independence in terms of its organizational base and in terms of its approach to knowledge. Public administration's fulfillment of this process has dealt with some particular challenges.

Organizationally, it has not always been easy to sever from the home department, whether it be law or political science. Currently, about half of the public administration programs in the United States are organizationally independent from political science; the same proportion of independent programs is found in Finland and the Netherlands. The remaining American public administration programs are embedded in political science departments as a more or less independent specialization; the same situation can be found in the Scandinavian countries (where these programs are a specialization in political science) and in Austria, France, Greece, and Spain (where they are a specialization in law). As in the United States, there are both independent and embedded public administration programs in Belgium, Germany, Italy, Ireland, Portugal, and the United Kingdom.

Of our nine authors, Taylor, Follett, Mayo, and Barnard are mainly identified (nowadays) with business administration, Lindblom with political science, and Gulick and Waldo with public administration. Simon started out in public administration but moved to other pastures, while Weber cannot reasonably be categorized. Thus, it is not surprising that, of these nine, only Waldo reflected in various places upon the separation of public administration and political science—and that was so because his interest had moved from reflections upon contemporary administration to chronicling the development of the study. Waldo's explanation for the separation was that political science had focused on "the historic Greek impulse" to disregard the administrative-bureaucratic component and the behavioral revolution of the 1950s and 1960s, while public administration found its interdisciplinarity.[31] He was, however, not the only one who noted, and sometimes lamented, the increasing separation of the two studies. It was a concern early on. For instance, Roscoe Martin posed the following question in 1952:

> Why should political science and political scientists concern themselves at all with the bothersome problems of public administration? One answer is to keep from going sterile. Another, to keep in touch with government in action. Another, to take advantage of the wide and inviting road for communication with the social sciences. Another, to participate in the exciting business of rethinking a field of knowledge. Another still, to profit from the enforced introspection which the process involves. As regards the last, public administration has shown a willingness, indeed an eagerness, to search its soul for basic meanings and significances.[32]

Thirty-six years later, James W. Fesler explored the symbiotic relation between the two studies and observed that, in both, scholars professed to doubt any benefit in their being related. Has political science expelled public administration because of the latter's combination of practical focus with academic interests? Or has public administration seceded from political science?[33]

The relationship between the two studies in the United States is still an uneasy one. On the one hand, public administration has long been missing as a subject matter in political science "state of the discipline" books[34] and has for years not been mentioned as an area of study in the annual report by the editor of the *American Political Science Review*. On the other hand, there is a thriving public administration section within the American Political Science Association, and the number of articles in the four leading political science journals on bureaucracy and public organization has been increasing.[35] How to reconcile these contradictory indicators is a puzzling question.

While the relationship between public administration and political science remains problematic in the United States, Australian and European scholars have taken up the challenge of (re)connecting the two studies. In his 1997 Gaus lecture, James March mentioned a variety of foreign authors by way of example: Michel Crozier and Jean-Claude Thoenig in France, Renate Mayntz and Fritz Scharpf in Germany, Johan Olsen in Norway, and John Halligan and Robert Goodin in Australia.[36] We should add a few more to enlarge the scope: Alex Kouzmin and Rod Rhodes (originally from the U.K.) and Paul 't Hart (originally from the Netherlands) in Australia; John Burns in Hong Kong; Geert Bouckaert and Christopher Pollitt in Belgium; Jens Hesse in Germany; Uri Rosenthal and Theo Toonen in the Netherlands; Tom Christensen and Per Laegreid in Norway; Jon Pierre in Sweden; and Christopher Hood and Edward Page in the United Kingdom. These and many other authors have identified sometimes with political science, sometimes with public administration, but most of the time they are engaged simply with an interesting research question. After all, their studies of the challenges of public management, of public decision making, of public policymaking, governance, crisis management, and so on cannot be pigeonholed as public administration or as political science, for they actually all concern government at large.

We mention these foreign authors because in the past thirty to forty years, relations among public administration scholars across the globe have intensified. Between the second and seventh decades of the twentieth century, American public administration scholarship was considered the leader in Western countries. Since the end of the 1960s, however, the study has come into its own in other Western countries. Scholars traditionally identifying with political science came to work in public administration departments.[37] These new departments recruited faculty from a variety of disciplinary backgrounds so as to emphasize their study's interdisciplinary nature (we return to this point later).

But, while public administration—to a larger (for instance, in the Netherlands and Finland) or smaller extent (as in France, Germany, Italy, and the United Kingdom)—became organizationally distinct, it maintained relations with political science, as is testified by various research projects that straddle both studies. One example is the extensive research into the nature and development of political-administrative relations;[38] another example is the study of civil service systems.[39] Both these projects are comparative, involving scholars from all over the globe rather than being dominated by one specific country. A third example is the Transatlantic Dialogue conferences since 2005, which have been jointly sponsored by the American Association for Public Administration (ASPA) and the European Group of Public Administration (EGPA) and have addressed such themes as ethics and integrity, public management, and leadership.[40] A fourth example is the publication of an international handbook of public administration with contributors from all over the world.[41] A fifth example is provided by comparative studies of policymaking, which may belong in either public administration or political science.[42] It is likely, moreover, that there are many other research projects and publications further testifying to these trends of an internationalizing public administration and of bridging with political science.

The biggest difference between American public administration and that in other Western countries is the degree of organizational separation of public administration from political science. Another, perhaps lesser, difference is the degree to which American public administration appears to be focusing on quantitative-statistical studies, on performance management, and on leadership studies. In the past fifteen years or so, there have been efforts in the United States at reviving interest in political theory and philosophy within public administration, and the most notable efforts in that direction have been made by scholars leaning toward or identified with postmodernism and/or critical theory.[43] Also, American public administration scholarship is rediscovering its relation to the study of law.[44] It is in these literatures that attention is rekindled as to the roles of, for instance, history, values, and constitutional and administrative law in public decision making and organizations. Nevertheless, it does appear that American public administration leans more toward the "hard," "science" side[45] of the endeavor at the expense of the "softer," humanist-liberal side, while Australian and European scholarship comes across as better balanced between these two approaches.

In the introduction to this volume, we wrote that "public administration is notoriously a borrowing discipline"; that "what cohesiveness it possesses [is derived] more from its object of analysis than [from] its intellectual parentage"; and that it is "cumulative rather than substitutive in its development." True, public administration borrows substantive interests as well as theoretical and methodological approaches from whatever discipline helps to advance its understanding of government; that borrowing makes it an interdisciplinary study. From this perception, it logically follows that its cohesiveness is, indeed, determined not by epistemology or methodology, but by its object of interest. Finally, where Kuhn's notion of paradigm clearly involves the substitution of one approach to knowledge for another—as, for instance, Newtonian physics was replaced by Einsteinian physics, so that Newtonian physics still applies after Einstein but under stricter *ceteris paribus* conditions—knowledge in public administration can only be cumulative.

All that being said, public administration has matured not only in terms of how it has learned to work with and tolerate a wide range of approaches, but also in the confidence with which it has transcended the initial substantive interests that are so well represented in this volume: principles of organizational structure and management, and processes of decision making and policymaking. The study now includes attention to historical development, to the relationship between law and administration, to the gendered nature of approaches, to ethics and integrity in the public sector, and so on, while not forgetting its traditional interests, which are nowadays especially well represented in New Public Management and performance measurement.

NOTES

1. This growth was predicted by Frederick C. Mosher in *Democracy and the Public Service* (New York: Oxford University Press, 1968), 219.
2. See Kenneth J. Meier, "The Public Administration of Politics, or, What Political Science Could Learn from Public Administration," *PS: Political Science & Politics* 60, no. 1 (2007): 3. On the same page, Meier reports that the best research in public administration is no longer published in political science journals but in public administration journals.
3. In some cases, we know that theorizing was also partially influenced by personal life experiences—see especially the Taylor, Follett, Mayo, and Simon chapters. That theory or concept formation might be the result of youthful experiences is not extensively investigated. Biography and intellectual thought may be more closely related than we want to realize. Yet, as a topic of study, it may be avoided because it is so difficult to capture, dependent as we are upon personal reflections and subsequent interpretations on the parts of both the author and the reviewer.
4. Francis W. Coker, "Dogmas of Administrative Reform as Exemplified in the Recent Reorganization in Ohio," *American Political Science Review* 16, no. 3 (1922): 408–409.
5. Charles E. Lindblom, "Concluding Comment: A Case Study of the Practice of Social Science," in *An Heretical Heir of the Enlightenment: Politics, Policy, and Science in the Work of Charles E. Lindblom*, ed. Harry Redner (Boulder, Colo.: Westview Press, 1993), 343–373, esp. 354.
6. Discussing the relation between science and tradition, Michael Polanyi recalls T.S. Eliot, who observed that when we ignore the difference between an author and her/his immediate predecessors, "… we shall often find that not only the best, but the most individual parts of his work may be those in which [the past] asserts its immortality most vigorously." Polanyi then writes that "Copernicus and Kepler told Newton where to find discoveries unthinkable to themselves"; see "The Republic of Science: Its Political and Economic Theory," *Minerva* 1 (1962): 69.
7. Cf. James G. March, "Administrative Practice, Organization Theory, and Political Philosophy: Ruminations on the *Reflections* of John M. Gaus," *PS: Political Science & Politics* 30, no. 4 (1997): 692.
8. The first public administration study is that by Veit Ludwig von Seckendorff, *Teutscher Fürsten Stat* (1656; Glashütten im Taunus: Verlag Detlev Auvermann, 1976). Cf. Jos C.N. Raadschelders, *Handbook of Administrative History* (New Brunswick: Transaction Publishers, 1998), 3–4; see also Helge Peukert (2005), "The Benevolent Prince in Veit Ludwig von Seckendorff's *Teutscher Fürsten Stat* with Special Consideration of the Prince's Revenues, Regalia, and Taxes," *European Journal of Law and Economics* 19, no. 2 (2005): 287–303, esp. 289.
9. Cf. Jos C.N. Raadschelders, *Government: A Public Administration Perspective* (Armonk, N.Y.: M.E. Sharpe, 2003), 102, 201–202. By way of example, the English and Dutch East and West India Companies exhibited features of a large private corporation, but their boards often had members who also held public office. Another example is the church officials appointed to public office—e.g., Cardinal Richelieu in France. Keep in mind that wherever a denomination was a state religion, its priests (as in France) or its

ministers (as in the Dutch Republic or Britain) were public officeholders even when only ministering to their flock.

10. For an excellent example of the abuse of power and trust by private corporations in the absence of government supervision, see how Henry Rogers and William Rockefeller made their first $39 million without spending any money of their own. In Robert L. Heilbroner, *The Worldly Philosophers: The Lives, Times, and Ideas of the Great Economic Thinkers* (New York: Touchstone, 1995), 215–217.

11. See March, "Administrative Practice, Organization Theory, and Political Philosophy," 691. March mentions the following examples: bounded rationality, pluralistic competition, muddling through, co-optation, resource dependence, garbage-can decision making, and loose coupling. He also mentions that Robert A. Dahl and Charles E. Lindblom anticipated studies of governance and transaction costs in their study, *Politics, Economics, and Welfare: Planning and Politico-Economic Systems Resolved into Basic Social Processes* (New York: Harper & Row, 1953).

12. Al Gore, *From Red Tape to Results: Creating a Government that Works Better and Costs Less*, Report of the National Performance Review (New York: Times Books, 1993). See also Jos C. N. Raadschelders, *Handbook of Administrative History* (New Brunswick, N.J.: Transaction, 2000), 248.

13. The argument here about the definition of science draws upon Jos C. N. Raadschelders, "Government and Public Administration: Challenges to and Need for Connecting Knowledge," *Administrative Theory & Praxis* 27, no. 4 (2005): 610–613.

14. Our authors' approaches to science have been discussed and referenced in the various chapters, so we will refrain from extensive footnotes in this paragraph.

15. Jeff Gill and Kenneth J. Meier, "Public Administration Research and Practice: A Methodological Manifesto," *Journal of Public Administration Research and Theory* 10, no. 1 (2000): 157–199.

16. Brian R. Fry and Lloyd Nigro, "Five Great Issues in the Profession of Public Administration," in *Handbook of Public Administration*, ed. Jack Rabin, W. Bartley Hildreth, and Gerald G. Miller (New York: Marcel Dekker, 1998), 1192.

17. See C. S. Hyneman, "Administrative Reorganization: An Adventure into Science and Theology," *Journal of Politics* 1, no. 1 (1939): 751, which mentions several authors going back to 1922; and E. O. Stene, "An Approach to a Science of Administration," *American Political Science Review* 35, no. 6 (1940): 1124–1137.

18. See Gary L. Wamsley, "A Public Philosophy and Ontological Disclosure as the Basis for Normatively Grounded Theorizing in Public Administration," in *Refounding Democratic Public Administration: Modern Paradoxes, Postmodern Challenges*, ed. Gary L. Wamsley and James F. Wolf (Thousand Oaks, Calif.: Sage, 1996), 366.

19. Dwight Waldo, "Public Administration," *Journal of Politics* 30, no. 2 (1968): 443. Interestingly, five years later, Vincent Ostrom also identified an identity crisis, but one concerned with the lack of understanding of the roots of American public administration; see *The Intellectual Crisis in American Public Administration* (University: University of Alabama Press, 1973).

20. E.g., Howard E. McCurdy and Robert E. Cleary, "Why Can't We Resolve the Research Issue in Public Administration," *Public Administration Review*

44, no. 1 (1984): 49–55; James L. Perry and Kenneth L. Kraemer, "Research Methodology in the *Public Administration Review*, 1975–1984," *Public Administration Review* 46, no. 2 (1986): 215–226; James L. Perry and Kenneth L. Kraemer, "Research Methodology in Public Administration: Issues and Patterns," in *Public Administration: The State of the Discipline*, ed. Naomi B. Lynn and Aaron Wildavsky (Chatham, N.J.: Chatham House, 1990), 347–372; Robert A. Stallings and James M. Ferris, "Public Administration Research: Work in *PAR*, 1940–1984," *Public Administration Review* 48, no. 1 (1988): 580–587; Jay D. White, "On the Growth of Knowledge in Public Administration," *Public Administration Review* 46, no. 1: 15–24; Jay D. White, "Dissertations and Public in Public Administration," *Public Administration Review* 46, no. 3 (1986): 227–234; David J. Houston and Sybil M. Delevan, "Public Administration Research: An Assessment of Journal Publications," *Public Administration Review* 50, no. 6 (1990): 674–681; David J. Houston and Sybil M. Delevan, "A Comparative Assessment of Public Administration Journal Publications," *Administration & Society* 26, no. 2 (1994): 252–271; Lewis C. Mainzer, "Public Administration in Search of a Theory: The Interdisciplinary Illusion," *Administration & Society* 26, no. 3 (1994): 359–394; Jay D. White, Guy B. Adams, and John P. Forrester, "Knowledge and Theory Development in Public Administration: The Role of Doctoral Education and Research," *Public Administration Review* 56, no. 5 (1996): 441–452; and Melvin J. Dubnick, "Demons, Spirits, and Elephants: Reflections on the Failure of Public Administration Theory" (paper delivered at the annual meeting of the American Political Science Association, Atlanta,1999).

21. Frank Marini, ed., *Toward a New Public Administration: The Minnowbrook Perspective* (Scranton, Pa.: Chandler, 1971); Dwight Waldo, ed., *Public Administration in a Time of Turbulence* (New York: Chandler, 1971); H. George Frederickson, *New Public Administration* (University: University of Alabama Press, 1980); Gary L. Wamsley, Robert N. Bacher, Charles T. Goodsell, Paul S. Kronenberg, John A. Rohr, Camilla M. Stivers, Orion F. White, and James F. Wolf, *Refounding Public Administration* (Newbury Park, Calif.: Sage, 1990); Gary L. Wamsley and James F. Wolf, ed., *Refounding Democratic Public Administration: Modern Paradoxes, Postmodern Challenges* (Thousand Oaks, Calif.: Sage, 1996); and Richard J. Stillman II, *Preface to Public Administration: A Search for Themes and Direction* (Burke, Va.: Chatelaine Press, 1999).

22. Frank H. Knight, *Risk, Uncertainty, and Profit* (Boston: Hart, Schaffner & Marx/Houghton Mifflin, 1921), 15.

23. The term "wicked problem" was coined by H. Rittel and M. Webber, in "Dilemmas in a General Theory of Planning," *Policy Sciences* 4, no. 1 (1973): 160.

24. To Thomas S. Kuhn, the concept of paradigm is closely linked to the concept of discipline; see *The Structure of Scientific Revolutions* (1962; Chicago: University of Chicago Press, 1973). Defining public administration as an interdiscipline logically means that a variety of paradigms exist. However, the term "paradigm" is so loosely applied in the study of public administration that it is of little use when attempting to characterize the study. See, i.a., Jos C.N. Raadschelders, "Understanding Government through Differentiated Integration in the Study of Public Administration," in *Retracing Public Administration*, ed. Mark R. Rutgers (Amsterdam: JAI Press, 2003), 342.

25. For the Harvard Negotiation Project, see R. Fisher and W. L. Ury, *Getting to Yes: Negotiating Agreement without Giving In* (Boston: Houghton Mifflin, 1981).

26. For information on American scholars traveling to Europe, see M. Curtis Hoffman, "Paradigm Lost: Public Administration at Johns Hopkins University, 1884–1896," *Public Administration Review* 62, no. 1 (2002): 12–23. For travels of American practitioners to Europe, see Pierre-Yves Saunier, "Les Voyages Municipaux Américains en Europe, 1900–1940: Une Piste d'Histoire Transnationale," in *Yearbook of European Administrative History* 15 (2003): 267–288. European ideas also found their way to Asia; see D. Eleanor Westney, *Imitation and Innovation: The Transfer of Western Organizational Patterns to Meiji Japan* (Cambridge, Mass.: Harvard University Press, 1987).

27. One example of this tendency is *The Federalist Papers*, which contrast English, French, and Dutch experiences in order to assess what not to do. Another good example is Dorman Eaton's proposal to reform the American civil service, based on his trip to England in 1877. Hoping to learn from the Northcote-Trevelyan reforms of 1853, Eaton ended up adapting the British example to a system that fitted the American style of governing.

28. Herbert A. Simon, *Administrative Behavior: A Study of Decision Making Processes in Administrative Organization*, 2nd ed. (New York: Free Press, 1957), 247. Emphasis added.

29. Waldo, *The Administrative State: A Study of the Political Theory of American Public Administration*, 2nd ed. (New York/London: Holmes and Meier, 1984), 203. Emphasis added.

30. Charles E. Merriam, *Civic Education in the United States* (New York: Scribner's, 1934), 97. Emphasis in original.

31. See Waldo, *Administrative State*, xxiii and liv.

32. Roscoe C. Martin, "Political Science and Public Administration: A Note on the State of the Union," *American Political Science Review* 46, no. 3 (1952): 676.

33. James W. Fesler, "The State and Its Study: The Whole and the Parts—The Third Annual John Gaus Lecture," *PS: Political Science and Politics* 21, no. 4 (1988): 892, 898.

34. E.g., Ira Katznelson and Helen V. Milner, eds., *Political Science: The State of the Discipline* (New York/London: Norton /APSA, 2002).

35. In "Conclusion: An Agenda for the Scientific Study of Bureaucracy," in *Politics, Policy, and Organizations: Frontiers in the Study of Bureaucracy*, ed. Kenneth J. Meier and George A. Krause (Ann Arbor: University of Michigan Press, 2003), 293 and 307, Meier and Krause observe that, in the past two decades, the four leading political science journals—*American Political Science Review, Journal of Politics, American Journal of Political Science*, and *British Journal of Political Science*—published 110 articles in which bureaucracy was a central feature. This amounts to less than 1.4 articles per journal per annum. In other words, the attention to bureaucracy is far greater in the mainstream public administration journals.

36. See March, "Administrative Practice, Organization Theory, and Political Philosophy," *PS: Political Science & Politics* 30, no. 4 (1997): 692.

37. For an overview of European public administration curriculums, see Tony Verheijen and Bernadette Connaughton, eds., *Higher Education Programmes in Public Administration: Ready for the Challenge of Europeanisation?*

Center for European Studies, University of Limerick, occasional paper no. 3, 1999.

38. This research was fueled especially by the publication of Joel D. Aberbach, Robert D. Putnam, and Bert A. Rockman, *Bureaucrats and Politicians in Western Democracies* (Cambridge, Mass.: Harvard University Press, 1981). For recent comparative studies, see Jos C. N. Raadschelders and Frits M. Van der Meer, eds., *Administering the Summit* (Brussels: IIAS, 1998), 13–33; E. C. Page and V. Wright, eds., *Bureaucratic Élites in Western European States* (Oxford: Oxford University Press, 1999); and idem, eds., *The Changing Role of the Senior Service in Europe* (Houndsmills, England: Palgrave, 2007).

39. Hans A. G. M. Bekke, James L. Perry, and Theo A. J. Toonen, eds., *Civil Service Systems in Comparative Perspective* (Bloomington: Indiana University Press, 1996); James L. Perry, ed., *Research in Public Administration*, vol. 5 (Stamford, Conn.: JAI Press, 1999); Tony Verheyen (with Alexander Kotchegura), eds., *Civil Service Systems in Central and Eastern Europe* (Cheltenham, England: Edward Elgar, 1999); Hans A. G. M. Bekke and Frits M. van der Meer, eds., *Civil Service Systems in Western Europe* (Cheltenham, England: Edward Elgar, 2000); John P. Burns and Bidhya Bowornwathana, eds., *Civil Service Systems in Asia* (Cheltenham, England: Edward Elgar, 2001); John Halligan, ed., *Civil Service Systems in Anglo-American Countries* (Cheltenham, England: Edward Elgar, 2004); and Jos C. N. Raadschelders, Theo A. J. Toonen, and Frits M. Van der Meer, eds., *The Civil Service in the 21st Century: Comparative Perspectives* (Houndsmills, England: Palgrave, 2007).

40. So far, two conferences at the University of Leuven in Belgium (2005 and 2006) and one in Delaware (2007) have not only involved ASPA and EGPA members but have also attracted scholars associated with the U.S.-based National Public Management Research Association (and its prime outlet: the *Journal of Public Administration Research and Theory*, or J-PART).

41. B. Guy Peters and Jon Pierre, eds., *Handbook of Public Administration* (London: Sage, 2003).

42. E.g., Francis G. Castles, *Comparative Public Policy: Patterns of Post-war Transformation* (Cheltenham, England: Edward Elgar, 1998).

43. For instance, one can think of the Blacksburg Manifesto (see Wamsley et al., *Refounding Public Administration*) and of Wamsley and Wolf as authors who label themselves "high modern" (this remark can be found in their *Refounding Democratic Public Administration*, pp. 22–24). Notable contributions to political theory in public administration have been credited to Michael W. Spicer; see, for instance, his *Public Administration and the State: A Postmodern Perspective* (Tuscaloosa: University of Alabama Press, 2001). Among postmodernists O. C. McSwite (a pseudonym for Orion S. White and Cynthia McSwain), David J. Farmer, Charles Fox and Hugh Miller, and Michael M. Harmon must be mentioned. For McSwite, see *Legitimacy in Public Administration: A Discourse Analysis* (Thousand Oaks, Calif.: Sage, 1997) and *Invitation to Public Administration* (New York: M. E. Sharpe, 2002). For Farmer, see *The Language of Public Administration: Bureaucracy, Modernity, and Postmodernity* (Tuscaloosa: University of Alabama Press, 1995) and *To Kill the King: Post-Traditional Governance and Bureaucracy* (Armonk, N.Y.: M. E. Sharpe, 2005). For Fox and Miller, see *Postmodern Public Administration* (Armonk, N.Y.: M. E. Sharpe, 2007). In *Responsibility as Paradox: A Critique of Rational Discourse on Government* (Thousand Oaks,

Calif.: Sage, 1995) and *Public Administration's Final Exam: A Pragmatist Restructuring of the Profession and the Discipline* (Tuscaloosa: University of Alabama Press, 2006), Harmon offers interesting thoughts about the dichotomous nature of the study, from what he labels a pragmatist perspective. Richard Box is the leading representative of critical theorists; see his *Critical Social Theory in Public Administration* (Armonk, N.Y.: M.E. Sharpe, 2005).

44. E.g., David H. Rosenbloom, *Administrative Law for Public Managers* (Boulder, Colo.: Westview Press, 2003); Robert K. Christensen and Charles E. Wise, "Law and Management: Comparatively Assessing the Reach of Judicialization," in Raadschelders, Toonen, and Van der Meer, *Civil Service in the 21st Century*, chap. 12.

45. Consider the content of J-PART. Also, half of all submissions to *PAR* can be grouped under one substantive category: performance measurement and performance management. Methodologically, submissions using quantitative-statistical methods balance those using qualitative methods.

Index